# The Master of the Ceremonies

*by*

George Manville Fenn

# The Master of the Ceremonies
## by George Manville Fenn

ISBN: 978-93-59951-17-1

**Published by**

# DOUBLE 9 BOOKS

2/13-B, Ansari Road
Daryaganj, New Delhi – 110002
info@double9books.com
www.double9books.com
Tel. 011-40042856

# ABOUT THE AUTHOR

George Manville Fenn was a very productive author of novels, a writer, an editor, and an educator from England. He was born on January 3, 1831, in Pimlico, London. He mostly learned on his own; he taught himself Italian, French, and German. During the years 1851-1854, he went to Battersea Training College for Teachers and then became the head of a state school in Alford, Lincolnshire. In the early 1850s, Fenn started to write short stories and pieces for newspapers and magazines. The Old Forest Ranger, his first book, came out in 1856. Afterward, he wrote more than 100 books, many of them for teenagers and young adults. He was one of the most famous writers of his time, and his books were well-liked and read by many people. I also worked as a reporter and writer for Fenn. Among the newspapers and magazines, he worked for was The Boy's Own Paper, which he ran from 1866 to 1874. He worked hard to make children's books better and was a strong supporter of education and reading. The Englishman Fenn passed away on August 26, 1909, in Isleworth.

# CONTENTS

# Volume one

# Chapter One
# His House

Early morning at Saltinville, with the tide down, and the calm sea shimmering like damasked and deadened silver in the sunshine. Here and there a lugger was ashore, delivering its take of iris-hued mackerel to cart and basket, as a busy throng stood round, some upon the sands, some knee-deep in water, and all eager to obtain a portion of the fresh fish that fetched so good a price amongst the visitors to the town.

The trawler was coming in, too, with its freight of fine thick soles and turbot, with a few gaily-scaled red mullet; and perhaps a staring-eyed John Dory or two, from the trammel net set overnight amongst the rocks: all choice fish, these, to be bought up ready for royal and noble use, for London would see no scale of any of the fish caught that night.

The unclouded sun flashed from the windows of the houses on the cliff, giving them vivid colours that the decorator had spared, and lighting up the downs beyond, so that from the sea Saltinville looked a very picture of all that was peaceful and bright. There were no huge stucco palaces to mar the landscape, for all was modest as to architecture, and as fresh as green and stone-coloured paint applied to window-frame, veranda and shutter could make it. Flowers of variety were not plentiful, but great clusters of orange marigolds flourished bravely, and, with broad-disked sunflowers, did no little towards giving warmth of colour to the place. There had been no storms of late—no windy nights when the spray was torn from the tops of waves to fly in showers over the houses, and beat the window-panes, crusting them afterwards with a coat of dingy salt. The windows, then, were flashing in the sun; but all the same, by six o'clock, Isaac Monkley, the valet, body-servant, and footman-in-ordinary to Stuart Denville, Esquire, MC, was busy, dressed in a striped jacket, and standing on the very top of a pair of steps, cloth in one hand and wash-leather in the other, carefully cleaning windows that were already spotless. For there was something in the exterior of the MC's house that suggested its tenant. Paint, glass, walls, and doorstep were so scrupulously clean that they recalled the master's face, and seemed to have been clean-shaven but an hour before.

Isaac was not alone in his task, for, neat in a print dress and snowy cap, Eliza, the housemaid, was standing on a chair within; and as they cleaned the windows in concert, they courted in a special way.

There is no accounting for the pleasure people find in very ordinary ways. Isaac and Eliza found theirs in making the glass so clear that they could smile softly at each other without let or hindrance produced by smear or speck in any single pane. Their hands, too, were kept in contact, saving for cloth and glass, and moved in unison, describing circles and a variety of other figures, going into the corners together, changing from cloth to wash-leather, and moving, as it were, by one set of muscles till the task was concluded with a chaste salute—a kiss through the glass.

Meanwhile, anyone curious about the house would, if he had raised his eyes, have seen that one of the upstairs windows had a perfect screen of flowers, that grew from a broad, green box along the sill. Sweet peas clustered, roses bloomed, geraniums dotted it with brilliant tiny pointless stars of scarlet, and at one side there was a string that ran up from a peg to a nail, hammered, unknown to the MC, into the wall. That peg was an old tooth-brush handle, and the nail had been driven in with the back of a hairbrush; but bone handle and string were invisible now, covered by the twining strands of so many ipomaeas, whose heart-shaped leaves and trumpet blossoms formed one of the most lovely objects of the scene. Here they were of richest purple, fading into lavender and grey; there of delicate pink with well-formed starry markings in the inner bell, and moist with the soft air of early morning. Each blossom was a thing of beauty soon to fade, for, as the warm beams of the sun kissed them, the edges began to curl; then there would be a fit of shrivelling, and the bloom of the virgin flower passed under the sun-god's too ardent caress.

About and above this screen of flowers, a something ivory white, and tinged with peachy pink, kept darting in and out. Now it touched a rose, and a shower of petals fell softly down; now a geranium leaf that was turning yellow disappeared; now again a twig that had borne roses was taken away, after a sound that resembled a steely click. Then the little crimson and purple blossoms of a fuchsia were touched, and shivered and twinkled in the light at the soft movements among the graceful stems as dying flowers were swept away.

For a minute again all was still, but the next, there was a fresh vibration amongst the flowers as this ivory whiteness appeared in a new place, curving round a plant as if in loving embrace; and at such times the blooms seemed drawn towards another and larger flower of thicker petal and of coral hue, that peeped out amongst the fresh green leaves, and then it was that a watcher would have seen that this ivory something playing about the window garden was a soft white hand.

Again a fresh vibration amongst the clustering flowers, as if they were trembling with delight at the touches that were once more to come. Then there was a brilliant flash as the sun's rays glanced from a bright vessel, the pleasant gurgle of water from a glass carafe, and once more stillness before the stems were slowly parted, and a larger flower peeped out from the leafy screen—the soft, sweet face of Claire Denville—to gaze at the sea and sky, and inhale the morning air.

Richard Linnell was not there to look up and watch the changes in the sweet, candid face, with its high white forehead, veined with blue, its soft, peachy cheeks and clear, dark-grey eyes, full of candour, but searching and firm beneath the well-marked brows. Was her mouth too large? Perhaps so; but what a curve to that upper lip, what a bend to the lower over that retreating dimpled chin. If it had been smaller the beauty of the regular teeth would have been more hidden, and there would have been less of the pleasant smile that came as Claire brushed aside her wavy brown hair, turned simply back, and knotted low down upon her neck.

Pages might be written in Claire Denville's praise: let it suffice that she was a tall, graceful woman, and that even the most disparaging scandalmonger of the place owned that she was "not amiss."

Claire Denville's gaze out to sea was but a short one. Then her face disappeared; the stems and blossoms darted back to form a screen, and the tenant of the barely-furnished bedroom was busy for some time, making the bed and placing all in order before drawing a tambour frame to the window, and unpinning a piece of paper that guarded the gay silks and wools. Then for the next hour Claire bent over her work, the glistening needle passing rapidly in and out as she gazed intently at the pattern rapidly approaching completion, a piece of work that was to be taken surreptitiously to Miss Clode's library and fancy bazaar for sale, money being a scarce commodity in the MC's home.

From below, time after time, came up sounds of preparation for the breakfast of the domestics, then for their own, and Claire sighed as she thought of the expenses incurred for three servants, and how much happier they might be if they lived in simpler style.

The chiming of the old church clock sounded sweetly on the morning air.

*Ting-dong*—quarter-past; and Claire listened attentively.

*Ting-dong*—half-past.

*Ting-dong*—quarter to eight.

"How time goes!" she cried, with a wistful look at her work, which she hurriedly covered, and then her print dress rustled as she ran downstairs to find her father already in the little pinched parlour, dubbed breakfast-room, standing thin and pensive in a long faded dressing-gown, one arm resting upon the chimney-piece, snuff-box in hand, the other raised level with his face, holding the freshly-dipped-for pinch—in fact, standing in a studied attitude, as if for his portrait to be limned.

# Chapter Two
# His Breakfast

"Ah, my child, you are late," said the Master of the Ceremonies, as Claire ran to meet him and kissed his cheek. "'Early to bed and early to rise makes a man healthy, wealthy, and wise.' It will do the same for you, my child, and add bloom to your cheek, though, of course, we cannot be early in the season."

"I am a little late, papa dear," said Claire, ringing a tinkling bell, with the result that Isaac, in his striped jacket and the stiffest of white cravats, entered, closed the door behind him, and then stood statuesque, holding a brightly-polished kettle, emitting plenty of steam.

"Any letters, Isaac?"

"No, sir, none this morning," and then Isaac carefully poured a small quantity of the boiling water into the teapot, whose lid Claire had raised, and stood motionless while she poured it out again, and then unlocked a very small tea-caddy and spooned out three very small spoonfuls—one apiece, and none for the over-cleaned and de-silvered plated pot. This done, Isaac filled up, placed the kettle on the hob, fetched a Bible and prayer-book from a sideboard, placed them at one end of the table and went out.

"Why is not Morton down?" said the MC sternly.

"He came down quite an hour ago, papa. He must have gone for a walk. Shall we wait?"

"Certainly not, my child."

At that moment there was a little scuffling outside the door, which was opened directly after by Isaac, who admitted Eliza and a very angular-looking woman with two pins tightly held between her lips—pins that she had intended to transfer to some portion of her garments, but had not had time. These three placed themselves before three chairs by the door, and waited till the MC had gracefully replaced his snuff-box, and taken two steps to the table, where he and Claire sat down. Then the servants took their seats, and then "Master" opened the Bible to read in a slow, deliberate way, and as if he enjoyed the names, that New Testament chapter on genealogies which to youthful ears seemed to be made up of a constant repetition of the two words, "which was."

This ended, all rose and knelt down, Isaac with the point of his elbow just touching the point of Eliza's elbow, for he comforted his conscience over this tender advance by the reflection that marriage, though distant, was a sacred thing; and he made up for his unspiritual behaviour to a great extent by saying the "Amens" in a much louder voice than Cook, and finished off in the short space of silence after the Master of the Ceremonies had read the last Collect, and when all were expected to continue their genuflexions till that personage sighed and made a movement as if to rise, by adding a short extempore prayer of his own, one which he had repeated religiously for the past four years without effect, the supplication being:

"And finally, may we all get the arrears of our wages, evermore. Amen."

Isaac had finished his supplementary prayer; the MC sighed and rose, and, the door being opened by the footman, the two maids stepped out. Isaac followed, and in a few minutes returned with a very coppery rack, containing four thin pieces of toast, and a little dish whose contents were hidden by a very battered cover. These were placed with the greatest form upon the table, and the cover removed with a flourish, to reveal two very thin and very curly pieces of streaky bacon, each of which had evidently been trying to inflate itself like the frog in the fable, but with no other result than the production of a fatty bladdery puff, supported by a couple of patches of brown.

Isaac handed the toast to father and daughter, and then went off with the cover silently as a spirit, and the breakfast was commenced by the MC softly breaking a piece of toast with his delicate fingers and saying:

"I am displeased with Morton. After yesterday's incident, he should have been here to discuss with me the future of his campaign."

"Here he is, papa," cried Claire eagerly, and she rose to kiss her brother affectionately as he came rather boisterously into the room, looking tall, thin and pale, but healthy and hungry, as an overgrown boy of nineteen would look who had been out at the seaside before breakfast.

"You were not here to prayers, Morton," said the MC sternly.

"No, father; didn't know it was so late," said the lad, beginning on the toast as soon as he was seated.

"I trust that you have not been catching—er—er—dabs, this morning." The word was distasteful when the fish was uncooked, and required an effort to enunciate.

"Oh, but I have, though. Rare sport this morning. Got enough for dinner."

The MC was silent for a few moments, and gracefully sipped his thin tea. He was displeased, but there was a redeeming feature in his son's announcement—enough fish for dinner. There would be no need to order anything of the butcher.

"Hush, Morton," said Claire softly, and she laid her soft little hand on his, seeing their father about to speak.

"I am—er—sorry that you should be so thoughtless, Morton," said his father; "at a time, too, when I am making unheard-of efforts to obtain that cornetcy for you; how can you degrade yourself—you, the son of a—er—man—a—er—gentleman in my position, by going like a common boy down below that pier to catch—er—dabs!"

"Well, we want them," retorted the lad. "A good dinner of dabs isn't to be sneezed at. I'm as hungry as hungry, sometimes. See how thin I am. Why, the boys laugh, and call me Lanky Denville."

"What is the opinion of boys to a young man with your prospects in life?" said his father, carefully ignoring the question of food supply. "Besides, you ought to be particular, sir, for the sake of your sister May, who has married so well."

"What, to jerry-sneaky Frank Burnett? A little humbug."

"Morton!"

"Well, so he is, father. I asked him to lend me five shillings the day before yesterday, and he called me an importunate beggar."

"You had no business to ask him for money, sir."

"Who am I to ask, then? I must have money. You won't let me go out to work."

"No, sir; you are a gentleman's son, and must act as a gentleman."

"I can't act as a gentleman without money," cried the lad, eating away, for, to hide the look of pain in her face, Claire kept diligently attending to her brother's wants by supplying him with a fair amount of thin tea and bread and butter, as well as her own share of the bacon.

"My dear son," said the MC with dignity, "everything comes to the man who will wait. Your sister May has made a wealthy marriage. Claire will, I have no doubt, do the same, and I have great hopes of your prospects."

"Haven't any prospects," said the lad, in an ill-used tone.

"Not from me," said the MC, "for I am compelled to keep up appearances before the world, and my fees and offerings are not nearly so much as people imagine."

"Then why don't we live accordingly?" said the lad roughly.

"Allow me, with my experience, sir, to know best; and I desire that you will not take that tone towards me. Recollect, sir, that I am your father."

"Indeed, dear papa, Morton does not mean to be disrespectful."

"Silence, Claire. And you, Morton; I will be obeyed."

"All right, father. I'll obey fast enough, but it does seem precious hard to see Ikey down in the kitchen stuffing himself, and us up in the parlour going short so as to keep up appearances."

"My boy," said the MC pathetically, "it is Spartan-like. It is self-denying and manly. Have courage, and all will end well. I know it is hard. It is my misfortune, but I appeal to you both, do I ever indulge myself at your expense? Do I ever spare myself in my efforts for you?"

"No, no, no, dear," cried Claire, rising with tears in her eyes to throw her arm round his neck and kiss him.

"Good girl!—good girl!" he said, smiling sadly, and returning the embrace. "But sit down, sit down now, and let us discuss these very weighty matters. Fortune is beginning to smile upon us, my dears. May is off my hands—well married."

Claire shook her head sadly.

"I say well married, Claire," said her father sternly, "and though we have still that trouble ever facing us, of a member of our family debauched by drunkenness, and sunk down to the degradation of a common soldier—"

"Oh! I say, father, leave poor old Fred alone," cried Morton. "He isn't a bad fellow; only unlucky."

"Be silent, sir, and do not mention his name again in my presence. And Claire, once for all, I forbid his coming to this house."

"He only came to the back door," grumbled Morton.

"A son who is so degraded that he cannot come to the front door, and must lower himself to the position of one of our servants, is no companion for my children. I forbid all further communication with him."

"Oh, papa!" cried Claire, with the tears in her eyes.

"Silence! Morton, my son, I have hopes that by means of my interest a certain person will give you a commission in the Light Dragoons, and—For what we have received may the Lord make us truly thankful."

"Amen," said Morton. "Claire, I want some more bread and butter."

"Claire," said the Master of the Ceremonies, rising from the table as a faint tinkle was heard, "there is the Countess's bell."

He drew the girl aside and laid a thin white finger upon her shoulder.

"You must give her a broader hint this morning, Claire. Six months, and she has paid nothing whatever. I cannot, I really cannot go on finding her ladyship in apartments and board like this. It is so unreasonable. A woman, too, with her wealth. Pray, speak to her again, but don't offend her. You must be careful. Delicately, my child—delicately. A leader of fashion even now. A woman of exquisite refinement. Of the highest aristocracy. Speak delicately. It would never do to cause her annoyance about such a sordid thing as money—a few unsettled debts of honour. Ah, her bell again. Don't keep her waiting."

"If you please, ma'am, her ladyship has rung twice," said Isaac, entering the room; "and Eliza says shall she go?"

"No, Isaac, your mistress will visit her ladyship," said the MC with dignity. "You can clear away, Isaac—you can clear away."

Stuart Denville, Esquire, walked to the window and took a pinch of snuff. As soon as his back was turned Isaac grinned and winked at Morton, making believe to capture and carry off the bread and butter; while the lad hastily wrote on a piece of paper:

"Pour me out a cup of tea in the pantry, Ike, and I'll come down."

Five minutes later the room was cleared, and the MC turned from the window to catch angrily from the table some half-dozen letters which the footman had placed ready for him to see.

"Bills, bills, bills," he said, in a low, angry voice, thrusting them unread into the drawer of a cabinet; "what am I to do? How am I to pay?"

He sat down gracefully, as if it were part of his daily life, and his brow wrinkled, and an old look came into his face as he thought of the six months' arrears of the lady who occupied his first floor, and his hands began to tremble strangely as he seemed to see open before him an old-fashioned casket, in which lay, glittering upon faded velvet, necklet, tiara, brooch, earrings and bracelets—large diamonds of price; a few of which, if sold, would be sufficient to pay his debts, and enable him to keep up appearances, and struggle on, till Claire was well married, and his son well placed.

Money—money—always struggling on for money in this life of beggarly gentility; while only on the next floor that old woman on the very brink of the grave had trinkets, any one of which—

He made a hasty gesture, as if he were thrusting back some temptation, and took up a newspaper, but let it fall upon his knees as his eyes lit upon a list of bankrupts.

Was it come to that? He was heavily in debt to many of the tradespeople. The epidemic in the place last year had kept so many people away, and his fees had been less than ever. Things still looked bad. Then there was the rent, and Barclay had said he would not wait, and there were the bills that Barclay held—his acceptances for money borrowed at a heavy rate to keep up appearances when his daughter May—his idol—the pretty little sunbeam of his house—became Mrs Frank Burnett.

"Barclay is hard, very hard," said the Master of the Ceremonies to himself. "Barclay said—"

He again made that gesture, a gracefully made gesture of repelling something with his thin, white hands, but the thought came back.

"Barclay said that half the ladies of fashion when short of money, through play, took their diamonds to their jeweller, sold some of the best, and had them replaced with paste. It took a connoisseur to tell the difference by candlelight."

Stuart Denville, poverty-stricken gentleman, the poorest of men, suffering as he did the misery of one struggling to keep up appearances, rose to his feet with a red spot in each of his cheeks, and a curious look in his eyes.

"No, no," he ejaculated excitedly as he walked up and down, "a gentleman, sir—a gentleman, if poor. Better one's razors or a pistol. They would say it was all that I could do. Not the first gentleman who has gone to his grave like that."

He shuddered and stood gazing out of the window at the sea, which glittered in the sunshine like—yes, like diamonds.

Barclay said he had often changed diamonds for paste, and no one but a judge could tell what had been done. Half a dozen of the stones from a bracelet replaced with paste, and he would be able to hold up his head for a year, and by that time how changed everything might be.

Curse the diamonds! Was he mad? Why did the sea dance and sparkle, and keep on flashing like brilliants? Was it the work of some devil to tempt him with such thoughts? Or was he going mad?

He took pinch after pinch of snuff, and walked up and down with studied dancing-master strides as if he were being observed, instead of alone in that shabby room, and as he walked he could hear the dull buzz of voices and a light tread overhead.

He walked to the window again with a shudder, and the sea still seemed to be all diamonds.

He could not bear it, but turned to his seat, into which he sank heavily, and covered his face with his hands.

Diamonds again—glistening diamonds, half a dozen of which, taken—why not borrowed for a time from the old woman who owed him so much, and would not pay? Just borrowed for the time, and paste substituted till fate smiled upon him, and his plans were carried out. How easy it would be. And she, old, helpless, would never know the difference—and it was to benefit his children.

"I cannot bear it," he moaned; and then, "Barclay would do it for me. He is secret as the tomb. He never speaks. If he did, what reputations he could blast."

So easy; the old woman took her opiate every night, and slept till morning. She would not miss the cross—yes, that would be the one—no, a bracelet better. She never wore that broad bracelet, Claire said, now she had realised that her arms were nothing but bone.

"Am I mad?" cried the old man, starting up again. "Yes, what is it?"

"Messenger from Mr Barclay, sir, to say he will call to-morrow at twelve, and he hopes you will be in."

"Yes, yes, Isaac; say yes, I will be in," said the wretched man, sinking back in his chair with the perspiration starting out all over his brow. And then, as he was left alone, "How am I to meet him? What am I to say?" he whispered. "Oh, it is too horrible to bear!"

Once more he started to his feet and walked to the window and looked out upon the sea.

Diamonds—glittering diamonds as far as eye could reach, and the Master of the Ceremonies, realising more and more the meaning of the word temptation, staggered away from the window with a groan.

# Chapter Three
# The Flickering Flame

"Draw the curtains, my dear, and then go into the next room, and throw open the French window quite wide."

It was a mumbling noise that seemed to come out of a cap-border lying on a pillow, for there was no face visible; but a long thin elevation of the bedclothes, showing that some one was lying there, could be seen in the dim light.

Claire drew the curtains, opened a pair of folding-doors, and crossed the front room to open the French window and admit the sweet fresh air.

She stepped out into the balcony supported by wooden posts, up which a creeper was trained, and stood by a few shrubs in pots gazing out at the brilliant sea; but only for a few moments, before turning, recrossing the skimpily furnished drawing-room, and going into the back, where the large four-post bedstead suddenly began to quiver, and the bullion fringe all round to dance, as its occupant burst into a spasmodic fit of coughing.

"He—he—he, hi—hi—hi, hec—hec—hec, ha—ha—ha! ho—ho! Bless my—hey—ha! hey—ha! hugh—hugh—hugh! Oh dear me! oh—why don't you—heck—heck—heck—heck—heck! Shut the—ho—ho—ho—ho—hugh—hugh—window before I—ho—ho—ho—ho!"

Claire flew back across the drawing-room and shut the window, hurrying again to the bedside, where, as she drew aside the curtains, the morning light displayed a ghastly-looking, yellow-faced old woman, whose head nodded and bowed in a palsied manner, as she sat up, supporting herself with one arm, and wiped her eyes—the hand that held the handkerchief being claw-like and bony, and covered with a network of prominent veins.

She was a repulsive-looking, blear-eyed old creature, with a high-bridged aquiline nose that seemed to go with the claw-like hand. A few strands of white hair had escaped from beneath the great mob of lace that frilled her nightcap, and hung over forehead and cheek, which were lined and wrinkled like a walnut shell, only ten times as deeply.

"It's—it's your nasty damp house," mumbled the old woman spitefully, her lips seeming to be drawn tightly over her gums, and her nose threatening to tap her chin as she spoke. "It's—it's killing me. I never had such a cough before. Damn Saltinville! I hate it."

"Oh, Lady Teigne, how can you talk like that!" cried Claire. "It is so shocking."

"What! to say damn? 'Tisn't. I'll say it again. A hundred times if I like;" and she rattled out the condemnatory word a score of times over, as fast as she could utter it, while Claire looked on in a troubled way at the hideous old wretch before her.

"Well, what are you staring at, pink face! Wax-doll! Baby chit! Don't look at me in that proud way, as if you were rejoicing because you are young, and I am a little old. You'll be like me some day. If you live—he—he—he! If you live. But you won't. You look consumptive. Eh?"

"I did not speak," said Claire sadly. "Shall I bring your breakfast, Lady Teigne?"

"Yes, of course. Are you going to starve me? Mind the beef-tea's strong this morning, and put a little more cognac in, child. Don't you get starving me. Tell your father, child, that I shall give him a cheque some day. I haven't forgotten his account, but he is not to pester me with reminders. I shall pay him when I please."

"My father would be greatly obliged, Lady Teigne, if you would let him have some money at once. I know he is pressed."

"How dare you! How dare you! Pert chit! Look here, girl," cried the old woman, shaking horribly with rage; "if another word is said to me about money, I'll go and take apartments somewhere else."

"Lady Teigne! You are ill," cried Claire, as the old woman sank back on her pillow, looking horribly purple. "Let me send for a doctor."

"What!" cried the old woman, springing up—"a doctor? Don't you mention a doctor again in my presence, miss. Do you think I'd trust myself to one of the villains? He'd kill me in a week. Go and get my beef-tea. I'm quite well."

Claire went softly out of the room, and the old woman sat up coughing and muttering.

"Worrying me for money, indeed—a dipperty-dapperty dancing-master! I won't pay him a penny."

Here there was a fit of coughing that made the fringe dance till the old woman recovered, wiped her eyes, and shook her skinny hand at the fringe for quivering.

"Doctor? Yes, they'd better. What do I want with a doctor? Let them get one for old Lyddy—wants one worse than I do, ever so much. Oh, there you are, miss. Is that beef-tea strong?"

"Yes, Lady Teigne, very strong."

Claire placed a tray, covered with a white napkin, before her, and took the cover from the white china soup-basin, beside which was a plate of toast cut up into dice.

The old woman sniffed at a spoonful.

"How much cognac did you put in?"

"A full wine-glass, Lady Teigne."

"Then it's poor brandy."

"No, Lady Teigne; it is the best French."

"Chut! Don't talk to me, child. I know what brandy is."

She threw some of the sippets in, and began tasting the broth in an unpleasant way, mumbling between the spoonfuls.

"I knew what brandy was before you were born, and shall go on drinking it after you are dead, I dare say. There, I shan't have any more. Give it to that hungry boy of yours. He looks as if he wanted it."

Claire could not forbear a smile, for the old woman had not left half a dozen spoonfuls at the bottom of the basin.

"Look here. Come up at two o'clock and dress me. I shall have a good many visitors to-day, and mind this: don't you ever hint at sending up Eliza again, or I'll go and take apartments somewhere else. We're getting proud, I suppose?"

There was a jingle of the china on the tray as the old woman threw herself down, and then a mumbling, followed by a fit of coughing, which soon subsided, and lastly there was nothing visible but the great cap-border, and a few straggling white hairs.

At two o'clock to the moment Claire went upstairs again, and for the space of an hour she performed the duties of lady's-maid without a murmur, building up the old relic of a bygone fashionable generation into a presentable form. There was an auburn set of curls upon her head, with a huge tortoise-shell comb behind. A change had been wrought in her mouth, which was filled with white teeth. A thick coating of powder filled up some of her wrinkles, and a wonderful arrangement of rich lace draped her form as she sat propped up in an easy-chair.

"Now my diamonds," she said, at last; and Claire fetched a casket from the dressing-table, and held a mirror before the old lady, as she wearied herself—poor old flickering flame that she was!—fitting rings on her thin fingers, the glittering necklet about her baggy throat, the diadem in her hair, and the eardrops in the two yellow pendulous adjuncts to her head.

"Shall I do, chit?" she said, at last.

"Yes," said Claire gravely.

"Humph! You don't look pleased; you never do. You're jealous, chit. There, half draw down the blinds and go, now. Leave the room tidy. I hate to have you by me at times like this."

Claire helped her to walk to the drawing-room, arranged a few things, and then left the room with the folding-doors closed, and it seemed as if life and youth had gone out of the place, leaving it to ghastly old age and death, painted with red lips and white cheeks, and looking ten times more awful than death in its natural solemn state.

Then for two hours fashionable Saltinville rattled the knocker, and was shown up by Isaac, in ones, and twos, and threes, and told Lady Teigne that she never looked better, and took snuff, and gossiped, and told of the latest scandals about Miss A, and Mr B, and Lord C, and then stopped, for Lord C came and told tales back; and all the while Lady Teigne, supported by Lady Drelincourt, her sister, ogled and smiled, and smirked under her paint and diamonds, and quarrelled with her sister every time they were left for a few minutes alone.

"It's shameful, Lyddy," said her ladyship, pinching her over-dressed sister; "an old thing like you, rolling in riches, and you won't pay my debts."

"Pay them yourself," was the ungracious reply. "Oh!"

This was consequent upon the receipt of a severe pinch from Lady Teigne, but the elderly sisters smiled again directly, for Isaac announced Major Rockley, and the handsome, dark officer came in, banging an imaginary sabre at his heels and clinking his spurs. He kissed Lady Teigne's hand, bent courteously over Lady Drelincourt, and then set both tittering over the latest story about the Prince.

The sisters might have been young from their ways and looks, and general behaviour towards the Major, whose attentions towards the venerable animated mummy upon the couch seemed marked by a manner that was almost filial.

He patted the cushions that supported the weak back; held her ladyship when a fit of coughing came on, and then had to find the necklet that had become unfastened and had slipped down beneath an Indian shawl, spread coverlet fashion, over the lady's trembling limbs.

"Thank you so much, Major. How clever you are!" cackled the old woman playfully, as he found the necklet, and clasped it about her throat. "I almost feel disposed to give you some encouragement, only it would make Lyddy furious."

Lady Drelincourt said "For shame!" and tapped her sister with her fan, and then Major Rockley had to give place to Captain Bray and Lieutenant Sir Harry Payne, officers in his regiment, the former a handsome, portly dandy who puzzled his dearest friends, he was so poor but looked so well.

Then followed other members of the fashionable world of Saltinville, till nearly six, when the knocker ceased making the passage echo, the last visitor had called, and Claire helped—half carried—her ladyship back to bed, and watched her relock her jewels in the casket, which was taken then to the dressing-table. Her ladyship was made comfortable, partook of her dinner and tea, and then waited for the coming of Claire for the last time that night.

# Chapter Four
# Clouds

Lady Teigne's drawing-room was in full progress, and Claire was working hard at her tambour frame, earning money respectably, and listening to the coming and going of the visitors, when there was a tap at her bedroom door, and the maid Eliza entered.

"If you please, miss," said Eliza, and stopped.

"Yes, Eliza," and the soft white hand remained suspended over the canvas, with the needle glittering between the taper fingers.

"If you please, miss, there's that young man at the kitchen door."

"That young man?"

"The soldier, miss; and he do look nice: Mr James Bell."

There was a flush in Eliza's face. It might have been that which fled from Claire's, leaving it like ivory.

"Where is your master?"

"He went out on the parade, miss."

"And Mr Morton?"

"Hush, miss! he said I wasn't to tell. He bought two herrings of Fisherman Dick at the back door, and I believe he've gone to the end of the pier, fishing."

"I'll come down, Eliza."

Eliza tripped off to hurry down to the handsome young dragoon waiting in the kitchen, and wonder whether he was Miss Claire's sweetheart, and wish he were hers, for he did look so lovely in his uniform and spurs.

As soon as Claire was alone she threw herself upon her knees beside her bed, to rise up at the end of a minute, the tears in her eyes, and a troubled look covering her handsome face with gloom.

Then she hurried down, barely escaping Major Rockley, who did contrive to raise his hat and direct a smile at her before she was gone—

darting in at the empty breakfast-room door, and waiting there trembling till the Major had passed the window and looked up in vain to see if she were there.

"What a coincidence," she thought, as her heart beat painfully, and a smarting blush came in her cheeks.

But the Major was gone; there was no fear of encountering him now; and she hurried into the kitchen, where a handsome, bluff-looking, fair young man of goodly proportions, who sat stiffly upright in his dragoon undress uniform, was talking to Eliza, who moved from the table against which she had been leaning, and left the kitchen.

"Oh, Fred dear," cried Claire, as the blond young soldier rose from his chair, took her in his arms, and kissed her tenderly.

"Why, Claire, my pet, how are you?" he cried; and Eliza, who had peeped through the key-hole, gave her foot a spiteful stamp.

"So miserable, Fred dear. But you must not come here."

"Oh, I won't come to the front, and disgrace you all; but hang it, you might let me come to the back. Getting too proud, I suppose."

"Fred! don't talk so, dear. You hurt me."

"Well, I won't, pet. Bless you for a dear, sweet girl. But it does seem hard."

"Then why not try and leave the service, Fred? I'll save all I can to try and buy you out, but you must help me."

"Bah! Stuff, little one! What's the good? Suppose I get my discharge. That's the good? What can I do? I shall only take to the drink again. I'm not fit for anything but a common soldier. No; I must stop as I am. The poor old governor meant well, Clairy, but it was beggarly work—flunkey work, and it disgusted me."

"Oh, Fred!"

"Well, it did, little one. I was sick of the fashionable starvation, and I suppose I was too fond of the drink, and so I enlisted."

"But you don't drink much now, Fred."

"Don't get the chance, little one," he said, with a bluff laugh. "There, I'll keep away. I won't disgrace you all."

"Dear Fred," said Claire, crying softly.

"And I won't talk bitterly to you, my pet. I say, didn't I see the Major come in at the front?"

"Yes, dear. He went up to see Lady Teigne. She is at home this afternoon."

"Oh, that's right. Didn't come to see you. Master comes in at the front to see the countess; Private James Bell comes in at the back to see you, eh?"

"Fred, dear, you hurt me when you talk like this."

"Then I'll be serious. Rum thing I should drift into being the Major's servant, isn't it? Makes me know him, though. I say, Clairy, you're a beautiful girl, and there's no knowing who may come courting."

"Hush, Fred!"

"Not I. Let me speak. Look here: our Major's one of the handsomest men in the town, Prince's favourite, and all that sort of thing; but if ever he speaks to you, be on your guard, for he's as big a scoundrel as ever breathed, and over head in debt."

"Don't be afraid, Fred," said the girl, smiling.

"I'm not, pet. So the old girl's at home, is she?"

"Yes."

"Sitting in her diamonds and lace, eh?"

Claire nodded.

"Wish I had some of them instead of that old cat—hang her!—for I'm awfully short of money. I say, dear, can you let me have a few shillings?"

Claire's white forehead wrinkled, and she looked at the young soldier in a troubled way, as she drew a little bead purse from her pocket, opened it, and poured five shillings into the broad hand.

"Thank ye," he said coolly, as his eyes rested on the purse. Then, starting up—"Hang it, no," he cried; "I can't. Here, catch hold. Good—bye; God bless you!"

He thrust the money back into her hand, caught her in his arms and kissed her, and before she could detain him he was gone.

That afternoon and evening passed gloomily for Claire. Her father, when he returned from his walk, was restless and strange, and was constantly walking up and down the room.

To make matters worse, her visitor of that afternoon went by two or three times on the other side of the road, gazing very attentively up at the house, and she was afraid that their father might see him.

Then Major Rockley went by, smoking a cigar, raised his hat to her as he saw her at the window, and at the same moment as she returned his salute she saw Private James Bell on the other side, looking at her with a frown full of reproach.

Bedtime came at last, after a serious encounter between the Master of the Ceremonies and his son Morton for staying out till ten. Claire had to go to Lady Teigne again to give her the sleeping-draught she always took, eighty years not having made her so weary that she could sleep; and then there was the wine-glass to half fill with water, and quite fill with salad oil, so that a floating wick might burn till morning.

"Good-night, Lady Teigne," said Claire softly.

There was no answer; and the young girl bent over the wreck of the fashionable beauty, thinking how like she looked to death.

Midnight, and the tide going out, while the waves broke restlessly upon the shingle, which they bathed with pallid golden foam. The sea was black as ink, with diamonds sparkling in it here and there reflected from the encrusted sky; and there was the glitter and sparkle of jewels in Lady Teigne's bedchamber, as two white hands softly lifted them from the wrenched-open casket.

That floating wick in the glass of oil looked like the condensation of some of the phosphorescence of the sea, and in its light the jewels glittered; but it cast as well a boldly-thrown aquiline shadow on the chamber wall. *Ching*!

The jewels fell back into the casket as a gasp came from the bed, and the man saw the light of recognition in the eyes that glared in his as the old woman sat up, holding herself there with her supporting hands.

"Ah!" she cried. "You?"

The word "Help!"—a harsh, wild cry—was half formed, but only half, for in an instant she was dashed back, and the great down pillow pressed over her face.

The tide was going out fast.

# Chapter Five
# A Night to be Remembered

There was a flush on Claire Denville's cheek as she turned restlessly upon her pillow. Her dreams were of pain and trouble, and from time to time a sigh escaped her lips.

The rushlight which burned in a socket set in the middle of a tin cup of water, surrounded by a japanned cylinder full of holes, sent curious shadows and feeble rays about the plainly furnished room, giving everything a weird and ghostly look as the thin rush candle burned slowly down.

All at once she started up, listened, and remained there, hardly breathing. Then, as if not satisfied, she rose, hurriedly dressed herself, and, lighting a candle, went down to Lady Teigne's room.

The position had been unsought, but had been forced upon her by the exacting old woman, and by degrees Claire had found herself personal attendant, and liable to be called up at any moment during one of the many little attacks that the great sapper and miner made upon the weak fortress, tottering to its fall.

Was it fancy, or had she heard Lady Teigne call?

It seemed to Claire, as she descended, that she had been lying in an oppressive dream, listening to call after call, but unable to move and master the unseen force that held her down.

She paused as she reached the landing, with the drawing-room door on her right, Lady Teigne's bedroom before her, and, down a short passage on her left, her father's room. Isaac slept in his pantry, by the empty plate-chest and the wineless cellar. Morton's room was next her own, on the upper floor, and the maids slept at the back.

The only sound to be heard was the faint wash of the waves as they curled over upon the shingle where the tide was going out.

"It must have been fancy," said Claire, after listening intently; and she stood there with the light throwing up the eager look upon her face, with her lips half parted, and a tremulous motion about her well-cut nostrils as her bosom rose and fell.

Then, drawing a breath full of relief, she turned to go, the horror that had assailed her dying off; for ever since Lady Teigne had been beneath their roof, Claire had been haunted by the idea that some night she would be called up at a time when the visit her ladyship insisted in every act was so far off had been paid.

Feeling for the moment, then, satisfied that she had been deceived, Claire ascended three or four stairs, her sweet face growing composed, and the soft, rather saddened smile that generally sat upon her lips gradually returning, when, as if moved by a fresh impulse, she descended again, listened, and then softly turned the handle of the door, and entered.

She did not close the door behind her, only letting it swing to, and then, raising the candle above her head, glanced round.

There was nothing to take her attention.

The curtain of the bed was drawn along by the head, and in an untidy way, leaving the end of the bolster exposed. But that only indicated that the fidgety, querulous old woman had fancied she could feel a draught from the folding-doors that led into the drawing-room, and she had often drawn them like that before.

"She is fast asleep," thought Claire.

The girl was right; Lady Teigne was fast asleep.

"If I let the light fall upon her face it will wake her," she said to herself.

But it was an error; the light Claire Denville carried was too dim for that. Still she hesitated to approach the bedside, knowing that unless she took her opiate medicine Lady Teigne's night's rest was of a kind that rendered her peevish and irritable the whole of the next day, and as full of whims as some fretful child.

She seemed to be sleeping so peacefully that Claire once more glanced round the room prior to returning to bed.

The folding-doors were closed so that there could be no draught. The glass of lemonade was on the little table on the other side of the bed, on which ticked the little old carriage-clock, for Lady Teigne was always anxious about the lapse of time. The jewel-casket was on the—

No: the jewel-casket was not on the dressing-table, and with a spasm of dread shooting through her, Claire Denville stepped quietly to the bedside, drew back the curtain, holding the candle above her head, let fall the curtain and staggered back with her eyes staring with horror, her lips apart, and her breath held for a few moments, but to come again with a hoarse sob.

She did not shriek aloud; she did not faint. She stood there with her face thrust forward, her right arm crooked and extended as if in the act of drawing back the curtain, and her left hand still holding the candlestick above her head—stiffened as it were by horror into the position, and gazing still toward the bed.

That hoarse sob, that harsh expiration of the breath seemed to give her back her power of movement, and, turning swiftly, she ran from the room and down the short passage to rap quickly at her father's door.

"Papa! Papa!" she cried, in a hoarse whisper, trembling now in every limb, and gazing with horror-stricken face over her shoulder, as if she felt that she was being pursued.

Almost directly she heard a faint clattering sound of a glass rattling on the top of the water-bottle as someone crossed the room, the night-bolt was raised, the door opened, and the Master of the Ceremonies stood there, tall and thin, with his white hands tightly holding his long dressing-gown across his chest.

His face was ghastly as he gazed at Claire. There was a thick dew over his forehead, so dense that it glistened in the light of the candle, and made his grey hair cling to his white temples.

He had evidently not been undressed, for his stiff white cravat was still about his neck, and the silken strings of his pantaloons were still tied at the ankles. Moreover, the large signet-ring that had grown too large for his thin finger had not been taken off. It was as if he had hastily thrown off his coat, and put on his dressing-gown; but, though the night was warm, he was shivering, his lower lip trembling, and he had hard work to keep his teeth from chattering together like the glass upon the carafe.

"Father," cried Claire, catching him by the breast, "then you have heard something?"

"Heard—heard something?" he stammered; and then, seeming to make an effort to recover his *sang froid*, "heard something? Yes—you—startled me."

"But—but—oh, papa! It is too horrible!"

She staggered, and had to hold by him to save herself from falling. But recovering somewhat, she held him by one hand, then thrust herself away, looking the trembling man wildly in the face.

"Did you not hear—that cry?"

"No," he said hastily, "no. What is the matter?"

"Lady Teigne! Quick! Oh, father, it cannot be true!"

"Lady—Lady Teigne?" he stammered, "is—is she—is she ill?"

"She is dead—she is dead!" wailed Claire.

"No, no! No, no! Impossible!" cried the old man, who was shivering visibly.

"It is true," said Claire. "No, no, it cannot be. I must be wrong. Quick! It may be some terrible fit!"

She clung to his hand, and tried to hurry him out of the room, but he drew back.

"No," he stammered, "not yet. Your—your news—agitated me, Claire. Does—wait a minute—does anyone—in the—in the house know?"

"No, dear. I thought I heard a cry, and I came down, and she—"

"A fit," he said hastily, as he took the glass from the top of the water-bottle, filled it, gulped the water down, and set bottle and glass back in their places. "A fit—yes—a fit."

"Come with me, father, quick!" cried Claire.

"Yes. Yes, I'll go with you—directly," he said, fumbling for his handkerchief in the tail of the coat thrown over the chair, finding his snuff-box, and taking a great pinch.

"Come, pray come!" she cried again, as she gazed at him in a bewildered way, his trembling becoming contagious, and her lips quivering with a new dread greater than the horror at the end of the passage.

"Yes—yes," he faltered—"I'll come. So alarming to be woke up—like this—in the middle of the night. Shall I—shall I ring, Claire? Or will you call the maids?"

"Come with me first," cried Claire. "It may not be too late."

"Yes," he cried, "it is—it is too late."

"Father!"

"You—you said she was dead," he cried hastily. "Yes—yes—let us go. Perhaps only a fit. Come."

He seemed to be now as eager to go as he had been to keep back, and, holding his child's hand tightly, he hurried with her to Lady Teigne's apartment, where he paused on the mat to draw a long, catching breath.

The next moment the door had swung to behind them, and father and daughter stood gazing one at the other.

"Don't, don't," he cried, in a low, angry voice, as he turned from her. "Don't look at me like that, Claire. What—what do you want me to do?"

Claire turned her eyes from him to gaze straight before her in a curiously dazed manner; and then, without a word, she crossed to the bedside and drew back the curtain, fixing her father with her eyes once more.

"Look!" she said, in a harsh whisper; "quick! See whether we are in time."

The old man uttered a curious supplicating cry, as if in remonstrance against the command that forced him to act, and, as if in his sleep, and with his eyes fixed upon those of his child, he walked up close to the bed, bent over it a moment, and then with a shudder he snatched the curtain from Claire's hand, and thrust it down.

"Dead!" he said, with a gasp. "Dead!"

There was an awful silence in the room for a few moments, during which the ticking of the little clock on the table beyond the bed sounded painfully loud, and the beat of the waves amid the shingle rose into a loud roar.

"Father, she has been—"

"Hush!" he half shrieked, "don't say so. Oh, my child, my child!"

Claire trembled, and it was as though a mutual attraction drew them to gaze fixedly the one at the other, in spite of every effort to tear their eyes away.

At last, with a wrench, the old man turned his head aside, and Claire uttered a low moan as she glanced from him to the bed and then back towards the window.

"Ah!" she cried, starting forward, and, bending down beside the dressing-table, she picked up the casket that was lying half hidden by drapery upon the floor.

But the jewel-casket was quite empty, and she set it down upon the table. It had been wrenched open with a chisel or knife-blade, and the loops of the lock had been torn out.

"Shall we—a doctor—the constables?" he stammered.

"I—I do not know," said Claire hoarsely, acting like one in a dream; and she staggered forward, kicking against something that had fallen near the casket.

She involuntarily stooped to pick it up, but it had been jerked by her foot nearer to her father, who bent down with the quickness of a boy and snatched it up, hiding it hastily beneath his dressing-gown, but not so quickly that Claire could not see that it was a great clasp-knife.

"What is that?" she cried sharply.

"Nothing—nothing," he said.

They stood gazing at each other for a few moments, and then the old man uttered a hoarse gasp.

"Did—did you see what I picked up?" he whispered; and he caught her arm with his trembling hand.

"Yes; it was a knife."

"No," he cried wildly. "No; you saw nothing. You did not see me pick up that knife."

"I did, father," said Claire, shrinking from him with an invincible repugnance.

"You did not," he whispered. "You dare not say you did, when I say be silent."

"Oh, father! father!" she cried with a burst of agony.

"It means life or death," he whispered, grasping her arm so tightly that his fingers seemed to be turned to iron. "Come," he cried with more energy, "hold the light."

He crossed the room and opened the folding-doors, going straight into the drawing-room, when the roar of the surf upon the shore grew louder, and as Claire involuntarily followed, she listened in a heavy-dazed way as her father pointed out that a chair had been overturned, and that the window was open and one of the flower-pots in the balcony upset.

"The jasmine is torn away from the post and balustrade," he said huskily; "someone must have climbed up there."

Claire did not speak, but listened to him as he grew more animated now, and talked quickly.

"Let us call up Isaac and Morton," he said. "We must have help. The doctor should be fetched, and—and a constable."

Claire gazed at him wildly.

"Did—did you hear anything?" he said hurriedly, as he closed the folding-doors.

"I was asleep," said Claire, starting and shuddering as she heard his words. "I thought I heard a cry."

"Yes, a cry," he said; "I thought I heard a cry and I dressed quickly and was going to see, when—when you came to me. Recollect that you will be called up to speak, my child—an inquest—that is all you know. You went in and found Lady Teigne dead, and you came and summoned me. That is all you know."

She did not answer, and he once more gripped her fiercely by the wrist.

"Do you hear me?" he cried. "I say that is all you know."

She looked at him again without answering, and he left her to go and summon Morton and the footman.

Claire stood in the drawing-room, still holding the candlestick in her hand, with the stiffening form of the solitary old woman, whose flame of life had been flickering so weakly in its worldly old socket that the momentary touch of the extinguisher had been sufficient to put it out, lying just beyond those doors; on the other hand the roar of the falling tide faintly heard now through the closed window. She heard her father knocking at the door of her brother's room. Then she heard the stairs creak as he descended to call up the footman from the pantry below; and as she listened everything seemed strange and unreal, and she could not believe that a horror had fallen upon them that should make a hideous gulf between her and her father for ever, blast her young life so that she would never dare again to give her innocent love to the man by whom she knew she was idolised, and make her whole future a terror—a terror lest that which she felt she knew must be discovered, if she, weak woman that she was, ever inadvertently spoke what was life and light to her—the truth.

"My God! What shall I do?"

It was a wild passionate cry for help where she felt that help could only be, and then, with her brain swimming, and a horrible dread upon her, she was about to open her lips and denounce her own father—the man who gave her life—as a murderer and robber of the dead. She turned to the door as it opened, and, deadly pale, but calm and firm now, Stuart Denville, Master of the Ceremonies at Saltinville, entered the room.

He uttered a low cry, and started forward to save her, but he was too late. Claire had fallen heavily upon her face, her hands outstretched, and the china candlestick she still held was shattered to fragments upon the floor.

At that moment, as if in mockery, a sweet, low chord of music rose from without, below the window, and floating away on the soft night air, the old man felt the sweet melody thrill his very nerves as he sank upon his knees beside his child.

# Chapter Six
# A Ghastly Serenade

"Gentlemen," said Colonel Lascelles, "I am an old fogey, and I never break my rules. At my time of life a man wants plenty of sleep, so I must ask you to excuse me. Rockley shall take my place, and I beg—I insist—that none will stir. Smith, send the Major's servant to see if he is better."

A smart-looking dragoon, who had been acting the part of butler at the mess table, saluted.

"Beg pardon, sir, James Bell is sick."

"Drunk, you mean, sir," cried the Colonel angrily. "Confound the fellow! he is always tippling the mess wine."

"Small blame to him, Colonel," said the Adjutant with tipsy gravity; "'tis very good."

"And disagreed with his master early in the evening," said the Doctor.

Here there was a roar of laughter, in which the greyheaded Colonel joined.

"Well, gentlemen, we must not be hard," he said. "Here, Smith, my compliments to Major Rockley, and if he is better, say we shall be glad to see him."

"Beg pardon, sir," said the man, "here is the Major."

At that moment the gentleman in question entered the room, and the brilliant illumination of the table gave a far better opportunity for judging his appearance than the blind-drawn gloom of Lady Teigne's drawing-room. He was a strikingly handsome dark man, with a fierce black moustache that seemed to divide his face in half, and then stood out beyond each cheek in a black tuft, hair highly pomatumed and curled, and bright black eyes that seemed to flash from beneath his rather overhanging brows. Five-and-thirty was about his age, and he looked it all, time or dissipation having drawn a good many fine lines, like tracings of future wrinkles, about the corners of his eyes and mouth.

"Colonel—gentlemen, a hundred apologies," he said. "I'm not often taken like this. We must have a fresh mess-man. Our cooking is execrable."

"And your digestion so weak," said the Doctor, sipping his port.

"There, there," said the Colonel hastily. "I want to get to bed. Take my place, Rockley; keep them alive. Good-night, gentlemen; I know you'll excuse me. Good-night."

The Colonel left his seat, faced round, stood very stiffly for a few moments, and then walked straight out of the room, while Major Rockley, who was still far from sober, took his place.

A good many bottles of port had been consumed that night, for in those days it was an English gentleman's duty to pay attention to his port, and after turning exceedingly poorly, and having to quit the table, the Major began by trying to make up for the past in a manner that would now be classed as loud.

"Gentlemen, pray—pray, pass the decanters," he cried. "Colonel Mellersh, that port is not to your liking. Smith, some more claret? Mr Linnell, 'pon honour, you know you must not pass the decanter without filling your glass. Really, gentlemen, I am afraid our guests are disappointed at the absence of Colonel Lascelles, and because a certain gentleman has not honoured us to-night. A toast, gentlemen: HRH."

"HRH" was chorused as every officer and guest rose at the dark, highly-polished mahogany table, liberally garnished with decanters, bottles, and fruit; and, with a good deal of demonstration, glasses were waved in the air, a quantity of rich port was spilled, and the fact was made very evident that several of the company had had more than would leave them bright and clear in the morning.

The mess-room of the Light Dragoon Regiment was handsome and spacious; several trophies of arms and colours decorated the walls; that unusual military addition, a conservatory, opened out of one side; and in it, amongst the flowers, the music-stands of the excellent band that had been playing during dinner were still visible, though the bandsmen had departed when the cloth was drawn.

The party consisted of five-and-twenty, many being in uniform, with their open blue jackets displaying their scarlet dress vests with the ridge of pill-sized buttons closely packed from chin to waist; and several of the wearers of these scarlet vests were from time to time pouring confidences into their neighbours' ears, the themes being two: "The cards" and "She."

"Colonel Mellersh, I am going to ask you to sing," said Major Rockley, after taking a glass of port at a draught, and looking a little less pale.

The Master of the Ceremonies | 39

He turned to a striking-looking personage at his right—a keen, aquiline-featured man, with closely-cut, iron-grey hair, decisive, largish mouth with very white teeth, and piercing dark-grey eyes which had rather a sinister look from the peculiarity of his fierce eyebrows, which seemed to go upwards from where they nearly joined.

"I'm afraid my voice is in no singing trim," said the Colonel, in a quick, loud manner.

"Come, no excuses," cried a big heavy-faced, youngish man from the bottom of the long table—a gentleman already introduced to the reader in Lady Teigne's drawing-room.

"No excuse, Sir Matt," cried the Colonel; "only an apology for the quality of what I am about to sing."

There was a loud tapping and clinking of glasses, and then the Colonel trolled forth in a sweet tenor voice an anacreontic song about women, and sparkling wine, and eyes divine, and flowing bowls, and joyous souls, and ladies bright, as dark as night, and ladies rare, as bright as fair, and so on, and so on, the whole being listened to with the deepest attention and the greatest of satisfaction by a body of gentlemen whose thoughts at the moment, if not set upon women and wine, certainly were upon wine and women.

It was curious to watch the effect of the song upon the occupants of the different chairs. The Major sat back slightly flushed, gazing straight before him at the bright face he conjured up; Sir Matthew Bray leaned forward, and bent and swayed his great handsome Roman-looking head and broad shoulders in solemn satisfaction, and his nearest neighbour, Sir Harry Payne, the handsome, effeminate and dissipated young dragoon, tapped the table with his delicate fingers and showed his white teeth. The stout Adjutant bent his chin down over his scarlet waistcoat and stared fiercely at the ruby scintillations in the decanter before him. The gentleman on his left, an insignificant-looking little civilian with thin, fair hair, screwed up his eyes and drew up his lips in what might have been a smile or a sneer, and stared at the gentleman on the Major's left, holding himself a little sidewise so as to peer between one of the silver branches and the épergne.

The young man at whom he stared was worth a second look, as he leaned forward with his elbows upon the table and his head on one side, his cheek leaning upon his clasped hands.

He was fair with closely curling hair, broad forehead, dark eyes, and what was very unusual in those days, his face was innocent of the touch of a razor, his nut-brown beard curling closely and giving him rather a peculiar appearance among the scented and closely-shaven dandies around.

As the song went on he kept his eyes fixed on Colonel Mellersh, but the words had no charm for him: he was thinking of the man who sang, and of the remarkable qualities of his voice, uttering a sigh of satisfaction and sinking back in his seat as the song ended and there was an abundance of applause.

"Come," cried Major Rockley, starting up again; "I have done so well this time, gentlemen, that I shall call upon my friend here, Mr Linnell, to give us the next song."

"Indeed, I would with pleasure," said the young man, colouring slightly; "but Colonel Mellersh there will tell you I never sing."

"No; Linnell never sings, but he's a regular Orpheus with his lute or pipe—I mean the fiddle and the flute."

"Then perhaps he will charm us, and fancy he has come into the infernal regions for the nonce; only, 'fore gad, gentlemen, I am not the Pluto who has carried off his Eurydice."

"Really, this is so unexpected," said the young man, "and I have no instrument."

"Oh, some of your bandsmen have stringed instruments, Rockley."

"Yes, yes, of course," cried the Major. "What is it to be, Mr Linnell? We can give you anything. Why not get up a quintette, and let Matt Bray there take the drum, and charming Sir Harry Payne the cymbals?"

"Play something, Dick," said Colonel Mellersh quietly.

"Yes, of course," said the young man. "Will you help me?"

"Oh, if you like," said the Colonel. "Rockley, ask your men to lend us a couple of instruments."

"Really, my dear fellow, we haven't a lute in the regiment."

"I suppose not," said the Colonel dryly. "A couple of violins will do. Here, my man, ask for a violin and viola."

The military servant saluted and went out, and to fill up the time Major Rockley proposed a toast.

"With bumpers, gentlemen. A toast that every man will drink. Are you ready?"

There was a jingle of glasses, the gurgle of wine, and then a scattered volley of "Yes!"

"Her bright eyes!" said the Major, closing his own and kissing his hand.

"Her bright eyes!" cried everyone but the Adjutant, who growled out a malediction on somebody's eyes.

Then the toast was drunk with three times three, there was the usual clattering of glasses as the gentlemen resumed their seats, and some of those who had paid most attention to the port began with tears in their eyes to expatiate on the charms of some special reigning beauty, receiving confidences of a like nature. Just then, the two instruments were brought and handed to the Colonel and Richard Linnell, a sneering titter going round the table, and a whisper about "fiddlers" making the latter flush angrily.

"Yes, gentlemen, fiddlers," said Colonel Mellersh quietly; "and it requires no little skill to play so grand and old an instrument. I'll take my note from you, Dick."

Flushing more deeply with annoyance, Richard Linnell drew his bow across the A string, bringing forth a sweet pure note that thrilled through the room, and made one of the glasses ring.

"That's right," said the Colonel. "I wish your father were here. What's it to be?"

"What you like," said Linnell, whose eyes were wandering about the table, as if in search of the man who would dare to laugh and call him "fiddler" again.

"Something simple that we know."

Linnell nodded.

"Ready, gentlemen," said the Major, with a sneering look at Sir Harry Payne. "Silence, please, ye demons of the nether world. 'Hark, the lute!' No: that's the wrong quotation. Now, Colonel—Mr Linnell, we are all attention."

Richard Linnell felt as if he would have liked to box the Major's ears with the back of the violin he held; but, mastering his annoyance, he stood up, raised it to his shoulder, and drew the bow across the strings, playing in the most perfect time, and with the greatest expression, the first bars of a sweet old duet, the soft mellow viola taking up the seconds; and then, as the players forgot all present in the sweet harmony they were producing, the notes came pouring forth in trills, or sustained delicious, long-drawn passages from two fine instruments, handled by a couple of masters of their art.

As they played on sneers were changed for rapturous admiration, and at last, as the final notes rang through the room in a tremendous vibrating chord that it seemed could never have been produced by those few tightly-drawn strings, there was a furious burst of applause, glasses were broken, decanters hammered the table, and four men who had sunk beneath, suffering from too many bottles, roused up for the moment to shout ere they sank asleep again, while the Major excitedly stretched out his hand first to one and then to the other of the performers.

"Gentlemen," he cried at last, hammering the table to obtain order, "I am going to ask a favour of our talented guests. This has come upon me like a revelation. Such music is too good for men."

"Hear! hear! hear! hear!" came in chorus.

"It is fit only for the ears of those we love."

"Hear!—hear!—hear!—hear!"

"We have drunk their health, to-night; each the health of the woman of his heart."

"Hear!—hear!—hear!—hear!"

"And now, as we have such music, I am going to beg our guests to come with us and serenade a lady whose name I will not mention."

"Hear!—hear!—hurrah!"

"It is the lady I am proud to toast, and I ask the favour of you, Colonel Mellersh, of you, Mr Linnell, to come and play that air once through beneath her window."

"Oh, nonsense, Rockley. My dear fellow, no," cried the Colonel.

"My dear Mellersh," said the Major with half-tipsy gravity. "My dear friend; and you, my dear friend Linnell, I pray you hear me. It may mean much more than you can tell—the happiness of my life. Come, my dear fellow, you'll not refuse."

"What do you say, Linnell?" cried the Colonel good-humouredly.

"Oh, it is so absurd," said Linnell warmly.

"No, no, not absurd," said the Major sternly. "I beg you'll not refuse."

"Humour him, Dick," said the Colonel in a whisper.

"You are telling him not to play," said the Major fiercely.

"My dear fellow, no: I was asking him to consent. Humour him, Dick," said the Colonel. "It's nearly two, and there'll be no one about. If we refuse it may mean a quarrel."

"I'll go if you wish it," said Richard Linnell quietly.

"All right, Major; we'll serenade your lady in good old Spanish style," said the Colonel laughingly. "Quick, then, at once. How far is it?"

"Not far," cried the Major. "Who will come? Bray, Payne, and half a dozen more. Will you be one, Burnett?"

"No, not I," said the little, fair man with the sneering smile; "I shall stay;" and he gave effect to his words by sinking back in his chair and then gliding softly beneath the table.

"Just as you like," said the Major, and the result was that a party of about a dozen sallied out of the barrack mess-room, crossed the yard, and were allowed to pass by the sentry on duty, carbine on arm.

It was a glorious night, and as they passed out into the fresh, pure air and came in sight of the golden-spangled sea, which broke amongst the shingle with a low, dull roar, the blood began to course more quickly through Linnell's veins, the folly of the adventure was forgotten, and a secret wish that he and the Colonel were alone and about to play some sweet love ditty, beneath a certain window, crossed his brain.

For there was something in the time there, beneath the stars that were glitteringly reflected in the sea! Did she love him? Would she ever love him? he thought, and he walked on in a sweet dream of those waking moments, forgetful of the Major, and hearing nothing of the conversation of his companions, knowing nothing but the fact that he was a man of seven and twenty, whose thoughts went hourly forth to dwell upon one on whom they had long been fixed, although no words had passed, and he had told himself too often that he dare not hope.

"Who is the Major's Gloriana, Dick?" asked the Colonel suddenly. "By Jove, I think we had better tune up a jig. It would be far more suited to the woman he would choose than one of our young composer's lovely strains."

"I don't know. He's going towards our place. Can it be Cora Dean?"

"Hang him, no," said the Colonel pettishly. "Perhaps so, though. I hope not, or we shall have your father calling us idiots—deservedly so—for our pains. Wrong, Dick; the old man will sleep in peace. Will it be Drelincourt?"

"Madame Pontardent, perhaps."

"No, no, no, my lad; he's going straight along. How lovely the sea looks!"

"And how refreshing it is after that hot, noisy room."

"Insufferable. What fools men are to sit and drink when they might play whist!"

"And win money," said Linnell drily.

"To be sure, my lad. Oh, you'll come to it in time. Where the dickens is he going? Who can the lady be?"

The Major evidently knew, for he was walking smartly ahead, in earnest converse with half a dozen more. Then came the Colonel and his companion, and three more of the party brought up the rear.

The Major's course was still by the row of houses that faced the sea, now almost without a light visible, and Richard Linnell was dreamily watching the waves that looked like liquid gold as they rose, curved over and broke upon the shingle, when all the blood seemed to rush at once to his heart, and then ebb away, leaving him choking and paralysed, for the Colonel suddenly said aloud:

"Claire Denville!"

And he saw that their host of the night had stopped before the house of the Master of the Ceremonies.

The blood began to flow again, this time with a big wave of passionate rage in Richard Linnell's breast. He was furious. How dared that handsome libertine profane Claire Denville by even thinking of her? How dared he bring him there, to play beneath the window—the window he had so often watched, and looked upon as a sacred temple—the resting-place of her he loved.

He was ready to seize the Major by the throat; to fight for her; to say anything; to dash down the instrument in his rage; to turn and flee; but the next moment the cool, calm voice of the Colonel brought him to his senses, and he recalled that this was his secret—his alone—this secret of his love.

"I did not know the Major was warm there. Well, she's a handsome girl, and he's welcome, I dare say."

Linnell felt ready to choke again, but he could not speak. He must get out of this engagement, though, at any cost.

As he was musing, though, he found himself drawn as it were to where the Major and his friends were standing in front of the silent house, and the Colonel said:

"Come, my lad, let's run through the piece, and get home to bed. I'm too old for such tom-fool tricks as these."

"I will not play! It is an insult! It is madness!" thought Richard Linnell; and then, as if in a dream, he found himself the centre of a group, fuming at what he was doing, while, as if in spite of his rage, he was drawing the sweet echoing strains from the violin, listening to the harmonies added by his friend, and all in a nightmare-like fashion, playing involuntarily on, and gazing at the windows he had so often watched.

On, on, on, the notes poured forth, throbbing on the night air, sounding pensive, sweet and love-inspiring, maddening too, as he tried to check his thoughts, and played with more inspiration all the while till the last bar, with its diminuendo, was reached, and he stood there, palpitating, asking himself why he had done this thing, and waiting trembling in his jealous rage, lest any notice should be taken of the compliment thus paid.

Did Claire Denville encourage the Major—that libertine whose amours were one of the scandals of the place? Oh, it was impossible. She would not have heard the music. If she had she would have thought it from some wanderers, for she had never heard him play. She would not notice it. She would not heed it. In her virgin youth and innocency it was a profanation to imagine that Claire Denville—sweet, pure Claire Denville—the woman he worshipped, could notice such an attention. No, it was impossible she would; and his eyes almost started as he gazed at the white-curtained windows, looking so solemn and so strange.

No, no, no; she would not notice, even if she had heard, and a strange feeling of elation came into the jealous breast.

"Come," he said hoarsely, "let us go."

"One moment, lad. Ah, yes," said the Colonel. "Gloriana has heard the serenade, and is about to respond to her lover's musically amatory call. Look, Dick, look."

Richard Linnell's heart sank, for a white arm drew back the curtain, and then the catch of the window fastening was pressed back, and a chord in the young man's breast seemed to snap; but it was only the spring of the window hasp.

*Click!*

# Chapter Seven
# After the Storm

The "ghastly serenade" it was called at Saltinville as the facts became known.

That night Richard Linnell was standing with his teeth set, his throat dry, and a feeling of despair making his heart seem to sink, watching the white hand that was waved as soon as the sash was opened. Half blind with the blood that seemed to rush to his eyes, he glared at the window. Then a sudden revulsion of feeling came over him as a familiar voice that was not Claire's cried, "Help!—a doctor!" and then the speaker seemed to stagger away.

The rest was to Richard Linnell like some dream of horror, regarding which he recalled the next morning that he had thundered at the door, that he had helped to carry Claire to her room, and that he had afterwards been one of the group who stood waiting in the dining-room until the doctor came down to announce that Miss Denville was better—that Lady Teigne was quite dead.

Then they had stolen out on tiptoe, and in the stillness of the early morning shaken hands all round and separated, the Major remaining with them, and walking with Colonel Mellersh and Richard Linnell to their door.

"What a horror!" he said hoarsely. "I would not for the world have taken you two there had I known. Good-night—good-morning, I should say;" and he, too, said those words—perhaps originated the saying—"What a ghastly serenade!"

Nine days—they could spare no more in Saltinville, for it would have spoiled the season—nine days' wonder, and then the news that a certain royal person was coming down, news blown by the trumpet of Fame with her attendants, raised up enough wind to sweep away the memory of the horror on the Parade.

"She was eighty if she was a day," said Sir Matthew Bray: "and it was quite time the old wretch did die."

"Nice way of speaking of a lady whose relative you are seeking to be," said Sir Harry Payne. "Sweet old nymph. How do you make it fit, Matt?"

"Fit? Some scoundrel of a London tramp scaled the balcony, they say. Fine plunder, the rascal! All those diamonds."

"Which she might have left her sister, and then perhaps they would have come to you, Matt."

"Don't talk stuff."

"Stuff? Why, you are besieging the belle. But, I say, I have my own theory about that murder."

"Eh, have you?" cried the great dragoon, staring open-mouthed.

"Egad! yes, Matt. It was not a contemptible robbery."

"Wasn't it? You don't say so."

"But I do," cried Sir Harry seriously. "Case of serious jealousy on the part of some lover of the bewitching creature. He came in the dead o' night and smothered the Desdemona with a pillow. What do you say, Rockley?"

The Major had strolled across the mess-room and heard these words.

"Bah! Don't ridicule the matter," he said. "Change the subject."

"As you like, but the feeble flame only wanted a momentary touch of the extinguisher and it was gone."

At the house on the Parade there had been terrible anguish, and Claire Denville suffered painfully as she passed through the ordeal of the examination that ensued.

But everything was very straightforward and plain. There were the marks of some one having climbed up the pillar—an easy enough task. The window opened without difficulty from without, a pot or two lay overturned in the balcony, a chair in the drawing-room, evidently the work of some stranger, and the valuable suite of diamonds was gone.

The constable arrested three men of the street tumbler and wandering vagrant type, who were examined, proved easily that they were elsewhere; and after the vote of condolence to our esteemed fellow-townsman, Stuart Denville, Esq, which followed the inquest, there seemed nothing more to be done but to bury Lady Teigne, which was accordingly done, and the principal undertaker cleared a hundred pounds by the grand funeral that took place, though it was quite a year before Lady Drelincourt would pay the whole of his bill.

So with Lady Teigne the horror was buried too, and in a fortnight the event that at one time threatened to interfere with the shopkeepers' and lodging-letters' season was forgotten.

For that space of time, too, the familiar figure of the Master of the Ceremonies was not seen upon the Parade. Miss Denville was very ill, it was said, and after the funeral Isaac had to work hard at answering the door to receive the many cards that were left by fashionable people, till there was quite a heap in the old china bowl that stood in the narrow hall.

But the outside world knew nothing of the agonies of mind endured by the two principal occupants of that house—of the nights of sleepless horror passed by Claire as she knelt and prayed for guidance, and of the hours during which the Master of the Ceremonies sat alone, staring blankly before him as if at some scene which he was ever witnessing, and which seemed to wither him, mind and body, at one stroke.

For that fortnight, save at the inquest, father and daughter had not met, but passed their time in their rooms. But the time was gliding on, and they had to meet—the question occurring to each—how was it to be?

"I must leave it to chance," thought the Master of the Ceremonies, with a shiver; and after a fierce struggle to master the agony he felt, he knew that in future he must lead two lives. So putting on his mask, he one morning walked down to the breakfast-room, and took his accustomed place.

Outwardly he seemed perfectly calm, and, save that the lines about his temples and the corners of his lips seemed deeper, he was little changed; but as he walked he was conscious of a tremulous feeling in the knees, and even when seated, that the curious palsied sensation went on.

On the previous night Morton had come in from a secret fishing excursion, to find the house dark and still, and he had stood with his hands in his pockets hesitating as to whether he should go and take a lesson in smoking with Isaac in the pantry, steal down to the beach, or creep upstairs.

He finally decided on the latter course, and going up to the top of the house on tiptoe, he tapped softly at Claire's bedroom door.

It was opened directly by his sister, who had evidently just risen from an old dimity-covered easy-chair. She was in a long white dressing-gown, and, seen by the light of the one tallow candle on the table, she looked so pale and ghastly that the lad uttered an ejaculation and caught hold of her thin, cold hands.

"Claire!—Sis!"

They were the first warm words of sympathy she had heard since that horrible night; and in a moment the icy horror upon her face broke up, her lips quivered, and, throwing her arms around her brother's neck, she burst into such a passion of hysterical sobbing that, as he held her to his breast, he grew alarmed.

He had stepped into the little white room where the flower screen stood out against the night sky, and as the door swung to, he had felt Claire sinking upon her knees, and imitating her action, he had held her there for some time till the attitude grew irksome, and then sank lower till he was seated on the carpet, holding his sister half-reclining across his breast.

"Oh! don't—don't, Claire—Sis," he whispered from time to time, as he kissed the quivering lips, and strove in his boyish way to soothe her. "Sis dear, you'll give yourself such a jolly headache. Oh, I say, what's the good of crying like that?"

For answer she only clung the tighter, the pent-up agony escaping in her tears, though she kissed him passionately again and again, and nestled to his breast.

"You'll make yourself ill, you know," he whispered. "I say, don't. The dad's ill, and you'll upset him more."

Still she sobbed on and wept, the outburst saving her from some more terrible mental strain.

"I wanted to come and comfort you," he said. "I did not know you'd go on like this."

She could not tell him that he was comforting her; that she had been tossed by a horrible life-storm that threatened to wreck her reason, and that when she had lain longing for the sympathy of the sister who now kept away, saying it was too horrible to come there now, she had found no life-buoy to which to cling. And now her younger brother had come—the elder forbidden the house—and the intensity of the relief she felt was extreme.

"Here, I can't stand this," he said at last, almost roughly. "I shall go down and send Ike for the doctor."

She clung to him in an agony of dread lest he should go, and her sobs grew less frequent.

"Come, that's better," he said, and he went on in his rough boyish selfishness, talking of his troubles and ignoring those of others, unconsciously strengthening Claire, as he awakened her to a sense of the duties she owed him, and giving her mental force for the terrible meeting and struggle that was to come.

For she dared not think. She shrank from mentally arguing out those two questions of duty—to society and to her father.

Was she to speak and tell all she knew?

Was she to be silent?

All she could do was to shrink within herself, and try to make everything pass out of her thoughts while she was sinking into the icy chains of idiocy.

But now, when she had been giving up completely, and at times gazing out to sea with horrible thoughts assailing her, and suggestions like temptations to seek for oblivion as the only escape from the agony she suffered, the life-raft had reached her hands, and she clung to it with all the tenacity of one mentally drowning fast.

There was something soothing in the very sound of her brother's rough voice speaking in a hoarse whisper; and his selfish repinings over the petty discomforts he had suffered came like words of comfort and rest.

"It has been so jolly blank and miserable downstairs," he went on as he held her, and involuntarily rocked himself to and fro. "Ike and Eliza have been always gossiping at the back and sneaking out to take dinner or tea or supper with somebody's servants, so as to palaver about what's gone on here."

A pause.

"There's been scarcely anything to eat. I've been half-starved."

"Oh, Morton, my poor boy!"

Those were the first words Claire had uttered since the inquest, and they were followed by a fresh burst of sobs.

"Oh, come, come. Do leave off," he cried pettishly. "I say it's all very well for the old man to growl at me for fishing, but if I hadn't gone catching dabs and a little conger or two, I should have been starved."

She raised her face and kissed him. Some one else was suffering, and her woman's instinct to help was beginning to work.

"What do you think I did, Sis? Oh, you don't know. I'd been up to Burnett's to see May, but the beggars had sneaked off and gone to London. Just like Franky Sneerums and wax-doll May. Pretty sort of a sister to keep away when we're in trouble."

"Oh, don't, my dear boy," whispered Claire in a choking voice.

"Oh, yes, I shall. They're ashamed of me and of all of us. Just as if we could help the old girl being killed here."

A horrible spasm ran through Claire.

"Don't jump like that, stupid," said Morton roughly. "You didn't kill her."

"Hush! hush!"

"No, I shan't hush. It'll do you good to talk and hear what people say, my pretty old darling Sis. There, there hush-a-bye, baby. Cuddle up close, and let's comfort you. What's the matter now?"

Claire had struggled up, with her hands upon his shoulders, and was gazing wildly into his eyes.

"What—what do people say?" she panted.

"Be still, little goose—no; pretty little white pigeon," he said, more softly, as he tried to draw her towards him.

"What—do they say?" she cried, in a hoarse whisper, and she trembled violently.

"Why, that it is a jolly good job the old woman is dead, for she was no use to anyone."

Claire groaned as she yielded once more to his embrace.

"Fisherman Dick says—I say, he is a close old nut there's no getting anything out of him!—says he don't see that people like Lady Teigne are any use in the world."

"Morton!"

"Oh, it's all right. I'm only telling you what he said. He says too that the chap who did it—I say, don't kick out like that, Sis. Yes, I shall go on: I'm doing you good. Fisherman Dick, and Mrs Miggles too, said that I ought to try and rouse you up, and I'm doing it. You're ever so much better already. Why, your hands were like dabs when I came up, and now they are nice and warm."

She caressed his cheek with them, and he kissed her as she laid her head on his shoulder.

"Dick Miggles said that the diamonds would never do the chap any good who stole 'em."

Once more that hysterical start, but the boy only clasped his sister more tightly, and went on:

"Dick says he never knew anyone prosper who robbed or murdered, or did anything wrong, except those who smuggled. I say, Sis, I do feel sometimes as if I should go in for a bit of smuggling. There are some rare games going on."

Claire clung to him as if exhausted by her emotion.

"Dick's been in for lots of it, I know, only he's too close to speak. I don't know what I should have done if it hadn't been for them. I've taken the fish I've caught up there, and Polly Miggles has cooked them, and we've had regular feeds."

"You have been up there, Morton?" said Claire wildly.

"Yes; you needn't tell the old man. What was I to do? I couldn't get anything to eat here. I nursed the little girl for Mrs Miggles while she cooked, and Dick has laughed at me to see me nurse the little thing, and said it was rum. But I don't mind; she's a pretty little tit, and Dick has taught her to call me uncle."

# Chapter Eight
# The First Meeting

It was the next morning that the Master of the Ceremonies made his effort, and went down to the breakfast-room, where he sat by the table, playing with the newspaper that he dared not try to read, and waiting, wondering, in a dazed way, whether his son or his daughter would come in to breakfast.

The paper fell from his hands, and as he sat there he caught at the table, drawing the cloth aside and holding it with a spasmodic clutch, as one who was in danger of falling.

For there was the creak of a stair, the faint rustle of a dress, and he knew that the time had come.

He tried to rise to his feet, but his limbs refused their office, and the palsied trembling that had attacked him rose to his hands. Then he loosened his hold of the table, and sank back in his chair, clinging to the arms, and with his chin falling upon his breast.

At that moment the door opened, and Claire glided into the room.

She took a couple of steps forward, after closing the door, and then caught at the back of a chair to support herself.

The agony and horror in his child's face, as their eyes met, galvanised Denville into life, and, starting up, he took a step forward, extending his trembling hands.

"Claire—my child!" he cried, in a husky voice.

His hands dropped, his jaw fell, his eyes seemed to be starting, as he read the look of horror, loathing, and shame in his daughter's face, and for the space of a full minute neither spoke.

Then, as if moved to make another effort, he started spasmodically forward.

"Claire, my child—if you only knew!"

But she shrank from him with the look of horror intensified.

"Don't—don't touch me," she whispered, in a harsh, dry voice. "Don't: pray don't."

"But, Claire—"

"I know," she whispered, trembling violently. "It is our secret. I will not speak. Father—they should kill me first; but don't—don't. Father—father—you have broken my heart!"

As she burst forth in a piteous wail in these words, the terrible involuntary shrinking he had seen in her passed away. The stiff angularity that had seemed to pervade her was gone, and she sank upon her knees, holding by the back of the chair, and rested her brow upon her hands, sobbing and drawing her breath painfully.

He stood there gazing down at her, but for a time he did not move. Then, taking a step forward, he saw that she heard him, and shrank again.

"Claire, my child," he gasped once more, "if you only knew!"

"Hush!—for God's sake, hush!" she said, in a whisper. "Can you not see? It is our secret. You are my father. I am trying so hard. But don't—don't—"

"Don't touch you!" he cried slowly, as she left her sentence unspoken. "Well, be it so," he added, with a piteous sigh; "I will not complain."

"Let it be like some horrible dream," she said, in the same low, painful whisper. "Let me—let me go away."

"No!" he cried, with a change coming over him; and he drew himself up as if her words had given him a sudden strength. "You must stay. You have duties here, and I have mine. Claire, you must stay, and it must be to you—to me, like some horrible dream. Some day you may learn the horrible temptations that beset my path. Till then I accept my fate, for I dare not confide more, even to you. Heaven help me in this horror, and give me strength!" he muttered to himself, with closed eyes. "I dare not die; I cannot—I will not die. I must wear the mask. Two lives to live, when heretofore one only has been so hard!"

Just then there was a quick step outside, and the tall figure of Morton Denville passed the window.

The Master of the Ceremonies glanced at Claire, who started to her feet, and then their eyes met.

"For his sake, Claire," he whispered, "if not for mine."

"For his sake—father," she answered, slowly and reverently, as if it were a prayer; and then to herself, "and for yours—the duty I owe you as your child."

"And I," he muttered to himself, as he stood with a white hand resting upon the table. "I must bear it to the end. I must wear my mask as of old, and wilt Thou give me pardon and the strength?"

Morton entered the room fresh and animated, and his eyes lit up as he saw that it was occupied.

"That's better!" he cried. "Morning, father," and he clasped the old man's hand.

"Good-morning, my dear boy," was the answer, in trembling tones; and then, with the ghost of a smile on the wan lips, "have you been—"

Morton had boisterously clasped Claire in his arms, and kissed her with effusion; and as he saw the loving, wistful look in his child's face, as she passionately returned the caress—one that he told himself would never again be bestowed on him—a pang shot through the old man's breast, and the agony seemed greater than he could bear.

"So—so glad to see you down again, my dear, dear, dear old Sis," cried Morton, with a kiss at almost every word. Then, half holding her still, he turned to the pale, wistful face at the other side of the room, and exclaimed:

"Yes, sir. Don't be angry with me. I *have* been down again, catching dabs."

# Chapter Nine
# Wearing His Mask

"Really, ladies, I—er—should—er—esteem it an honour, but my powers here are limited, and—"

"Rubbish!"

"You'll pardon me?"

"I say—rubbish, Denville."

"Mamma, will you hold your tongue?"

"No, miss; if it comes to that, I won't! Speaking like that to your own mother, who's always working for you as I am, right out here on the open cliff, where goodness knows who mayn't—"

"Mother, be silent!"

"Silent, indeed!"

"Ladies, ladies, you'll pardon me. I say my powers here are—er—very limited."

"Yes, I know all about that, but you must get invitations for mamma and me for the next Assembly."

"I'll try, Miss Dean, but—you'll pardon me—"

"There, don't shilly-shally with him, Betsy; it's all business. Look here, Denville, the day the invitations come there'll be five guineas wrapped up in silver paper under the chayny shepherdess on my droring-room mantelpiece, if you'll just call and look under."

"Really, Mrs Dean, you—you shock me. I could not think of—er—really—er—I will try my best."

"That you will, I know, Mr Denville. Don't take any notice of mamma I hope Miss Denville and Mrs Burnett are well."

"In the best of health, Miss Dean, I thank you. I will—er—do my best. A lovely morning, Mrs Dean. Your humble servant. Miss Cora, yours. Good-morning."

"A nasty old humbug; but he'll have the invitations sent," said Mrs Dean, a big, well-developed, well-preserved woman of fifty, with bright dark eyes that glistened and shone like pebbles polished by the constant attrition of the blinking lids.

"I wish you would not be so horridly coarse, mother; and if you don't drop that 'Betsy' we shall quarrel," said the younger lady, who bore a sufficient likeness to the elder for anyone to have stamped them mother and daughter, though the latter was wanting in her parent's hardness of outline, being a magnificent specimen of womanly beauty. Dark and thoroughly classic of feature, large-eyed, full-lipped, perhaps rather too highly coloured, but this was carried off by the luxuriant black hair, worn in large ringlets flowing down either side of the rounded cheeks they half concealed, by her well-arched black brows and long dark lashes, which shaded her great swimming eyes. Her figure was perfect, and she was in full possession of the ripest womanly beauty, as she walked slowly and with haughty carriage along the cliff, beside the elder dame.

Both ladies were dressed in the very height of the fashion, with enormous wide-spreading open bonnets, heavy with ostrich plumes, tightly-fitting dresses, with broad waistbands well up under the arms, loose scarves, long gloves and reticules ornamented with huge bows of the stiffest silk, like Brobdingnagian butterflies.

"Horrid, coarse indeed! I suppose I mustn't open my mouth next," said the elder lady.

"It would be just as well not," said the younger, "when we are out."

"Then I shall open it as wide as I like, ma'am, and when I like, so now then, Betsy."

"As you please; only if you do, I shall go home, and I shall not go to Assembly or ball with you. It was your wish that I should be Cora."

"No, it wasn't. I wanted Coral, or Coralie, miss."

"And I preferred Cora," said the younger lady with languid hauteur, as if she were practising a part, "and you are always blurting out Betsy."

"Blurting! There's a way to speak to your poor mother, who has made the lady of you that you are. Carriages and diamonds, and grand dinners, and—"

"The smell of the orange peel, and the candles, and the memory of the theatre tacked on to me. 'Actress!' you can see every fine madam we pass say with her eyes, as she draws her skirt aside and turns from me as if I polluted the cliff. I've a deal to be proud of," cried the younger woman fiercely. "For heaven's sake, hold your tongue!"

"Don't go on like that, Betsy—Cora, I mean, my dear. Let 'em sneer. If your poor, dear, dead father did keep a show—well, there, don't bite me, Bet—Cora—*theatre*, and make his money, it's nothing to them, and you'll make a marriage yet, as'll surprise some of 'em if you plays your cards proper!"

"Mother!"

"Say mamma, my dear, now; and do smooth down, my beauty. There, there, there! I didn't mean to upset you. There's Lord Carboro' coming. Don't let him see we've been quarrelling again. I don't know, though," she added softly, as she noticed her child's heightened colour and heaving bosom; "it do make you look so 'andsome, my dear."

"Pish!"

"It do, really. What a beauty you are, Cora. I don't wonder at the fools going mad after you and toasting you—as may be a countess if you like."

"Turn down here," said Cora abruptly. "I don't want to see Carboro'."

"But he made me a sign, my dear; with his eyeglass, dear."

"Let him make a hundred," cried Cora angrily. "He is not going to play with me. Why, he's hanging about after that chit of Denville's."

"Tchah! Cora dear. I wouldn't be jealous of a washed-out doll of a thing like that. Half-starved paupers; and with the disgrace of that horrid murder sticking all over their house."

"Jealous!" cried Cora, with a contemptuous laugh; "jealous of her! Not likely, mother; but I mean to make that old idiot smart if he thinks he is going to play fast and loose with me. Come along."

Without noticing the approaching figure, she turned up the next street, veiling her beautiful eyes once more with their long lashes, and gliding over the pavement with her magnificent figure full of soft undulations that the grotesque fashion of the dress of the day could not hide.

"Oh, Cora, my darling," said her mother, "how can you be so mad and obstinate!—throwing away your chances like that."

"Chances? What do you mean?" cried the beauty.

"Why, you know, my dear. He has never married yet; and he's so rich, and there's his title."

"And are we so poor that we are to humble ourselves and beg because that man has a title?"

"But it is such a title, Betsy," whispered the elder woman.

"And he is so old, and withered, and gouty, and is obliged to drive himself out in a ridiculous donkey-chaise."

"Now, what does that matter, dear?"

"Not much to you, seemingly."

"Now, my lovely, don't—don't. To think that I might live to see my gal, Betsy Dean, a real countess, and such a one as there ain't anywhere at court, and she flying in my face and turning her back upon her chances."

"Mother, do you want to put me in a rage."

"Not in the street, dear; but do—do—turn back!"

"I shall not."

"Then I know the reason why," cried the elder woman.

"What do you mean?"

"You're thinking of that nasty, poverty-stricken, brown-faced fiddler of a fellow, who hasn't even the decency to get himself shaved. I declare he looks more like a Jew than a Christian."

"You mean to make me angry, mother."

"I don't care if I do. There, I say it's a sin and a shame. A real Earl—a real live Lord as good as proposing to you, and you, you great silly soft goose, sighing and whining after a penniless pauper who won't even look at you. Oh! the fools gals are!"

Cora Dean's lips were more scarlet than before, and her beautiful eyes flashed ominously, but she said nothing.

"Going silly after a fellow like that, who's for ever hanging about after Denville's gal. Oh! I hav'n't patience."

She said no more, for her daughter walked so fast that she became short of breath.

"Egad! Juno's put out," said James, Earl of Carboro', peer of the realm, speaking in a high-pitched voice, and then applying one glove to his very red lips, as if he were uneasy there. "What a magnificent figure, though! She's devilish handsome, she is, egad! It's just as well, perhaps. I won't follow her. I'll go on the pier. Let her come round if she likes, and if she doesn't—why, demme, I don't care if she doesn't—now that—"

He smacked his lips, and shook his head, and then drew himself up, rearranging his quaint beaver hat that came down fore and aft, curled up tightly at the sides, and spread out widely at the flat top. He gave his ancient body a bit of a writhe, and then raised his gold eyeglass to gaze at the pier, towards which people seemed to be hastening.

"Eh? Egad, why, what's the matter? Somebody gone overboard? I'll go and see. No, I won't; I'll sit down and wait. I shall soon know. It's deuced hot. Those railings are not safe."

He settled himself on the first seat on the cliff, and, giving the wide watered-silk ribbon a shake, used his broad and square gold-rimmed eyeglass once more, gazing through it at the long, old-fashioned pier that ran down into the sea, amongst whose piles the bright waves that washed the chalky shore of fashionable Saltinville were playing, while an unusual bustle was observable in the little crowd of loungers that clustered on the long low erection.

Meanwhile the Master of the Ceremonies of the fashionable seaside resort honoured of royalty had continued his course towards the pier.

The trouble at his house seemed to be forgotten, and in the pursuit of his profession to serve and be observed—gentleman-in-waiting on society—he looked to-day a tall, rather slight man, with nut-brown hair, carefully curled and slightly suggestive of having been grown elsewhere, closely-shaven face of rather careworn aspect, but delicate and refined. He was a decidedly handsome, elderly man, made ridiculous by a mincing dancing-master deportment, an assumed simpering smile, and a costume in the highest fashion of George the Third's day. His hat has been already described, for it was evidently moulded on the same block as my Lord Carboro's, and the rest of the description will do for the costume of both—in fact, with allowances for varieties of colour and tint, for that of most of the gentlemen who flit in and out in the varied scenes of this story of old seaside life.

His thin, but shapely legs were in the tightest of pantaloons, over which were a glossy pair of Hessian boots with silken tassels where they met the knee. An extremely tight tail coat of a dark bottle green was buttoned over his breast, leaving exposed a goodly portion of a buff waistcoat below the bottom buttons, while the coat collar rose up like a protecting erection, as high as the wearer's ears, and touched and threatened to tilt forward the curly brimmed hat. Two tiny points of a shirt collar appeared above the sides of an enormous stock which rigidly prisoned the neck; a delicate projection of cambric frilling rose from the breast; the hands were tightly gloved, one holding a riding-whip, the top of which was furnished with a broad-rimmed square eyeglass; and beneath the buff vest hung, suspended by a broad, black watered-silk ribbon, a huge bunch of gold seals and keys, one of the former being an enormous three-tabled topaz, which turned in its setting at the wearer's will.

Such was the aspect of the Master of the Ceremonies in morning costume—the man whose services were sought by every new arrival for introduction to the Assembly Room and to the fashionable society of the day—the man who, by unwritten canons of the fashionable world, must needs be consulted for every important fête or dance, and whose offerings from supplicants—he scorned to call them clients—were supposed to yield him a goodly income, and doubtless would do so, did the season happen to be long, and society at Saltinville in force.

Parting from the ladies he had met, he passed on with a feeble smirk, growing more decided, his step more mincing, to bow to some lady, a proceeding calling for grace and ease. The raising and replacing of the hat was ever elaborate, so was the kissing of the tips of the gloves to the horsemen who cantered by. There was quite a kingly dignity full of benevolence in the nods bestowed here and there upon fishers and boatmen in dingy flannel trousers rising to the arm-pits, trousers that looked as if they would have stood alone. Then there was an encounter with a brace of beaux, a halt, the raising and replacing of their hats, and the snuff-box of the Master of the Ceremonies flashed in the bright autumn sunshine as it was offered to each in turn, and pinches were taken of the highly-scented Prince's Mixture out of the historical prince's present—a solid golden, deeply-chased, and massive box. Then there was a loud snuffling noise; three expirations of three breaths in a loud "Hah!" three snappings of three fingers and three thumbs, the withdrawal of three bandanna silk, gold, and scarlet handkerchiefs, to flip away a little snuff from three shirt frills; then the snuff-box flashed and glistened as it was held behind the Master of the Ceremonies, with his gold-mounted whip; three hats were raised again and replaced, their wearers having mutually decided that the day was charming, and Sir Harry Payne, officer of dragoons in mufti, like his chosen companion, Sir Matthew Bray, went one way to "ogle the gyurls," the Master of Ceremonies the other to reach the pier.

Everyone knew him; everyone sought and returned his bow. Fashion's high priest, the ruler of the destinies of many in the season, he was not the man to slight, and the gatekeeper drew back, hat in hand, and the bandmaster bowed low, as with pointed toes, graceful carriage, snuff-box in one hand, eyeglass and whip for the horse he never rode in the other, Stuart Denville walked behind the mask he wore, mincing, and bowing, and condescending, past the groups that dotted the breezy resort.

Half-way down the pier, but almost always hat in hand, and the set smile deepening the lines about his well-cut mouth, he became aware of some excitement towards the end.

There was a shriek and then a babble of voices talking, cries for a boat, and a rush to the side, where a lady, who had arrived in a bath-chair, pushed by a tall footman in mourning livery, surmounted by a huge braided half-moon hat, was gesticulating wildly and going to and fro, now fanning herself with a monstrous black fan, now closing it with a snap, and tapping lady bystanders with it on the shoulder or arm.

"He'll be drowned. I'm sure he'll be drowned. Why is there no boatman? Why is there no help? Oh, here is dear Mr Denville. Oh! Mr Denville, help, help, help!"

Here the lady half turned round, and made with each cry of "help!" a backward step towards the Master of the Ceremonies, who had not accelerated his pace a whit, for fear of losing grace, and who was only just in time—the lady managed that—to catch her as she half leaned against his arm.

"Dear Lady Drelincourt, what terrible accident has befallen us here?"

"My darling!" murmured the lady. "Save him, oh, save him, or I shall die!"

# Chapter Ten
# A Small Rescue

Small matters make great excitements among idle seaside people, and as Denville gracefully helped Lady Drelincourt to a chair, and stepped mincingly to the side of the pier, he found that the little crowd were gazing down upon the black, snub-nosed, immature bull-dog physiognomy of an extremely fat Chinese pug dog, who, in a fit of playfulness with another fashionable dog, had forgotten his proximity to the extreme edge of the pier and gone in with a splash.

He had swum round and round, evidently mistrustful of his powers to reach the shore, and, in a very stolid manner, appeared to enjoy his bath; but growing tired, he had ceased to swim, and, throwing up his glistening black muzzle, had begun to beat the water with his forepaws, uttering from time to time a dismal yelp, while a bell attached to his collar gave a ting. Ignorant of the fact that he was fat enough to float if he only kept still, he was fast approaching the state when chicken legs and macaroons would tempt in vain, when his stiffened jaws would refuse to open to the tiny ratafia well soaked in milk, and digestion pains would assail him no more, after too liberal an indulgence in the well-fried cutlet of juicy veal. The bell-hung pagoda in Lady Drelincourt's drawing-room was likely to be vacant till another pet was bought, and as the Master of the Ceremonies gazed down at poor Titi through his glass, it was in time to see a rough fisherman throw a rope in rings to the drowning beast, evidently under the impression that the dog would seize the rope and hold on till he was drawn up, for no boat was near.

The rope was well aimed, for it struck the pet heavily, knocking him under, and the rough boatman took off his glazed hat, and scratched a very rough head, staring in wonderment at the effect of his well-meant effort.

But Titi came up again and yelped loudly, this time with a sweet, silvery, watery gurgle in his throat.

Then he turned over, and a lady shrieked. Then he paddled about on his side, and made a foam in the water, and in spite of the helpless, sympathising glances given through the gold-rimmed eyeglass of the

Master of the Ceremonies, Titi must have been drowned had there not been a sudden splash from the staging of the pier somewhere below, a loud exciting cry, and a figure seen to rise from its plunge, swim steadily to the drowning dog, reach it amidst a storm of delighted cries, swim back to the staging, and disappear.

This was the correct time, and Lady Drelincourt fainted dead away, with her head resting upon her shoulder, and her shoulder on the back of her chair. Immediately there was a rustling in bow-decked reticules, smelling salts were drawn, and Lady Drelincourt's nose was attacked. She was almost encircled with cut-glass bottles.

The Master of the Ceremonies looked on, posed in an attitude full of eager interest, and he saw, what was nothing new to his attentive gaze, that Time had behaved rudely to Lady Drelincourt; that art had been called in to hide his ravages, and that her ladyship's attitude caused cracks in the thickened powder, and that it differed in tone from the skin beneath; that there was a boniness of bust, and an angularity of shoulder where it should have been round and soft; and that if her ladyship fainted much more he would not be answerable for the consequences to her head of hair.

But Lady Drelincourt was not going to faint much more. The dog had been saved, and she had fainted enough, so that at the first approach of a rude hand to loosen the fastenings at her throat, she sighed and gasped, struggled faintly, opened her eyes of belladonna brilliancy, stared wildly round, recovered her senses, and exclaimed:

"Where is he? Where is my Titi? Where is his preserver?" and somebody said, "Here!"

There was a hurried opening of the circle, and Stuart Denville, Esquire, Master of the Ceremonies, struck a fresh attitude full of astonishment, but, like the rest of the well-dressed throng, he shrank away, as a tall, fair youth, dripping with water, which made his hair and clothes cling closely, came from an opening that led to the piles below, squeezing the pug to free him from moisture, and gazing from face to face.

"You rascally prodigal!" whispered the Master of the Ceremonies, as the youth came abreast, "you've been fishing for dabs again!"

"Well, suppose I have," said the youth sulkily.

"Where is his preserver? Give me back my darling Titi," wailed Lady Drelincourt; and catching the wet fat dog to her breast, regardless of the effect upon her rich black silk dress and crape, the little beast uttered a satisfied yelp and nestled up to her, making a fat jump upwards so as to lick a little of the red off the lady's lips.

"And who was it saved you, my precious?" sobbed the lady.

"Lady Drelincourt," said the Master of the Ceremonies, taking the youth's hand gingerly, with one glove, "allow me to introduce your dear pet's preserver—it was Morton Denville, Lady Drelincourt, my son. I am sorry he is so very wet."

"Bless you—bless you!" cried Lady Drelincourt with effusion. "I could embrace you, you brave and gallant man, but—but—not now."

"No, no—not now. Lady Drelincourt, let me assist you to your chair. Morton," he whispered, "you're like a scarecrow: quick, be off. You dog, if you mind me now, your fortune's made."

"Oh, is it, father? Well, I'm precious glad. I say, isn't it cold?"

"Yes: quick—home, and change your things. Stop; where are you going?"

"Down below, to fetch the dabs."

"Damn the dabs, sir," whispered the Master of the Ceremonies excitedly; "you'll spoil the effect. Run, sir, run!"

The youth hesitated a moment and then started and ran swiftly towards the cliff, amidst a shrill burst of cheers, the ladies fluttering their handkerchiefs, and fisherman Dick Miggles wishing he had been that there boy.

"Denville—dear Denville," said her ladyship, "how proud you must be of such a son!"

"The idol of my life, dear Lady Drelincourt," said the Master of the Ceremonies, arranging her dress in the bath-chair. "Shall I carry the poor dog?"

"No, no—no, no, my darling Titi!" cried the lady, to his great relief. "Thomas, take me home quickly," she said, as the wet dog nestled in her crape lap and uttered a few snuffles of satisfaction. "Quick, or Titi will take cold Denville, see me safely home. My nerves are gone."

"The shock, of course."

"Yes, Denville, and I shall never forget your gallant son," sobbed her ladyship hysterically, as they passed through a lane of promenaders; "but I must not cry."

It was indeed quite evident that such a giving way to natural feeling would have had serious results, and she was not veiled. So the rising tear was sent back, and Denville saw her safely home, forgetting for the moment his domestic troubles in his exultation, and making out a future for his son, as the rich Lady Drelincourt's protégé—a commission—a handsome allowance. Perhaps—ah, who knew! Such unions had taken place before now.

For the next half-hour he was living artificially, seeing his son advanced in life, and his daughter dwelling in a kind of fairy castle that had been raised through Lady Drelincourt's introduction.

Then as he approached home a black cloud seemed to come down and close him in, the artificiality was gone, age seemed to be attacking him, and he moaned as he reached the door.

"Heaven help me, and give me strength to keep up this actor's life, for I'm very, very weak."

# Chapter Eleven
# The Opening of a Vein

"Well, young Denville," said Dick Miggles, the great swarthy fisherman, whose black hair, dark eyes, and aquiline features told that his name was a corruption of Miguel, and that he was a descendant of one of the unfortunates who had been wrecked and imprisoned when the Spanish Armada came to grief, and had finally resolved to "remain an Englishman."

Dick Miggles rarely did anything in the daytime but doze and smoke. Of course, he ate and drank, and, as on the present occasion, nursed the little girl that Mrs Miggles, who was as round and snub and English of aspect as her lord was Spanish, had placed in his arms. At night matters were different, and people did say—but never mind.

"Well, young Denville," said Fisherman Dick, as he sat on the bench outside his whitewashed cottage with the whelk-shell path, bordered with marigold beds, one of which flowers he picked from time to time to give the child.

"Well, Dick, where are my dabs?"

"Haw-haw," said the fisherman, laughing. "I say, missus, where's them dabs?"

Mrs Miggles was washing up the dinner things, and she came out with a dish on which were a number of fried heads and tails, with a variety of spinal and other bones.

"What a shame!" cried Morton, with a look of disgust. "I do call that shabby, Dick."

"How was I to know that you would come after 'em, lad? I'd ha' brote 'em, but I don't like to come to your house now."

"I say, Dick, don't be a fool," cried the lad. "What's the good of raking up that horrid affair, now it's all dead and buried?"

"Nay," said Dick, shaking his head. "That ar'n't all dead and buried, like the old woman, my lad. There's more trouble to come out o' that business yet."

"Oh, stuff and nonsense!"

"Nay, it isn't, my lad. Anyhow, I don't like coming to your place now, and there's other reasons as well, ar'n't there, missus?"

"Now, I do call that shabby, Dick. Just because there's a bill owing for fish. I've told you I'll pay it some day, if papa does not; I mean, when I have some money."

"Ay, so you did, lad, and so you will, I know; but I didn't mean that, did I, missus?"

"No," came from within.

"What did you mean, then?"

"Never mind. You wait and see. I say, the old gentleman looks as if he'd got over the trouble, Master Morton. He was quite spry to-day."

"No, he hasn't," said Morton. "It's quite horrible at home. He's ill, and never hardly speaks, and my sister frets all day long."

"Do she though! Poor gal! Ah, she wants it found out, my lad. It wherrits her, because you see it's just as if them jools of the old lady's hung like to your folk, and you'd got to account for 'em."

"Get out! Why, what nonsense, Dick."

"What, dropped it agen, my pretty?" said the great fisherman, stooping to pick up a flower, and place it in the little fat hand that was playing with his big rough finger. "Ah, well, perhaps it be, but never mind. I say, though, the old gentleman looked quite hisself agen. My! he do go dandy-jacking along the cliff, more'n the best of 'em. He do make me laugh, he do. Why, hello, Master Morton, lad, what's matter?"

"If you dare to laugh at my father, Dick," cried the boy, whose face was flushed and eyes flashing, "big as you are, I'll punch your head."

"Naw, naw, naw, don't do that, my lad," said the fisherman, growing solemn directly. "I were not laughing at him. I were laughing at his clothes."

"And if my father dresses like the Prince and the Duke and all the fashionable gentlemen, what is there to laugh at then? Suppose I were to laugh at you for living in that great pair of trousers that come right up under your arms?"

"Well, you might, lad, and welcome; they're very comf'table. P'r'aps you'd like to laugh at my boots. Haw, haw, haw, Master Morton, what d'yer think I did yes'day? I took little flower here, after missus had washed her, and put her right into one o' my boots, and she stood up in it with her head and arms out, laughing and crowing a good 'un. Ar'n't she a little beauty?"

"Yes," said Morton, looking down and playing with the child. "Whose is she?"

"Dunno. Ask the missus."

"And she won't tell me, Dick."

"That's so. But look here, lad. I'm sorry I laughed at Master Denville, for he's a nice gentleman, and always has a kind word and a smile, if he doesn't pay his bill."

"Dick!"

"All right, my lad, all right. You'll pay that when you're rich. I say: chaps sez as you'll marry Lady Drelincourt, now, after saving her dog, and—"

"Don't be a fool, Dick. Here, what were you going to say?" said the lad, reddening.

"You won't want a bit of fishing then, I suppose?"

"Look here; are you going to speak, Dick, or am I to go?"

"All right, my lad. Look here; we eat your dabs, but never mind them. I shall just quietly leave a basket at your door to-night. You needn't know anything about it, and you needn't be too proud to take it, for a drop in the house is worth a deal sometimes, case o' sickness. It's real French sperit, and a drop would warm the old gentleman sometimes when he is cold."

"Smuggling again, Dick?"

"Never you mind about that, Master Morton, and don't call things by ugly names. But that ar'n't all I've got to say. You lost your dabs, but if you'll slip out to-night and come down the pier, the tide'll be just right, and I'll have the bait and lines ready, and I'll give you as good a bit of fishing as you'd wish to have."

"Will you, Dick?"

"Ay, that I will. They were on last night, but they'll be wonderful to-night, and I shouldn't wonder if we ketches more than we expex."

"Oh, but I couldn't go, Dick."

"Why not, lad?"

"You see, I should have to slip out in the old way—through the drawing-room, and down the balcony pillar."

"Same as you and Master Fred used, eh?"

"Don't talk about him," said the lad.

"Well, he's your own brother."

"Yes, but father won't have his name mentioned," said the boy sadly. "He's to be dead to us. Here, what a fool I am, talking so to you!"

"Oh, I don't know, my lad; we was always friends, since you was quite a little chap, and I used to give you rides in my boat."

"Yes; you always were a friend, Dick, and I like you."

"On'y you do get a bit prouder now you're growing such a strapping chap, Master Morton."

"I shan't change to you, Dick."

"Then come down to-night, say at half arter 'leven."

Morton shook his head.

"Why, you ar'n't afraid o' seeing the old woman's ghost, are you?"

"Absurd! No. But it seems so horrible to come down that balcony pillar to get out on the sly."

"Why, you never used to think so, my lad."

"No, but I do now. Do you know, Dick," he said in a whisper, "I often think that the old lady was killed by some one who had watched me go in and out that way."

"Eh?" cried the fisherman, giving a peculiar stare.

"Yes, I do," said the lad, laying his hand on the big fellow's shoulders. "I feel sure of it, for that murder must have been done by some one who knew how easy it was to get up there and open the window."

"Did you ever see anyone watching of you?" said the fisherman in a hoarse whisper.

"N-no, I'm not sure. I fancy I did see some one watching one night."

"Phew!" whistled the fisherman; "it's rather hot, my lad, sitting here in the sun."

"Perhaps some day I shall find out who did it, Dick."

"Hah—yes," said the man, staring at him hard. "Then you won't come?"

"Yes, I will," cried Morton. "It's so cowardly not to come. I shall be there;" and, stopping to pick up the flower the child had again dropped, the pretty little thing smiled in his face, and he bent down and kissed it before striding away.

"Think o' that, now," said Mrs Miggles, coming to the door.

"Think o' what?" growled her lord, breaking off an old sea-ditty he was singing to the child.

"Why, him taking to the little one and kissing it. How strange things is!"

# Chapter Twelve
# Mrs Burnett Makes a Call

"Gad, but the old boy's proud of that chariot," said Sir Matthew Bray, mystifying his sight by using an eyeglass.

"Yes," said Sir Harry Payne, who was lolling against the railings that guarded promenaders from a fall over the cliff; and he joined his friend in gazing at an elegantly-appointed britzka which had drawn up at the side, and at whose door the Master of the Ceremonies was talking to a very young and pretty woman. "Yes; deuced pretty woman, May Burnett. What a shame that little wretch Frank should get hold of her."

"Egad, but it was a good thing for her. I say, Harry, weren't you sweet upon her?"

"I never tell tales out of school, Matt. 'Fore George, how confoundedly my head aches this morning."

Just then the Master of the Ceremonies drew back, raising his hat with the greatest of politeness to the lady, and waving his cane to the coachman, who drove off, the old man going in the other direction muttering to himself, but proud and happy, while the carriage passed the two bucks, who raised their hats and were rewarded with the sweetest of smiles from a pair of very innocent, girlish-looking little lips, their owner, aptly named May, being a very blossom of girlish prettiness and dimpled innocency.

"Gad, she is pretty," said Sir Matthew Bray. "Come along, old lad. Let's see if Drelincourt or anyone else is on the pier."

"Aha! does the wind blow that way, Matt? Why were you not there to save the dog?"

"Wind? what way?" said the big, over-dressed dandy, raising his eyebrows.

"Ha—ha—ha! come, come!" cried Sir Harry, touching his friend in the side with the gold knob of his cane, "how innocent we are;" and, taking Sir Matthew's arm, they strolled on towards the pier.

"I didn't ask you who the note was for that we left at Mother Clode's," said Sir Matthew sulkily.

"No; neither did I ask you where yours came from—you Goliath of foxes," laughed Sir Harry. "But I say. 'Fore George, it was on mourning paper, and was scented with musk. Ha—ha—ha!"

Sir Matthew scowled and grumbled, but the next moment the incident was forgotten, and both gentlemen were raising their ugly beaver hats to first one and then another of the belles they passed.

Meanwhile the britzka was driven on along the Parade, and drew up at the house of the Master of the Ceremonies, where the footman descended from his seat beside the coachman, and brought envious lodging-letters to the windows on either side by his tremendous roll of the knocker and peal at the bell.

Isaac appeared directly.

Yes, Miss Denville was in, so the steps were rattled down, and Mrs Frank Burnett descended lightly, rustled up to the front door, and entered with all the hauteur of one accustomed to a large income and carriage calling.

"Ah, Claire darling!" she cried, as she was shown into the drawing-room; "how glad I shall be to see you doing this sort of thing. Really, you know, it is time."

"Ah, May dear," said Claire, kissing her sister affectionately, but with a grave pained look in her eyes, "I am so glad to see you. I was wishing you would come. Papa will be so disappointed: he has gone up the town to see the tailor about Morton."

"What, does that boy want new clothes again? Papa did not say so."

"Have you seen him, then?"

"Yes. How well he looks. But why did you want to see me?"

For answer Claire took her sister's hand, led her to the chintz-covered sofa, and seated herself beside her, with her arm round May's waist.

"Oh, do be careful, Claire," said Mrs Burnett pettishly; "this is my lute-string. And, my dear, how wretchedly you do dress in a morning."

"It is good enough for home, dear, and we are obliged to be so careful. May dear, I hardly like to ask you, but could you spare me a guinea or two?"

"Spare you a guinea or two? Why, bless the child! what can you want with a guinea or two?"

"I want it for Morton. There are several things he needs so much, and I want besides to be able to let him have a little pocket-money when he asks."

"Oh, really, I cannot, Claire. It is quite out of the question. Frank keeps me so dreadfully short. You would never believe what trouble I have to get a few guineas from him when I am going out, and there is so much play now that one is compelled to have a little to lose. But I must be off. I have some shopping to do, and a call or two to make besides. Then there is a book to get at Miss Clode's. I won't ask you to come for a drive this morning."

"No, dear, don't. But stay a few minutes; I have something to say to you."

"Now, whatever can you have to say, Claire dear? Nothing about that—that—oh, don't, pray. I could not bear it. All the resolution I had was needed to come here at all, and, as I told you in my letter, it was impossible for me to come before. Frank would not let me."

"I want to talk to you very—very seriously."

"About that dreadful affair?"

"No," said Claire, with a curiously solemn look coming over her face, and her voice assuming a deep, tragic tone.

"Then it is about—oh, Claire!" she cried passionately, as she glanced up at a floridly painted portrait of herself on the wall; "I do wish you would take that picture down."

"Why should you mind that? You know papa likes it."

"Because it reminds me so of the past."

"When you were so weak and frivolous with that poor fellow Louis."

"Now I did not come here to be scolded," cried the childlike little thing passionately. "I don't care. I did love poor Louis, and he'd no business to go away and die."

"Hush, hush, May, my darling," said Claire, with a pained face. "I did not scold you."

"You did," sobbed the other; "you said something about Louis, and that you had something to talk to me about. What is it?" she cried with a look of childish fright in her eyes. "What is it?" she repeated, and she clung to her sister excitedly.

"Hush, hush, May, I was not going to scold, only to talk to you."

"It will keep, I'm sure," cried May, with the scared look intensifying.

"No, dearest, it will not keep, for it is something very serious—so serious that I would not have our father know it for the world."

"Lack-a-day, Claire," cried Mrs Burnett, with assumed mirth forming pleasant dimples in her sweet childish face, "what is the matter?"

"I wanted to say a few words of warning to you, May dear. You know how ready people are to gossip?"

"Good lack, yes, indeed they are. But what—?" she faltered, "what—?"

"And several times lately they have been busy with your name."

"With my name!" cried Mrs Burnett, with a forced laugh, and a sigh of relief.

"Yes, dear, about little bits of freedom, and—and—I don't like to call it coquetry. I want you, dearest, to promise me that you will be a little more staid. Dear May, it pains me more than I can say."

"Frump! frump! frump! Why you silly, weak, quakerish old frump, Claire! What nonsense to be sure! A woman in my position, asked out as I am to rout, and kettledrum, and ball, night after night, cannot sit mumchance against the wall, and mumble scandal with the old maids. Now, I wonder who has been putting all this in your head?"

"I will not repeat names, dear; but it is some one whom I can trust."

"Then she is a scandalous old harridan, whoever she is," cried Mrs Burnett with great warmth. "And what do you know about such matters?"

"I know it pains me to hear that my dear sister's name is mentioned freely at the officers' mess, and made a common toast."

"Oh, indeed, madam; and pray what about yours? Who is talked of at every gathering, and married to everyone in turn?"

"I know nothing of those things," said Claire coldly.

"Ah, well, all right; but, I say, when's it to be, Claire? Don't fribble away this season. I hear of two good opportunities for you; and—oh, I say, Claire, they do tell me that a certain gentleman said—a certain very high personage—that you were—"

"Shame, sister!" cried Claire, starting up as if she had been stung. "How can you—how dare you, speak to me like that?"

"Hoity-toity! What's the matter, child?"

"Child!" cried Claire indignantly. "Do you forget that you have always been as a child to me—my chief care ever since our mother died? Oh, May, May, darling, this is not like you. Pray—pray be more guarded in what you say. There, dearest, I am not angry; but this light and frivolous manner distresses me. You are Frank Burnett's honoured wife—girl yet, I know; but your marriage lifts you at once to a position amongst women, and these light, flippant ways sit so ill upon one like you."

"Oh, pooh! stuff! you silly, particular old frump!" cried May sharply. "Do you suppose that a married woman is going to be like a weak, prudish girl? There, there, there; I did not come to quarrel, and I won't be scolded. I say, they tell me that handsome Major Rockley is likely to throw himself away on Cora Dean."

"Oh, May, May, my darling!"

"You are a goose not to catch him in your own net."

"Major Rockley?"

"Yes; he is rich and handsome. I wish I'd had him instead of Frank."

"May, dear May!"

"Oh, I know: it's only talk. But, I say, dear, have you heard about old Drelincourt? So shocking! In mourning, too. They say she is mad to marry some one. There, good-bye. Don't crush my bonnet. Oh, of course; yes, I'm going to be as prudish as you, and so careful. Well, what is it?"

"May, you cannot deceive me; you have something on your mind."

"I? Nonsense! Absurd!"

"You were going to tell me something; to ask me to help you, I am sure."

"Well—perhaps—yes," said the little thing, with scarlet face. "But you frightened me out of it. I daren't now. Next time. Good-bye; good-bye; good-bye."

She rattled these last words out hastily, kissed her sister, and hurried, in a strangely excited manner, from the room.

Claire watched the carriage go, and then sank back out of sight in a chair, to clasp her hands upon her knees, and gaze before her with a strangely old look upon her beautiful face.

For there was trouble, not help, to be obtained from the wilful, girlish wife who had so lately left her side.

# Chapter Thirteen
# A Night-Bird Trapped

It was, as Morton Denville said, cold and cheerless at his home, and the proceedings that night endorsed his words, as at half-past ten, after the servants had been dismissed, his father rose to seek his sleepless couch.

Claire rose at the same moment, starting from a silent musing fit, while Morton threw down the book he had been reading in a very ill-used way.

"Good-night, my son," said Denville, holding out his hand, and grasping the lad's with unusual fervour. "Good-night, father."

"And you'll mind and be particular now, my boy. I am sure that at last I can advance your prospects."

"Oh, yes, father, I'll be particular."

"Don't let people see you fishing there again." "No, father, I'll take care. Good-night. Coming Claire?" Claire had put away her needlework, and was standing cold and silent by the table.

"Good-night, Claire, my child," said Denville, with a piteous look and appeal in his tone.

"Good-night, father."

She did not move as the old man took a couple of steps forward and kissed her brow, laying his hands afterwards upon her head and muttering a blessing.

Then, in spite of her efforts, a chill seemed to run through her, and she trembled, while he, noting it, turned away with a look of agony in his countenance that he sought to conceal, and sank down in the nearest chair.

He seemed to be a totally different man, and those who had seen him upon the cliff and pier would not have recognised in him the fashionable fribble, whose task it was to direct the flight of the butterflies of the Assembly Room, and preside at every public dance.

"Aren't you going to bed, father?" said Morton, trying to speak carelessly.

"Yes, yes, my son, yes. I only wish to think out my plans a little—your commission, and other matters."

"I hope he won't be long," muttered Morton as he left the room. "Why, Claire, how white and cold you are! There, hang me if it isn't enough to make a fellow sell himself to that old Lady Drelincourt for the sake of getting money to take care of you. If I'd got plenty, you should go abroad for a change."

Claire kissed him affectionately.

"Hang me if I don't begin to hate May. She doesn't seem like a sister to us. Been here to-day, hasn't she? I heard they'd come back."

"Yes," said Claire with a sigh.

"It was cowardly of them to go off like that, when you were in such trouble. You did not have a single woman come and say a kind word when—*that* was in the house."

"Don't speak of it, dear," said Claire. "Mrs Barclay came, though."

"Rum old girl! I always feel ready to laugh at her."

"She has a heart of gold."

"Old Barclay has a box of gold, and nice and tightly he keeps it locked up. I say, he'll sell us up some day."

"Morton dear, I can't bear to talk to you to-night; and don't speak like that of May. She has her husband to obey."

"Bless him!" cried Morton musingly. "Good-night, Sis."

He kissed her affectionately, and a faint smile came into Claire's wan face, as it seemed to comfort her in her weary sorrow. Then they parted, and she went to her room, opened the window, and sat with her face among the flowers, watching the sea and thinking of some one whom she had in secret seen pass by there at night.

That was a dream of the past, she told herself now, for it could never be. Love, for her, was dead; no man could call her wife with such a secret as she held in her breast, and as she thought on, her misery seemed greater than she could bear.

The tide was well up, and the stars glittered in the heaving bosom of the sea as she sat and gazed out; and then all at once her heart seemed to stand still, and then began beating furiously, for a familiar step came slowly along the cobble-paved walk in front of the house, along by the railed edge of the cliff, and then for a moment she could see the tall, dark figure she knew so well, gazing wistfully up at the window.

She knew he loved her; she knew that her heart had gone out to him, though their acquaintance was of the most distant kind. She knew, too, how many obstacles poverty had thrown in the way of both, but some day, she had felt, all would be swept away. Now all that was past. She must never look at him again.

She shrank from the window, and sank upon her knees, weeping softly for the unattainable, as she felt how he must love her, and that his heart was with her in sympathy with all her trouble.

"Dead—dead—dead," she moaned; "my love is dead, and my life-course broadly marked out, so that I cannot turn to the right or left."

She started and shuddered, for below her there was the tread of a heavy foot. She heard her father's slight cough, and his closing door, and at the same moment, as if it were he who separated them, the step outside could be heard returning, and Claire arose and crept to the window again to listen till it died away.

"Dead—dead—my love is dead," she moaned again, and closing the window, she strove to forget her agony of mind and the leaden weight that seemed to rest upon her brow in sleep.

Eleven had struck, and two quarters had chimed before Morton Denville dared to stir. He had waited with open door, listening impatiently for his father's retiring; he had listened to the steps outside; and then at last, with all the eagerness of a boy, in spite of his near approach to manhood, and excited by the anticipations of the fishing, and the romance of the little adventure, he stole forth with his shoes in his hands, after carefully closing the catch of his well-oiled door.

The crucial part was the passing of the end of the passage leading to his father's room, and here he paused for a few moments, but he fancied he could hear a long-drawn breathing, and, after a hasty glance at the door of the back drawing-room, erst Lady Teigne's chamber, he opened the drawing-room door, stepped in and closed it.

He breathed more freely now, but a curious chill ran through him, and he felt ready to retreat as he saw that the folding-doors were not closed, and that the faint light from the back window made several articles of furniture look grotesque and strange.

"Here am I, just twenty, and as cowardly as a girl," he muttered. "I won't be afraid."

All the same, though, his heart beat violently, and he shrank from moving for some minutes.

"And Dick waiting," he muttered.

Those words gave him the strength he sought, and, going on tiptoe across the room, half feeling as if a hand were going to be laid upon his shoulder to keep him back, he drew aside the blind, opened the French window, passed out, closed it after him, and stood there in the balcony, gazing at the heaving, star-spangled sea.

"I can't be a man yet," he said to himself. "If I were I shouldn't feel so nervous. It is very horrid, though, the first time after that old woman was killed; and by some one coming up there. Ugh! it's very creepy. I half fancied I could hear the old girl snoring as she used."

He leaned over the balcony rails and looked to right and left, but all seemed silent in the sleeping town, and after listening for a minute or two he seized the support of the balcony roof, stepped over the rails, lowered himself a little, and clasping the pillar with his legs, slid easily down, rested for a moment on the railings with his feet between the spikes, and then, clasping the pillar, dropped lightly down upon the pavement, to be seized by two strong hands by arm and throat, a dark figure having stepped out of the doorway to hold him fast.

# Chapter Fourteen
## Something Thrown in the Sea

"What—"

"Hush! Who are you? What are you doing here? Why, Morton Denville!"

"Richard Linnell! Is it you? Oh, I say, you did give me a scare. I thought it was that chap come again."

"What do you mean?"

"Why, the fellow who did that, you know," said the lad with a nod upwards.

"But why have you stolen down like this, sir?"

"Don't talk so loud; you'll wake the old man. Only going fishing."

"Fishing? Now?"

"Yes. Fisherman Dick's waiting for me on the pier."

"Is this true?" asked Linnell sternly. "True! What do you mean?" said the lad haughtily. "Did you ever know a Denville tell a lie?"

"No, of course not. But it looks bad, young fellow, to see you stealing out of the house like this, and after that ghastly affair."

"Hush, don't talk about it," said the lad with a shudder. "But, I say, how came you here?"

"I—I—" stammered Linnell. "Oh, I was walking along the cliff and I saw the window open. I thought something was wrong, and I crossed to see."

"Did you think some one had come to run away with my sister, Mr Linnell?" said the lad with a sneering laugh. "Ah, well, you needn't have been alarmed, and if they had it would have been no business of yours."

Richard Linnell drew his breath with a faint hiss.

"That's rather a sneering remark, young gentleman," he said coldly; "but there, I don't want to quarrel with you."

"All the same to me if you did, only if you will take a bit of good advice, stop at home, and don't be hanging about gentlemen's houses at this time of night. It looks bad. There, now you can knock at the door and ring them up and tell them I've gone fishing. I don't care."

He thrust his hands in his pockets and strutted away, trying to appear very manly and independent, but nature would not permit him to look like anything but a big, overgrown boy.

Richard Linnell drew his breath again with the same low hiss, and stood watching the retiring figure, after which he followed the boy along the cliff till he saw him reach the pier, where a gruff voice greeted him; and, satisfied that the truth had been spoken, he turned off and went home.

"Thought you wasn't coming, lad," said Fisherman Dick. "Here, just you ketch hold o' yon basket, and let's get to work."

Morton seized the basket of bait, and together they walked to the very end of the pier, at one corner of which was a gangway and some steps, down which they went to a platform of open beams, moist with spray, and only about a foot above the water now the tide was high, the promenade forming the ceiling above their heads.

It was very dark, and the damp, salt smell of the weed that hung to the piles was floating around, while the misty spray every now and then moistened their hands and faces. On all sides huge square wooden piles rose up, looking grim and strange in the gloom, and before them the star-spangled sea heaved and sank, and heaved and sighed and whispered in amongst the woodwork, every now and then seeming to give a hungry smack as if the waves were the lips of some monstrous mouth, trying to seize upon the two fishers for its prey.

"Didn't I tell you?" said Dick Miggles: "Sea's just right, and the fish'll bite like anything. We ought to get ten shillings' worth to-night. There you are; go ahead."

Dick had been busy unwinding a line, whose hooks he had already baited; and then, for the next quarter of an hour they were busy catching and hauling in whiting and large dabs, and every now and then a small conger, the basket filling rapidly.

Then, all at once, the fish ceased biting, and they sat waiting and feeling the lines, trying to detect a touch.

"Some one coming," said Dick suddenly, in a low whisper. "What's he want to-night?"

"Sh!" whispered back Morton. "Don't speak, or I shall be found out."

"Right," answered Dick in the same low tone; and as they sat there in the darkness with the water lapping just beneath them, and a wave coming in among the piles every now and then with a hiss and a splash, they could hear the slow, firm tread of some one coming down the pier, right to the end, to stand there as if listening, quite still above their heads.

All at once the night-breeze wafted to them the scent of a good cigar, and they knew that whoever it was must be smoking.

At the same moment, Morton felt a tug at his line, and he knew a fish had hooked itself.

It was all he could do to keep from dragging it in; but he was, in spite of his boasting, afraid of his nocturnal expedition coming to his father's ears, and he remained still.

Fisherman Dick had moved so silently that Morton had not heard him; but all at once the planks overhead seemed veined with light, and the figure of the fisherman could be seen dimly, with his face close up to a hole in the planking. The light died out as quickly as it shone, and the odour of tobacco diffused itself again, while the man overhead began to walk slowly up and down.

Tug-tug-tug! How that fish—a big one, too—did pull! But Morton resisted the temptation, and waited, till all at once it seemed to him that the smoker must have heard them, and was about to come down, for he was evidently listening.

Then there was a shuffling of feet, a curious expiration of the breath, and a sort of grunt, followed by utter silence; and then, some fifty yards away, right in front of where Morton sat, there was a faint golden splash in the sea, and the noise of, as it were, a falling stone or piece of wood.

Almost at the same moment Morton noticed that his line had become phosphorescent, and he could see it for some distance down as the fish he had hooked dragged it here and there.

Then there was a sigh overhead as of relief, and the steps were heard again, gradually going back along the pier, and dying slowly away.

Simultaneously, Morton Denville and the fisherman began hauling in their lines, the former listening the while, to make sure that the promenader did not return; and then, as all was silent, their captives were drawn on to the open planking, to break the silence with flapping and beating and tangling the lines.

"What light was that, Dick?" said Morton, as he threw his fish into the basket.

"Dunno, zackly. Some way o' lighting another cigar."

"Who was it—could you see?"

"How's it likely I could see, squintin' through a hole like that? Some 'un or 'nother stretching his legs, 'cause he ain't got no work to do, I s'pose."

"But couldn't you see his face?"

"See his face? Is it likely? Just you get up and look through that hole. Why, I had to look straight up, then sidewise, and then straight up again, and that bends your sight about so as you couldn't even do anything with a spyglass."

"I believe you could see who it was, and won't tell me."

"Hear that, now! Why shouldn't I want to tell? Says you, I'm out on the sly, and nobody mustn't know I'm here."

"No, I didn't," said Morton shortly.

"Well, lad, not in words you didn't; but that's how it seemed to be, so I kep' as quiet as I could, and whoever it was didn't hear us."

"What did he throw into the water?"

"Stone, I s'pose. Some o' them dandy jacks, as looks as if they couldn't move in their clothes, once they gets alone, nothing they likes better than throwing stones in the water. If it wasn't that the waves washes 'em up again, they'd have throwed all Saltinville into the sea years ago."

Two hours later, after a very successful night's sport, Morton parted from Fisherman Dick at the shore end of the pier, and ran home, while the owner of the lines and the heavy basket sat down on the lid, and rubbed the back of his head.

"Yes, I did see his face, as plain as I ever see one, but I warn't going to tell you so, Master Morton, my lad. What did he chuck inter the sea, and what did he chuck it there for?"

Fisherman Dick sat thinking for a few minutes, and shaking his head, before saying aloud:

"No; it didn't sound like a stone."

After which he had another think, and then he got up, shouldered his basket, and went homeward, saying:

"I shall have to find out what that there was."

# Chapter Fifteen
# Miss Clode's Library

Miss Clode's library and fancy bazaar stood facing the sea—so near, indeed, that on stormy days she was occasionally compelled to have the green shutters up to protect the window-panes from the spray and shingle that were driven across the road. But on fine days it was open to the sunshine, and plenty of cane-seated chairs were ranged about the roomy shop.

The back was formed of a glass partition, pretty well covered with books, but not so closely as to hide the whole shop from the occupants of the snug parlour, where little, thin Miss Clode sat one fine morning, like a dried specimen of her niece, Annie Slade, a stout young lady nicknamed Dumpling by the bucks who made the place a sort of social exchange.

The shop was well fitted and carpeted. Glass cases, filled with gaily-dyed wools and silks, were on the counter. Glass cases were behind filled with knick-knacks and fancy goods, papier-maché trays and inkstands bright with mother-of-pearl, and ivory and ebony specimens of the turner's art. Look where you would, everything was brightly polished, and every speck of dust had been duly hunted out. In fact, Miss Clode's establishment whispered of prosperity, and suggested that the little eager-eyed maiden lady must be in the circumstances known as comfortable.

Business had not been very brisk that morning, but several customers had called to make purchases or to change books, and two of these latter had made purchases as well. In fact, it was rather curious, but when certain of her clients called, and Miss Clode introduced to their notice some special novelty, they always bought it without further consideration.

"You are such a clever business woman, auntie," drawled her niece. "I wish I could sell things as fast as you."

"Perhaps you will some day, my dear."

"Lady Drelincourt bought that little Tunbridge needle-book for half a guinea, didn't she, aunt?"

"Yes, my dear," said Miss Clode, pursing up her thin lips.

"She couldn't have wanted it, auntie," drawled the girl. "I don't believe she ever used a needle in her life."

"Perhaps not, my dear, but she might want it for a present."

"Oh, so she might; I never thought of that. Customers!" added the girl sharply, and rose to go into the shop.

"I'll attend to them, my dear," said Miss Clode quickly, and she entered the shop to smilingly confront Sir Harry Payne and Sir Matthew Bray.

"Well, Miss Clode, what's the newest and best book for a man to read?"

"Really, Sir Harry, I am very sorry," she said. "The coach has not brought anything fresh, but I expect a parcel down some time to-day. Perhaps you'd look in again?"

"Ah, well, I will," he said. "Come along, Bray."

"Have you seen these new card-cases, Sir Matthew?" said the little woman, taking half a dozen from a drawer. "They are real russia, and the gilding is of very novel design. Only a guinea, Sir Matthew, and quite new."

"Ah, yes, very handsome indeed. A guinea, did you say?" he said, turning the handsome leather case over and over.

"Yes, Sir Matthew. May I put it down to your account?"

"Well, ah, yes—I—ah, yes, I'll take this one."

"Thank you, Sir Matthew. I'll wrap it up, please, in silver paper;" and, with deft fingers, the little woman wrapped up the purchase, handed it over with a smile, and the two friends strolled out for Sir Harry to give his friend a light touch in the side with the head of his cane, accompanied by a peculiar smile, which the other refused to see.

"How very anxious Sir Harry seems to be to get that new book, auntie," drawled Annie, coming into the shop where Miss Clode was busily making an entry on her slate; "that makes twice he's been here to-day."

"Yes, my dear, he's a great reader. But now, Annie, the time has come when I think I may take you into my confidence."

"La, auntie, do you?"

"I do, and mind this, child: if ever you are foolish or weak, or do anything to betray it, you leave me directly, and that will be a very serious thing."

Miss Slade's jaw fell, and her mouth opened widely, as did her eyes.

"Ah, I see you understand, so now come here with me."

Miss Slade obeyed, and followed her aunt into the middle room at the back, where, by means of a match dipped into a bottle of phosphorus. Miss Clode obtained a light and ignited a little roll of wax taper, and then, as her niece watched her with open eyes as they sat at the table, the lady took a small letter from her pocket and laid it with its sealed side uppermost on the table.

"Why, I saw Sir Harry Payne give you that letter this morning, auntie, when he came first."

"Oh, you saw that, did you?" said Miss Clode.

"Yes, auntie, and I thought first he had given it to you to post, and then as you didn't send me with it, I wondered why he had written to you."

"He did give it to me to post, my dear," said Miss Clode with a curious smile, "and before I post it I am bound to see that he has not written anything that is not good for the la—person it is for."

"Oh, yes, auntie, I see," said Miss Slade, resting her fat cheeks on her fat fingers, and watching attentively as her aunt took out a seal from a tin box, one that looked as if it were made of putty, and compared it with the sealing-wax on the letter.

This being satisfactory, she cleverly held the wax to the little taper till it began to bubble and boil, when it parted easily, the paper being drawn open and only some silky threads of wax securing it, these being at once brushed aside.

"Oh, you have got it open lovely, auntie," said the girl.

"Yes, my dear; and now I am going to read it," said Miss Clode, suiting the deed to the word, skimming through the note rapidly, and then refolding it.

"Oh, I say, auntie, what does he say?" said the girl with her eyes sparkling. "Is it about love?"

"Don't ask questions, and you will not get strange answers," said Miss Clode austerely, as she deftly melted the wax once more, and applied the well-made bread seal, after which there was nothing to show that the letter had been opened. "I see, though, that it was quite time I did trust you, my dear, and I hope I shall have no cause to repent."

Just then a customer entered the shop, and again Miss Clode went to attend.

"I know it was a love-letter," said Annie quickly; "and it was Sir Harry Payne wrote it. I wonder who it was to. I wish he'd make love to me."

Miss Clode came back directly with a volume of poems in her hand—a new copy, and looking significantly at her niece she said:

"I'm going to post that letter, my dear. Don't you touch it, mind."

As she spoke she thrust the note between the leaves, and then walked into the shop with her niece, and placed the book upon a shelf.

"There, if you behave yourself you shall see who buys those poems; but, once more, never a word to a soul."

"Oh, no, auntie, never," said the girl, with her big eyes rolling. "But oh, I say, auntie, isn't it fun?"

"Isn't what fun?"

"I know," giggled the girl; "there was a letter in that card-case you sold. I saw you put it there."

"Well, well, perhaps there was, my dear. I must oblige customers, and the profits on things are so small, and rents so high. We must live, you see. And now mind this: if Mrs Frank Burnett comes, you call me."

"Couldn't I sell her that volume of poems, auntie?" said the girl eagerly.

"No, certainly not; and now look here, miss. Don't you ever pretend to be simple any more."

"No, auntie," said the girl, "I won't;" and she drew her breath thickly and gave a smack with her lips, as if she were tasting something very nice.

Loungers dropped in, and loungers dropped out, coming for the most part to meet other loungers, and, like the Athenians of old, to ask whether there was anything new. Sometimes Miss Clode was consulted, and when this was the case, her way was soft, deprecating, and diffident. She thought she had heard this; she believed that she had heard that; she would endeavour to find out; or, yes, to be sure, her ladyship was right: it was so, she remembered now. While when not invited to give opinions, she was busy in the extreme over some item connected with her business, and hearing and seeing nothing, with that bended head so intent upon arranging, or booking, or tying up.

There was very little, though, that Miss Clode did not hear, especially when some one of a group said, "Oh, fie!" or "No, really, now!" or "How shocking!" and there was a little burst of giggles.

In due time, just as Miss Clode was instructing her niece in the art of tying up a packet of wools, so that one end was left open and the dealer could see at a glance what colours it contained, Annie's jaw dropped, and seemed to draw down the lower lids of her eyes, so that they were opened to the fullest extent, for Frank Burnett's handsome britzka drew up at the door, the steps were rattled down, *flip, flop, flap*, with a vigorous action that would bring people to the windows to see, and, all sweetness in appearance and odour, like the blossom she was, the MC's idol stepped daintily rustling down, the very model of all that was *naïve* and girlish.

"Who'd ever think she was a wife?" said Miss Clode to herself.

"Oh my! isn't she pretty?" said Annie.

"Go on tying up those packets, and don't take any notice," said Miss Clode; and then, with the greatest of deference, wished her visitor good-morning, and begged to know how she was.

"Not very well, Miss Clode: so tired. Society is so exacting. Can you recommend me any book that will distract me a little?"

"Let me see, ma'am," said Miss Clode, turning her head on one side in a very bird-like way, and bending forward as if she were going to peck a seed off the counter.

"Something that will really take me out of myself."

"The last romance might be too exciting, ma'am?"

"Do you think it would?"

"Ye-e-e-es. Oh, yes, decidedly so in your case, ma'am," said Miss Clode, in quite the tone of a female physician. "Poems—soft, dreamy, soothing poems, now, would I think be most suited."

"Oh, do you think so?" said Mrs Burnett half pettishly.

"Yes, ma'am, I have a volume here, not included in the library, but for sale—'Lays of the Heart-strings'—by a gentleman of quality. I should recommend it strongly."

"Oh, dear no," exclaimed the visitor, as Miss Clode took the work from the shelf. "I don't think a—well, I will look at it," she said, blushing vividly, as she saw that the book did not thoroughly close in one part. "Perhaps you are right, Miss Clode. I will take it. What is the price?"

"Half a guinea, ma'am, to subscribers, and I will call you a subscriber. Shall I do it up in paper?"

"Yes, by all means. What delightful weather we are having!"

"Delightful, indeed, ma'am," said Miss Clode, whose face was simply business-like. There was not a nerve-twitch, not a peculiar glance to indicate that she was playing a double part; and it was wonderfully convenient. Visitors both ladies and gentlemen, liked it immensely, and patronised her accordingly, for no Artesian well was ever so deep and dark as Miss Clode, or as silent. She knew absolutely nothing. Mrs Frank Burnett had bought a volume of poems at her establishment, that was all. Anybody might have slipped the note inside. While as to seeking a client's confidence, or alluding in the mildest way to any little transaction that had taken place for the sake of obtaining further fee or reward, any client would have told you that with the purchase of book, album, card-case, or needle-housewife, every transaction was at an end; and so Miss Clode's business throve, and Lord Carboro' called her the Saltinville sphinx.

"Is there any particular news stirring, Miss Clode?"

"Really, no, ma'am," said that lady, pausing in the act of cutting the twine that confined the book. "A new family has come to the George; and, by the way, I have to send their cards to Mr Denville."

"Oh, of course, I don't want to know anything about that," said Mrs Burnett hastily.

"The officers are talking of getting up a ball before long, and they say that a certain person will be there."

"Indeed!" said the visitor, flushing.

"Yes, ma'am, I was told so, and—ahem!—here is Lord Carboro'. Half a guinea, ma'am, if you please."

Surely there was no occasion for a lady to look so flushed in the act of extricating a little gold coin from her purse; but somehow the ordinary sweet ingenuous look would not come back to May Burnett's face, any more than the coin would consent to come out of the little, long net purse with gold tassels and slides; and the colour deepened as the keen little eyes of the old man settled for a moment on the tied-up book, and then on Miss Clode's face.

"What an old sphinx it is," he thought to himself. "The day grows brighter every hour, Mrs Burnett," he said gallantly. "It has culminated in the sight of you."

"Your lordship's compliments are overpowering," said the lady, with a profound curtsey; and then she secured her book and would have fled, but his lordship insisted upon escorting her to her carriage, hat in hand, and he cursed that new pomade in a way that was silent but not divine, for it lifted one side of his hair as if he were being scalped when he raised his hat.

"Good-morning, good-morning!" he said, as the carriage drove off. "Little wretch," he muttered as he watched the equipage out of sight, but with his hat on now. "I hate scandal, but if we don't have a toothsome bit before long over that little woman, I'm no man. It's vexatious, too," he said angrily, "doosid vexatious. I don't like it. So different to the other, and our sweet Christians here will throw dirt at both. Can't help it; can't help it. Well, Miss Clode, anything you want to recommend to me?"

"Yes, my lord, I have a very charming little tortoise-shell-covered engagement-book or two. Most elegant and very cheap."

"I don't want cheap things, my dear little woman. Let me see, let me see. Oh, yes, very nice indeed," he said, opening the case, and letting a scented note drop out on the counter. "Same make, I see, as the cigar-case I bought last week."

"No, my lord, it is French."

"No, no—no, no; don't tell me—English, English. People have stuck their advertisement in. Send it back to 'em. Do for some one else."

"Then your lordship does not like the case?"

"My dear little woman, but I do, doosidly, but don't offer me any more with that person's circular inside. There, there, there; take the price out of that five-pound note. Two guineas? And very cheap too. Doosid pretty little piece of art, Miss Clode. Doosid pretty little piece of art."

"Wouldn't he have old Mrs Dean's pink note, auntie?" said Annie, as soon as his lordship had gone.

"My dear child, this will never do. You see and hear far too much."

"Please auntie, I can't help it," drawled the girl. "I shouldn't speak like that to anyone else."

"Ah, well, I suppose not; and I have done right, I see. No; he would not have the pink note. This is the second he has refused. Old Mrs Dean will be furious, but she must have known that it would not last long."

"I know why it is," said Annie eagerly. "I know, auntie."

"You know, child?"

"Yes, auntie; old Lord—"

"Hush! don't call people old."

"Lord Carboro' has taken a fancy to some one else."

"Well, perhaps so," said Miss Clode, tapping her niece's fat cheek, and smiling. "People do take fancies, even when they are growing older," she added with a sigh. "Well, he hasn't taken a fancy to you."

"Ugh! Oh, gracious, auntie, don't," said the girl with a shudder. "He's such a horrid old man. I can't think how it was that beautiful Miss Cora Dean could like him."

"I can," said Miss Clode shortly. "Now go and see about the dinner, and don't talk so much."

# Chapter Sixteen
# Mrs Dean's Drive

May Burnett, with her little palpitating heart full of trouble, pretty butterfly of fashion that she was, was flitting through the sunshine one afternoon for the second time to confide her troublesome secret to her sister and obtain her help, but her heart failed her again. The right road was so steep and hard, so she turned down the wrong one once more, laughed at Claire, and left her with saddened face, as in response to the again-repeated question, "Why did you come?" she replied:

"Oh, I don't know. Just to try and make people forget what a horrible house this has been. I almost wonder, though, that I dare to call."

She gave her sister a childlike kiss, and away she went full sail, and with no more ballast than she possessed two years before, at the time she was so severely taken to task for flirting with Louis Gravani, when the handsome young artist painted her portrait and that of her father, hers to hang in the drawing-room, that of the Master of the Ceremonies in the ante-room at the Assembly Rooms.

Claire went to the window to gaze down over the flowers in the balcony at her sister, as she stepped lightly into her carriage, just as manly, handsome Richard Linnell came by on the other side, to raise his hat gravely to each of the sisters in turn, with the effect of making Claire shrink back more into the room, so that she only heard the door of the britzka banged to, and the horses start off, while Richard Linnell went on with bended head and knitted brows, thinking of the part he had taken in the serenade on that terrible night.

"Goose!" said May Burnett to herself angrily, as she ordered the footman to go to Miss Clode's. "I believe she'd be ready to throw herself away on that penniless fellow. I haven't patience with her, and—"

Here she had to bend to a couple of ladies with a most gracious smile. A few yards further and she encountered Lord Carboro', whose hat was carefully raised to her, and on turning the bend where the cliff curved off to the north, she came suddenly upon a handsome pony carriage, driven by Cora Dean in a dazzling new costume of creamy silk and lace, while her mother leaned back in ruby satin, with her eyes half-closed, a small groom behind, seated upon a very tiny perch, having his arms closely folded, and his hat cocked at a wonderful angle.

The driver of the high-stepping pair of ponies stared hard at May Burnett, while that lady leaned back languidly, and quite ignored the presence of the handsome actress.

"Little upstart!" muttered Cora, as she gave her ponies a sharp cut, making them tear along. "I'm not good enough for her to even see; but maybe smuts will fall on the whitest snow. Who knows, my pretty baby madam? Get on with you then!"

*Whish-swish*, and the ponies sent the chalky dust flying as they tore along.

"Now, lookye here, Betsy, once for all," said Mrs Dean angrily; "if you are going to drive like that, I stay at home. I like my bones, though they do ache sometimes, and I'm not going to have them broke to please you."

Cora frowned, and softly took up the second rein with the effect of checking the ponies' rattling gallop just as heads were being turned and gentlemen on horseback were starting off in pursuit.

"I ain't easily frightened, Betsy, you know," said Mrs Dean, panting. "Speaking as a woman as has faced a whole company in the bad days on treasury night, when there's been nothing in the cash-box, and your poor father off his head, I say I ain't easily frightened."

"Now, mother—I mean mamma—how are we to get into society if you will refer so constantly to those wretched old days?"

"They weren't wretched old days, my dear, and I was a deal happier then than I am now. But never mind; we've got our tickets. I knew old Denville would get 'em, and my Betsy'll startle some of 'em at the ball, I know. Hold 'em in tighter, my dear, do."

"Don't be so foolishly nervous, mother. I have them well in hand."

"But why does that one keep laying down its ears and squeaking, and trying to bite t'other one?"

"Play," said Cora shortly.

"Then I wish he'd play in the stable, and behave himself when he comes out on the cliff. My word, look at that old Drelincourt, Bet—Cora," said the old woman, giving her daughter a nudge. "Look at the nasty old thing in black. If she'd had any decency, she'd have left the place when her old sister was killed, instead of being pushed about in her chair like that."

"But she has a house here of her own," said Cora shortly, as she guided her ponies in and out among the fashionable equipages, not one of whose lady occupants noticed her.

"Look at 'em," whispered Mrs Dean, nudging her daughter again. "They're a-busting with envy, but they shall be civil to you yet. I did grudge the money for the turn out, and I told Ashley it was a swindle, but they do show off, and I'm glad I bought 'em. Look at the fine madams in that broosh; they're as envious as can be. Hit'm up, Cora, and make 'em go. I should like to see anybody else's gal with such a turn-out."

Too showy, and with a suspicion of the circus in the style of the harness and the colours of the rosettes; but Cora Dean's pony carriage, driven as it was in masterly style, created no little sensation in Saltinville; and if, in addition to the salutes of the gentlemen, which she acknowledged very superciliously, only one lady would have bowed in recognition, Cora Dean would have enjoyed her drive, and probably have gone more slowly.

As it was, in obedience to her mother's nudges and admonitions to "Hit 'm up again," she gave the ponies flick after flick with the whip, and increased the restiveness consequent upon plenty of spirit and too much corn.

It was a risky drive with restive beasts along that cliff with so slight a railing, and the archives of the town told how one Sir Rumble Thornton had gone over with his curricle and pair on to the shingle below, to be killed with his horses. But Cora Dean and her mother thought only of making a show, and the well-bred little ponies seemed to be kept thoroughly in hand by their mistress, though they were fretting and champing their bits and sending flakes of foam all over their satin coats.

"I'm getting used to it now, Cora, my dear," panted the old woman. "I don't feel so squirmy inside, and as if I should be obliged to go home for a drop of brandy. Humph! I wish you wouldn't bow to him."

"Why not? He's our neighbour," said Cora tartly, as Richard Linnell took off his hat. "He's the most thorough gentleman in this town."

"P'raps he is, but I don't think anything of such gentlemen as he is— now Betsy, do a' done. Don't drive like that. I was getting used to it, but now you've made my pore 'art fly up into my mouth."

A sharp snatch at the reins had made the ponies rear up, and Richard Linnell, who was looking after them, started to go to Cora's help, but a cut of the whip sent the two ponies on again, and the carriage spun along, past the wide opening to the pier, down which Richard Linnell turned to think out how he might get over the prejudice he knew that Mr Denville had against him, and to wonder why Claire had grown so cold and strange.

"I am getting well used to it now, Betsy," said Mrs Dean, as they drove right along the London road for a mile or two; "but, I say, hadn't you better turn their heads now? Let's get back on the cliff, where they can see us. I hate these fields and hedges. Let's go back by the other road, down by Lord Carboro's house, and through the street down to the pier."

"Very well," said Cora shortly; and she turned the ponies, and took the upper road.

Now, it so happened that after a short promenade Lord Carboro' had found out that it was going to rain, by a double barometer which he carried in his boots.

"Confound these corns!" he grumbled. "Ah, Barclay," he cried to a thick-set man whom he met at that moment, "collecting your dues? It's going to rain."

"Yes, my lord. My corns shoot horribly."

"So do mine; doosid bad. I'm going to get the carriage and have a drive. Can't walk."

He nodded and went back to his handsome house and grounds, contenting himself with sitting down in the lodge portico while the gardener's wife ordered the carriage to be got ready.

"It isn't handsome, but it suits me," his lordship used to say, "and it's comfortable. If I can't have things as I like with my money, and at my time of life, why it's doosid strange."

So he waited till a groom brought the carriage down the drive, and then looked at it as it came.

"Don't do to go wooing in," he said, with a chuckle, as he got in and took the reins; and certainly it did not look like the chariot of love, for it was a little, low basket carriage, big enough to hold one, and shaped very much like a bath-chair. It was drawn by a very large, grey, well-clipped donkey with enormous ears, quite an aristocrat of his race, with his well-filled skin and carefully blackened harness.

"Thankye, John. Thankye, Mrs Roberts," said his lordship, as he shook the reins. "Go on, Balaam."

Balaam went deliberately on, and just as they were going out of the great iron gates, and his lordship was indulging in a pinch of snuff, there was the rattle of wheels to his right, and Cora Dean came along with her ponies at a smart trot, her mother looking like an over-blown peony by her side.

"Juno, by Jove!" said his lordship, preparing to raise his hat.

But just then—it was a matter of moments—Balaam stood stock still, drew his great flap ears forward and pointed them at the ponies, and staring hard, lifted his tail, and, showing his teeth, uttered with outstretched neck a most discordant roaring—*Hee-haw—Hee-haw*!

Cora's ponies stopped short, trembling and snorting. Then, with a jerk that threatened to snap the harness, and as if moved by the same impulse, they plunged forward and tore down the road that, a hundred yards further on, became busy street, and went down at a sharp angle right for the pier.

"Betsy!" shouted Mrs Dean.

Cora sat firm as a rock, and caught up the second rein to pull heavily on the curb, when—*snap!*—the rein parted at the buckle, and with only the regular snaffle rein to check the headlong gallop, the driver dragged in vain.

The road became street almost like a flash; the street with its busy shops seemed to rush by the carriage; a bath-chair at a shop door, fortunately empty, was caught, in spite of Cora's efforts to guide the ponies, and smashed to atoms, the flying pieces and the noise maddening the ponies in their headlong race.

It was a steep descent, too, and with such bits even a man's arm could not have restrained the fiery little animals as they tore on straight for the sea.

"By Jove!" panted Lord Carboro', jumping out of his little carriage, and, forgetful of all infirmities, he began to run; "they'll be over the cliff. No, by all that's horrible, they'll go right down the pier!"

# Chapter Seventeen
## Miss Dean's Ponies

Richard Linnell was very blind as he walked down the pier, stopping here and there to lay his hand upon the slight rail, and watch the changing colours on the sea, which was here one dazzling sheen of silver, there stained with shade after shade of glorious blue, borrowed from the sky, which was as smiling now as it was tearful but a few days back, when it was clouded over with gloom.

Then he gazed wistfully at a mackerel boat that could not get in for want of wind, and lay with its mast describing arcs on the ether, while its brown sails kept filling out and flapping, and then hanging empty from the spars.

It was a glorious day; one that should have filled all young and buoyant hearts with hope, but Richard Linnell's was not buoyant, for it felt heavy as lead.

He told himself that he loved Claire Denville truly a man could love; and time back she had been ready to respond to his bows; her eyes, too, had seemed to look brightly upon him; but since that dreadful night when he had been deluded into making one of the half-tipsy party gathered beneath her window, and had played that serenade, all had been changed.

It was horrible! Such a night as that, when, judging from what he could glean, the agony and trouble of father and daughter must have been unbearable. And yet he had been there like some contemptible street musician playing beneath her window, and she must know it was he.

That white hand that opened the window and waved them away was not hers, though, but old Denville's, and that was the only relief he found.

He was very blind, or he would have seen more than one pair of eyes brighten as he sauntered down the pier, and more than one fan flutter as he drew near, and its owner prepare to return his bow while he passed on with his eyes mentally closed.

He was very blind, for he did not see one of the attractive ladies, nor one of those who tried to be attractive as he dawdled on, thinking of the face that appeared, somehow, among the flowers at Claire Denville's window; then of pretty little blossom-like May Burnett, who people said was so light and frivolous.

Then he asked himself why he was frittering away his life in Saltinville with his father instead of taking to some manly career, and making for himself a name.

"Because I'm chained," he said, half aloud, as he returned a couple of salutes from Sir Harry Payne and Sir Matthew Bray—rather coldly given, condescending salutations that brought a curl of contempt to his lip.

These gentlemen were near the end of the pier, and he passed them, and went on to look out to sea on the other side, where a swarthy-looking man was wading nearly to his arm-pits, and pushing a pole before him, while a creel hung upon his back.

"I tell you what," said a loud voice, "let's go back now, Josiah, and wait till he comes ashore, and then you can buy a pint o' the live s'rimps, and I'll see them boiled myself."

"No, no. Here's Major Rockley," said the speaker's companion, Josiah Barclay, twitching his heavy brows. "He wants to see me about some money. Why he looks as if he was going to buy shrimps himself. How do, Mr Linnell!"

Richard bowed to the thick-set busy-looking man, and to his pleasant-faced plump lady, who smiled at him in turn, and then passed on, walking back and passing the Major, who did not see him, but watched the fisherman as he lifted his net, picked out the shrimps, shook it, and plunged it in again to wade on through the calm water, and pushing it before him as he went.

There were other looks directed at the handsome young fellow, who seemed so unconscious, and so great a contrast to the bucks and beaux who were waving clouded canes, taking snuff from gold boxes, and standing in groups in studied attitudes.

Even Lady Drelincourt in her deep mourning, and with a precaution taken against any further mishap to her pet, in the shape of a delicately thin plated chain, smiled as Richard Linnell drew near, and waited for an admiring glance and a bow, and when they did not come, said "Boor!" half audibly and closed her fan with a snap.

"Beg pardon, m'lady," said the tall footman.

"Turn the chair and go back."

The tall footman in black, with the great plaited worsted aiguillettes looped so gracefully up to the buttons on his breast, did not turn the chair, but turned round and stared with parted lips and a look of bewildered horror towards the shore end of the pier, from whence came all at once a rushing sound, shrieks, cries, and then the rapid beating of horses' feet, sounding hollow upon the boards, and the whirr of wheels.

"Take care!"

"Run!"

"Keep to the side!"

"No. Get to the end."

There was a rush and confusion. Ladies shrieked and fainted. Gentlemen ran to their help, or ran to their own help to get out of the way. Sir Harry Payne and his friend climbed over the railing and stood outside on the edge of the pier, holding on to the bar to avoid a fall into the water. Major Rockley did likewise on the other side, and all the while the rush, the trampling, and the hollow sound increased.

It was only a matter of moments. Cora Dean's handsome ponies had not gone right over the cliff; but in response to a desperate tug at the reins given by their driver, had swerved a little and dashed through the pier gateway, and then the loungers saw the beautiful woman, with her lips compressed, sitting upright, pulling at the reins with both hands, while her mother in her rich satin dress crouched down with her eyes shut and her full florid face horribly mottled with white.

It was a case of *sauve qui peut* for the most part, as the frantic ponies, growing more frightened by the shouts and cries and the hollow beating of their hoofs, tore on to what seemed to be certain death.

"Here, old girl, quick, down here!" cried Barclay, as he saw the coming danger; and he thrust his trembling wife into one of the embayments at the side of the pier, where there was a shelter for the look-out men and the materials for trimming the pier-lights were kept. "Bravo! bravo, lad!" he cried hoarsely, as he saw Richard Linnell dash forward, and, at the imminent peril of his life, snatch at the bearing rein of one of the ponies, catch hold and hang to it, as the force with which the animals were galloping on took him off his legs.

It was a score of yards from Barclay, who was going to his aid when the rein broke, and Richard Linnell fell and rolled over and over to strike against a group of shrieking women clinging to the side railings. The ponies tore on past Barclay, whose well-meant efforts to check them were vain, and before the danger could be thoroughly realised Cora Dean's little steeds had blindly rushed at the rotting railings at the end of the pier, and gone through them. There was a hoarse, wild shriek from half a hundred voices, a crash, a plunge, and ponies, carriage, and the occupants were in the sea.

"A boat!"

"The life-buoy!"

"Ropes here, quick."

"Help!—help!"

Cries; the rush of a crowd to the end of the pier.

A very Babel of confusion, in the midst of which a man was seen to plunge off the end of the pier and swim towards where Cora Dean could be seen clinging to the broad splashboard of the carriage, drawn through the water, while, after rising from their plunge, the ponies swam together for a few moments, and then began to snort and plunge, and were rapidly drowning each other.

"Oh, horrid, horrid, horrid!" cried a woman's voice. "Help! help! Josiah, come back! He'll be drowned!"

For Josiah Barclay had seized a life-buoy, and throwing off his coat, boldly plunged in after the first man had set an example.

"A good job if he is," muttered Sir Matthew Bray—a kindly wish echoed by several lookers-on who thought of certain slips of paper (stamped) that the money-lender had in his cash-box at home.

But Josiah Barclay did not find a fair amount of stoutness interfere with his floating powers, as he held on to the life-buoy with one hand, swimming with the other towards what looked like a patch of red in the sea, surrounding a white face; and a roar of cheers rose from the crowd who were watching him as he reached Mrs Dean, who had rolled from the carriage, and now gripped the life-buoy as it was pushed towards her, and fainted away.

But the majority were watching the daring man who was striving after the ponies, which were now about fifty yards from the pier, and instead of swimming away, pawing the water frantically, so that the end of the accident seemed near.

Boats were putting off from the shore, but it would be long enough before they could do any good. The chances were that the end would have come before they reached the spot, and Richard Linnell was now within half a dozen yards.

"Let go," he shouted to Cora. "Try and throw yourself out this side, and I'll get you ashore."

She only turned a dazed, despairing look in his direction, too much paralysed by the horror of her situation to even grasp his meaning.

"All right, Master Linnell, sir," growled a deep voice. "Take it coolly, and we'll do it."

Linnell glanced aside, and saw that the swarthy fisherman who had been shrimping was not a couple of yards behind him.

"Look ye here, sir. Let the lady be. I'll go round t'other side. You go this. Mind they don't kick you. Take care. Wo-ho, my pretties; wo-ho, my lads," he cried to the ponies, as, perfectly at his ease in the water, he swam past their heads, well clear of their beating and pawing hoofs, and got to the other side.

In cases of emergency, whether the order be right or wrong, one that is given by a firm, cool man is generally obeyed, and it was so here, for Linnell took a stroke or two forward towards the off-side pony, leaving Cora clinging to the front of the little carriage.

"Wo-ho, my beauties. Steady, boys," cried the big fisherman soothingly.

"Woa, lad, woa, then," cried Linnell, in imitation of his companion.

The ponies, the moment before snorting and plunging desperately, seemed to gather encouragement from the voices, and ceasing their frantic efforts, allowed themselves to sink lower in the water, let their bits be seized, and with outstretched necks, and nostrils just clear of the water, began to swim steadily and well.

"That's it, lads, steady it is!" cried the fisherman. "Lay out well clear of 'em, Master Linnell, sir. Mind they don't kick you. I'll steer 'em, and we shall do it. You hold on, mum; it's all right."

Cora's head and shoulders were above the water and the ponies were swimming well now, and obeying the pressure of the fisherman's hand, though they needed little guidance now they were making steadily for the shore.

"I thought they'd do it, Master Linnell, sir. Good boys, then. Good lads. Pity to let 'em drown," said the fisherman coolly.

"Right," cried Linnell, easing the pony on his side by swimming with one hand. "Keep still, Miss Dean. We shall soon be ashore. There's no danger now. Yes, there is," he muttered. "Those boats."

Cora turned her eyes upon him with a frightened look, but she was growing more calm, though she could not speak, and the ponies kept on snorting loudly as they swam on.

"Keep quiet, will you, you fools!" grumbled Dick Miggles, as bursts of cheers kept rising from the pier, answered by a gathering crowd on the beach about where they were expected to land, while the cliff was now lined with people who had heard of the accident on the pier.

"Here! hoy!" roared Dick Miggles, who had grasped the danger. "Wo-ho, my boys, I'm with you. It's all right."

"Ahoy!" came from the nearest boat, whose occupants were rowing with all their might.

"Back with you. D'ye hear! Wo-ho, lads; it's all right. Back, I say. You'll frighten the horses again."

"We're coming to help you," came from the boat.

"Go back, curse yer!" roared Dick. "Don't you see what you're doing."

The ponies were getting scared by the shouting, but by dint of patting and soothing words, they were calmed down once more, and the boatmen, in obedience to the orders given, ceased rowing.

"Go back, and bid 'em hold their row," cried Dick, as he guided the ponies. "We must get in quiet, or the horses'll go mad again."

The men rowed back, communicating their orders to the other boats, whose occupants rested on their oars, while, like some sea-queen, Cora was drawn on in her chariot towards the shore, but looking terribly unaccustomed to the mode of procedure, as she still clung to the front of the little carriage.

"Miggles."

"'Ullo?"

"Can you manage them alone? The lady."

"All right, Master Linnell, sir. They'll go now. We shall be ashore directly."

He had turned his head and seen what was wrong as Richard Linnell loosed his hold of the pony's head, letting it swim on, though the frightened beast uttered a snorting neigh and tried to follow him, till its attention was taken up by the soothing words of Dick Miggles, and it struck out afresh for the shore.

Meanwhile Richard had caught Cora Dean as she loosened her grasp of the front of the carriage, for he had seen that something was coming as her countenance changed and her eyes half-closed.

It was an easy task, for he had only to check her as she was floating out of the carriage, and take hold of the front with his right hand to let himself be drawn ashore.

She opened her eyes again with a start, as if she were making an effort to master her emotion, and they rested on Linnell's as he held her tightly to his breast. Then she shivered and clung to him, and the next minute the ponies' hoofs touched the shingly bottom, and people began to realise how it was that the carriage had not sunk in the deep water and dragged the ponies down.

It was plain enough. There was nothing but the slight body with its seats, which had been torn from springs, axle-trees, and wheels, giving it more than ever the aspect of a chariot drawn by sea-horses through the waves.

The ponies were for making a fresh dash as soon as they felt the yielding shingle beneath their hoofs, but a dozen willing hands were at their heads; the remains of the carriage were drawn up the beach, and the traces were loosened and twisted up, while Cora was borne by a couple of gentlemen to one of several carriages offered to bear her home.

As for Linnell, he was surrounded by an excited crowd of people eager to shake hands with him, but none of whom could answer his questions about Mrs Dean.

"Mrs Dean?" said a wet, thick-set man, elbowing his way through. "All right; sent home in Lord Carboro's donkey-carriage. Mr Linnell, sir, your hand, sir. God bless you, sir, for a brave gentleman! Nice pair of wet ones, aren't we?"

"Oh, never mind, Mr Barclay," cried Linnell, shaking hands. "I'm only too thankful that we have got them safe ashore."

"With no more harm done than to give the coachbuilder a job, eh? Ha, ha!"

"Three cheers for 'em!" shouted a voice; and they were heartily given.

"And three more for Fisherman Dick!" cried Linnell.

"Don't, Master Richard, sir—please don't!" cried the swarthy fisherman modestly.

"He did more than I did."

"No, no, Master Richard, sir," protested Dick, as the cheers were heartily given; and then a horrible thought smote Linnell:

"The boy—Mrs Dean's little groom! Where is he?"

"Oh, I'm all right, sir," cried a shrill voice. "When I see as missus couldn't stop the ponies, I dropped down off my seat on to the pier."

"Hurray! Well done, youngster!" cried first one and then another,

"Look here, Mr Richard," cried Barclay; "my place is nearest; come there, and send for some dry clothes."

"No, no; I'll get back," said Linnell. "Thanks all the same. Let me pass, please;" and as Cora Dean's ponies were led off to their stable, and Barclay went towards where plump Mrs Barclay was signalling him on the cliff, the young man hurried off homeward, followed by bursts of cheers, and having hard work to escape from the many idlers who were eager to shake his hand.

# Chapter Eighteen
# Unreasonable Children

"Claire, Claire! Quick, Claire!"

Pale and very anxious of aspect, Claire hurried down from her room, to find her father, in his elaborate costume, standing in an attitude before one of the mirrors, not heeding her, so wrapped was he in his thoughts.

Her brow contracted, and she looked at him wonderingly, asking herself was his memory going, or was something more terrible than the loss of memory coming on? for he appeared to have forgotten that which was an agony to her, night and day.

Something had happened to please him, she knew, for his countenance at such times was easy to read; but all the same, his worn aspect was pitiable, and it was plain that beneath the mask he wore the terrible care was working its way.

"What is it, papa?" she said, in the calm, sad way which had become habitual with her.

"What is it?" he cried, in his mincing, artificial style.

"Success! Assured fortune! The wretched fribbles who have been disposed to slight me and refuse my offices will now be at my feet. A brilliant match for you, and a high position in the world of fashion."

"Father!"

"Hush, child, and listen. The position of both of you is assured; a peaceful and more prosperous fortune for me! The few trifles I ask for: my snuff, a glass of port—one only—my cutlet, a suit of clothes when I desire a change, without an insulting reference to an old bill, the deference of tradespeople, freedom from debt. Claire, at last, at last!"

"Oh, papa!" cried the girl, with the tears welling over and dropping slowly from her beautiful eyes, while her sweet mouth seemed all a-tremble, and her agitated hands were stretched out to clasp the old man's arm.

But he waved her off.

"Don't, don't, Claire," he said quickly. "See there. I do detest to have my coat spotted. It is so foolish and weak."

Claire smiled—a sweet, sad smile—as she drew a clean cambric handkerchief from the pocket of her apron, shook it out, showing a long slit and a series of careful darns, removed the pearly drop before it had time to soak the cloth, and exclaimed:

"Then the town has conferred a salary upon you?"

"Pah! As if I would condescend to take it, girl!" cried the old man, drawing himself up more stiffly.

"A legacy?"

The Master of the Ceremonies shook his head.

"A commission for Morton?"

"No, no, no."

"Then—"

The old man waved his cane with a graceful flourish, placed it in the hand that held his snuff-box, opened the latter, and, after tapping it, took a pinch, as if it were a matter calling forth long study of deportment to perform, closed the box with a loud snap, and said, in a haughty, affected tone:

"Half an hour since, on a well-filled parade, I encountered His Royal Highness and a group of friends."

He paused, and took out a silk handkerchief, embroidered here and there with purple flowers by his child.

"And then—"

There was a flourish of the handkerchief, and the flicking away of imaginary specks from the tightly-buttoned coat.

"His Royal Highness—"

"Yes, papa," said Claire piteously, as he looked at her as if asking her attention.

At that moment Morton entered, looking weary and discontented; but, seeing his father's peculiar look, he checked the words he was about to say, and watched his face as he gave his handkerchief another flourish, replaced it, and took his cane from his left hand to twirl it gracefully.

"His Royal Highness shook hands with me."

"Oh!" exclaimed Morton, while Claire's brow grew more rugged.

"Shook hands with you, father?" said Morton eagerly.

"And asked me for a pinch of snuff."

There was a dead silence in the room as Claire clasped her hands together and trembled, and seemed about to speak, but dared not; while Morton screwed up his mouth to whistle, but refrained, looking half contemptuously at his father the while.

"Fortune has thrown a magnificent chance in our way."

"I say, dad, what do you mean with your magnificent chance?"

"I have hopes, too, for Claire. I cannot say much yet, but I have great hopes," he continued, ignoring the question of his son.

"Oh, papa!"

"Yes, my child, I have. I can say no more now, but I have hopes."

Claire's careworn face grew more cloudy as she uttered a low sigh.

"But look here, father; what do you mean," repeated Morton, "by your magnificent chance?"

The Master of the Ceremonies coughed behind one delicate hand, brushed a few imaginary specks from his sleeve, then took out his snuff-box, and refreshed himself with a pinch in a very elaborate way.

"You are a man now, Morton, and I will speak plainly to you, as I have before now spoken plainly to your sisters. My only hope for the future is to see you both make good marriages."

"Why, that won't send you to heaven, father," said the lad, grinning.

"I mean my—our—earthly future, sir," said the old man. "This is no time for ribald jest. Remember your duty to me, sir, and follow out my wishes."

"Oh, very well, father," said Morton sulkily.

"But, papa dear, you surely do not think of Morton marrying," said Claire anxiously.

"And why not, madam, pray? Younger men have married before now, even princes and kings, when it was politically necessary, at twelve and fifteen; my memory does not serve me at the moment for names, but let that pass."

"But have you any fixed ideas upon the subject, papa?"

"My dear Claire! How dense you are! Did I not tell you about Morton's providential rescue of Lady Drelincourt's favourite, and of her impassioned admiration of his bravery? She saw him at great disadvantage then; but I am going to arrange with—er—one of the principal tailors, and Morton must now take his place amongst the best dressed bucks on the Parade. With his manly young person, and a few touches in deportment that I can give him, his prospect is sure, I will answer for it."

"Ha—ha—ha—ha—ha—ha!" roared Morton, bursting out into a fit of uncontrollable laughter.

"Morton!" and the old man turned round fiercely.

"Why, you don't want me to marry that old female Guy Fawkes, father!"

"Morton! my son! you grieve and pain me. How dare you speak like that of a leader of society—a lady of title, sir—of great wealth. Why, her diamonds are magnificent. I will be plain with you. You have only to play your cards well, and in due course others will be issued—Mr Morton Denville and the Countess of Drelincourt."

"Why, father, all the fellows would laugh at me."

"Sir, a man with horses, carriages, servants, a town mansion and country seat, and a large income can laugh at the world."

"Oh, yes, of course, father; but she's fifty or sixty, and I'm not twenty."

"What has that to do with it, sir! How often do men of sixty marry girls of seventeen, eighteen, and nineteen?"

"But she paints, and wears false hair."

"Matters of which every gentleman, sir, would be profoundly ignorant as regards a lady of title."

"But, papa dear, surely you are not serious?" said Claire, who had listened with horror painted in every feature.

"I was never more serious in my life, child. Lady Drelincourt is not young, but she is a most amiable woman, with no other weakness than a love for play."

"And little beasts of dogs," said Morton contemptuously.

"Of course, because there is a void in her womanly heart. That void, my son, you must try and fill."

"Oh, nonsense, father!"

"Nonsense! Morton, are you mad? Are you going to throw away a fortune, and a great position in society? Of course, I do not say that such an event will follow, but it is time you began to assert your position. You did well the other day on the pier."

"Yes," said Morton with a sneer. "I fished out a dog. Now Dick Linnell did something worth—"

"Silence, sir! Do not mention his name in my presence, I beg," said the old man sternly; and he left the house.

"Well, I tell you what it is, Sis," said Morton, speaking from the window, where he had gone to see his father mince by, "the old dad hasn't been right since that night. I think he's going off his head."

There was no reply, and, turning round, it was to find that he was alone, for Claire, unable to bear the strain longer, had glided from the room.

# Chapter Nineteen
# Miss Clode's Hero

No one would have called Miss Clode pretty, "but there were traces," as the Master of the Ceremonies said. She was thin and middle-aged now, but she had once been a very charming woman; and, though the proprietress of the circulating library at Saltinville, a keen observer would have said that she was a lady.

Richard Linnell entered her shop on the morning after the carriage accident, and a curious flush came into her little thin face. There was a light in her eye that seemed to make the worn, jaded face pleasanter to look upon, and it seemed as if something of the little faded woman's true nature was peeping out.

She did not look like the little go-between in scores of flirtations and intrigues; but as if the natural love of her nature had come to the surface, from where it generally lay latent, and her eyes seemed to say:

"Ah, if I could have married, and had a son like that."

It is the fashion, nowadays, for ladies to attempt a strong-minded *rôle*, and profess to despise the tyrant man; to take to college life and professorship; to cry aloud and shout for woman's rights and independence; for votes and the entry to the school board, vestry, and the Parliamentary bench; when all the time Nature says in her gentle but inflexible way: "Foolish women; it was not for these things that you were made to tread the earth."

Study! Yes, nothing is too abstruse, nowadays. The pretty maidens, who used to learn a little French with their music and drawing, now take to Greek and Latin and the higher mathematics, but they cannot stitch like their grandmothers.

"And," says a strong-minded lady, "are they any worse companions now for men than they were then?"

"Opinions are various, madam." I used to write that as a text-hand copy in a nicely-ruled book that I used to blot with inky fingers. You, madam, who claim your rights, surely will not deny me mine—to have my own opinion, which I will dare to give, and say:

"Yes; I think they have not improved. Somehow one likes softness and sweetness in a woman, and your classic young ladies are often very sharp and hard.

"If you combat my opinion upon the main idea of women's purpose here, add this to your study—the aspect of a woman when she is most beautiful.

"And when is that?—in her ball dress?—in her wedding costume?—when she first says 'yes?'

"Oh, no; none of these, but when she is alone with the child she loves, and that sweet—well, angelic look of satisfied maternity is on her face, and there is Nature's own truth stamped indelibly as it has been from the first.

"Men never look like that. They never did, and one may say never will. It is not given to us, madam. Study that look; it is more convincing than all the speeches women ever spoke on woman's rights."

Just such a look was upon the face of little thin white-faced Miss Clode, as the frank, manly young fellow strode suddenly into her shop, making her start, change colour, and set down on the counter something she was holding, taking it up again directly with trembling hands.

"Ah, Miss Clode," he said cheerfully, "here I am again. Is it the weather, or are your strings bad?"

"Do they break so, then?" she said, hurriedly producing a tin canister, which refused to give up its lid; and Richard had to take it, and wrench it off with his strong fingers, when a number of oily rings of transparent catgut flew out on to the glass case.

"How clumsy I am," he said.

"No," she said softly; "how strong and manly. How you have altered these last ten years!"

"Well, I suppose so," he said, smiling down at the little thin, upturned, admiring face. "But you'll ruin me in strings, Miss Clode."

"I wish you would not pay for them," she said plaintively. "I get the very best Roman strings. I send on purpose to a place in Covent Garden, London, and they ought to be good."

"And so they are," he said, taking up half a dozen rings on his fingers and examining them to see which were the clearest, smoothest, and most transparent.

"But they break so," she sighed. "You really must not pay for these."

"Then I shall not have any," he said.

She gazed tenderly in his face, and her eyes were very intent as she watched him. Then, coughing slightly, and half turning away, she said gently:

"And your father—is he quite well?"

"Oh yes, thank you. Very well. Well as a man can be who has such a great idle, useless son."

Miss Clode shook her little curls at him reproachfully, and there was something very tender in her way as she cried, "You should not say that." Then, in a quiet apologetic manner, she lowered her tone and said:

"You can't help being so tall and strong and manly, and—and—and—I'm only an old woman, Mr Linnell," she said, smiling in a deprecating way, "and I've known you since you were such a boy, so I shall say it—you won't be vain—so handsome."

"Am I?" he said, laughing. "Ah well, handsome is that handsome does, Miss Clode."

"Exactly," she said, laying her hand upon his arm and speaking very earnestly, "and I have three—three notes here."

"For me?" he said, blushing like a woman, and then frowning at his weakness.

"Yes, Mr Linnell, for you."

"Tear them up, then," he said sharply. "I don't want them."

Miss Clode gave vent to a sigh of relief.

"Or no," he said firmly. "They were given to you to deliver. Give them to me."

She passed three triangular notes to him half unwillingly, and he took them, glanced at the handwritings, and then tore them across without opening them.

"No lady worth a second thought would address a man like that," he said sharply. "Where shall I throw this stuff?"

Miss Clode stooped down and lifted a waste-paper basket from behind the counter, and he threw the scraps in.

"We are old friends, Miss Clode," he said. "Burn them for me, please, at once. I should not like to be so dishonourable as to disgrace the writers by letting them be seen."

"People are talking about you so, sir."

"About me?" he cried.

"Yes, Mr Linnell; they say you behaved like a hero."

"Absurd!"

"When you swam out to the pony carriage and helped to rescue those—er—ladies."

"My dear Miss Clode, would not any fisherman on the beach have done the same if he had been near? I wish people would not talk such nonsense."

"People will talk down here, Mr Linnell. They have so little else to do."

"More's the pity," said Richard pettishly.

"And is—is Mrs Dean quite well again, Mr Linnell?"

"Oh yes," he said coolly. "She was more frightened than hurt."

"Does Miss Dean seem any worse, sir? Does she look pale?"

The little woman asked these questions in a hesitating way, her hands busy the while over various objects on her counter.

"Pale—pale?" said Richard, turning over the violin strings and looking to see which were the most clear. "Really, I did not notice, Miss Clode."

"He would not speak so coolly if this affair had ripened into anything more warm than being on friendly terms," thought the little woman, and she seemed to breathe more freely.

"I'm afraid I've been very rude," continued the young man. "I ought to have asked after them this morning."

Miss Clode gave another sigh of relief.

"No one shall see those scraps, Mr Linnell," she said quietly; and the look of affectionate pride in him seemed to intensify. "It is quite right that a young gentleman like you should have some one to love him, but not in such a way as that."

"No," he replied shortly, and the colour came into his cheeks again, making them tingle, so that he stamped his foot and snatched up the violin strings again to go on with his selection. "There, I shall have these four," he said, forcing a smile, "and if they don't turn out well I shall patronise your rival, Miss Clode."

"My rival!" exclaimed the little woman, turning pale. "Oh, I understand. Yes, of course, Mr Linnell. Those four. Let me put them in paper."

"No, no. I'll slip them in this little case," he said, and he laid four shillings on the counter.

"I'd really much rather you did not pay for them," she protested, and very earnestly too.

"Then I won't have them," he said; and, with a sigh, Miss Clode placed the money in her drawer.

"I hope you were not one of the party who serenaded a certain lady on that terrible night of horrors, Mr Linnell," she said, smiling; and then, noticing quickly the start he gave, "Why, fie! I did not think you thought of such things."

"Yes; don't talk about it, I beg," he exclaimed. "It was by accident. I did not know I was going there."

"But surely, Mr Linnell, you don't think—Oh!"

She stood gazing at him with her lips apart.

"Miss Clode," he said firmly, "I do not confide to people what I think. Good-morning."

"No, no: stop," she said earnestly; and he turned, wondering at her tone of voice, and agitation.

"What do you mean?" he said.

"Only—only—that I have known you so long, Mr Linnell, I can't help—humbly, of course—taking a little interest in you—you made me feel so proud just now—when you tore up those foolish women's letters—and now—"

"Well, and now?" he said sternly.

"It troubled me—pray don't be angry with me—it troubled me—to think—of course it was foolish of me, but I should not—should not like to see you—"

"Well, Miss Clode, pray speak," for she had stopped again.

"See you make an unworthy choice," she faltered.

"Miss Clode, this is too much," he said, flushing angrily, and he turned and left the shop, the little thin pale woman gazing after him wistfully and sighing bitterly as he passed from her sight.

"I'm—I'm very fond of him," she said as she wiped a few weak tears from her eyes. "Such a brave, upright, noble young fellow, and so gentle one moment, and so full of spirit the next. Dear, dear, dear, what a thing it is! He never wastes money in gambling, and wine and follies. Perhaps he would though, if he were as rich as the rest of them. And he ought to be."

She wiped her eyes again, and as she did so the woman's entire aspect changed. For just then Miss Cora Dean was driven by in a hired carriage, her dark eyes flashing, half veiled as they were by the long fringe of lashes, and then she was gone.

"Ah!" exclaimed Miss Clode angrily, "you are a beauty, sitting up there as haughty as a duchess, and your wicked old mother lying back there in her silks and satins and laces, as if all Saltinville belonged to you, instead of being drowned. But mind this, my fine madams, I may be only little Miss Clode at the library, but if you work any harm between you to those I love I'll have you both bundled neck and crop out of the place, or I'll know the reason why.

"A wretch!" she said, after a pause. "She'd like nothing better than to tempt him to follow her. But he won't! No; he's thinking of that girl Claire, and she is not half good enough for him. I don't like them and their fine ways. I don't like Denville with his mincing, idiotic airs. How that man can go about as he does with the stain of that poor old woman's death at his house astounds me.

"Well, poor wretch," she said scornfully, "it is his trade, as this miserable go-between business is mine. Perhaps he has fallen as low as I have; but I don't live as he does—as if he had thousands a year, when they are next door to starving and horribly in debt.

"Ah, well, it is to make a good show in his shop," she went on, speaking very bitterly—"to dress the window, and sell his girls, and start his boys.

"Nice bargain he has made in selling one. There's something more about that wretched little empty-headed child than I know, but I shall find out yet. Surely he does not think of that boy and Drelincourt. Oh, it would be too absurd. I've not seen the other brother lately. What a family! And for that boy to be taken with—oh, I must stop it if I can.

"Mrs Burnett? Yes, I must know about her. There was a great deal going on with that poor young artist who went away—and died. There was some mystery about that, I know, and—"

"What are you talking about, auntie? I thought there was some one in the shop, and came to see if you wanted me."

"Talking? I talking? Oh, nonsense, my dear. I was only thinking aloud."

"Well, auntie, it was very loud, for I heard you say you would have to find out something about Mrs Burnett."

"You heard me say that? Nonsense!"

"But I did, auntie; and, do you know, I could tell you something so funny about her."

"You could, child?" cried the little woman fiercely.

"Yes, and about Mr Richard Linnell, too."

Miss Clode caught the girl by the arm, and held her tightly while she seemed to be gasping for breath.

"About May Burnett? about Richard Linnell?"

"Yes, auntie, for do you know the other night as I was going down by the lower cliff to see if Fisherman Dick had—"

"Hush!" cried Miss Clode, pressing her arm so sharply that the girl winced. "Here she is."

# Chapter Twenty
# Barclay's Tenants

"It was scandalous," Saltinville said, "that she should accept it."

But she did: a handsome little carriage that came down from Long Acre, and was sent round to the stables, where Cora Dean's ponies were put up and kept now on a shorter allowance of corn.

The note was a simple one, written in a very large hand that was decidedly shaky. There was a coronet on the top, and its owner, Lord Carboro', begged Miss Dean's acceptance of the little gift, with his sorrow that he was the cause of the mishap, and his congratulations that she was not hurt.

This was all very refined and in accordance with etiquette. The postscript looked crotchety.

"P.S.—Tell your people not to give them so much corn."

Cora did so, and said that she should drive out to show the people of Saltinville that she was no coward.

"Then I'll go with you, Betsy," said Mrs Dean, "to show 'em I ain't, too: and, you mark my words, this'll be the making of you in society."

So Cora took her drives as of old, found that she was very much noticed by the gentlemen, very little by the ladies, but waited her time.

The Deans lodged at one of the best houses in the Parade—a large, double-fronted place facing the sea, with spacious balcony and open hall door, and porch ornamented with flowers.

The little groom sprang down and ran to the ponies' heads as his mistress alighted, and after sweeping her rich dress aside, held out his hand for her mother, who got out of the carriage slowly, and in what was meant for a very stately style, her quick beady eyes having shown her that the windows on either side of the front door were wide open, while her sharp ears and her nose had already given her notice that the lodgers were at home—a low buzzing mellow hum with a wild refrain in high notes, announcing that old Mr Linnell was at work with his violoncello to his son's violin, and a faint penetrating perfume—or smell, according to taste—suggesting that Colonel Mellersh was indulging in a cigar.

Mrs Dean's daughter was quite as quick in detecting these signs, and, raising her head and half closing her eyes, she swept gracefully into the house, unconscious of the fact that Richard Linnell drew back a little from the window on one side of the door, and that Colonel Mellersh showed his teeth as he lay back in his chair beside a small table, on which was a dealt-out pack of cards.

"I should like to poison that old woman," said the Colonel, gathering together the cards.

"I wish Mr Barclay had let the first floor to some one else, Richard," said a low pleasant voice from the back of the room. *P-r-r-rm, Pr-um!*

The speaker did not say *Pr-r-rm, Pr-um!* That sound was produced by an up and down draw of the bow across the fourth string of the old violoncello he held between his legs, letting the neck of the instrument with its pegs fall directly after into the hollow of his arm, as he picked up a cake of amber-hued transparent rosin from the edge of a music stand, and began thoughtfully to rub it up and down the horse-hair of the bow.

The speaker's was a pleasant handsome face of a man approaching sixty; but though his hair was very grey, he was remarkably well-preserved. His well-cut rather effeminate face showed but few lines, and there was just a tinge of colour in his cheeks, such as good port wine might have produced: but in this case it was a consequence of a calm, peaceful, seaside life. He was evidently slight and tall, but bent, and in his blue eyes there was a dreamy look, while a curious twitch came over his face from time to time as if he suffered pain.

"It would have been better, father," said Richard Linnell, turning over the leaves of a music-book with his violin bow, "but we can't pick and choose whom one is to sit next in this world."

"No, no, we can't, my son."

"And I don't think that we ought to trouble ourselves about our neighbours, so long as they behave themselves decorously here."

"No, no, my son," said Linnell, senior, thoughtfully. "There's a deal of wickedness in this world, but I suppose we mustn't go about throwing stones."

"I'm not going to, father, and I'm sure you wouldn't throw one at a mad dog."

"Don't you think I would, Dick?" with a very sweet smile; and the eyes brightened and looked pleased. "Well, perhaps you are right. Poor brute! Why should I add to its agony?"

"So long as it didn't bite, eh, father?"

"To be sure, Dick; so long as it didn't bite. I should like to run through that *adagio* again, Dick, but not if you're tired, my boy, not if you're tired."

"Tired? No!" cried the young man. "I could keep on all day."

"That's right. I'm glad I taught you. There's something so soul-refreshing in a bit of music, especially when you are low-spirited."

"Which you never are, now."

"N-no, not often, say not often, say not often. It makes me a little low-spirited though about that woman and her mother, Dick."

"I don't see why it should."

"But it does. Such a noble-looking beautiful creature, and such a hard, vulgar, worldly mother. Ah, Dick, beautiful women are to be pitied."

"No, no: to be admired," said Richard, laughing.

"Pitied, my boy, pitied," said the elder, making curves in the air with his bow, while the fingers of his left hand—long, thin, white, delicate fingers—stopped the strings, as if he were playing the bars of some composition. "Your plain women scout their beautiful sisters, and trample upon them, but it is in ignorance. They don't know the temptations that assail one who is born to good looks."

"Why, father, this is quite a homily."

"Ah, yes, Dick," he said, laughing. "I ought to have been a preacher, I think, I am always prosing. Poor things—poor things! A lovely face is often a curse."

"Oh, don't say that."

"But I do say it, Dick. It is a curse to that woman upstairs. Never marry a beautiful woman, Dick."

"But you did, father."

The old man started violently and changed colour, but recovered himself on the instant.

"Yes, yes. She was very beautiful. And she died, Dick; she died."

He bent his head over his music, and Richard crossed and laid his hand upon his shoulder.

"I am sorry I spoke so thoughtlessly."

"Oh, no, my boy; oh, no. It was quite right. She was a very beautiful woman. That miniature does not do her justice. But—but don't marry a beautiful woman, Dick," he continued, gazing wistfully into his son's face. "Now that *adagio*. It is a favourite bit of mine."

Richard Linnell looked as if he would have liked to speak, and there was a troubled expression on his face as he thought of Claire Denville's sweet candid eyes; but he shrank from any avowal. For how dare he, when she had given him but little thought, and—well, she was a beautiful woman, one of those against whom he had been warned.

He looked up and found his father watching him keenly, when both assumed ignorance of any other matter than the *adagio* movement, the sweet notes of which, produced by the thrilling strings, floated out through the open window, and up and in that of the drawing-room floor overhead, where on a luxurious couch Mrs Dean had thrown herself, while her daughter was slowly pacing the room with the air of a tragedy queen.

"Buzz-buzz; boom-boom! Oh, those horrid fiddlers!" cried Mrs Dean, bouncing up and crossing to the fireplace, where she caught up the poker; but only to have her hand seized by her daughter, who took the poker away, and replaced it in the fender.

"What are you going to do?"

"What am I going to do? Why thump on the floor to make them quiet. Do you suppose I'm going to sit here and be driven mad with their scraping! This isn't a playhouse!"

"You will do nothing of the sort, mother."

"Oh, won't I? Do you think I'm going to pay old Barclay all that money for these rooms, and not have any peace? Pray who are you talking to?"

"To you, mother," said Cora sternly; and the stoutly-built, brazen-looking virago shrank from her daughter's fierce gaze. "You must not forget yourself here, among all these respectable people."

"And pray who's going to? But I don't know so much about your respectability. That Colonel, with his queer looks like the devil in 'Dr Faustus,' is no better than he should be."

"The Colonel is a man of the world like the rest," said Cora coldly.

"Yes, and a nice man of the world, too. And that old Linnell's living apart from his wife. I know though—"

"Silence!"

"Now look here, Betsy, I won't have you say *silence* to me like that. This here isn't the stage, and we aren't playing parts. Just you speak to me proper, madam."

"Mother, I will not have you speak of Mr Linnell like that."

"Ho, indeed! And why not, pray? Now, look here, Betsy," she cried, holding up a warning finger, "I won't have no nonsense there. I'm not a fool. I know the world. I've seen you sighing and looking soft when we've passed that young fellow downstairs."

Cora's eyes seemed to burn as she fixedly returned her mother's look.

"Oh, you may stare, madam; but I can see more than you think. Why, you ought to be ashamed of yourself, making eyes at a poor, penniless fiddler, when you might—"

"I—I don't want to quarrel, mother," cried Cora, "but if you dare to speak to me again like that I'll not be answerable for myself."

"There!—there!—there! There's gratitude!"

"Gratitude? Where should I have been but for Mr Linnell's bravery, and which of the wretched dressed-up and titled dandies stirred to save me the other day? Richard Linnell is a brave, true-hearted man, too good to marry an actress."

"She's mad—she's mad—she's mad! There's grace; and to her mother, too, who's thought of nothing but getting her on in the world, and brought her forward, so that now she can live on the best of everything, in the handsomest of rooms, and keep her carriage. She flies in her poor mother's face, and wants to get rid of her, I suppose. Oho—oho—oh!"

Mrs Dean plumped herself down into a gilded chair, and began to howl very softly.

"Don't be a fool, mother," said Cora. "I don't want to quarrel, I tell you, so hold your tongue."

"After the way I've brought her up, too," howled Mrs Dean—softly, so that the sound should not be heard downstairs.

"After the way you've brought me up!" cried Cora fiercely. "Yes; brought me up to be sneered at by every lady I meet—brought me up so that I hate myself, and long sometimes to be one of the poor women we see knitting stockings on the beach."

"Don't be a fool, Cory, my handsome, beautiful gal," cried Mrs Dean, suddenly starting up in her seat, dry-eyed and forgetful of her grief. "How can you be so stupid!"

"Stupid!" cried Cora bitterly. "Is it stupid to wish myself a woman that some true-hearted man could love, instead of looking forward to a life of acting."

"Oh, how you do go on to be sure. I am surprised at you, Cory. I know what you'd say about the life as them leads as ar'n't in the profession, but don't you be a fool, Betsy. 'Your face is your fortune, sir, she said,' as the song says; working your fingers to the bone won't keep you out of the workus. Don't tell me. I know. I've known them as has tried it. Let them work as likes. I like a cutlet and a glass of fine sherry, and some well-made coffee with a noo-laid egg in it, and it ain't to be got by folks as works their fingers to the bone."

"And who wants to work their fingers to the bone, mother?" cried Cora, tearing off and flinging down her handsome feathered hat. "In every face I see there's the look—'You're only one of the stage-players—a rogue and a vagabond.' I want to lead some life for which I need not blush."

"As she needn't blush for! Oh, dear, oh, dear! When her father trod the boards and her mother was born on 'em! What a gal you are, Betsy," said Mrs Dean, who professed high good humour now, and she rocked herself to and fro, and pressed her hands on her knees as she laughed. "Oh, I say, Cory, you are a one. You will act the injured fine lady in private life, my dear. Why, what a silly thing you are. Look at that hat you've chucked down. Didn't it cost five guineas?"

"Yes, mother, it cost five guineas," said Cora wearily.

"And you can have whatever you like. Oh, I say, my lovely gal, for you really are, you know, don't get into these silly fits. It's such stuff. Why, who knows what may happen? You may be right up atop of the tree yet, and how about yon folks as passes you by now? Why, they'll all be as civil and friendly as can be. There, there, come and kiss me, ducky, we mustn't quarrel, must we? I've got my eyes open for you, so don't, don't, there's a dear. I know what these things means—don't go chucking yourself at that young Linnell's head."

"Let Mr Linnell alone, mother."

"But I can't, my luvvy; I know too well what these things mean. Why, there was Julia Jennings as was at the Lane—it was just afore you was born. There was a dook and a couple of lords, and carridges and horses, and livery suvvants, and as many jewels and dymonds and dresses as she liked to order; and if she didn't kick 'em all over and marry a shopman, and lived poor ever after. Now do, my luvvy, be advised by me. I know what the world is, and—Gracious goodness! there's somebody coming up the stairs."

Mrs Dean threw herself into an attitude meant to be easy, and Cora smoothed her knitted brows as there was a knock at the door, and, after a loud "Come in," a neat-looking maid entered.

"Mr Barclay, please, ma'am."

"Show him up, Jane," said Mrs Dean sharply; and then, as the door closed, "The old rip's come after his rent. How precious sharp he is."

"Morning, ladies," said Barclay. "I heard you were in. Glad to see you are no worse for your accident the other day."

He glanced at Cora, who bowed rather stiffly, and said "Not at all."

"I can't say that, Mr Barclay. I'm a bit shook; but, as I said to my daughter, I wasn't going to show the white feather, and the ponies go lovely now."

"Well, I'm glad of that."

"And I'm so much obliged to you for helping of me. Do you know, it was just like a scene in a piece we—er—saw once at the Lane."

"Oh, it was nothing ma'am, what I did. Miss Dean, there, she took off all the honours. No cold, I hope."

Cora did not answer.

"Plucky fellow, young Linnell; but poor, you know, poor."

"So I've heard," said Mrs Dean maliciously. "I was thinking of sending him ten guineas."

"Oh, I wouldn't do that, ma'am," said Barclay.

"Oh, well, I must say *thankye* some other way. Very kind of you to call. I said to my daughter, 'There's Mr Barclay come for his rent,' but I was wrong."

"Not you, ma'am," said Barclay, whose eyes were rapidly taking in the state of the room. "Business is business, you know," and he took another glance at the rich furniture and handsome mirrors of the place.

"Oh, it's all right, Mr Barclay. We're taking the greatest care of it all, and your rent's all ready for you, and always will be, of course."

"Yes, yes, I know that, ma'am. I've brought you a little receipt. Saves trouble. Pen and ink not always ready. I keep to my days. So much pleasanter for everybody. Nice rooms, ain't they?" he added, turning to Cora.

"Yes, Mr Barclay, the rooms are very nice," she said coldly and thoughtfully.

"Anything the matter with her?" said Mr Barclay, leaning forward to Mrs Dean, and taking the money she handed in exchange for a receipt. "Not in love, is she?"

Mrs Dean and her visitor exchanged glances, and smiled as Cora rose and walked to the window to gaze out at the sea, merely turning her head to bow distantly when the landlord rose to leave.

"I'm a regular scoundrel, 'pon my soul I am," said Josiah Barclay, rubbing his nose with the edge of a memorandum book; "but they pay very handsomely, and if I were to refuse to let a part of a house that I furnish on purpose for letting, without having the highest moral certificates of character with the people who want the rooms, I'm afraid I should never let them at all. Bah! it's no business of mine."

He went back to the front door and knocked, to be shown in directly after to where Colonel Mellersh was sitting back in his chair, having evidently just thrown down the pack of cards.

"Morning, Shylock," he said, showing his white teeth. "Want your pound of flesh again?"

"No, thank ye, Colonel; rather have the ducats. I say, though, I wish you wouldn't call me Shylock. I'm not one of the chosen, you know."

"That I'll take oath you're not, Barclay," said the Colonel, looking at his visitor with a very amused smile. "Your future is thoroughly assured. I'm sorry for you, Barclay, for I don't think you're the worst scoundrel that ever breathed."

"I say, you know, Colonel, this is too bad, you know. Come, come, come."

"Oh, I always speak plainly to you, Barclay. Let me see; can you let me have a hundred?"

"A hundred, Colonel?" said the other, looking up sharply; "well, yes, I think I can."

"Ah, well, I don't want it, Barclay. I know you'd be only too glad to get a good hold of me."

"Wrong, Colonel, wrong," said Barclay, chuckling as he glanced at the cards. "You do me too much good for that."

"Do I?" said the Colonel, smiling in a peculiarly cynical way. "Well, perhaps I do influence your market a little. There," he said, taking some notes from his little pocket-book, and handing them to his visitor, "now we are free once more."

"Thankye, Colonel, thankye. You're a capital tenant. I say, by the way, after all these years, I shouldn't like to do anything to annoy you: I hope you don't mind the actors upstairs."

"No," said the Colonel, staring at him.

"Because if you did complain, and were not satisfied, I'd make a change, you know."

"Don't trouble the women for my sake," said the Colonel gruffly. "Look here, Barclay, how would you play this hand?"

He took up the cards as he spoke, shuffled them with an easy, graceful movement, the pieces of pasteboard flying rapidly through his hands, before dealing them lightly out upon the table, face upwards, and selecting four thirteens.

"Now," he said, "look here. Your partner holds two trumps—six, nine; your adversaries right and left have knave and ace; B on your right leads trumps—what would you do?"

Barclay knit his brow and took the Colonel's hand, gazing from one to the other thoughtfully, and then, without a word, played the hand, the Colonel selecting those cards that would be played by the others till the hand was half through, when Barclay hesitated for a moment, and then seemed to throw away a trick.

"Why did you do that?" said the Colonel sharply.

"Because by losing that I should get the next two."

"Exactly!" cried the Colonel with his eyes flashing. "That endorses my opinion. Barclay, I shan't play against you if I can help myself. Money-lending seems to sharpen the wits wonderfully. What a clever old fox you are!"

"One's obliged to be clever now a days, Colonel, if one wants to get on. Well, I must go. I have to see your neighbours. Rents are very bad to get in."

"I suppose so," said the Colonel drily. "Good-morning."

"I wonder what he makes a year by his play," said Barclay to himself, as he went back to the front door to knock for the third time. "I believe he plays square, too, but he has a wonderful head, and he's practising night and day. Now for old Linnell."

He was shown into Mr Linnell's room the next minute, to find that he was expected, and that he was gravely and courteously received, and his rent paid, so that there was nothing for him to do but say "Good-morning." But Josiah Barclay's conscience was a little uneasy, and in spite of the fact that his tenant was far from being a rich man, there was something in his grave refined manner that won his respect.

"Wish you'd come and see us sometimes, Mr Linnell, just in a friendly way, you know. Chop and glass o' sherry with Mrs Barclay and me; and you'd join us too, Mr Richard, eh?"

"Thank you, Mr Barclay, no," said Richard's father; "I never go out. Richard, my son, here, would, I dare say, accept your invitation."

"Oh, but can't you too, eh? Look here, you know, you're a man who loves bits of old china, and I've quite a lot. Really good. Come: when shall it be?"

"Don't press me now, Mr Barclay," said his tenant gravely. "Perhaps some other time."

"Then you're offended, Mr Linnell. You're a bit hipped because of the other lodgers, you know."

"Mr Barclay, I have made no complaints," said the elder Linnell quietly.

"No, you've made no complaints, but you show it in your way, don't you see. It wasn't for me to be too strict in my inquiries about people, Mr Linnell. I'm sorry I offended you; but what can I do?"

"Mr Barclay has a perfect right to do what he pleases with his own house," replied the elder Linnell with dignity. "Good-day."

"Now I could buy that man up a hundred times over," grumbled Barclay as he walked away, richer by many pounds than when he started on his journey that morning; "but he always seems to set me down; to look upon me with contempt; and young Richard is as high and mighty as can be. Ah, well, wait a bit!—'Can you oblige me with fifty pounds, Mr Barclay, on my note of hand?'—and then p'raps they'll be more civil.

"Things ain't pleasant though, just now. One house made notorious by a murder, and me letting a couple of actresses lodge in another. Well, they pay regular, and I dare say she'll make a good match somewhere before long; but I'm afraid, when the old lady gets to know they're stage people, there'll be a bit of a breeze."

# Chapter Twenty One
# Dick Catches Shrimps

There was quite a little crowd at the end of the pier to see Fisherman Dick and some others busy with boathooks searching for the fragments of Cora Dean's pony carriage, and for want of something better to stare at, the fastening of a rope to first one pair of wheels and then to the other, and the hauling ashore, formed thrilling incidents.

Two rich carriage-cloaks were cast ashore by the tide, miles away, and the rug was found right under the pier, but there were several articles still missing. Cora's reticule, containing her purse and cut-glass scent-bottle; a little carriage-clock used by Mrs Dean, who was always very particular about the lapse of time, and that lady's reticule and purse.

It was Fisherman Dick's special task to search for them when the tide was low, and this he did by going to work as a setter does in a field, quartering the ground and hunting it all over to and fro.

But Fisherman Dick did his work with a shrimping-net, and one day he took home the little carriage-clock and showed it to his wife.

Another day he found Mrs Dean's reticule, and caught a great many shrimps as well.

Then the tide did not serve for several days, and he had to wait, shaking his head and telling Mrs Miggles he was afraid the sand would have covered everything.

"Then give it up," said Mrs Miggles, who was trying to sew with the little girl in her lap, but was prevented by the tiny thing making dashes at her broad-brimmed silver spectacles, which it kept taking off and flourishing in one little plump hand.

"Well done, little 'un," cried the fisherman, grinning. "No, missus, I don't like being beat."

He went off, looking very serious, with his net over one shoulder, the creel over the other, and after going to and fro patiently waist and often breast deep, he was successful in finding Cora Dean's reticule, with its purse and cut-glass bottle; and that night he went home amply rewarded,

Cora having been very generous, and Mrs Dean saying several times over that she wouldn't have believed that a great rough man like that would have been so honest.

"I declare, Betsy, he's just like a man in a play—the good man who finds the treasure and gives it up. Why, he might have kep' your puss, and my puss too, and nobody been a bit the wiser."

That was all that was missing; but every day for a week, during the times that the tide was low, Fisherman Dick was busy, pushing his shrimping-net before him, and stopping every now and then to raise it, throw out the rubbish, and transfer the few shrimps he caught to his creel.

It was not a good place for shrimping—it was too deep; but he kept on with his laborious task, wading out as far as ever he could go; and more than one of his fellow-mermen grinned at his empty creel.

"Why don't you try the shallows, Dick?" said one of the blue-jerseyed fellows, who seemed to be trying to grow a hump on his back by leaning over the rail at the edge of the cliff.

"'Cause I like to try the deeps," growled Fisherman Dick.

"Ah, you want to make your fortune too quick, my lad; that's plain."

Dick winked, and went home; and the next day he winked, and went out shrimping again, and caught very few, and went home again, put on his dry clothes, and said:

"Give us the babby."

Mrs Miggles gave him the "babby," and Dick took her and nursed her, smiling down at the little thing as she climbed up his chest, and tangled her little fingers in his great beard; while Mrs Miggles gave the few shrimps a pick over and a shake up before she consigned the hopping unfortunates to the boiling bath that should turn them from blackish grey to red.

"What is it, old man?" said Mrs Miggles; "sperrits?"

Fisherman Dick shook his head, and began to sing gruffly to the child about a "galliant" maiden who went to sea in search of her true "lovy-er along of a British crew."

"What is it, then—lace?"

Fisherman Dick shook his head again, and bellowed out the word "crew," the little child looking at him wonderingly, but not in the least alarmed.

"I never did see such an oyster as you are, old man," said Mrs Miggles. "You're the closest chap in the place."

"Ay!" said Fisherman Dick; and he went on with his song.

He went shrimping off the end of the pier for the delectation of the mincing crowd of promenaders twice more. Lord Carboro' saw him; so did Major Rockley and Sir Harry Payne. Sir Matthew Bray was too busy dancing attendance upon Lady Drelincourt to pay any attention.

The Master of the Ceremonies saw him too, as he bowed to one, smiled upon a second, and took snuff with a third; and several times, as he watched the fisherman wading out there, he followed his movements attentively, and appeared to be gazing without his mask of artificiality.

The man's calm, dreamy ways seemed to have an attraction, as if he were wishing that he could change places with him, and lead so simple and peaceful a life. And as he watched him, very far out now, Dick raised his net, emptied it, shook it with his back to the people, and then began to wade in quite another direction, going back no more to the ground off the pier.

The Master of the Ceremonies did not look himself that day, and twice over he found himself on the edge of the pier gazing out to sea, where everything seemed so peaceful and still.

There was a buzz of voices going on about him, but he heard nothing, till all at once a voice, quite familiar to him, exclaimed sharply:

"Well, what is it?"

"Message from Mr Barclay, sir."

"Well?"

"I took your note, sir, and he'll be glad to see you to-morrow morning at twelve."

"That will do. Now take the other."

Stuart Denville could not restrain himself as he heard those voices just behind, and it was as if some power had turned him sharply round to see Major Rockley in conversation with one of the private dragoons of his regiment.

The man had delivered his message to his master, and then turned stiffly to go, coming face to face with Denville, whose whole manner changed. He turned deadly pale, of an unwholesome pallor, and then the blood seemed to flush to his face and head. His eyes flashed and his lips parted as if to speak, but the dragoon saluted, turned upon his heel, and strode away.

"Anything the matter, Denville?" said the Major, who had seen something of the encounter.

"Matter, matter," said the old man hoarsely, and he now began to tremble violently. "No—no,—a little faint. You'll pardon me,—a chair,—a—"

The old man would have fallen, but the Major caught his arm and helped him to a seat, where a crowd of fashionables surrounded him, and did all they possibly could to prevent his recovery from his fit by keeping away every breath of air, and thrusting at him bottles of salts, vinaigrettes, and scents of every fashionable kind.

"What's the matter with the old fellow?" said the Major, as he twirled his moustache. "Could he have known about the note? Impossible; and if he had known, why should he turn faint? Bah! Absurd! The heat. He's little better than a shadow, after all."

# Chapter Twenty Two
# A Surreptitious Visitor

"Major Rockley's servant to see you, miss."

Claire started from her seat and looked at Footman Isaac with a troubled expression that was full of shame and dread.

She dropped her eyes on the instant as she thought of her position.

It was four o'clock, and the promenade on cliff and pier in full swing. Her father would not be back for two hours, Morton was away somewhere, and it was so dreadful—so degrading—to be obliged to see her brother, the prodigal, in the servants' part of the house.

For herself she would not have cared, but it was lowering her brother; and, trying to be calm and firm, she said:

"Show him in here, Isaac."

"In here, miss?"

"Yes."

"Please ma'am, master said—"

"Show him in here, Isaac," said Claire, drawing herself up with her eyes flashing, and the colour returning to her cheeks.

The footman backed out quickly, and directly after there was the clink of spurs, and a heavy tread. Then the door opened and closed, and Major Hockley's servant, James Bell, otherwise Fred Denville, strode into the room; and Isaac's retreating steps were heard.

"Fred!" cried Claire, throwing her arms round his neck, and kissing the handsome bronzed face again and again.

"My darling girl!" he cried, holding her tightly to his breast, while his face lit up as he returned her caresses.

"Oh, Fred!" she said, as she laid her hands then upon his shoulders and gazed at him at arm's length, "you've been drinking."

"One half-pint of ale. That's all: upon my soul," he said. "I say, I wish it were not wicked to commit murder."

If he had by some blow paralysed her he could not have produced a greater change in her aspect, for her eyes grew wild and the colour faded out of her cheeks and lips.

"Don't look like that," he said, smiling. "I shan't do it—at least, not while I'm sober; but I should like to wring that supercilious scoundrel's neck. He looks down upon me in a way that is quite comical."

"Why did you come, dear?" said Claire sadly. "Oh, Fred, if I could but buy you out, so that you could begin life again."

"No good, my dear little girl," he said tenderly. "There's something wrong in my works. I've no stability, and I should only go wrong again."

"But, if you would try, Fred."

"Try, my pet!" he said fiercely; "Heaven knows how I did try, but the drink was too much for me. If we had been brought up to some honest way of making a living, and away from this sham, I might have been different, but it drove me to drink, and I never had any self-command. I'm best where I am; obliged to be sober as the Major's servant."

There was a contemptuous look in his eyes as he said this last.

"And that makes it so much worse," sighed Claire with a sad smile. "If you were only the King's servant—a soldier—I would not so much mind."

"Perhaps it is best as it is," he said sternly.

"Don't say that, Fred dear."

"But I do say it, girl. If I had been brought up differently—Bah! I didn't come here to grumble about the old man."

"No, no, pray, pray don't. And, Fred dear, you must not stop. Do you want a little money?"

"Yes!" he cried eagerly. "No! Curse it all, girl, I wish you would not tempt me. So you are not glad to see me?"

"Indeed, yes, Fred; but you must not stay. If our father were to return there would be such a scene."

"He will not. He is on the pier, and won't be back these two hours. Where's Morton?"

"Out, dear."

"Then we are all right. Did you expect me?"

"No, dear. Let me make you some tea."

"No; stop here. Didn't you expect this?"

He drew a note from his breast.

"That note? No, dear. Who is it from?"

Fred Denville looked his sister searchingly in the face, and its innocent candid expression satisfied him, and he drew a sigh full of relief.

"If it had been May who looked at me like that, I should have said she was telling me a lie."

"Oh, Fred!"

"Bah! You know it's true. Little wax-doll imp. But I believe you, Claire. Fate's playing us strange tricks. I am James Bell, Major Rockley's servant, and he trusts me with his commissions. This is a *billet-doux*—a love-letter—to my sister, which my master sends, and I am to wait for an answer."

Claire drew herself up, and as her brother saw the blood mantle in her face, and the haughty, angry look in her eyes as she took the letter and tore it to pieces, he, too, drew himself up, and there was a proud air in his aspect.

"There is no answer to Major Rockley's letter," she said coldly. "How dare he write to me!"

"Claire, old girl, I must hug you," cried the dragoon. "By George! I feel as if I were not ashamed of the name of Denville after all. I was going to bully you and tell you that my superior officer is as big a scoundrel as ever breathed, and that if you carried on with him I'd shoot you. Now, bully me, my pet, and tell your prodigal drunken dragoon of a brother that he ought to be ashamed of himself for even thinking such a thing. I won't shrink."

"My dear brother," she said tenderly, as she placed her hands in his.

"My dear sister," he said softly, as he kissed her little white hands in turn, "I need not warn and try to teach you, for I feel that I might come to you for help if I could learn. There—there. Some day you'll marry some good fellow."

She shook her head.

"Yes, you will," he said. "Richard Linnell, perhaps. Don't let the old man worry you into such a match as May's."

"I shall never marry," said Claire, in a low strange voice; "never."

"Yes, you will," he said, smiling; "but what you have to guard against is not the gallantries of the contemptible puppies who haunt this place, but some big match that—Ah! Too late!"

He caught a glimpse of his father's figure passing the window, and made for the door, but it was only to stand face to face with the old man, who came in hastily, haggard, and wild of eye.

Fred Denville drew back into the room as his father staggered in, and then, as the door swung to and fastened itself, there was a terrible silence, and Claire looked on speechless for the moment, as she saw her brother draw himself up, military fashion, while her father's face changed in a way that was horrible to behold.

He looked ten years older. His eyes started; his jaw fell, and his hands trembled as he raised them, with the thick cane hanging from one wrist.

He tried to speak, but the words would not come for a few moments.

At last his speech seemed to return, and, in a voice full of rage, hate, and horror combined, he cried furiously:

"You here!—fiend!—wretch!—villain!"

"Oh, father!" cried Claire, darting to his side.

"Hush, Claire! Let him speak," said Fred.

"Was it not enough that I forbade you the house before; but, now—to come—to dare—villain!—wretch!—coldblooded, miserable wretch! You are no son of mine. Out of my sight! Curse you! I curse you with all the bitterness that—"

"Father! father!" cried Claire, in horrified tones, as she threw herself between them; but, in his rage, the old man struck her across the face with his arm, sending her tottering back.

"Oh, this is too much," cried Fred, dropping his stolid manner. "You cowardly—"

"Cowardly! Ha! ha! ha! Cowardly!" screamed the old man, catching at his stick. "You say that—you?"

As Fred strode towards him, the old man struck him with his cane, a sharp well-directed blow across the left ear, and, stung to madness by the pain, the tall strong man caught the frail-looking old beau by the throat and bore him back into a chair, holding him with one hand while his other was clenched and raised to strike.

# Chapter Twenty Three
# Father and Daughter

"Strike! Kill me! Add parricide to your other crimes, dog, and set me free of this weary life," cried the old man wildly, as he glared in the fierce, distorted face of the sturdy soldier who held him back.

But it wanted not Claire's hand upon Fred Denville's arm to stay the blow. The passionate rage fled as swiftly as it had flashed up, and he tore himself away.

"You shouldn't have struck me," he cried in a voice full of anguish. "I couldn't master myself. You struck her—the best and truest girl who ever breathed; and I'd rather be what I am—scamp, drunkard, common soldier, and have struck you down, than you, who gave that poor girl a cowardly blow. Claire—my girl—God bless you! I can come here no more."

He caught her wildly in his arms, kissed her passionately, and then literally staggered out of the house, and they saw him reel by the window.

There was again a terrible silence in that room, where the old man, looking feeble and strange now, lay back in the chair where he had been thrown, staring wildly straight before him as Claire sank upon the carpet, burying her face in her hands and sobbing to herself.

"And this is home! And this is home!"

She tried to restrain her tears, but they burst forth with sobs more wild and uncontrolled; and at last they had their effect upon the old man, whose wild stare passed off, and, rising painfully in his seat, he glared at the door and shuddered.

"How dare he come!" he muttered. "How dare he touch her! How—"

He stopped as he turned his eyes upon where Claire crouched, as if he had suddenly become aware of her presence, and his face softened into a piteous yearning look as he stretched out his hands towards her, and then slowly rose to his feet.

"I struck her," he muttered, "I struck her. My child—my darling! I—I— Claire—Claire—"

His voice was very low as he slowly sank upon his knees, and softly laid one hand upon her dress, raising it to his lips and kissing it with a curiously strange abasement in his manner.

Claire did not move nor seem to hear him, and he crept nearer to her and timidly laid his hand upon her head.

He snatched it away directly, and knelt there gazing at her wildly, for she shuddered, shrank from him, and, starting to her feet, backed towards the door with such a look of repulsion in her face that the old man clasped his hands together, and his lips parted as if to cry to her for mercy.

But no sound left them, and for a full minute they remained gazing the one at the other. Then, with a heartrending sob, Claire drew open the door and hurried from the room.

"What shall I do? What shall I do?" groaned Denville as he rose heavily to his feet. "It is too hard to bear. Better sleep—at once and for ever."

He sank into his chair with his hands clasped and his elbows resting upon his knees, and he bent lower and lower, as if borne down by the weight of his sorrow; and thus he remained as the minutes glided by, till, hearing a step at last, and the jingle of glass, he rose quickly, smoothed his care-marked face, and thrusting his hand into his breast, began to pace the room, catching up hat and stick, and half closing his eyes, as if in deep thought.

It was a good bit of acting, for when Isaac entered with a tray to lay the dinner cloth, and glanced quickly at his master, it was to see him calm and apparently buried in some plan, with not the slightest trace of domestic care upon his well-masked face.

"Mr Morton at home, Isaac?" he said, with a slightly-affected drawl.

"No, sir; been out hours."

"Not gone fishing, Isaac?"

"No, sir; I think Mr Morton's gone up to the barracks, sir. Said he should be back to dinner, sir."

"That is right, Isaac. That is right. I think I will go for a little promenade before dinner myself."

"He's a rum 'un," muttered the footman as he stood behind the curtain on one side of the window; "anyone would think we were all as happy as the day's long here, when all the time the place is chock full of horrors, and if I was to speak—"

Isaac did not finish his sentence, but remained watching the Master of the Ceremonies with his careful mincing step till he was out of sight, when the footman turned from the window to stand tapping the dining-table with his finger tips.

"If I was to go, there'd be a regular wreck, and I shouldn't get a penny of my back wages. If I stay, he may get them two well married, and then there'd be money in the house. Better stay. Lor', if people only knew all I could tell 'em about this house, and the scraping, and putting off bills, and the troubles with Miss May and the two boys, and—"

Isaac drew a long breath and turned rather white.

"I feel sometimes as if I ought to make a clean breast of it, but I don't like to. He isn't such a bad sort, when you come to know him, but that—ugh!"

He shuddered, and began to rattle the knives and forks upon the table, giving one a rub now and then on his shabby livery.

"It's a puzzler," he said, stopping short, after breathing in a glass, and giving it a rub with a cloth. "Some day, I suppose, there'll be a difference, and he'll be flush of money. I suppose he daren't start yet. Suppose I—No; that wouldn't do. He'll pay all the back, then, and I might—"

Isaac shuddered again, and muttered to himself in a very mysterious way. Then, all at once:

"Why, I might cry halves, and make him set me up for life. Why not? She was good as gone, and—"

He set down the glass, and wiped the dew that had gathered off his brow, looking whiter than before, for just then a memory had come into Isaac's mental vision—it was a horrible recollection of having been tempted to go and see the execution of a murderer at the county town, and this man's accomplice was executed a month later.

"Accomplice" was an ugly word that seemed to force itself into Isaac's mind, and he shook his head and hurriedly finished laying the cloth.

"Let him pay me my wages, all back arrears," he said. "Perhaps there is a way of selling a secret without being an accomplice, but I don't know, and—oh, I couldn't do it. It would kill that poor girl, who's about worried to death with the dreadful business, without there being anything else."

# Chapter Twenty Four
# Pressed for Money

As a rule, a tailor is one who will give unlimited credit so long as his client is a man of society, with expectations, and the maker of garments can charge his own prices; but Stuart Denville, Esq, MC, of Saltinville, paid a visit to his tailor to find that gentleman inexorable.

"No, Mr Denville, sir, it ain't to be done. I should be glad to fit out the young man, as he should be fitted out as a gentleman, sir; but there is bounds to everything."

"Exactly, my dear Mr Ping, but I can assure you that before long both his and my accounts shall be paid."

"No, sir, can't do it. I'm very busy, too. Why not try Crowder and Son?"

"My dee-ar Mr Ping—you'll pardon me? I ask you as a man, as an artist in your profession, could I see my son—my heir—a gentleman who I hope some day will make a brilliant match—a young man who is going at once into the best of society—could I now, Mr Ping, see that youth in a suit of clothes made by Crowder and Son? Refuse my appeal, if you please, my dear sir, but—you'll pardon me—do not add insult to the injury."

Mr Ping was mollified, and rubbed his hands softly. This was flattering: for Crowder and Son, according to his view of the case, did not deserve to be called tailors—certainly not gentlemen's tailors; but he remained firm.

"No, Mr Denville, sir, far be it from me to wish to insult you, sir, and I thank you for the amount of custom you've brought me. You can't say as I'm unfair."

"You'll pardon me, Mr Ping; I never did."

"Thank you, sir; but as I was a saying, you've had clothes of me, sir, for years, and you haven't paid me, sir, and I haven't grumbled, seeing as you've introduced me clients, but I can't start an account for Mr Denville, junior, sir, and I won't."

The MC took snuff, and rested first on one leg and then on the other; lastly, he held his head on one side and admired two or three velvet waistcoat pieces, so as to give Mr Ping time to repent. But Mr Ping did not want time to repent, and he would not have repented had the MC stayed an hour, and this the latter knew, but dared not resent, bowing himself out at last gracefully.

"Good-morning, Mr Ping, good-morning. I am sorry you—er—but no matter. Lovely day, is it not?"

"Lovely, sir. Good-morning—poor, penniless, proud, stuck-up, half-starved old dandy," muttered the prosperous tradesman, as he stood in his shirt-sleeves at the door, his grey hair all brushed forward into a fierce frise, and a yellow inch tape round his neck like an alderman's chain. "I wouldn't trust his boy a sixpence to save his life. Prospects, indeed. Fashion, indeed. I expect he'll have to 'list."

The MC went smiling and mincing along the parade, waving his cane jauntily, and passing his snuff-box into the other hand now and then to raise his hat to some one or another, till he turned up a side street, when, in the solitude of the empty way, he uttered a low groan, and his face changed.

"My God!" he muttered. "How long is this miserable degradation to last?"

He looked round sharply, as if in dread lest the emotion into which he had been betrayed should have been observed, but there was no one near.

"I must try Barclay. I dare not go to Frank Burnett, for poor May's sake."

A few minutes later he minced and rolled up to a large, heavy-looking mansion in a back street, where, beneath a great dingy portico, a grotesque satyr's head held a heavy knocker, and grinned at the visitor who made it sound upon the door.

"Hallo, Denville, you here?" said Mr Barclay, coming up from the street. "Didn't expect to see you. I've got the key: come in."

"A little bit of business, my dear sir. I thought I'd come on instead of writing. Thanks—you'll pardon me—a pinch of snuff—the Prince's own mixture."

"Ah yes." *Snuff, snuff, snuff.* "Don't like it though—too scented for me. Come along."

He led the way through a large, gloomy hall, well hung with large pictures and ornamented with pedestals and busts, up a broad, well-carpeted staircase and into the drawing-room of the house—a room, however, that looked more like a museum, so crowded was it with pictures, old china, clocks, statues, and bronzes. Huge vases, tiny Dresden ornaments, rich carpets, branches and lustres of cut-glass and ormolu, almost jostled each other, while the centre of the room was filled with lounges, chairs and tables, rich in buhl and marqueterie.

At a table covered with papers sat plump, pleasant-looking Mrs Barclay, in a very rich, stiff brocade silk. Her appearance was vulgar; there were too many rings upon her fat fingers, too much jewellery about her neck and throat; and her showy cap was a wonder of lace and ribbons; but Nature had set its stamp upon her countenance, and though she was holding her head on one side, pursing up her lips and frowning as she wrote in the big ledger-like book open before her, there was no mistaking the fact that she was a thoroughly good-hearted amiable soul.

"Oh, bless us, how you startled me!" she cried, throwing herself back, for the door had opened quietly, and steps were hardly heard upon the soft carpet. "Why, it's you, Mr Denville, looking as if you were just going to a ball. How are you? Not well? You look amiss. And how's Miss Claire? and pretty little Mrs Mayblossom—Mrs Burnett?"

"My daughters are well in the extreme, Mrs Barclay," said the MC, taking the lady's plump extended hand as she rose, to bend over it, and kiss the fingers with the most courtly grace. "And you, my dear madam, you?"

"Oh, she's well enough, Denville," said Barclay, chuckling. "Robust's the word for her."

"For shame, Jo-si-ah!" exclaimed the lady, reddening furiously. She had only blushed slightly before with pleasure; and after kicking back her stiff silk dress to make a profound curtsey. "You shouldn't say such things. Why, Mr Denville, I haven't seen you for ever so long; and I've meant to call on Miss Claire, for we always get on so well together; but I'm so busy, what with the servants, *and* the dusting, *and* the keeping the books, *and* the exercise as I'm obliged to take—"

"And don't," said Barclay, placing a chair for the MC, and then sitting down and putting his hands in his pockets.

"For shame, Jo-si-ah. I do indeed, Mr Denville, and it do make me so hot."

"There, that'll do, old lady. Mr Denville wants to see me on business. Don't you, Denville?"

"Yes—on a trifle of business; but I know that Mrs Barclay is in your confidence. You'll pardon me, Mrs Barclay?"

A looker-on would have imagined that he was about to dance a minuet with the lady, but he delicately took her fingers by the very tip and led her back to her seat, into which she meant to glide gracefully, but plumped down in a very feather-beddy way, and then blushed and frowned.

"Oh, Mr Denville won't mind me; and him an old neighbour, too, as knows how I keep your books and everything. It isn't as if he was one of your wicked bucks, and bloods, and macaronies as they calls 'em."

"Now, when you've done talking, woman, perhaps you'll let Denville speak."

"Jo-si-ah!" exclaimed the lady, reddening, or to speak more correctly, growing more red, as she raised a large fan, which hung by a silken cord, and used it furiously.

"Now then, Denville, what is it?" said Barclay, throwing himself back in his chair, and looking the extreme of vulgarity beside the visitor's refinement.

"You'll pardon me, Mr Barclay?" said the MC, bowing. "Thanks. The fact is, my dear Barclay, the time has arrived when I must launch my son Morton upon the stream of the fashionable world."

"Mean to marry him well?" said Barclay, smiling.

"Exactly. Yes. You'll pardon me."

He took snuff in a slow, deliberate, and studied mode that Mrs Barclay watched attentively, declaring afterwards that it was as good as a play, while her husband also took his pinch from his own box, but in a loud, rough, frill-browning way.

"I have high hopes and admirable prospects opening out before him, my dear Barclay. Fortune seems to have marked him for her own, and to have begun to smile."

"Fickle jade, sir; fickle jade."

"At times—you'll pardon me. At times. Let us enjoy her smiles while we can. And now, my dear Barclay, that I wish to launch him handsomely and well—to add to his natural advantages the little touches of dress, a cane and snuff-box, and such trifles—I find, through the absence of so many fashionable visitors affecting my fees, I am troubled, inconvenienced for the want of a few guineas, and—er—it is very ridiculous—er—really I did not know whom to ask, till it occurred to me that you, my dear sir, would oblige me with, say, forty or fifty upon my note of hand."

"Couldn't do it, sir. Haven't the money. Couldn't."

"Don't talk such stuff, Jo-si-ah," exclaimed Mrs Barclay, fanning herself sharply, and making a sausage-like curl wabble to and fro, and her ribbons flutter. "You can if you like."

"Woman!" he exclaimed furiously.

"Oh, I don't mind you saying 'woman,'" retorted the lady. "Telling such wicked fibs, and to an old neighbour too. If it had been that nasty, sneering, snickle dandy, Sir Harry Payne, or that big, pompous, dressed-up Sir Matthew Bray, you'd have lent them money directly. I'm ashamed of you."

"Will you allow me to carry on my business in my own way, madam?"

"Yes, when it's with nobodies; but I won't sit by and hear you tell our old neighbour, who wants a bit of help, that you couldn't do it, and that you haven't the money, when anybody can see it sticking out in lumps in both of your breeches' pockets, if they like to look."

"'Pon my soul, woman," said Barclay, banging his fist down upon the table, "you're enough to drive a man mad. Denville, that woman will ruin me."

Mrs Barclay shut up her fan and sat back in her chair, and there was a curious kind of palpitating throbbing perceptible all over her that was almost startling at first till her face broke up in dimples, and the red lips parted, showing her white teeth, while her eyes half-closed. For Mrs Barclay was laughing heartily.

"Ruin him, Mr Denville, ruin him!" she cried. "Ha, ha, ha, and me knowing that—"

"Woman, will you hold your tongue?" thundered Barclay. "There, don't take any notice of what I said, Denville. I've been put out this morning and money's scarce. You owe me sixty now and interest, besides two years' rent."

"I do—I do, my dear sir; but really, my dear Barclay, I intend to repay you every guinea."

"He's going to lend it to you, Mr Denville," said Mrs Barclay. "It's only his way. He always tells people he hasn't any money, and that he has to get it from his friend in the City."

"Be quiet, woman," said Barclay, smiling grimly. "There, I'll let you have it, Denville. Make a memorandum of it, my gal. Let's see: how much do you want? Twenty-five will do, I suppose?"

"My dear friend—you'll pardon me—if you could make it fifty you would confer a lasting obligation upon me. I have great hopes, indeed."

"Fifty? It's a great deal of money, Denville."

"Lend him the fifty, Josiah, and don't make so much fuss about it," said the lady, opening the ledger, after drawing her chair to the table, taking a dip of ink, and writing rapidly in a round, clear hand. "Got a stamp?"

"Yes," said Barclay, taking a large well-worn pocket-book from his breast, and separating one from quite a quire. "Fill it up. Two months after date, Denville?"

"You'll pardon me."

"What's the use of doing a neighbour a good turn," said Mrs Barclay, filling up the slip of blue paper in the most business-like manner, "and spoiling it by being so tight. 'Six months—after—date—interest—at—five—per—centum'—there."

Mrs Barclay put her quill pen across her mouth, and, turning the bill stamp over, gave it a couple of vigorous rubs on the blotting-paper before handing it to her husband, who ran his eye over it quickly.

"Why, you've put five per cent, *per annum*," he cried. "Here, fill up another. Five per cent."

"Stuff!" said Mrs Barclay stoutly; "are you going to charge the poor man sixty per cent? I shan't fill up another. Here, you sign this, Mr Denville. Give the poor man his money, Josiah."

"Well," exclaimed Barclay, taking a cash-box from a drawer and opening it with a good deal of noise, "if ever man was cursed with a tyrant for a wife—"

"It isn't you. There!" cried Mrs Barclay, taking the bill which the visitor had duly signed, and placing it in a case along with some of its kin.

"There you are, Denville," said Barclay, counting out the money in notes, "and if you go and tell people what a fool I am, I shall have to leave the town."

"Not while I live, Mr Barclay," said the MC, taking the notes carefully, but with an air of indolent carelessness and grace, as if they were of no account to such a man as he. "Sir, I thank you from my very heart. You have done me a most kindly action. Mrs Barclay, I thank you. My daughter shall thank you for this. You'll pardon me. My visit is rather short. But business. Mr Barclay, good-day. I shall not forget this. Mrs Barclay, your humble servant."

He took the hand she held out by the tips of the fingers, and bent over it to kiss them with the most delicate of touches; but somehow, just then there seemed to be a catch in his breath, and he pressed his lips firmly on the soft, fat hand.

"God bless you!" he said huskily, and he turned and left the room.

"Poor man!" said Mrs Barclay after a few moments' pause, as she and her lord listened to the descending steps, and heard the front door close. "Why, look here, Josiah, at my hand, if it ain't a tear."

"Tchah! an old impostor and sham. Wipe it off, woman, wipe it off. Kissing your hand, too, like that, before my very face."

"No, Jo-si-ah, I don't believe he's a bad one under all his sham and fuss. Folks don't know folkses' insides. They say you are about the hard-heartedest old money-lender that ever breathed, but they don't know you as I do. There, it was very good of you to let him have it, poor old man. I knew you would."

"I've thrown fifty pounds slap into the gutter."

"No, you haven't, dear; you've lent it to that poor old fellow, and you've just pleased me a deal better than if you'd given me a diamond ring, and that's for it, and more to come."

As she spoke she threw one plump arm round the money-lender's neck, and there was a sound in the room as of a smack.

# Chapter Twenty Five
# A Revelation

"Oh, May, May! As if I had not care and pain enough without this. Surely it cannot be true."

"Hush! don't make a fuss like that, you silly thing. You'll have the people hearing you down in the street. How could I help it?"

"Help it? May, you must have been mad."

"Oh! no, I wasn't," said Mrs Burnett, nestling into a corner of the couch in her father's drawing-room. "I believe he was, though, poor fellow."

She gazed up at her portrait with her pretty girlish face wrinkling up, and these wrinkles seeming to have had work to get the better of the dimples in her baby cheeks and chin.

"He was dreadfully fond of me, Claire," she continued, "and I was very fond of him. And then, you see, we were both so young."

Claire clasped her hands together and gazed at her sister with a face full of wonder, she seemed so calm and unconcerned, as if it were some one else's trouble and not her own that had brought the tears into her eyes.

"But, May, why did not you confide in me?"

"Likely! You were always scolding and snubbing me, as it was. I don't know what you would have said if you had known. Besides, I was afraid of you in those days."

"May, you will drive me mad," said Claire, pacing the room.

"Nonsense; and don't go on running up and down the room like that. Be sensible, and help me."

"Why have you not told me before?"

"I've been going to tell you heaps of times, but you've always had something or other to worry about, and I've been put off."

"Till you knew that detection was inevitable; and now you come to me," cried Claire reproachfully.

"Look here, Claire, are you going to talk sensibly, or am I to go to some lady friend to help me? There's Mrs Pontardent."

"No, no," cried Claire excitedly. "You must not take anyone else into your confidence. Tell me all. But May, May, is this really true, or is it some miserable invention of your own?"

"Oh, it's true enough," said May sharply, as she arranged her bonnet strings, and bent forward to catch a glimpse of her great ostrich feather.

Claire looked at her with her face drawn with care and horror, while she wondered at the indifference of the little wife, and the easy way in which she was trying to shift the trouble and responsibility of her weakness and folly upon her sister.

"Why, May, you could not have been seventeen."

"Sixteen and a half," said May. "Heigho! I begin to feel quite an old woman now."

"But, Frank? Do you ever think of the consequences if he were to know?"

"Why, of course I do, you silly thing. Haven't I lain in bed and quaked hundreds of times for fear he should ever find out? How can you talk so? Why do you suppose I came to you, if it was not that I was afraid of his getting to know?"

"May, it would drive our father mad if all came out."

"Of course it would. Now you are beginning to wake up and understand why I have come."

"How could you accept Frank Burnett, and deceive him so?"

"How could I marry him? What would papa have said if I had refused? Don't talk stuff."

Claire's brow knit more and more, as she realised her sister's utter want of principle, and her heart seemed rent by anger, pity, and grief.

"Besides, do you suppose I wanted to stop here and pinch and starve when a rich husband and home were waiting for *me*? Poor Louis was dead, and if I'd cried my eyes out every week and said I'd be a widow for ever and ever, it would not have brought him to life."

Claire did not speak. Her words would not come, and she gazed in utter perplexity, struggling to realise the fact that the girlish little thing before her could possibly have been a widow and mother before she became Mrs Burnett.

"When—when did this begin?" said Claire at last.

"Now, don't talk to me like that, Claire, or you'll set me off crying my eyes blind, and I shall go home red and miserable, and Frank will find it all out."

"He must be told."

"Told?" cried May, starting up. "Told? If he is told, I'll go right down to the end of the pier and drown myself. He must never know, and papa must never know. Do you think I've kept this a secret for more than two years for them to be told?"

"They will be sure to know."

"Yes, if you tell them. Oh, Claire, Claire, I did think I could find help in my sister, now that I am in such terrible trouble."

"I will help you all I can, May," said Claire sadly; "but they must know."

"I tell you they must not," cried May angrily, and speaking like a spoiled child. "Frank would kill me, and as for poor, dear, darling papa, with all his troubles about getting you married and Morton settled, and Fred turning out so badly, it would kill him, and then you'd have a nice time of it, far worse than poor old mummy Teigne being killed."

"Oh, hush, May!" said Claire, with a horrified look.

"That moves you, does it, miss? Well, then, be reasonable. I don't know what to make of you of late, Claire; you seem to be so changed. Ah, you'll find the difference when you're a married woman."

Claire gazed down at her, with the trouble and perplexity seeming to increase, while May Burnett arranged the folds of her dress, as she once more nestled in the corner of the old sofa, and seemed as if she were posing herself to be pitied and helped.

Then she lifted her eyes towards the florid portrait on the wall, and sighed.

"Poor Louis! How he did flatter me. But he always did that, and I suppose it was his flattering words made me love him so. I was very fond of him."

"May," said Claire excitedly, "when was it you were married?"

"Oh, it was such fun. It was while I was staying at Aunt Jerdein's, and taking the music lessons. I went out as usual, to go to Golden Square for my lesson as aunt thought, and Louis was waiting for me, and he took me in a hackney coach with straw at the bottom and mouldy old cushions, and one of the windows broken. And we went to such a queer old church somewhere in the city, and were married—a little old church that smelt as mouldy as the hackney coach; and the funny old clergyman took snuff all over his surplice, and he did mumble so."

"And then?"

"Oh, Louis left Saltinville, you know, when I went up to London, and gave lessons at Aunt Jerdein's, and we used to see as much of each other as we could, till he had to go back to Rome, and there, poor boy, you know he died of fever."

Claire did not speak, but stood with her hands clasped before her, listening to the calm, cool, selfish words that seemed to come rippling out from the prettily-curved mouth as if it were one of the simplest and most matter-of-fact things in the world.

"It was a great trouble to me, of course, dear," May continued; and she raised herself a little, to spread her handsome dress, so that it should fall in graceful folds. "I used to cry my eyes out, and I don't know what I should have done if it had not been for Anne Brown."

"Anne Brown? Aunt Jerdein's servant?" said Claire bitterly. "You trusted her, then, in preference to your own sister."

"No, I didn't, baby. She found me out. And besides, I daren't have told you. How you would have scolded me, you know," continued May. "Anne was very good to me, and I went and stayed with her mother when baby was born, and then Anne left aunt soon after. Aunt thought, you know, that I'd come down home, and, of course, you all thought I was still at aunt's. Anne Brown managed about the letters."

"Go on," said Claire, who listened as if this were all some horrible fiction that she was forced to hear.

"Then I did come home, and Anne Brown took care of poor baby with her mother, and it was terribly hard work to get money to send them, but somehow I did it; and then you know about Frank Burnett, how poor dear papa brought all that on."

Claire uttered a sigh that was almost a groan, but the pretty little rosebud of a wife went prattling on, in selfish ignorance of the agony she was inflicting, dividing her attention between her dress and the picture of herself that was smiling down at her from the wall.

"I suffered very much all that time, Claire dear, and, whenever I could, I used to go upstairs, lock myself in my room, and put on a little widow's cap I had—a very small one, dear, of white crape—and have a good cry about poor Louis. It was the only mourning I ever could wear for him, and it was nearly always locked up in the bottom drawer; but I used to carry a bit of black crape in my dress pocket, and touch that now and then. It was a little strip put through my wedding ring and tied in a knot. There it is," she said, fishing it out of her dress pocket; "but the strip of crape only looks like a bit of black rag now."

She held out a tiny, plain gold ring for her sister to see, and it looked so small that it seemed as if it had been used sometime when a little girl had been playing at being married with some little boy, or at one of the child weddings that history records.

"Poor Louis!" sighed May. "I was very fond of him. Then, when I was married again, of course I was able to send money up every week easily enough till Frank began to grow so stingy, when I've often had no end of trouble to get it together. But I always have managed somehow. Oh, dear me! This is a wearisome place, this world."

Claire stood gazing down at her, and May went on:

"Then all went smoothly enough till that stupid Anne's mother took a cold or something, and died; then Anne sent me word that she was going to be married, and I must fetch poor baby away."

The sisters' eyes now met as May continued:

"So, as I didn't know anyone else, I went to Mrs Miggles out there on the cliff, and told her how I was situated. She wouldn't help me at first. She said I was to tell you; but when I told her I dared not, and promised her I'd pay her very regularly, she came round, and she went up to London by the coach and fetched baby, and a great expense it was to me, for she had to come back inside. Do open the window, Claire; this room is stifling."

Claire slowly crossed the room and threw open the window and then returned to stand gazing at her sister.

"And your little innocent child is there at that fisherman's hut on the cliff?"

"Yes, dear," said May calmly; and then, for the first time, her face lit up, and she showed some trace of feeling as she exclaimed:

"And, oh, Claire dear, she is such a little darling."

Claire looked at her in a strangely impassive way. It was as if the story she had heard of her sister's weakness and deception had stunned her, and, instead of looking at her, she gazed right away with wistful eyes at the past troubles culminating in Fred's enlistment, and then that horror, the very thought of which sent a shudder through her frame.

And now this new trouble had come, one that might prove a terrible disgrace, while the future looked so black that she dared not turn her mental gaze in that direction.

"Well," said May, at last, "why don't you speak—though you need not, if you are only going to scold."

"Why have you come to tell me this now—this disgraceful story of deceit and shame?"

"Do you wish to send me back broken-hearted, Claire—crying my eyes out so that Frank is sure to know?"

"I say, why have you come to me, May?"

"Because I am in dreadful trouble at last, and don't know what to do. I daren't communicate with those people or go near the cottage, for I'm sure Frank is watching me and suspecting something."

"You will have to confess everything, May; he loves you and will forgive you."

"But he doesn't love me, and he never would forgive me," cried May excitedly. "You can't think how we quarrel. He's a horribly jealous little monster, and I hate him."

"May!"

"I don't care: I do. Now, look here, Claire, it's of no use for you to boggle about it, because you must help me. If it were to come out it would be social ruin for us all, and I've had quite enough poverty, thank you. I dare not go and see the little thing again, and if some one does not take the Miggleses some money regularly, likely as not they'll turn disagreeable and begin to talk. I shall bring you money, of course, and as some one must go and see that my poor darling is properly cared for, why you must."

"I?"

"Yes, dear, you. The poor little thing shall not be neglected, I'm determined upon that; and as my situation prevents me, why it is your duty, Claire."

"Who knows that this is your little girl, May?" said Claire coldly.

"Nobody."

"Not even the fisherman's wife?"

"Well, I dare say she thinks something; but those people never say anything so long as you pay them regularly. But there, I dare not stay any longer. There's a guinea, Claire; it's all I have to-day. Take that to Mrs

Miggles, and see how the darling is. I must be off. I'll come in to-morrow and hear."

"May, I cannot—I dare not—try to cloak this shameful story."

"But you must, I tell you. Now, don't be so silly. Why, I'd do as much for you."

"I tell you I dare not do this. I must tell papa—or, there, I'll be your help in this; I'll come with you, and you shall confess to Frank."

"Why, he'd kill me. I know it has been a surprise to you, and you are a bit taken aback, but think about it, and you will see that it is your duty to help me now. Good-bye, Claire dear," she continued, as she kissed her sister. "Nobody knows anything about this but you, and it is our secret, mind. Good-bye."

Claire hardly heard the door close as May rustled out of the room, hot and excited by the confidence she had had to make, but evidently quite at her ease, as her bright eyes and smile showed, when she looked up from her carriage and nodded at her sister.

Claire looked down at her, drawn involuntarily to the window; and as the carriage drove off, and she still remained gazing straight before her, an officer passed and raised his hat.

Claire had an instinctive feeling that it was Major Rockley, but she neither looked nor moved, for the face of a tiny child seemed to be looking up at her, smiling, and asking her sympathy.

Then she started into life as there was another footstep on the boulder path, and another hat was raised, and an eager appealing look met hers, making her shrink hastily away, with her erst blank face growing agitated as she drew back trembling and fighting hard to keep down the sobs that rose.

For all that was past now for her. With the secrets she had held within her breast before, how dared she to think of his love? Now there was another—a secret so fraught with future trouble that she hardly dared dwell upon all that she had heard. It had come upon her that morning like a thunderclap—this new trouble, known only to herself and the fisherman's wife. So May had said: for she had gone to her sister to demand her aid in happy ignorance of this part of her miserable story being known, beside much more, to little library-keeping Miss Clode.

# Chapter Twenty Six
# The Money-Lender at Home

"Who is it?"

"It's that Major Rockley, Jo-si-ah, and he's walking up and down, switching his riding-whip about, and he'll be knocking down some of the chimney if you don't make haste."

"Let him wait a minute," said Barclay, finishing a letter.

"I do 'ate that man, Jo-si-ah—that I do," said Mrs Barclay.

"I wish you wouldn't talk so, old lady, when I'm writing."

"I can't help it, Jo-si-ah. That man, whenever I meet him, makes me begin to boil. So smooth, and polite, and smiling, and squeeze-your-handy, while all the while he's laughing at you for being so fat."

"Laughing at me for being so fat?"

"No, no. You know what I mean—laughing at me myself for being so fat. I 'ate him."

"Well, I don't want you to love him, old lady."

"I should think not, indeed, with his nasty dark eyes and his long black mustarchers. Ugh! the monster. I 'ate him."

"Handsomest man in Saltinville, my dear."

"Handsome is as handsome does, Jo-si-ah. He's a black-hearted one, if ever there was one, I know."

"Now, you don't know anything of the kind, old girl."

"Oh, yes, I do, Jo-si-ah. I always feel it whenever he comes anigh one, and if I had a child of my own, and that man had come and wanted to marry her, I'd have cut her up in little pieces and scattered them all about the garden first."

"Well, then, I suppose I ought to be very, very glad that we never had any little ones, for, though I should be very glad to get rid of you—"

"No, you wouldn't, Jo-si-ah," said Mrs Barclay, showing her white teeth.

"Yes, I should, but I shouldn't have liked to see you hung for murder."

"Don't talk like that, Jo-si-ah. It gives me the shivers. That word makes me think about old Lady Teigne, and not being safe in my bed."

"Stuff and nonsense!"

"It isn't stuff and nonsense, Jo-si-ah. I declare, ever since that dreadful affair, I never see a bolster without turning cold all down my back; and I feel as if it wasn't safe to put my head upon my pillow of a night. There: he's ringing because you're so long."

"Then I shall be longer," growled Barclay, putting a wafer in his mouth.

"How that poor Claire Denville can stop in that house of a night I don't know."

"Ah, that puts me in mind of something: I wish you wouldn't be so fond of that Claire Denville."

"Why not? I must be fond of somebody."

"Be fond of me, then, I'm ugly enough."

"So I am fond of you, Jo-si-ah, and you are not ugly, and I should like to hear anyone say you were to my face."

"I don't like that Denville lot."

"No more do I, Jo-si-ah, only poor dear Claire. Her father ain't bad, but she's as good as gold."

"I don't know so much about that," muttered Barclay.

"And now, Jo-si-ah, just you be careful with that Major Rockley. He owes you a lot now."

"Yes, but I've got him tight enough."

"And if you let him have more you get him tighter. He's a bold, bad man, always gambling and drinking, and doing worse."

"Oh, I'm very fond of him, old lady," said Barclay, chuckling. "I love him like a son, and—there he is again. I must go now."

It was only into the next room, but there were double doors, and as Barclay entered the Major's countenance did not look at all handsome, but very black and forbidding.

"Come, Barclay," he cried, with a smile; "I thought you were going to put me off. Here, I've been hard hit again. I'm as poor as Job, and I must have a hundred."

For answer Barclay shrugged his shoulders, took out a fat pocket-book, and began to draw out the tuck.

"Put that away," cried the Major impatiently; and he gave the book a flick with his riding-whip, but not without cutting right across Barclay's fingers, and making a red mark.

The money-lender did not even wince, but he mentally made a mark against his client's name, intimating that the cut would have to be paid for some day or another.

"I know all about that. I've had five hundred of you during the past two months. Never mind that; the luck must turn sometime. Cards have been dead against me lately. That Mellersh has the most extraordinary luck; but I shall have him yet, and we'll soon be square again. Come, I want a hundred."

"When?"

"Now, man, now."

"Can't be done, Major, really."

"Don't talk nonsense, man. I tell you I must have it."

"Your paper's getting bad, Major. Too much of it in the market."

"Look here, Barclay; do you want to insult me?"

"Not I, sir; never thought of such a thing."

"Then what do you mean?"

"I mean? Only that you've had five hundred pounds of my money during these last three months."

"For which you hold bills for seven hundred and fifty."

"You put down five hundred pounds now in Bank of England notes, Major Rockley, and you shall have the lot."

"Then you do mean to insult me, sir?"

"No, Major."

"What do you mean, then?"

"Only that I won't part with another five-pound note till I get some of that money back."

Major Rockley's dark brows came down over his eyes as he glared at Barclay with a peculiarly vindictive expression, while the money-lender thrust his hands deep down into his drab breeches' pockets, and whistled softly.

"I shall not forget this, Barclay," he said slowly, and, turning upon his heels, he walked out of the place beating his boot viciously with his whip.

"Oh, the monster!" cried Mrs Barclay, entering the room.

"Why, you've been listening."

"Well, didn't you leave the door open on purpose for me to listen, Jo-si-ah? Oh, what a bad, evil-looking man, Jo-si-ah. I believe he wouldn't stop at anything to get money from you now."

"Black mask and a pair of pistols, on a dark night in a country road, eh, old lady? Stand and deliver; money or your life, eh?"

"Well, you may laugh, Jo-si-ah; but he looks just the sort of man who wouldn't stop at anything. I am glad you wouldn't let him have any money, for I'm sure you'd never get it back."

"I don't know so much about that, old lady, but whether or no, I wasn't going to let him have any this morning. He has been short lately, and no mistake. Some one I know's making a nice thing out of them at the mess."

"Colonel Mellersh?"

"Mum!"

"Oh, there's no one to hear us now. But, I say, Jo-si-ah, why is he so friendly with Miss Clode?"

"Because she sells packs of cards, old girl."

"Ah, but there's something more than that. I went in there one day, and he had hold of her hand across the counter; and I could see, though she turned it off, that she had been crying."

"Asking her to wed, and let him succeed to the business," said Barclay, with a chuckle.

"Don't talk nonsense, Jo-si-ah. I wish I had a good, clear head like you, and was as clever, and then perhaps I could make this out."

"What?"

"About Miss Clode. I'm sure she has seen better days."

"That she has," said Barclay, chuckling. "She looks pretty shabby now, a newsy, gossiping old hag!"

"I don't dislike Miss Clode," said Mrs Barclay thoughtfully. "There's much worse in Saltinville."

"I dare say," he said, laughing. "I've only one thing against her."

"What's that?"

"She hates poor Claire Denville like poison."

# Chapter Twenty Seven
# Fisherman Dick Stares

Major Rockley had counted upon getting a hundred pounds from Barclay, and the refusal annoyed him to so great an extent that he determined upon having a sharp walk to calm himself. So setting off at a good rate towards the main cliff to reach the downs beyond the town, he had not gone far before he saw a graceful figure, in a white dress, with black scarf and plain straw bonnet going in the same direction.

"Claire Denville as I'm a sinner!" he cried, his pale cheeks flushing, and a curious light shining in his dark eyes.

"Yes, without doubt," he muttered. "Off for a walk to the downs. Lucky accident. At last!"

He checked himself, walking slowly, so as not to overtake her until she was well out of the town, and thinking that perhaps it would be as well to keep back until she turned, and then meet her face to face.

"The jade! How she has kept me at a distance. Refused my notes, and coquetted with me to make me more eager for the pursuit. The old man's lessons have not been thrown away. I'm to approach in due form, I suppose. Well, we shall see."

Claire went straight on, walking pretty quickly, and without turning her head to right or left. The streets were left behind; the row of houses facing the sea had come to an end; and she was getting amongst the fishermen's cottages, while below the cliff the fishing boats were drawn high up on the shingle, and long, brown filmy nets spread out to dry, looking like square shadows cast by invisible sails, and mingled with piles of tarred barrels, lobster baskets, and brown ropes, bladders and corks.

Every here and there, on the railing at the cliff edge, hung oilskins to soften in the sunshine, and in one place a giant appeared to be sitting astride the rail, with nothing to be seen of him but a huge pair of boots. Farther on fish were drying in the air, and farther still there came up a filmy cloud of grey smoke from the shingle, along with a pleasant smell of Stockholm tar, for Fisherman Dick was busy paying the bottom of a boat turned upside down below the cliff.

These matters did not interest Major Rockley any more than the grey gulls that wheeled overhead and descended, to drop with a querulous cry upon a low spit of shingle where the sea was retiring fast.

For the fluttering white dress took up all his attention, and now that they were well beyond the promenaders, he was about to hasten his steps—too impatient to wait until she turned—when he uttered an impatient oath, for Claire suddenly stopped by a cottage where a woman was sitting knitting a coarse blue garment and nursing a little child.

It was all so sudden that it took the officer by surprise. The woman jumped up hastily on being spoken to, and curtseyed, and they went in at once, leaving the Major by the rails.

"Well, I can wait," he said, smiling and taking out his cigar-case. "I can study the tarring of boats till her ladyship appears."

He slowly chose and lit a cigar, and then, going close to the edge of the cliff, leaned upon the rails and gazed down at Fisherman Dick, who was working away busily, dipping his brush in a little three-legged iron pot, and carefully spreading the dark-brown odorous tar.

He was about forty feet below the Major, and for some time he went on steadily with his work, but all at once he stopped short, and turned his face upwards as if he felt that he was being watched; and as he did so his straw hat fell off and he stood fixed by the Major's eyes as if unable to move.

The sensation was mutual, for Major Rockley felt attracted by the dark, Spanish-looking face, and the keen eyes so intently fixed upon his.

"Confound the fellow! how he stares," said the Major, at last, as he seemed to wrench himself away, and turned his back.

As he did so, leaning against the rail, Dick Miggles drew a long breath, stared now at his iron tar-kettle, and carried it to the fire of old wreck-wood to re-heat it, as he stood by and thoughtfully scratched his head.

He looked up for a moment, and saw that the Major's back was towards him, and then bent over his kettle again, and began pushing half-burned scraps of wood beneath, making the fire roar and the pitch heat quickly, and he did not look up again till the Major had walked away, when he began to brush again at the boat as if relieved, ending by giving one leg a tremendous slap, and stopping short as if to think.

The Major had some time to wait, and he passed a good deal of it walking up and down, as if watching a sail in the offing, till fortune favoured him; so that as he was approaching the cottage again, Claire came out quickly, and, seeing him, started and turned to walk in the other direction, out on the downs and round by the London Road into the town.

She repented on the instant, and wished that she had faced him boldly and passed on. But she was excited and confused by her visit, which had to her a curious suggestion of wrong-doing in it; and she was leaving the place, feeling agitated and guilty, when, seeing the Major, she had turned sharply to walk on, trembling, and hoping that he had not seen her. The hope died out on the instant, for she heard his steps, with the soft *clink, clink* of the rowels of his spurs; but he kept his distance till they were well beyond the cottages, and then rapidly closed up.

What would he think of her visit there? What would he say? were the questions Claire asked herself as she walked rapidly on to reach the stile that bounded the cornfield she would have to turn into and cross to get into the London Road; and all the time, *clink, clink — clink, clink,* those spurs rang on her ears, and came nearer and nearer.

The stile at last; and, trembling with eagerness, she was about to cross, when the Major passed her quickly, leaped over, and turned smilingly to face her with:

"Allow me, my dear Miss Denville. We meet at last." ~C

# VOLUME TWO

## Chapter One
## An Officer and a Gentleman

Claire shrank back for a moment, and her natural womanly timidity urged her to turn and hurry home by the way she had come.

But that would be showing Major Rockley that she was afraid of him, and this she wished to keep a secret in her own breast.

Bowing slightly, then, she declined the offer of his hand, stepped over the stile, and went on.

With anyone else Rockley would have felt bound to retire, but he only laughed. Claire was the daughter of the poor minister of fashion, who lived by the fees and offerings he received from new-comers; and he did not feel himself called upon to treat her as a lady.

"Why, my dear Miss Denville," he said, laughing, "what have I done that you should try to cut me like this? I am ignorant. Come, shake hands."

He held his out, as he walked by her side, and she turned upon him a look full of indignation.

"Are you not making a mistake, sir?" she said coldly.

"Mistake? No. My dear Claire, why do you treat me like this? How absurd it is to refuse my letters, and play coquette when we meet. Here have I been watching for such an opportunity as this for weeks."

Claire's eyes flashed at his assumption, but she made no reply, and walked on.

"How can you be so absurd," he whispered, as he kept pace with her step for step, "when you know how I love you?"

"Major Rockley!" she cried, stopping short and facing him, "by what right do you insult me like this?"

"How beautiful she is!" he said in a low tone.

Claire bit her lips, and, divining that he was disposed to treat her as one in an entirely different rank of life, she hurried on along the path, with the tall corn waving on either side, trembling with dread and indignation, as she realised that he was behaving to her as he might to some servant-girl.

"Say what you like to me. Be angry. Punish me. I cannot help it," he whispered. "Your beauty maddens me, as it has done all these weary months, and I must speak to you now."

"Major Rockley, I am alone and unprotected. I ask you, as a gentleman, to leave me."

"And as an officer and a gentleman I would leave you, but my passion masters me. Sweet Claire, whom I love so dearly, how can you be so cruel and so hard?"

He tried to take her hand, but she shrank from him and turned back.

"No, no, little one, you are not going to serve me like that!" he cried, darting before her. "Come, how can you be so absurd?" he whispered. "We are quite alone. No one can see our meeting, and yet you are trifling with me, and wasting golden moments. You know I love you."

"Once more, Major Rockley, will you leave me? You insult me by staying."

"No, I will not leave you," he whispered excitedly; "and I do not insult you."

"I am alone now, sir, but I have a father—brothers, who shall call you to account for this!" she cried, with her eyes full of indignation.

"Don't," he whispered imploringly. "You make your eyes flash and your face light up in a way that drives me frantic. Claire, if you speak to me like that again, I shall risk being seen, and take you to my heart to cover those lips with kisses. No, no; don't shrink away; only be gentle with me, and talk sensibly. Let us be closer friends, dear. Come, let there be an end to all this coy nonsense. There, we understand one another now. That's better."

He seized her hand, and drew it through his arm; but, with a display of strength that he had not expected, she snatched it away, and stood pale with anger and indignation.

She hurried forward the next moment, but he laughingly kept at her side.

Claire turned and retreated, but he was still there; and, choking down her sobs, she walked as fast as she could towards the stile she had crossed.

It seemed evident to her that the Major must know the reason for her visit to the fisherman's cottage, or he would never have dared to treat her with such bold insolence; and as she walked on he kept close beside her, pressing his suit in the most daringly insulting manner, while she ceased her protests now, and walked on in silence.

"It is the only way to deal with her," he said to himself; "and, after this outburst to keep up appearances, we shall be on the best of terms."

Claire had gone farther in her excitement than she had thought possible, and it seemed now that she would never reach the stile. Beyond that, there might be people who would help her; and in any case, the fishermen's cottages were not many hundred yards away.

In spite of her silence, the Major kept on his passionate addresses and protestations, pleading his inability to obtain a hearing from her before; and at last, irritated by her silence, he caught her by the arm and held it fast.

"No, no; you are not going yet," he said, speaking angrily. "What sort of a man do you take me for, that you play with me like this?"

"Major Rockley, will you loose my arm?"

"Claire Denville, will you promise to meet me to-night where I will name?"

"I am a defenceless woman, sir, and this is an insult—an outrage. Will you loose my arm?"

"You are a cruel coquette," he cried passionately. "Is this your treatment, after the months of glances you have given me to lure me on?"

"Will you loose my arm, sir?"

"Will you be a sensible girl?" he whispered. "How can you be so absurd? Look about you: we are too far off for anyone to see who we are, and if they could see us, why should we care? What is the world to us? Come, Claire, my darling."

He tried to draw her towards him, but she struggled to get free and reach the stile in the tall hedge that separated them from the bare downs beyond.

The tears of rage and indignation were in Claire's eyes as she felt her helplessness, and saw how thoroughly she was in Rockley's power. There seemed to be nothing she could do but scream for help, and from that she shrank.

Turning suddenly upon him, with her eyes flashing, she exclaimed:

"Major Rockley! as a gentleman I ask you to cease this cowardly pursuit."

"Claire Denville, as the woman I adore and have set my mind to win, I ask you to cease this silly heroic nonsense. My dear child, is it to make terms?"

She snatched her hand by an angry movement from his grasp, and reached the stile; but he was too quick for her, catching her and drawing her back to clasp her in his arms.

"You shall not say I wasted my opportunity," he whispered. "If I am to be punished by you, it shall be for something more than words. This kiss is to be the first of millions that you shall pay me back, and—Curse the fellow!"

There was a quick step, a hand was laid on the stile, and Richard Linnell vaulted over, white with jealous anger. For, coming along the downs, he had seen Claire cross the stile, followed by Rockley, and, half mad with rage, he had gazed at them for a moment or two, and then, feeling that all was over, and that there was no more love for him in the world, since the woman he had worshipped could be so light as to make appointments with the greatest libertine in the town, he walked straight back for the parade.

It was all plain enough; there had been an understanding between Claire and the Major, and hence that serenade. But for the horrible accident that night Claire would have come to the window and answered to the musical call.

What a boyish, childish idiot he had been: dreaming always of a vain, weak, frivolous woman, whom he had in his blind idolatry endowed with all the beauties and virtues of her sex.

"Well," he said with a scornful laugh, "I ought to have known how artificial she would be. Like father, like daughter; but it is cruel, cruel work."

He laughed bitterly.

"What an idiot I am!" he cried angrily. "A boy in such matters—a child. Well, it is a lesson. I might have known that she would be as ready to receive attentions as her sister, and now I may go, and console myself by making love to the handsome actress who is ready to make love to me."

"Another actress," he said aloud, as he strode on with his jealous anger up to boiling-point, his face flushed, and his teeth set fast.

"Liar!" he exclaimed. "Fool! Idiot again! I will not believe it. Claire Denville is too true and sweet to listen to a man like that."

He turned and went back faster than he had come, but he had walked some distance, and the return journey gave him time to cool a little and to ask himself whether he was going to watch—to act the eavesdropper—and whether this was a manly part to play.

His indecision increased as he approached the down side of the stile, and he was about to turn and retreat when an excited voice, speaking loudly, sent a thrill through him, and running to the opening he leaped over into the cornfield.

At the sight of Linnell, Claire, who had been up to now strong and heroic, grew feeble and helpless.

"Mr Linnell! Help!" she cried, as she struggled to reach him; and as Rockley, white with fury at the interruption, loosed his hold, Richard Linnell was upon him, striking him a blow full in the chest, which sent him staggering back to fall amongst the corn.

Linnell would have followed, but he caught sight of Claire tottering towards the stile, and he turned to help her, but Rockley had sprung up and, with a hoarse cry of rage, struck at Linnell with his riding-whip, the plaited whalebone falling upon his cheek, and making a weal right across his face.

Major Rockley had better have restrained his rage, for in an instant that blow transformed Richard Linnell, the calm and quiet, into a savage.

He turned round with a roar more than a cry, and sprang upon Rockley; there was a fierce struggle, ending in the riding-whip being torn from its owner's grasp, and for the space of a couple of minutes there was the sound of the lash cutting through the air, and the blows that fell upon the tight undress uniform.

No words were uttered, but there was the scuffling of feet, the hoarse panting of excited men, and the corn was trampled down.

"There," cried Linnell at last, flinging Rockley from him, and throwing the whip in his face, "dog and coward! You have had the thrashing you deserved. Strike me again if you dare."

Major Rockley picked up the whip, and brushed the dust from his uniform. He strove hard to make his convulsed face smooth and to force a smile, while he mastered the desire to writhe and utter impatient cries, so keen was the agony he felt.

"No," he said, in a low hissing whisper, "you are a stronger man than I, and when we meet again it shall be on equal terms."

He accompanied his words with a vindictive look that told Richard Linnell plainly enough how they would encounter next.

He repressed a shudder, and then a pang that seemed to pierce his heart shot through him, for with a malicious smile Rockley said:

"I did not know the lady had made an appointment with you. Of course, she had to keep up appearances. But there: I'll say no more."

He raised his cap mockingly, and went off across the cornfield, leaving Richard Linnell stung to the heart, his brow knit, and his eyes fixed upon Claire, who, white as ashes, and her face convulsed by the agony within her breast, crouched where she had sunk upon the lower steps of the stile.

# Chapter Two
# "Impossible!"

"Claire—Miss Denville," cried Richard Linnell, mastering the cruel thoughts suggested by Rockley's words, "how dared that scoundrel insult you like this!"

"Hush!" said Claire agitatedly. "Don't—pray don't speak to me. I cannot bear it."

"You are ill. You are faint. Let me help you over these bars and get you to one of the cottages."

"No; I shall be better directly. Don't speak to me now."

She bent down, covered her face with her hands, and the tears came now in a passionate burst, while he went down on his knee beside her, laid one hand upon her arm, and, his doubts and suspicions all driven away by her grief, tried to whisper words of comfort as he bade her be calm.

Major Rockley had walked with jaunty military stride for the first two or three hundred yards with assumed calmness; then he gave vent to his rage in a torrent of oaths, and strode on rapidly out of sight, beating the air fiercely with his whip, and leaving the fields clear of his presence as Richard Linnell knelt by the sobbing girl.

"Miss Denville—Claire," he said again, as he now possessed himself of her hand, while in his anger and remorse at having doubted her he poured forth his words in quick, excited tones.

"I had not thought to speak to you like this, and at such a time, but I cannot bear to see you weep—it cuts me to the heart, for I love you—Claire, dear Claire, I love you dearly as man can love."

"Oh, hush, hush!" she moaned piteously, weak now with her emotion and the scene she had gone through.

"I must speak now," he went on. "I have no opportunities of seeing you and telling you all I feel. Claire, I would have come and asked permission to address you, but I have been obliged to feel that my presence was not welcome to Mr Denville, and you—you have been so cold and distant to me of late."

She did not speak, but kept one hand to her bent-down face, while he held the other tightly clasped in his.

"You do not speak," he whispered. "Claire—you are not angry? I have suffered so—there, I confess—such jealous thoughts, such bitter cruel thoughts, though I had no right—no claim upon your love. But now, forgive me—only tell me—there was nothing between you and that man?"

She raised her head quickly, and dropped her hand.

"You ask me that!" she said proudly.

"Forgive me. You would if you knew all. I felt that you had come to meet him, and I was tortured with these jealous doubts, but I would not believe, and I came, as you saw. And now, Claire, one word—my love!"

Her eyes half closed as he drew her towards him; her lips trembled, and her colour went and came. Then, as if her memory, that had been veiled for the moment, tore aside the film of forgetfulness, she thrust him from her, and, with a look of anguish in her eyes, started to her feet.

"No, no!" she cried with a shiver; "it is impossible!"

"Hush! don't say that," he whispered. "Claire, I could not bear it. I know I am not well-to-do, but I love you. I cannot offer you a rich home, but I give you a love that is wholly yours. Don't—don't refuse me—don't make me think that you despise me."

"No, no, it is not that," she sobbed wildly. "You must not speak to me. It is impossible."

"Impossible?" he cried, holding her hands tightly.

"Yes, impossible."

"No," he said with a quiet smile, "it is not impossible. You will grow to the knowledge by-and-by that there is one who lives for your sake, whose every thought is yours, and these little obstacles will melt away when you know me as I am. Claire, I only ask for a little hope—to go away with the thought that I have no rival for your love."

"Don't speak to me—don't think of me again!" she cried, with a wild look in her face. "Heaven bless you, Mr Linnell! Think well of me, whatever comes, but all that is over now."

"Over? No, no; don't say that. Claire—my love!"

He still held her hands in his, and as their eyes met her lips quivered, and her sweet face was drawn with anguish. It was a hard fight, but she conquered, and tearing herself away, she crossed the stile, and he saw her with bent head hurrying towards her home.

"It is impossible—impossible," he muttered, as he stood leaning against the stile. "No; she may say that a thousand times, but I shall hold to my faith, and this affair will give me strength."

He walked slowly homeward, dreaming for a time of Claire's anguished face, and then the sight of a uniform brought back the thought of the Major, and the punishment he had received.

"Will he resent it?" he asked himself.

The answer was awaiting him later on at home, where he encountered Cora Dean just going out for a drive.

The pony-carriage was at the door, and there was nothing for it but to hand the ladies in, Mrs Dean receiving the attention with a most ungracious look, while Cora smiled and looked flushed and pleased as she drove off, with Sir Harry Payne, in Colonel Mellersh's room, watching her with admiring eyes.

"Won't be long, you know. Very kind of you to see me about it; as it's his father he lives with," said Sir Harry. "Handsome woman that, Colonel. Precious unfortunate, all this. I say, how lucky you were at the tables last night. Very handsome woman that. Ever act now, do you know?"

"Every day," said Colonel Mellersh drily. "Here, I'll ask Linnell to step in."

# Chapter Three
# No Better than a Fiddler

"But you can't fight a fellow like that, Rockley," said Sir Harry, who had been summoned to his brother-officer's room.

"Not fight him? I'll fight him, and kill him."

"But he's only a fiddler."

"Enough of the gentleman for my purpose, I tell you," roared Rockley fiercely. "I'll kill him."

"Nonsense, man alive. If you must meet, wing him, or pink him, or spoil the blackguard's good looks. You can't kill a man!"

"Can't kill a man!" said the Major, in a low hissing voice; "can't kill a man!"

"I say, Rockley! Hang it all, don't look the diabolical like that: you give me the cold shivers. Why, I wouldn't be called out by you on any consideration."

"Ha-ha-ha!" laughed Rockley, with a ghastly attempt at mirth. "Did I look queer?"

"Queer? You looked queer multiplied ten thousand times. Why, Rockley, one of you with a face like that would scare a regiment of French cuirassiers. I say, what was the row about—a woman?"

"Curse her!" cried Rockley, flashing out into uncontrolled rage again, as he writhed with mental and bodily pain. "I'll bring her to her senses for this. Treat me as if I were some gawky boy, to be held off and coaxed on, and then bidden to keep my distance!"

"What girl was it?"

"Curse you! don't ask questions."

"Bah! What a fire-eater you are, Rockley. As if I did not know. So the fairy Clairy has been saying, 'How dare you, sir?' Ha—ha—ha!"

"Do you want to quarrel, man?" said the Major, with an angry look in his eye.

"Not I, old lad; not with you in that temper. So she has been riding the high horse, and bidding you keep your distance; and, just in the nick of time, she had her dear friend Dick Linnell there, and the strong-armed fool horsewhipped you."

Rockley turned upon him savagely, and gripped him by the arm so fiercely that Sir Harry Payne involuntarily shrank away.

"Don't!" cried the Major hoarsely. "Don't! or I can't answer for myself."

"Why, Rockley!"

"Don't speak to me. Man, I feel as if that Linnell had roused a devil in me, and till I see him on the turf helpless I shall know no rest. Were you ever beaten—cut—and wealed with your own whip?"

"Well, egad, not to put too fine a point on it, old lad, it was not with a whip; it was a walking cane."

"And did it cut deep down into your very soul, and make you feel as if nothing but blood would heal the pain?"

"Well, egad, no. It hurt a good deal, but I was obliged to pocket it all. Lady's husband was a bit put out, you see. But that's a long time ago. And do you really mean to fight?"

"Fight? If I don't I shall lie in wait for the scoundrel and shoot him like a dog."

"You couldn't do that, my dear Rockley. Behaviour unworthy of an officer and a gentleman."

"And as for that woman," continued Rockley, striding up and down the room as if he were some savage beast confined in a cage, "my God! she shall smart for this!"

"My dear Rockley," said Sir Harry, "you went the wrong way to work."

"Silence, idiot!" roared the Major fiercely. "You would, of course, have won. She would have gone down on her knees to you. You are so handsome—so irresistible. Oh, damn it! No one could withstand you!"

"Sneer away, old fellow. I'm not going to boast," said Sir Harry with a quiet, self-satisfied smile. "I'm not the man to kiss and tell; but—never mind."

"Go on and settle that at once. No shirking; no excuses, mind. He shall meet me, and then—"

"Then—poor devil!" murmured Sir Harry Payne, as he sauntered out of the room and away across the parade ground. "What a temper he has! By

George! if he were little May's husband I'm afraid I should be disposed to abdicate in favour of some one, who might flirt to his heart's content for me.

"Now what's to be done? Shall I tell the Colonel? No. Wouldn't do. The matter must go on. He'll be cooler when they meet, and it will only mean a wing or a leg. That's all."

He went jauntily down to the parade, and exchanged pinches of snuff with old Lord Carboro', who looked after him and muttered, "Fashionable fool! I wonder how much he owes Barclay. I must see. Clode tells me things are going too far, and I'm not going to have some one's fair fame smirched through that idiot. A few months in a debtor's prison would do him good."

In happy ignorance of the remarks made behind his back, Sir Harry Payne went on to the house on the Parade, and Lord Carboro' trotted off, snuff-box in hand, slightly uneasy in mind, but at rest compared to what he would have been had he known of the encounter that had taken place, and of Sir Harry Payne's mission.

Richard Linnell had not returned, so Sir Harry bethought himself of Colonel Mellersh, found him at home, began chatting with him concerning cards, and the company staying in the place, firmly resolved not to give the Colonel a hint about his mission—and in ten minutes he had told him all.

"Tut—tut—tut!" ejaculated the Colonel. "I'm very sorry. About Claire Denville, you say?"

"Egad, Mellersh, what a fellow you are! You pump a man dry. Well, yes. Rockley's dead on her. You remember the serenade?"

"Ah, yes; that horrible night!"

"Well, he's a close fellow, as a rule, about his amours, but he raves about that girl."

"Had she gone to meet him?"

"I don't know; suppose so. Then the other lover comes; and it's tom-cats."

"They came to blows!"

"Blows?" said Sir Harry, bending forward and taking the Colonel by a button: "as far as I can make out, Linnell took his riding-whip from him, and he is lashed from head to foot."

"And all about that girl of Denville's," said the Colonel, with a contemptuous look.

"Yes. But, my dear boy, you must own that she is devilishly handsome."

"Oh yes, she's handsome enough. Then the affair is serious?"

"Serious?" said Sir Harry, lowering his voice. "Rockley swears he'll kill him."

Colonel Mellersh looked very grave.

"They'll have to meet, then?"

"Meet, my dear sir! Rockley says he'll lie in wait for him and shoot him like a dog if he doesn't come out. Fancy, you know, beaten like that before a lady!"

"And such a lady as Claire Denville," said Colonel Mellersh, with a sneer. "Well," he added, changing his manner, "I'm very sorry."

"Yes, so am I. Rockley's deuced haughty, and bullying, and overbearing, particularly lately—things seem to have gone wrong with him—but he's not a bad fellow."

"As men go," said the Colonel with a sneer.

"Exactly—as men go," replied Sir Harry, whose brains were not very analytical as regarded *double entendre*.

Just then Richard Linnell reached the door, encountered Cora Dean, and was finally beckoned into Colonel Mellersh's room.

"My dear Linnell," said the Colonel gravely, as the others exchanged distant bows, "Sir Harry Payne has called on behalf of Major Rockley—as his friend."

He watched Linnell's face intently, but there was only a slight contraction of the brows.

"Bravo!" said the Colonel to himself. "He's staunch."

"Mellersh," said Linnell gravely, "I have no friend to whom I can appeal but you in a case like this."

"I would far rather leave it," said Colonel Mellersh slowly; "but perhaps if you leave the affair in my hands, Sir Harry Payne and I may be able to arrange for a peaceful issue. Major Rockley may be ready to withdraw or apologise."

"S'death, sir!" cried Sir Harry; "apologise for being horsewhipped!"

"I beg pardon," said the Colonel. "You see, I am not properly acquainted with the matter."

"There can be no apology, Colonel Mellersh," said Linnell, with a grave dignity that made the Colonel's eyes light up. "I leave myself in your hands, and I shall be most grateful."

"But—"

"I need say no more," said the young man. "Of course, I know what Sir Harry Payne's visit means, and I am ready when and where you will."

He bowed and left the room with all the formality of the time; and when, about a quarter of an hour later, Sir Harry Payne went away, the young officer uttered a contemptuous sneer.

"'Pon my soul," he muttered, "it is horribly degrading for Rockley. The fellow really is no better than a fiddler after all."

# Chapter Four
# A Lesson in Pistol Practice

The reason for Sir Harry Payne's sneering remark was patent to Colonel Mellersh as soon as he opened the door, for from the Linnells' rooms came the sweet harmonies of a couple of exquisitely-played violins, and for a few minutes the Colonel seemed to forget the trouble on hand, as he stood with his face softened, and one delicate hand waving to the rhythm of the old Italian music.

"Poor lad!" he said, as his face changed, and a look of pain crossed his brow. "And for her, too. Weak, foolish lad! He's infatuated—as we all are at some time or other in our lives."

He stood in his doorway, thoughtful, and with brow knit.

"That chattering pie will spread it all over the town. Clode will get to know, and then—well, we must take care."

He crossed the hall, tapped lightly on the opposite door, and then entered.

"Bravo—bravo!" he cried, clapping his delicate white hands. "Admirable!"

"Ah, Mellersh, come and join us," said the elder Linnell, raising his glasses on to his forehead. "Just in time for a trio."

"No, no, not to-day. Impossible. My head is terrible this morning. Late hours—cards—strong coffee. I came to ask Dick here if he would be my companion for a six-mile walk to Shankley Wood."

The elder Linnell looked from one to the other with a smile.

"Oh, I'm sure he will," he said. "Eh, Dick?"

"Of course, father, of course."

"And out all the morning, too! Well, well, fresh air for health."

"Why don't you get more then, Linnell?"

"I—I?" said the grave, elderly man slowly. "I don't know. I don't want fresh air. I'm very well as I am. I shall do for my time here."

"Why, father," said Richard merrily, as he clapped him on the shoulder, "what a tone to take."

He exchanged a quick, agonised glance with Mellersh, and then proceeded to replace his violin and bow in the case.

"Come to me, Dick," said the Colonel; "I want to go to my room:" and he went out, busied himself for a few minutes in his bedroom, and then came out again into the hall, to find Mrs Dean disappearing up the staircase, and Cora giving some orders to her little groom.

He waited till she turned and came towards him with a scornful look in her eyes.

"Well," he said, in a low voice, and with a longing undertook in his eyes that he evidently tried to conceal, "how many poor fellows slain this morning?"

"How many are there here worth slaying?" she said, in the same low tone.

"A matter of taste," he said, gravely. "A matter of taste, Miss Cora Dean."

"Not one," she said, giving him her hand in response to his own held out.

"I don't know," he said, looking very keenly in her eyes, "anger—love—jealousy."

She snatched her hand away.

"Don't fool!" she cried angrily. "I? Jealous?"

"Yes, you—jealous," he said; and then as she hurried up the stairs, "and there would be another emotion to trouble you, Cora Dean, if you knew all that I know now. Ah, Dick! Ready?"

"Yes. Who was that, here?"

"Your fair enslaver—Cora Dean!"

Richard looked up at him keenly and laughed as they left the house, ignorant of the fact that Cora was watching them intently, and Mrs Dean was keeping up a running fire of comment on what she called her "gal's foolery."

Mellersh led the way at a good brisk pace along the parade, and they had not gone far before they became aware of the tall figure of the Master of the Ceremonies showing himself, as was his wont, king of the place apparently, and bowing and acknowledging bows.

Richard Linnell drew his breath with a slight hiss, but there was no avoiding the encounter, and as they drew near and raised their hats, there was a smile and most courteous bow for Colonel Mellersh, and the most distant of salutes for his companion.

"Old impostor," said the Colonel, as they took the first turning and made for the country beyond the Downs.

"No," said Richard Linnell gravely, "I don't think him that. He is a gentleman at heart, fond of his children, and his ways are forced upon him by his position."

"Fond of his children! Bah! As objects of merchandise. I tell you, Dick, I hate the man."

"And when you hate a man you are unjust."

"Not here. My dear Dick, you look at old Denville through rose-coloured glasses. Pah! I detest him, and, by Jove, sir, I don't acquit him of some knowledge of that terrible affair at his house."

"Colonel Mellersh!"

"My dear boy!"

They walked on in silence for a few minutes, and then, clear now of the town, Colonel Mellersh exclaimed:

"My dear Dick, you have always known my feelings regarding this unfortunate attachment."

"Yes," said the young man sadly.

"She is very beautiful, but see how she has been brought up. Look at her sister—a weak, vain, foolish child more than a married woman, about whom there is bound to be some scandal soon."

"Can the sister help that?"

"Look at the brother; that careless young ne'er-do-weel, who is to be trained up in his father's steps."

"Poverty seems to be their greatest sin," replied Richard quietly.

"Then, there is another son, who quarrelled with the father and went off and enlisted. My dear Dick, is such a family one that you ought to enter?"

"My dear Colonel," said Richard with a sad smile, "I do not seem likely to enter it. You saw the look old Denville gave me. But, for heaven's sake, don't throw out hints again about that murder."

"Very well, but you must promise me that there shall be an end to all this infatuation. I speak as your father's oldest and dearest friend, and as one who feels as if he had a share in you—you reckless wild young scapegrace."

"I can promise nothing," said Richard coldly.

"Not now that you have been dragged into this serious affair?"

"Miss Denville has dragged me into no serious affair. Her conduct to me has always been that of a refined and modest lady."

"My dear boy! Have you forgotten that this has been going on between her and Rockley for months?"

"There is nothing between Major Rockley and Miss Denville," said Richard hoarsely; and his cheeks began to burn and his eyes to flash.

"Dick! Have you forgotten the serenade that night?"

"Have I forgotten it!" cried Richard fiercely.

"Well, what does that show?"

"That this scoundrel—this *roué*—this libertine—dared to cast his vile eyes on as sweet and pure a girl as ever breathed. Look here, Colonel Mellersh—no, no—my dear old friend—I found that dog insulting Miss Denville."

"Where?"

"Away there, beyond the Downs, out past the fishermen's cottages."

"How came Claire Denville out there alone with one of the wildest officers at the barracks?"

"Heaven knows," cried Richard. "I tell you I found him grossly insulting her, and I took the dog's whip from him, and thrashed him till my arm ached."

"And the lady flung herself into your arms, called you her gallant, her brave preserver, and you embraced and swore fidelity, while the wicked villain, the dog that you had thrashed, sneaked off snarling, with his tail between his legs."

Richard turned upon him fiercely, but he checked his anger as he met the Colonel's mocking eyes.

"You do not know Claire Denville," he said coldly.

"But, Dick, lad, come—there was the embracing and thanks?"

"Miss Denville is a sweet, true lady," said Richard, "whom I fear I may never win."

"Never win!" said the Colonel mockingly. "Dick, Dick, what a child you are! I used, a year or two back, to be glad you were so different to the other men here; but now I almost regret that you have not led a faster life. You are such an innocent boy."

"Shall we turn back?" said Richard abruptly.

"Turn back, man, no. We have not said a word yet about your meeting. Don't be angry with me, lad. Believe me, I am one of your truest friends."

"I know it," cried Richard warmly; "but don't talk of my love affair. We shall never agree till the scales of prejudice have dropped from your eyes."

"Till the scales of a boyish folly have dropped from yours, Dick. Well, we shall be in accord some day. If I'm wrong I'll humbly ask your pardon."

"And if I'm wrong I will yours," cried Richard. "Now, then, what of Payne's visit?"

"You will have to meet the Major," said the Colonel gravely.

"Yes, I suppose so. He could not forgive such an insult as that."

"You treat it very lightly, Dick. The consequences may be very grave."

"I hope not," said Richard. "I am not a soldier, but I am not going to show the white feather, even if I wear it in my heart."

"Not you," said the Colonel, as he tapped his companion on the shoulder. "But I should have liked you to be fighting on account of some other lady."

"And I should not," cried Richard. "Is this likely to be serious?"

"I should be no true friend to you, my lad, if I concealed the truth from you. It may be very serious."

"For me?"

"I don't say that."

"But I never fired a pistol in my life, and I fence horribly."

"It will be pistols, Dick. I arranged that it should be. But you will be cool?"

"I hope I shall be just as I am now," said Richard calmly.

The Colonel looked at him intently, but no nerve showed a tremor.

"A good walk will do you good," he said, and after telling him the preliminaries, and the place where they were to meet, the conversation was changed and they walked slowly on till the edge of the Downs was reached, and they soon after entered an extensive wood, walking down a leafy glade where all seemed wonderfully peaceful, and its solemnity was so soothing to Richard Linnell that he was about to throw himself upon the turf when Colonel Mellersh stopped short, and pointing to a gnarled beech of stunted growth, exclaimed:

"That will do exactly."

"Do?" said Linnell. "Do for what?"

"Why, my dear boy, do you suppose I have brought you out here for nothing? No; since the abominable code for furbishing up injured honour exists, and a man may be called out, it is our duty to prepare for emergencies. You cannot use a pistol?"

"No," said Richard, shaking his head.

"I can. I have been out six times, and I'm going to show you how to hit your man and save yourself."

"I don't want to hit Major Rockley."

"But I want you to hit him and save yourself. My dear boy, you are worth five thousand Major Rockleys to your father, and we must not have you hurt."

As he spoke, to Richard's great surprise, he took out a brace of duelling pistols with flask and bullets, and after loading skilfully he took a few cards from his breast, and going to the stunted tree, tacked one on each of two boughs about on a level with a man's outstretched arms, another on the trunk, and another higher still, where the head would be.

"I used to practise with the pistol a great deal at one time, Dick, and I could hit either of those address cards as many times as I liked."

"Then I will not quarrel with you and call you out."

"Don't," said the Colonel, handing him a pistol, and proceeding to step out fifteen paces. "There," he said, "stand there and aim at that card on the trunk. That is where a man's heart would be. I will count slowly, and when I come to three, raise your pistol quickly and fire."

"One—two—*three*!"

Richard Linnell raised his pistol, and drew the trigger, but there was no report.

"It will not go off," he said.

"No," replied the Colonel; "pistols never will, unless you cock them."

"Pish!" ejaculated Richard, repairing the omission. "Again."

The Colonel counted once more; there was a flash, a sharp report, and a leaf or two fell from high up a tree to the right of the target.

"Take the other," said the Colonel quietly; "hold it a little more firmly, and raise it slowly. The moment your eye glances straight along the barrel, press the trigger softly, so as not to jerk the pistol. Ready? Now—one—two—*three!*"

There was another sharp report, and the Colonel smiled.

"That's better," he said. "Your first bullet went over the enemy's head twenty feet or so. That one would have him in the shoulder. Try again."

The Colonel busied himself loading the pistols with all the quickness of an adept as his pupil fired, keeping him at it for quite a couple of hours, with intervals of rest. Now he made him fire at one card, then at another, practising as at his adversary's arms, head, and body, till Richard looked at him wearily.

"Yes; that will do now," said Colonel Mellersh. "You may congratulate yourself, Dick, upon being a horribly bad shot; but you will be able to handle your pistol properly, and raise it like a man who is used to the weapon."

"What is the use of that," said Richard, smiling, "if I cannot aim straight?"

"A great deal. If you had taken hold of your pistol in a bungling way to-morrow, Rockley would have felt that he had you at his mercy, and he would have been as cool as a fish. Now he will see that you know what a pistol is, and be perfectly ignorant of the fact that you are unskilful of aim. He will think he has a dangerous adversary before him, and be more likely nervous than cool."

"I see," said Richard, with his eyes lighting up. "I've had my turn at the scoundrel, and I'm satisfied. Of course I don't want to hit him, but at the same time I don't want him to hit me."

"Oh!" said the Colonel drily, "I thought you did."

"What! want him to hit me! Why?"

"You seemed so cool over it."

"Oh, but I'm not," said Richard gravely. "I suppose a good shot would hit one of those cards?"

"Time was, Dick, when I could have put half a dozen shots in either of them. I don't know that I could hit one now."

He raised the pistol he had been loading as he spoke, took a quick aim, and hit the centre card just on the edge, driving it into the bark of the tree.

"Bad!" he said. "Let's try another."

He aimed at the card representing the enemy's right arm fired, and struck it also about a quarter of an inch from the edge.

"Out of practice, Dick," he said, thrusting the pistols into their dark cloth bags, and replacing them in his pocket. "There, my lad, let's get home. Dine lightly this evening, go to bed in good time, and have a long night's rest."

"When is the meeting?" said Richard calmly.

"At six to-morrow morning."

"Where did you say?"

"On the sands, two miles out below the east cliff."

"Why there?"

"We shall want an excuse for going out so early, my lad. We can be going to bathe, and so be unnoticed, and there will be no fear of an interruption," said the Colonel grimly. "This is to be no play affair, Dick. An officer in His Majesty's service cannot submit to a horse-whipping from a civilian without trying to get ample satisfaction."

He looked at Richard with a grave air of pity in his countenance.

"Did you ever shoot a man?" said Richard, as they were walking briskly back.

"Do you mean wounded or killed?"

"The latter."

"Once, Dick."

The young man's countenance contracted, and he looked at his companion almost in horror.

"Yes," said the Colonel; "it is horrible, Dick, and the remembrance that the man was an utter scoundrel does not make the fact much less horrible after all these years."

They walked on for some distance in silence, before Richard Linnell broke in upon his companion's reverie.

"Was the duel about—a lady?"

The Colonel uttered a harsh laugh.

"It's an arrangement of nature, my dear Ulysses," he said. "If you see a couple of stags smashing their antlers, a couple of bulls goring each other, or two rams battering one another's heads, a brace of pheasants or barn-door cocks pecking and spurring each other to death, what's it about? A lady. The same with mankind, Dick; a duel is almost invariably more or less directly about a lady."

Richard Linnell went on thoughtfully for a time, and then turned with a sad smile to the Colonel.

"So even you had to do battle once in such a cause?"

"Not exactly, Dick; it was upon another's behalf. An utter scoundrel, just such a fellow as Rockley, did my best friend a mortal wrong. One day, Dick, it was a happy, peaceful home that I used to visit, where as sweet-natured, true, and gentle a man as ever breathed lived in happy trust and faith in his sweet young wife; the next there was a stain—an indelible stain—upon that hearth-stone, and my poor friend lay stricken down by the shock, and nearly died of the brain fever that ensued."

Richard Linnell looked at him with a curious feeling of horror—he knew not why—troubling his breast.

"Do you want to know any more?" said the Colonel roughly.

"Yes; go on."

"I did not see either of them for two years: the young wife or the scoundrel I had introduced to the house as my friend. Then I had a letter from the lady—a piteous, appealing letter to me to help her. She told me she was starving in London, Dick, and that the villain who had won her into leaving her home had forsaken her at the end of six months, and that, since then, she had been striving to get a living by teaching, but that now she was prostrate on a sick bed, helpless and alone."

There was a few moments' pause, and then the Colonel went on:

"I went to see her, Dick—poor, little, weak woman. Her good looks were gone, and she lay sick unto death for want of medical help and ordinary nutriment."

The Colonel stopped again, for his mouth seemed dry, and he passed his tongue over his fevered lips before he went on.

"I did what was necessary, and went straight to the man who had done all this wrong. I told him everything, and that it was his duty to make some reparation at least by providing for the lady's needs, and ensuring that she should not want in the future."

"Well?" said Richard hoarsely.

"He laughed at me. He refused so utterly that I lost my temper and called him villain and scoundrel. He retorted by insulting me with a vile charge as to the cause of my taking an interest in that poor woman, and he struck me, and then—"

"Well," said Richard, "and then?"

"I horsewhipped him, Dick, as you horsewhipped that man."

"And he challenged you, and you fought, and—"

"Yes, heaven forgive me," said Mellersh in a low voice, "I shot him dead!"

"You did this for the woman you did not love," said Richard Linnell, as if speaking to himself. "Yes, for the woman I did not love."

"What I did was for the woman I love with all my heart."

# Chapter Five
# A Retired Spot for a Bathe

It was a cold grey morning as Colonel Mellersh and Richard Linnell went out on to the parade, quite unaware that a pair of dark eyes were watching from behind an upper blind; but the fact that each man carried a towel in his hand disarmed suspicion, and the owner of the eyes went back to the couch in her room as the gentlemen passed out of sight.

"I was afraid," she said to herself softly. "Perhaps there was no truth in it after all."

Meanwhile, the Colonel and Richard Linnell went briskly on past the pier, with no one yet astir upon the parade; but farther on there were boats putting out to sea, and fishermen carrying oars and baskets down to those lying on the shingle.

As they went on along the cliff, Fisherman Dick was down by his upturned boat, trying the pitch, to find out whether it was hardened, and hearing the voices, he looked up and saw the two men pass.

"Master Richard Linnell—the Colonel," he said to himself. "Bathing, eh? Well, it's lonesome enough out there."

The mist hung over the sea, and the waves came in with a mournful sound upon the shore, the pebbles rattling together as they were driven up and rolled back with the retiring waters, sounding in the distance as if they were whispering together about the meeting that was about to take place a mile or so onward, beyond the chalk bluff, where the land trended inward, and formed a little bay.

Fisherman Dick found the bottom of his boat rather sticky, but he did not seem to be thinking about it, but to be putting that and that together.

"Master Richard Linnell give that Major Rockley an out and out good welting yonder in the cornfield, and if he'd been with him instead of that tother one, I should say there was going to be a fight with pistols; but I suppose it means a bit of a swim, and—"

Dick Miggles bent down over his boat, and seemed to be paying not the least heed, for just then he saw four people coming down the cliff path on to the beach, and as they passed he saw that they were Rockley, Sir Harry Payne, a gentleman he did not know, and the Major's dragoon servant, James Bell, carrying something under his military cloak.

"It's a fight," said Dick Miggles, as they passed him, picking their way down over the shingle to the firmer ground, close to the water's edge, where there were long stretches of sand, and it was better walking.

"Now, what shall I do?" said Fisherman Dick; "go and tell the constables? They'd be abed, and it would take me an hour to get back with them, and the mischief would be done before then. Anyhow, I'll go and see what's going on."

By this time Mellersh and Linnell had passed out of sight along the shore, and the second party were a hundred yards away.

Fisherman Dick did not hesitate, but, going back up the cliff path, he reached the top, and walked swiftly along eastward for some distance. Then, throwing himself down, he crawled flat on the ground, taking off his hat and leaving it behind him.

In a few seconds he was at the edge of the cliff, where the soft shore turf ended, and the chalk was broken away, going sheer down perpendicularly to the shingle beach and rough rock débris that had fallen from time to time after undermining by the sea. As he expected, the two little parties were below.

"They're going to fight, sure enough," muttered the fisherman. "I may as well go and see fair. Where'll they do it?"

He lay still for a few moments thinking.

"Why, they'll make for the sand patch in Jollick's Cove," he said aloud. "Don't know much about it, or they'd have took the path and the short cut and gone down the chalk steps."

He smiled as some thought occurred to him, and, drawing back from the edge of the cliff, he crawled back to where the beaten path showed faintly, and where at intervals the turf had been cut away down to the chalk, and a white patch made, as a guide for travellers in the dark, lest they should stray from the slight sheep-track and go over the cliff to certain death.

Along this path Fisherman Dick ran at a brisk trot for quite a mile, while the cliff rose slightly into a bold bluff, but the fisherman did not climb this, but plunged down suddenly behind a clump of furze into a ravine where a slight path showed that there was a way to the shore.

He went down this a few yards, and then turned, took two great strides, climbed up the face of the ravine a little way, stepped behind a huge mass of chalk, went in and out among some débris from the cliff, and then stepped into what looked like a rain gully which led to an opening in the rock, forming a rough half hole, half cavern, with the light coming from the side through a large irregular opening, partly natural, partly reduced by the arrangement of blocks of chalk, so that there was plenty of room for a dozen men to be in shelter, and where, unseen, they had full view of the open sea for miles on either side, and of the smooth patch of sand in the little cove, fifty feet or so below.

"There, as long as they don't shute up this way," said the fisherman, "I shall be all right and can see them all. I hope young Linnell won't be hurt. Don't suppose he will, for pistols is mortal stupid tools to work with."

Linnell and Mellersh came into sight soon after, and paused on reaching the sandy cove, a place admirably suited for the purpose in hand, for though from the rough look-out above, the shore could be commanded for some distance either way, those who occupied the sandy patch were hidden from either east or west.

"I'd have given something to have prevented this, Dick," said Mellersh huskily; "but you were bound to meet him."

"Yes," said Richard gravely. "It was unavoidable. Hush! don't talk to me. I'm firm now, and,"—he smiled as he spoke—"I want to do you justice."

"Well," said Sir Harry Payne, in a low voice, as the second party came upon the ground, "how do you feel now, Rockley? What do you mean to do?"

"To the man who struck me, and came between me and Claire Denville?"

"Yes."

"I shall shoot him like a dog."

# Chapter Six
# James Bell is Confidential

Sir Harry Payne looked at the stony face before him, and read fierce, implacable determination written plainly there. He felt that his companion was a soldier who would face death without a moment's hesitation, and that there was not a tremor in any pulse.

He had but little time for thought, for there were salutations to make, everything being carried out in the most cold-blooded style; after which Sir Harry took an oblong box from the Major's servant.

"You can go now," he said.

"Not stay with my master, sir?"

"I said go, fellow," cried Sir Harry sharply; and, in spite of his jaunty manner, he looked cold and pale.

"Back, Sir Harry?"

"No—anywhere. There, up the cliff. Be within call."

The man saluted, turned on his heel, and, walking to where a roughly-cut path of steps led up the cliff into the little ravine, began to mount as quickly as he could.

About half-way up he turned, saw that he was out of sight, and then, following Fisherman Dick's steps as if he were familiar with the way, climbed right into the rough cavern, and came suddenly upon the man, who started round in surprise.

"Hullo!" he growled. "What are you doing here?"

"Same to you," said the young dragoon, in a low voice. "What are you going to do?"

"See the fight, if you must know," said Fisherman Dick. "Like my place, p'raps."

"Yes," said the young soldier quickly, "I should;" and, stepping forward, he looked down cautiously on the group below.

"Why, it's Fred Denville, sure*ly*," cried Fisherman Dick.

"Hush, man!" said the young soldier, catching him by the arm; "James Bell now. Not a word to a soul about me."

"What, not to your young brother, Master Fred?"

"Hist! I'm only a common soldier now, Dick. You won't betray me, I know."

"Not I, lad. Troost me."

"I will, Dick, with my name, and—"

He placed his lips close to the fisherman's ear, and whispered.

Fisherman Dick brought a broad hand down softly on his knee, and laughed a silent laugh. But the next moment he turned preternaturally solemn, and whispered:

"It wouldn't be fair."

"Fair!" whispered back Fred: "is it fair for that poor fellow to stand and be shot down by a man who can snuff a candle at a dozen paces? I've seen him do it."

"I've done, my lad, and you're safe with me. I'm closer as you used to know."

Meanwhile the preparations had been going on below, and were so far advanced that the preliminaries had been all settled, the pistols charged, the ground stepped out, and the men were standing back to back, twelve paces apart.

Rockley was deadly pale, but not with the pallor of fear, as he stood exactly below the hollow where the two men were looking down. There was a savage look of rage in his eyes, and his lip was white where he pressed his teeth upon it firmly, longing the while to receive the weapon that was to be the minister of his vengeance upon the man he hated with an intense and ardent hate.

The doctor had drawn aside, walking down towards the sea, and the two seconds were together, every step in the progress of the drama being taken with a cold formality that was awful.

At last the seconds parted, each bearing one of the loaded weapons, and walking firmly towards his principal.

"Here you are, Rockley," said Sir Harry, in a voice that was husky, and not quite firm. "You'll wing him, won't you, or give him a ball through one of his legs?"

"If I can shoot straight," said Rockley coldly—"and my arm is pretty firm this morning—there shall be a funeral in Saltinville next Sunday."

"No, no. Gad, man, don't do that. Think of yourself if you killed him."

"I could get over it," was the reply. "The Prince would help me; and if he wouldn't—curse that Linnell, I'd sacrifice anything to pay him back his debt."

"Yes, you're firm enough, Dick. Mind: as Payne gives the word, raise your pistol and fire at once. You will not hit him, but the quick flash will spoil his aim. I will not consent to another shot. If he wants another it shall be at me. Now then; you understand?"

"Yes," said Linnell firmly, "I understand, Mellersh. I shall not fire at him. If I fall—badly hit—tell Claire Denville I sent her my dear love."

"Be firm, man. You will not fall," said the Colonel, pressing his hand. Then, glancing at Sir Harry Payne, who was waiting, he walked away towards a certain prearranged point, where he and Sir Harry stood together in the grey morning light; while, back to back, there were the principals, each grasping his heavy duelling pistol, with the chalk cliff towering above, and, fifty yards away, the waves uttering their low, whispering sound.

Just then a couple of gulls floated by, grey and ghostly in the dull mist, uttering their faint and peevish cry, and a few drops of rain began to fall.

"Are you ready, gentlemen?" said Sir Harry Payne hoarsely.

No one spoke, but the principals bowed their heads.

"When I say 'three,'" said Sir Harry, "you will turn round and fire. One—two—three!"

As the last word left Sir Harry Payne's lips, the principals turned quickly round, and almost simultaneously came two sharp echoing reports following the faint puffs of smoke that shrouded the duellists for the moment.

Then, as the seconds were starting forward, Mellersh saw that Rockley was looking up at the face of the cliff. Then he looked down at Richard Linnell, who, as the shots were fired, twisted himself sharply round, dropping his pistol, and now stood with one hand pressed to his temple.

Mellersh saw a curious smile on Rockley's face, and a hoarse gasp came from his throat.

"It is my fate to shoot another man—dead!" he muttered; and he was just in time to catch Richard Linnell as he reeled and was about to fall.

The doctor was coming up quickly, and Sir Harry had run to his principal.

"You've killed him," he whispered.

"I hope so," was the cool reply. "I'm not sure, though. That cursed piece of chalk fell from the cliff as I fired, and spoiled my aim. Go and see where he is hurt."

As Sir Harry ran off, Rockley stooped and picked up a piece of chalk rock as big as his fist, and then threw it down, dusting his hand afterwards, and then removing the mark of the chalk where it had struck him upon his right shoulder.

"Pah!" he exclaimed, pressing his handkerchief to his lip, which was cut; "the thing bounced up. I hope it has not saved Mr Richard Linnell's life."

Judging from appearances it had not, for Richard Linnell lay upon the sand with his eyes half closed, and the blood trickling from a wound over the right temple, just where the hair began to grow.

"Is he much hurt?" whispered Sir Harry.

"Don't know yet," said the doctor sharply, as he examined the fallen man. "Not Rockley's fault if he is not."

"He's a perfect devil," muttered Sir Harry, as, looking very white, he gazed from one to the other, while the Major slowly walked down towards the sea and back.

"Well?" said Colonel Mellersh, as the doctor ceased his examination.

"Had my man better be off at once?" said Sir Harry. "Give him a chance to get away."

"If you do get him away, Sir Harry Payne, let me know where he is gone. I may have a few words to say to Major Rockley."

"I can't tell what may supervene. There may be concussion of the brain," said the surgeon. "Yes, he is coming to now. The bullet has only scored his head. It was a marvellous escape."

"Blast!" muttered Major Rockley, as the news was conveyed to him. "Here, let's be off back, I want my breakfast. Curse him, I've not done with him yet, Payne. There are other ways to touch the heart of a greenhorn like that, than with bullets. I'd got him dead as a hammer. My arm felt like steel, and my shot would have had him right in the chest if that piece of chalk had not struck me and jerked my arm. Come along."

"Hadn't I better go and see if I can be of any help?"

"Hadn't you better go and nurse the scoundrel, and read to him a bit? Bah! Come along, man. He has his second, and they can fetch help from the fishermen's cottages if they want it."

Sir Harry followed him up the cliff steps and along the Down path without a word.

"So, I shall not want a post-chaise," said Rockley, with a laugh. "No rushing up to town and hiding for a while in chambers in St. James's, or running over to Boulogne. Good job, too. Save the money. I'm fearfully short. Why, man, you look white."

"Do I? It's cold. I'm glad that the affair has terminated so well."

"Terminated?" cried the Major, grasping him by the arm, "It has only begun. I tell you there are other ways than bullets to touch a man's heart, and I'll pierce his, curse him! so that he shall rue the day he ever crossed my path."

Sir Harry looked at him uneasily.

"Payne," he continued, "I'm a firm friend to those who help me—and lend me money," he added, with a laugh—"but I never forgive an insult, or a woman's slight."

Down on the beach, Colonel Mellersh was kneeling with the great drops of perspiration standing on his face, holding Richard Linnell's hand, while the surgeon was looking on anxiously at the returning signs of knowledge of his position on his patient's part.

The other principal and second had been gone some minutes when footsteps were heard, and James Bell and Fisherman Dick came quickly down the cliff.

"Is he much hurt, sir?" said the former, with real signs of trouble in his face.

"No, my man: you may tell the Major that it was a narrow escape."

"Poor lad!" muttered the soldier, going down on one knee, and making Colonel Mellersh look at him with surprise, as he took one cold hand, to hold it between his own for a few moments.

"Can we carry him to my house, gen'lemen," said Fisherman Dick roughly. "'Taint very far."

"No, my man, no," said the doctor; "he has only been stunned. Narrow escape, though. He'll walk home."

"Do you mean it, sir?" cried James Bell. "Beg pardon, sir. Only glad the Major won't have to go. I'll get back to barracks now. He'll be wanting me."

"All right, my man. Take those confounded pistols with you. There: be off."

The soldier placed the pistols in the case, and, saluting both gentlemen, hurried away by the shore, while Fisherman Dick touched his hat again, and said in a whisper:

"I've got a drop of right Nantes sperrit at my cottage, gentlemen, if you can bring him in there."

"No, no," said the doctor. "There, he's coming round fast now," and he pointed to Linnell's staring eyes.

The doctor was right. Half an hour later, with no worse trouble to combat than a fierce headache, and the wound smarting under its strapping, Richard Linnell was able to take the Colonel's arm and walk home, a warning to other young men not to attempt to climb up the cliff to the Downs, and risk falling and cutting their heads!

For that was the version of Richard Linnell's mishap that ran through the town.

# Chapter Seven
# Miss Clode is Overcome

It was a vain effort, for such an event was sure to be known to others besides the parties concerned.

Sent on a special mission by her aunt that morning, to see whether Mr Miggles had any fish, and with a basket to obtain a small bottle of a peculiar water that Fisherman Dick secretly supplied to a few friends whom he could trust, simple-faced Annie picked up some news.

"You don't want any more brandy, aunty," the girl had said; "there are two bottles not opened, and you said you wouldn't have any more fish for ever so long."

"Oh, Annie!" cried Miss Clode, "I thought you were beginning to be of a little use to me."

The girl's mouth opened wide, and her nose turned red; but directly after a cunning smile came in her face, and her eyes nearly closed.

"Oh, I say, aunty," she said softly, "I know what you mean now. You mean go and make that an excuse for getting to know about pretty Miss Denville going to see about the little girl."

"Worse and worse, Annie," cried Miss Clode. "Don't you understand that a still tongue makes a wise head?"

"Oh, yes, aunty, I know now;" and nodding her head very knowingly, Annie went off on her mission.

She returned very quickly, with a face quite scarlet with heat and excitement, full of the news she had picked up from Mrs Miggles, who had determined not to say a word of what she knew, and ended by telling all.

Miss Clode was in a state of excitement, for she had heard from a customer that young Mr Linnell, of the Parade, had fallen from the cliff that morning and cut his head, and the news turned the little woman pale, and she staggered and felt sick. When Annie came back she had recovered, but only ready on hearing her niece's news to faint dead away and lie insensible, just as stout Mrs Barclay came in about a new account-book, and to purchase a couple of pounds' worth of bill-stamps.

"Poor little woman!" cried Mrs Barclay sympathetically. "Here, don't make a fuss, my dear; I'll help you. Let's get her on the sofa. It's only fainting, and the smelling-salts will bring her round. That's the way," she panted and puffed as she helped to carry the slight little woman into the inner room. "Worse disasters at sea. Not so bad as Mr Linnell tumbling off the cliff this morning and cutting his head."

"He didn't tumble off the cliff," said Annie, round-eyed and trembling with eagerness, as she whispered in Mrs Barclay's ear.

"Oh, yes, he did, my dear."

"No, he didn't," whispered Annie, as Miss Clode lay quite senseless. "Hearing about it all upset aunty."

"Did it? What, his fall?"

"No, no, it wasn't a fall; but I mustn't say anything."

"You don't know anything," said Mrs Barclay contemptuously.

"Oh yes, I do," whispered Annie. "It's very horrid. Major Rockley shot him in a duel this morning for horse-whipping him after Major Rockley had insulted Miss Denville. There!"

"Hush!" whispered Mrs Barclay, whose face was now as red as Annie's. "Your aunt is coming to."

"Don't say I told you. She would be so cross."

Mrs Barclay nodded; and, after saying a few comforting words to the sufferer as she came to, contented herself with buying the bill-stamps, and left the shop, while, as soon as she had recovered sufficiently, Miss Clode wrote a few hasty lines to Colonel Mellersh, and strictly enjoining her to hold her tongue, sent her niece off to deliver the note on the Parade.

Colonel Mellersh was not within, but Cora Dean and her mother were alighting from the pony-carriage, and Annie greeted them with a smile and a curtsey, which made Mrs Dean tap the girl on the shoulder with a formidable fan.

"Here, you come in, and walk upstairs. I want a word with you."

"No, no, not now, mother," said Cora hastily.

"Now, just you let me have my own way for once in my life, please, Betsy," said Mrs Dean; and to avoid having words in the hall, where they could easily be overheard, Cora gave way, and in due time, to her intense delight, Annie was seated in one of Josiah Barclay's gilded easy-chairs, with a piece of cake in her hand, and a glass of ginger wine before her.

"Which is quite good enough for her," Mrs Dean had said to herself.

Cora had not taken off her things, but had gone to the window, to stand looking out, and biting her lips with shame and rage, as she heard her mother's words to the girl.

"Trust me, ma'am?" Annie said, with her mouth half full of sweet Madeira cake, "that you may, ma'am, as much as you would aunty. Oh, yes, I'm sure aunty gave his lordship the notes, and he only laughed."

Cora's beautiful white teeth gritted together as, ill-bred as she was, she knew well enough that had she wished Lord Carboro's openly-manifested admiration to ripen to her profit, her mother's open invitations to him to call would have destroyed her chance.

Then she tried to shut her ears to what was going on, and stood there wondering whether Richard Linnell would go out while she stood there—why it was the house had been so quiet that morning, for she generally listened for an hour to him playing duets with his father.

Then she wondered rather bitterly whether he would ever care for her, and his coldly polite way be changed. He was always civil and pleasant, and chatted with her when they met, but that was all, and at times it mortified her, as she thought how beautiful she was, making her vow that she would be revenged upon him, while at other times all this made her sit down and sob by the hour together.

"Why should I trouble about him?" she was asking herself just then, as she gazed from the window, and ignored the low buzzing of Annie's voice, which came huskily through Madeira cake, "I, who might accept almost any man I like. I've good looks, and money, and there are hundreds of men who would be only too glad of a smile. As for—"

"Mr Linnell, ma'am? Oh, yes, it's quite true," Annie was whispering, and the name sent a thrill through Cora.

"But he lives downstairs, girl, and we should have known."

"Oh, yes, ma'am, I learn by heart—aunty makes me—where all the fashionable people live. I know Mr Linnell—two Mr Linnells—live downstairs. It's in our visitor's list, along with you, and Colonel Mellersh, and it's quite true."

What was quite true about Richard Linnell? If it was about Claire Denville, she would tear him from her; she would crush her. How dare she presume to think of her idol—the true, brave fellow who had dashed into the sea and saved her when she was drowning?

Poor Fisherman Dick, like many more, not being young and handsome, was forgotten after that ten-pound note.

Cora's eyes flashed, her cheeks burned, and she looked as beautiful as an artist's idea of Juno, listening now with all the concentration of her passionate nature.

"I oughtn't to talk about it, ma'am, and I wouldn't tell anyone but you," Annie went on. "They said he fell over the cliff this morning and cut his head."

Cora Dean saw blood upon a white forehead, and she clutched the back of a chair, for the room seemed to be turning, and she felt sick.

"But he didn't, ma'am."

"Isn't he hurt, then?"

"Yes, ma'am, badly. I wonder you didn't know. You see, he met Major Rockley—you know him, ma'am?—handsome dark gentleman with mustachios."

"Yes, yes, I know," said Mrs Dean, revelling in the bit of gossip. "Have some more cake."

"Thank you, ma'am. Major Rockley was out walking with Miss Claire Denville out on the Downs—"

Cora's faintness passed away, and the room ceased to glide round as her eyes brightened, and she felt as if she could have embraced that handsome *roué*, who always, bowed to her with such a look of insolent contempt.

"And then Mr Linnell came up and took Major Rockley's whip away and beat him."

Cora's cheeks burned with jealous rage now. How dare Richard Linnell do that? And yet she liked him for it. He was so brave. But for Claire Denville! Her eyes flashed again.

"Then they met this morning, ma'am, down on the sands, and fought a real duel, and Major Rockley shot Mr Linnell."

"It is not true!" cried Cora excitedly, and once more the room began to turn.

"Yes, ma'am, it's quite true," said Annie, with her mouth now full of cake.

Shot!—injured by Major Rockley! and she—she could not go down to him to wait upon him, and show him by her every act how she loved him.

A minute before she had been ready to bless Major Rockley. Now, curses were in her heart, as she thought of him raising his hand against Richard Linnell to strike him down.

"No, ma'am, he isn't very bad," Annie went on, in answer to a question of Mrs Dean.

"It can't be true," Cora said to herself, as her brain seemed to become a chaos of love, jealousy, hatred, and pride in the brave young fellow who had saved her life, and, civilian though he was, showed himself ready to meet such a notorious fire-eater as the Major.

Just then she gave a gasp, for she saw a stiff, military-looking man, whom she knew to be the regimental surgeon, come up to the door.

It was true, then; and it was all she could do to keep from bursting into an hysterical fit of sobbing.

But a thought came directly that gave her strength, and she felt joy and elation together as she said to herself:

"He found them together, and horsewhipped the Major. Well, so much the better. He can never think of Claire Denville again. If he did—"

She uttered a low unpleasant laugh, as Annie found that she must go back, for she could eat no more cake; and as soon as they were alone Mrs Dean exclaimed:

"Don't, for goodness' sake, laugh like that, my dear; it gives me the cold shivers all down my back. It's just like Metalina in 'The Haunted Vampire,' where she takes an oath as she'll kill her rival or perish in the attempt."

# Chapter Eight
# Mrs Barclay is Puzzled

"Oh, my dear, and do you know how they're all a-talking about you?" cried Mrs Barclay, as she sat panting beneath the florid portrait of May Burnett in the MC's shabby drawing-room.

Claire looked up appealingly in the pleasant, plump face, and her brow knit.

"You see, it all comes to me, my dear, and it worries me because I like you so."

"You were always very kind to me, Mrs Barclay."

"Not half so kind as I should like to be, my dear. I wanted to have you home when the mur—"

"Oh, hush!"

"Of course, my dear. That's my way. So vulgar and thoughtless. Think of me now bringing that up to you who live here; and us sitting in the very next room."

"Mrs Barclay!"

"Yes, I won't say another word, my dear. Not that I believe in sperrits or anything of that kind. But you were saying about me being kind. Why, you won't let me be, my dear. I'm sure the dresses I'd buy you, and the things I'd give you, if you'd let me, would make some of them stare."

"But I could not let you, Mrs Barclay," said Claire, smiling.

"No; you're so proud, my dear, that's it. You see, Josiah lets me have so much for housekeeping, that I've always plenty to spare; and as to jewellery, why, I might wash in diamonds if I liked, but I don't."

"Let us be as usual, Mrs Barclay," said Claire, with more animation, "and never mind about what people say, or fashion, or dress, or any of the nonsense."

"I'm sure I should like to be, my dear; but you being a motherless girl, I don't like to hear people talking about you."

Claire's face grew flushed.

"Don't look like that, Claire, my dear. I'm not cross with you, but when people talk about you being out walking with that horrid black Major Rockley, it hurts me."

"I could not help it, Mrs Barclay," said Claire.

"Then it's all true, then, about young Mr Linnell horse-whipping him?"

"Yes, yes; but this is so cruel to me. He did beat him for insulting me."

"Bless him then. I always liked him, my dear. How he must love you!"

"Oh, hush, hush!" cried Claire, in agony.

"I don't see why. I'm sure he's everything that's good and brave; and you need not sob like that, my dear, for, from what I can hear, he isn't very badly hurt."

Claire started. A dread that had been hanging over her was beginning to assume form.

"But they say it's a mercy that the Major's bullet did not go an inch lower."

"Bullet? The Major! They have had a meeting?"

"Yes, my dear. I thought you must know, and I came to talk to you about even speaking to—there—there, what a woman I am. I came to do good, and I'm doing nothing but harm. Now, she's going to faint."

"No, no!" cried Claire agitatedly; "it is nothing. I am not going to faint, Mrs Barclay, indeed. There, you see, I am quite calm now."

"Yes, and I am sorry, my dear; but I am such a thoughtless woman. Barclay's quite right; I haven't no head at all."

"No head?" said Claire, smiling, as she sat down close to her visitor and laid her hands upon her arm. "Perhaps it is because you have so much heart."

"Heart, my dear! why—no; I declare I'm most afraid to speak, for fear of saying something that may hurt your feelings."

"If you will not speak about—about—"

"Mr Linnell, my dear?"

"Yes, but only to tell me that he is not much hurt—you said so, did you not?" cried Claire.

"Yes, my dear; he's not much hurt. But, Claire, my dear, wouldn't it be better if you—so pretty and young as you are—did care very much for some one as nice and good as he is?"

"No, no," cried Claire excitedly. "Pray, pray say no more. It is impossible."

"Well, you know best, my dear," said Mrs Barclay sadly; "and you want me to talk about something else. Well, I'll talk about you, only you must not mind if I say something stupid. It's my way."

"I am sure you would not say anything to wound me," said Claire, kissing her.

"Indeed I wouldn't, my dear: and, do you know, ever since I found out how you people here were situated, through Mr Denville coming to see my Josiah, who is the real best of men, I seemed to take to you like. I went home and had a good cry after I'd been here the first time, and seen you managing your poor father, and your sister and brother so well."

Claire's brow grew troubled, but her visitor prattled on.

"You had another brother, hadn't you, my dear, who couldn't agree with your father like, and then went away?"

"Yes," said Claire, bowing her head to hide her face.

"Ah, my Josiah told me so. Well, well, there's troubles in every family, my dear; and so long as pa has got you he has not much cause for complaint."

Claire looked up, trying to smile, but it was a sorry attempt; and soon after her guest rose, assuring her that she need not be uneasy about Mr Linnell.

"One word before I go, my dear, though, just as a secret. It isn't that I'm curious, because I don't care who it is marries, or whom they marry; but I've no girls of my own, and I do take an interest in you. Now, just in a whisper like. I am an old friend."

"Yes, yes—indeed, you are. The only dear friend I have."

"Then tell me now; put your lips close to my ear—it is to be Mr Linnell, is it not?"

"Never!" said Claire firmly.

"Oh, my! And I told you to whisper. I won't believe it's that horrible Major."

"Mrs Barclay," said Claire, putting her arms round her homely friend's neck, "they say that every woman has her duty in life: mine is to watch over and help my father, and to be such protection as I can to my sister and brothers."

"What, and not get married at all?" cried Mrs Barclay, in a tone of disappointment.

"And never be any man's wife," said Claire sadly. "Oh!"

"Stop one moment, Mrs Barclay," whispered Claire, in a strangely hesitating manner, "you do like me, I know."

"Indeed, I do, my dear, though I must say you disappoint me horribly."

"Then I want you—whatever comes to pass—whatever people may say of me—to try and think the best of me."

"Why, my darling!"

"Yes: I know you will; but your confidence may be sorely tried, and I want you to think well of me always. I cannot do all I wish, and—and—I cannot explain myself; only think the best you can of me. Good-bye, good-bye!"

"She is the strangest girl I ever did meet," said Mrs Barclay, as she panted away in her thick silk and enormous open bonnet. "Think well of her, whatever comes to pass! Why, of course I will, poor girl!"

# Chapter Nine
# An Interested Patron

"Well, Denville," said Lord Carboro', "I wanted to see you."

"In what way can I serve your lordship?" said the MC, with his best bow.

"A pinch of your snuff."

The pinch was taken, and the box snapped and returned.

"Your arm."

Denville's breast swelled as he offered his arm to the elderly beau, and a flush of hope rose into his cheeks. The sun must be coming out at last.

It was a pleasant thing to be seen walking along the Parade in so familiar a way with Lord Carboro', and to his great delight Denville saw that the Parade was well filled.

He expected that this would be only a temporary condescension from the wealthy old nobleman; but Lord Carboro' held on tightly, made a few very nasty remarks about some of the people they passed, and then said suddenly:

"Drelincourt has been asking me to interest myself with the Prince to get your boy a commission."

"Indeed, my lord?"

"Yes, indeed. 'Nother pinch of snuff."

The box—*sniff—snuff—snap.*

"Like to know what I said to her?"

"My lord, I am a father."

"Yes, Denville, I know it. Well."

The old man changed the conversation to make another remark or two about some visitors, and then said, suddenly returning to the subject:

"Drelincourt asked me to get the lad a commission."

"Yes, my lord."

"You don't think of letting that old harpy claw up the boy?"

"Oh, my lord!"

"Of course, it would be madness. I told her I'd see her ladyship made a mummy first."

The MC's heart sank.

"She means to marry fat Matt Bray. I hope she will. I said I'd see her ladyship made a mummy first, Denville; and—he, he, he! she showed real colour. It came up in her cheeks, all round the rouge. Poor old girl! she is as bad as her sister was: hates to hear about dying. Doosid awkward thing, old Teigne being killed in your house. I wonder who got her diamonds."

Denville's hands began to tremble, and the beads of perspiration to stand upon his forehead.

"Must all die some day, I suppose. Great nuisance to think about if the weather's fine, Denville; but when it's a cold, easterly wind, or one's gout's bad, I often feel as if I shouldn't mind being tucked up comfortably. How do you feel about it, Denville? You're not a chicken."

"My lord, I feel sometimes as if, once I could see my boy settled, and my daughter well married, it would be a relief to lie down and take the long sleep," said the MC solemnly.

"Denville," said Lord Carboro', after a pause, during which he held on tightly to his companion's arm. "I've gone on for years calling you an artificial old humbug, with your deportment and niminy-piminy ways. I hadn't the common sense to see that they were like my wig and stock, sir— put on. I beg your pardon, Denville. I do, sir: I beg your pardon. You've the right stuff in you after all, and, sir—I'm very proud to tell you that what I wouldn't do for that old harpy, Drelincourt, I would do on my own account."

"My lord!"

"Yes, sir; asked His Royal Highness, myself, and he said nothing would give him greater pleasure. Denville, your son has a commission in the Light Dragoons."

"My lord, I—I—"

"Don't, don't, Denville," said the old man, pressing his arm. "Hold up man, or some of these idiots will be seeing that you are moved. Take a pinch of snuff, man—of mine, and let's walk out upon the Downs, out here beyond the fishermen's cottages, and my sight isn't what it was, or I should have said that was Miss Claire going into yon fisherman's hut."

"Impossible, my lord. Will you allow me to express my—"

"No, no, no. Not a word, Denville. Why, man, you are husky with emotion now, real emotion. Don't say another word about it. Only make the boy do us justice."

"He shall, my lord," said the MC in a broken voice.

"And now, look here, Denville; I'm about one of the most selfish old fellows that ever breathed, and I want to see if I can't have a little recompense for all my miseries and disappointments."

"Yours, my lord?"

"Yes, sir, mine," said the old beau. "Do you think because I'm rich I'm happy? Not a bit of it. I haven't long to live though now, and I want to make the best of the time left."

"My lord!"

"Hold your tongue and listen. I heard all about Rockley meeting Miss Claire and young Linnell thrashing him."

"It was a most unfortunate affair, my lord."

"I don't know that either. Pity young Linnell couldn't shoot and pop off that scoundrel Rockley. By the way, he looked daggers at me for getting your boy appointed to his regiment; but the boy shan't disgrace the corps, if I find him money myself."

Denville paused where they stood upon the Downs and gazed wonderingly at the old Earl.

"I make you stare, Denville. Well, I'll be frank with you, and you shall be frank with me."

The MC bowed and wiped his streaming face.

"Of course she does not care for Rockley."

"Good heavens, my lord; no!"

"Nor for young Linnell?"

The MC hemmed twice before he spoke.

"I, too, will be frank with you, my lord," he said. "It was in dead opposition to my wishes, but I'm afraid there was something between my daughter and Mr Richard Linnell."

Lord Carboro' looked at the speaker searchingly.

"It was an unspoken attachment, my lord, nothing more; and since that terrible event at my house—I am obliged to name it," he said, with quivering lip—"whatever intimacy existed has been broken off."

"Humph! Sure, Denville?"

"I have my daughter's word, my lord. That duel set me thinking; and like another father, my lord, of whom we read, I bespoke her roundly."

"Oh! come, Denville, don't compare yourself to Polonius, man. He— he—he!"

"Only to that extent, my lord. As I say, I spoke to her, and she assured me that there was nothing whatever between her and Mr Linnell, but gratitude towards a gentleman who saved her from insult."

"Denville, that Mellersh is his friend; he ought to have shown the boy how to shoot the scoundrel."

The MC was trembling with excitement. He was between hope and dread, for he could not but divine what was coming, and in spite of the glittering future it held up to his view he shrank from it with fear.

# Chapter Ten
# An Elderly Suitor

"Gratitude, eh?" said Lord Carboro' suddenly.

"Yes, my lord," said the MC, who was perspiring profusely.

"Deuced dangerous thing, Denville. Are you sure?"

"My lord, I have my child's word, and that is sacred."

"Hah!" ejaculated Lord Carboro', "you are right. Bless her! she is as sweet and true as she is beautiful. She stands alone here in her youthful dignity. Damme, Denville, I always look upon her as some beautiful Greek goddess, and I would have sooner gone to her funeral than seen that *roué* Rockley win her. I would, damme."

"My lord, so would I," said Denville huskily.

"And you would sooner go to her funeral than see her my wife, eh?" said the old beau abruptly.

"My lord, I did not say so."

"Nor think it?"

Stuart Denville, MC of Saltinville, stood there out on the hazy Downs, trembling, obsequious, tossed by his emotions. It was so dazzling, this suggestion of an offer for his child's hand. May had married a rich man; but for Claire, his beautiful child, to become the wife of a wealthy nobleman— to become Countess of Carboro'! It was such an exaltation—greater than his highest dreams. But before him stood that withered old man, scanning him with his sharp eyes, and ready to probe him with his bitterly venomed tongue. He, to be the husband of his beautiful child. It was sacrilege.

"We agreed to be quite frank," said Lord Carboro' sharply.

Denville drew a long breath, and biting his lip, called up before his mental vision the sweet soft face of his child wearing a new horror as he bore her this news, and trampling down, as it were, the great temptation, he cast off his mincing ways, his servile politeness, and in a quick, firm voice exclaimed:

"Will your lordship commence and set me the example? What do you mean?"

"Come, I like that, Denville. Spoken like a man. Well, I'll be frank. I have long been thinking of your child, and watching her, and as I have watched her I have loved—no, that is absurd at my age—my liking for her has grown. I have put it off and it has come back, and I have put it off again as I have heard some bit of scandal, but she has always come out of it so spotless and well that I have grown more—well, infatuated."

He paused for a minute, and then went on speaking earnestly.

"Then came that horror at your house, just as I had made up my mind to speak to you; and I said no: it was impossible; but the feeling grew. Yes, man, even at my age."

Denville bowed, and drew himself up very stiffly.

"I waited, Denville, and was about to speak to you when this affair with Rockley and the duel took place, and I stopped at home and swore horribly; but the feeling still grew and grew, and as that has all passed away, I now ask you if you will give me your consent. I ask you as a gentleman, Denville, to address her and ask her if she will be my wife."

Denville did not answer, for a tremendous struggle was going on within his breast, and it was hard to say which side would win.

"Hah!" said Lord Carboro', speaking quickly; "you say I am very old. Granted. That I ought to think of my coffin instead of a wife. Granted. That I am an old fool; but there I join issue."

Denville had raised his hands deprecatingly.

"I am not an old fool, Denville."

"No, my lord, you are not."

"I'll tell you why. I have said to myself that if this beautiful young creature swore to be my faithful wife I could trust her. She would be a sweet companion for my declining years; and, God bless her! if she consented, I would repay her for the sacrifice. In a few years I should leave her young, rich, titled, and free to choose some more suitable companion than the old man she had tended to his grave."

There were no marks lying on the ground as those two elderly men stood face to face alone on the short turf of the Downs; but it seemed as if they must have dropped a tear.

Neither spoke for some minutes, and then it was the Master of the Ceremonies.

"My lord," he said firmly, "you have given me this commission for my son as a bribe."

"No, no, Denville, I swear I have not."

"Take it back, my lord, for what you ask is impossible."

"Impossible?"

"Fate has been very hard to me, my lord, and the burden has been too heavy at times to bear; but I cannot do this thing. I love my child too well."

They stood gazing out to sea for some minutes, and only the rushing of the wind was heard, or the wailing cry of the gulls, but at last Lord Carboro' spoke.

"Denville, I did not know you," he said gravely. "I thought I had to deal with a different man; but don't let us be hasty. As to the commission, it is your boy's, and may he deserve it. As to what we have said, let us wait. Don't refuse me absolutely, and don't say a word to Miss Denville. Give me leave to visit at your house, and let matters slide for a few months. Things may shape themselves so that you may change your mind; do you consent to this?"

"It would be like buoying your lordship up with false hopes."

"That is my look-out, sir; do you consent?"

"I am your lordship's obedient, humble servant."

"You are the man I offer to make my father-in-law? Answer me, sir, like a man."

"I consent."

"That's better. Denville, your hand. In future I shall know you as the man I have seen to-day. I never respected you one half so much before."

# Chapter Eleven
# James Bell's Decision

It was in honour of Morton Denville's reception into the regiment that the Master of the Ceremonies received. There had been some difficulty in the matter, but on the very first night that the young man dined at the mess, when, urged by Major Rockley, his brother-officers had decided to send him to Coventry, it so happened that "a certain gentleman" was at Saltinville and had expressed his intention to Colonel Lascelles of looking in.

Consequently, it was decided not to transport the young subaltern to the Midlands that night; and as it happened His Royal Highness asked the Colonel who the tall youth was, ordered him to be introduced, and shook hands with the young man.

"Devilish gentlemanly fellow, your father, my lad. Always looks a gentleman, and carries a devilish good pinch of snuff. My compliments to him, and tell him I was glad to oblige Carboro'."

"They were all as civil to me as could be, after that, Clairy," said Morton, relating the meeting at home. "Even Rockley shook hands after dinner, when we'd had a lot of claret, and he apologised about being carried away, he called it, and said we were brother-officers now, and must be good friends. I don't like him, though."

Claire turned pale.

"I say, though, Clairy, I haven't said a word to the dad, but what am I to do? I turned cold and hot, and queer as could be yesterday. Whom do you think I met?"

Claire knew what was coming, but she did not speak.

"Fred. I'd half forgotten about him, and he's in my troop."

"Did—did Fred speak, Morton?"

"No; he cut me dead, and of course he is James Bell in the regimental books; but, I say, isn't it awkward? I can't know him, you see, as my brother: what shall I do?"

"Fred has shown you," said Claire huskily, as her troubles seemed to be on the increase. "I will try and persuade him to leave the regiment. We must buy him out."

"Yes, to be sure," cried the boy. "Oh, I say, what a clever old girl you are, Sis! Why, you're better than a mother."

Claire smiled sadly as he kissed her and left the house.

That night she wrote to Private James Bell about the difficulty—a long sisterly letter, offering to get the money to buy his discharge, and alluding to everything as tenderly as the subject would allow.

In due time a crisp short reply came back:

"Dear Claire,

"No, I shall not leave the regiment. I want to keep my eye on the Major. Tell Morton not to be afraid. I am only James Bell, and I shall never presume. I am too well disciplined for that. Take care of your dear self.

"Good-bye, F."

Claire wept over the letter, and hid it with her treasures. The difficulty seemed to have passed away, and she felt lighter at heart.

She had to prepare too for the evening that the Master of the Ceremonies had determined to give, not because he could afford it, but nominally, as intimated, in honour of his son's receiving a commission, more especially because Lord Carboro' had wished it, and said that he should come.

With such a visitor to give *éclat* to the proceedings, the difficulty was how to arrange to issue invitations, for Denville, with throbbing breast, felt that no one would decline.

He was in a tremor for days, as he thought the matter over, and was swayed by his ambition and his true manhood, to and fro.

At times he raised his eyes to find that Claire was watching him, and her cold candid look made him shrink within himself, as he thought of the past, and he shivered in dread lest she should display that terrible repugnance again, instead of the sad, half despondent distance that had become her manner and her bearing towards him.

She never kissed him, but, when he took her hand, she suffered him to press his lips to her brow without flinching as she had at first, and he sighed and accepted his fate.

There had been times of late when the entanglement of his younger son's position in the regiment, with an elder brother a private in the ranks, had half driven him mad, keeping him awake night after night; and Claire had lain weeping despairingly as she had heard him pace his room, but the horrible difficulty he had been anticipating did not seem to come home, and he waited for the Nemesis that would some day arrive, hoping that he might be allowed time to complete his plans before the bolt fell.

He sat one morning, deciding with Claire to whom invitations were to be issued. Lady Drelincourt would come of course, as Lord Carboro' would be there, and several other notables had been invited.

"Then the officers of the regiment, of course."

Claire half rose and looked in her father's face.

"We must forget that, my child," he said imploringly. "Major Rockley is a gentleman, and he has in some sort apologised to Morton. He told me so. To leave him out would be to insult him. He must be asked. His good sense will keep him away. You must ask Colonel Mellersh, too. He is a great friend of Colonel Lascelles."

"You will ask Mr and Mrs Barclay, father?" said Claire.

"Oh, yes, we must. Dreadfully vulgar people, but it is a necessity."

Claire sighed as she thought of what was behind Mrs Barclay's vulgarity, and the note was written.

A couple of days passed, and everyone without exception had expressed his or her intention of being present, when, as he was on the Parade, Colonel Mellersh met the MC, and said:

"By the way, Denville, I want you to invite my young friend Linnell to your party."

"I shall be charmed," said Denville, with a smile, for he could not refuse; and in due course Richard Linnell received an invitation and replied.

A little farther on, Denville came upon Lady Drelincourt in her chair.

"Ah, Denville, bad man," she said, tapping him with her folded fan. "I feel as if I could not come to your house. My poor dear sister!"

The houses on the Parade seemed to reel before the MC's eyes.

"But one cannot grieve for ever. I shall come. Have you asked that wicked Rockley?"

Denville bowed.

"And Sir Matthew Bray?"

"All the officers whom duty will allow are coming."

"That's well; and now, Denville, you must send an imitation with apologies to Mrs Pontardent."

"Lady Drelincourt!"

"I can't help it. She wishes to come, and I have promised that she shall."

The result was that Mrs Pontardent was invited, and in turn she expressed a wish that her dear friends the Deans, whom Mr Denville had introduced to her, should not be left out.

The Master of the Ceremonies had the deciding who should be in society, and who should not; and here he was making a stand when Lord Carboro' came up—it was on the pier—and was appealed to by Mrs Pontardent.

"Oh, yes, Denville," he said good-humouredly; "ask Mrs and Miss Dean."

The Master of the Ceremonies ruled the roost, but he was everybody's slave; and, in this case, the only way out of the difficulty after they had been neglected so long was to call with Claire and invite them personally.

"If you wish it, papa," Claire said, when spoken to on the subject.

"I do not, my dear," he replied, with a sigh. "My position compels it."

They went trembling: Claire in agony lest she should encounter Richard Linnell; her father about the expenses into which he was drifting, for the tradespeople were giving him broad hints, especially the confectioner, that money must be forthcoming if the refreshments were to be supplied.

Cora Dean's eyes flashed with pride and jealousy as the visitors were shown in, but she received Claire courteously, and the wonderfully different pair were left together by the open window, while Mrs Dean drew the Master of the Ceremonies aside.

"I am pleased, Mr Denville," she whispered. "This is real good of you. I knew you would get us into society at last. Mrs Pontardent has been very kind, but she ain't everybody. I wanted my Bet—my Cora—to meet my Lady Drelincourt and the other big ones. After this, of course, it's all plain sailing, and we shall go on. I say, just look at 'em."

Denville turned with a sigh towards the bay window where Claire and Cora were seated, talking quietly, but with eyes that seemed to fight and fence, as if each feared the other.

"You go into a many houses and don't see such a pair as that."

"Your daughter is a beautiful woman, Mrs Dean."

"*Lady*," said the latter correctively; "and so's yours, only too cold and pale. And now, look here, Denville, as friends—I know what's what."

"Really, Mrs Dean, you puzzle me."

"Hush! Don't speak so loud. Look here, you've done me a thoroughly good turn, and I'm a warm woman, and not ungrateful. As I said before, I know what's what—Parties ain't done well for nothing, and expenses comes heavy sometimes. If you want to borrow thirty or forty pounds—there, stuff! you must have your fees. I'm going to put half a dozen five-pound notes under the chany ornament in the back room. You can look round and admire the rooms and get it."

His spirit rebelled, but his breeches pocket gaped horribly, and wincing in spirit, he rose and went forward to talk to Cora in his society way, starting, in spite of himself, as he heard the chink of china on marble, while, after a time, he began in the most graceful way to gaze through his eyeglass at the pictures and china from Mr Barclay's ample store, ending by securing the notes in the most *nonchalant* way.

After letting a sufficient time elapse, the Denvilles took their leave, and Mrs Dean broke out in ecstasy:

"There, Betsy, at last. You'll be a real lady now."

"Yes, mother," said Cora dreamily.

"I say, Denville isn't a bad one, only he has to be paid."

"It's the custom, mother."

"Oh, yes. You know what 'Amlet says, as your poor father used to make jokes about, and call breeches; but I say, isn't she a milk-and-water chit beside you, my gal? Didn't you feel as if you 'ated her?"

"No, mother," said Cora thoughtfully. "She's different to what I expected. I don't think she'll live."

"Don't talk like that. Now, let's see what about your noo dress."

"And yours, mother?"

"Of course. And feathers."

And as this conversation went on, Stuart Denville and his daughter Claire walked homeward, the latter with the gloom deepening, so it seemed, over her young life, the former with the six crisp notes riding lightly in his pocket, and the load of misery and shame growing heavier day by day.

# Chapter Twelve
## In Society

It was a proud time for the MC, and he knew how it would be canvassed in Saltinville. All the principal people would have honoured his little home, and in the future he saw his fees and offerings doubled, and Claire well married—to Lord Carboro'. No, he could not say that, though the bait was glittering still before his eyes.

He was in the drawing-room waiting, with pretty May smiling out of her curls, hanging in her tawdry frame upon the wall; but Claire was not yet down.

If she would only forget that night and not avoid him as she did, how much less difficult this burden would be to bear.

He rang, and Isaac, in a new suit of livery, appeared.

"Send word to your mistress that it is time she was down, Isaac."

"Yes, sir."

"Is everything ready?"

"Yes, sir."

"The cards on the tables?"

"Yes, sir."

"And the refreshments?"

"Yes, sir."

"You will ask Lady Drelincourt's servant to stop and help wait."

"Yes, sir."

"And the Earl of Carboro's."

"Yes, sir."

"Perhaps it would be as well to keep Mr Burnett's man also."

"Yes, sir."

"I need say no more, Isaac, only that you will see that the tea and coffee are hot, and that the refreshments in the dining-room are ready in relays."

"Yes, sir; everything shall be done, sir; and would you mind casting your eye over that, sir?"

"Certainly, I will do so, Isaac. Hem! An account, Isaac?"

"Yes, sir—wages, sir; and if you would make it convenient—"

"My good Isaac," said the MC blandly, "as you must be aware, gentlemen are in the habit sometimes of taking rather long credit, and of often being in debt. I might cite to you His Royal Highness. But no one troubles thereon, because it is well known that sooner or later His Royal Highness will pay his debts."

"Yes, sir; of course, sir; but wages, sir—"

"Are wanted, Isaac, of course. Now, my good Isaac, you must have seen how much occupied I have been of late. No: say no more now. I will look over your statement, and you shall be paid."

A tremendous knock and ring cut short this little scene, and Denville wiped the dew from his face as he uttered a low sigh of relief.

"She will come down now.—Ah, my dear Mrs Barclay; my dear Barclay. Delighted to see you both."

"I say, Denville, old fellow, you're going it, eh?"

"My dear Barclay, a sheer necessity. You see how I have placed my son."

"Umph! yes," said the money-lender, with a chuckle; "but I'm no better off. You are. One less to keep, but at my expense."

"But, my dear Barclay—"

"All, it's all very well, but you came to me to find the money for his outfit."

"Now, look here, Jo-si-ah," cried Mrs Barclay, who was a wonder of satin, feathers, and jewellery, "Mr Denville has been kind enough to ask us to his party, and I will not have another word said about bills and money. I've come to enjoy myself, and I mean to. There!"

"Bless the woman!" sighed Denville.

"And where's Miss Claire? Oh, here she is. Oh, my dear, how lovable you look in your plain pearl satin. Oh, I never did! Only oughtn't you to have a necklace on? I say, take me to your room, and let me lend you mine."

She placed her plump hand upon a magnificent ruby necklet that she wore, but Claire checked her.

"No, no, no, Mrs Barclay," she whispered.

"Well, p'raps you're right, my dear. Nothing wouldn't make you look better."

"Let me compliment you too, Miss Denville," said Barclay in his brusque way; and, after a smile and a few words, he turned back to talk to his host.

"I say, Denville—why, it was in that back room that—why, you've made it into a back drawing-room."

"For God's sake, Barclay!"

Denville caught at his visitor's arm, and looked at him in a ghastly way.

"Eh? Why, you look scared. Ah, well, it was stupid to mention it at a time like this. Mustn't allude to it when they are all here, eh?"

"For heaven's sake, no."

"All right, I won't. I say, Denville, what do you think of that?"

He drew a case from his pocket, opened it, and displayed a necklace of large single diamonds, the sight of which made the MC start and shiver.

"Magnificent!" he faltered.

"I should think they are. All choice picked stones, sir. Belonged to a Countess."

"To a Countess?" said Denville, in a faltering voice.

"Yes, sir. I say, your bread's beginning to be buttered thick. Look here."

He drew out another case as they stood alone in the front room.

"There's a set of pearls, sir. There's lustre and regularity. Two fifty guineas, Denville."

"But, my dear Barclay," said the host, striving to recover his equanimity, "why have you brought those here?"

"Why have I brought 'em? Don't you know? Well, I'll tell you. Old Carboro' wants to pay a delicate attention to a lady he admires, and he bade me bring two or three things here to choose from. I mean to sell old Drelincourt the one he does not take. Look, I've two more lots."

"But, my dear Barclay, surely you will not attempt to sell or barter here—in my house," said Denville piteously.

"Not try? Oh, won't I, though! Why, my dear Denville, you don't suppose I came to waste time, do you? Not I."

There was an announcement here, and Denville had to hide the feeling of annoyance mingled with pleasure that came upon him, for there could be no doubt in his own mind for whom the jewels were intended.

How would Claire treat the offer?

The guests began to arrive fast now, and the shabbiness of the candle-decked room was soon turned into a suitably subdued setting to the rich dresses which Mrs Barclay scanned in turn, and decided were not so good as her own.

The incident about the jewels troubled Denville more and more, and he found himself glancing from time to time at the beautiful woman in her simple, pearl-tinted satin, who was doing the honours of his house so gracefully.

"Yes," he sighed, "worthy to be a Countess, but—" He drew his breath hard. Poor as he was, it seemed too terrible a sacrifice.

Then the temptation came upon him very strongly again. Rich, admired, beautiful, an enviable position; and, once she was married, the terrible disclosure that would some day perhaps come would not affect her.

"Colonel Mellersh; Mr Richard Linnell," announced Isaac; and a feeling of jealous anger against the young man he had been obliged to invite came over him, but had to be hidden by a smile as the two new-comers advanced to Claire.

Denville watched them keenly; but Claire's face was as calm as if they had been total strangers. She gave them both a most courteous greeting. That was all.

"Lord Carboro'," announced Isaac.

There was a little excitement here, as the wealthy old beau entered, looking very keen and sharp, but very old; and as Denville saw him take Claire's hand, the feeling of elation was swept away by a cold, despairing chill. It was impossible.

And yet, as his lordship stood chatting to the beautiful girl, Denville noticed that there was a change in her. She seemed brighter and more animated. She smiled at the old man's remarks, and once more the impossible seemed to be growing possible, for Claire was only a woman, after all.

Colonel Mellersh saw this too, and half sneeringly turned to Richard Linnell.

"There," he said, "much good you've done by making me bring you. I believe your syren has captivated old Carboro'."

"Just look at the old man," whispered Mrs Barclay to her husband. "Why, I declare, he's quite gallant."

"Hold your tongue, and don't you let it go, old woman. Here he is."

"Pinch of your snuff, Barclay," said the old dandy, coming up smiling. "My compliments to you, Mrs Barclay. You look charming."

"Oh, my lord!" said Mrs Barclay, rising to curtsey, and saying to herself, "As if I didn't know better than that."

"I can't think what you were about to marry such an ugly old scoundrel as Barclay here. Have you brought anything?"

He took Barclay's arm, and they walked into the back drawing-room, where there were a couple of card-tables.

"Dick," said Colonel Mellersh, "old Carboro's going to borrow money, or else—by Jove, he's getting a present from him for your beloved."

"I thought you were my friend, Mellersh," said Linnell, with his brow knitting.

"So I am. Look."

"I am not a spy," said Linnell coldly, and he turned away.

"What have you brought?" said Lord Carboro'.

"These diamonds, my lord, this string of pearls, and a large diamond bracelet. Look at these diamonds, my lord—"

"Don't talk. I don't want everybody to see. Lay them on the table. No: show me the pearls."

"They are perfect, my lord, and—"

"Hold your tongue, man. That will do."

"I'll slip out this bracelet, my lord. No; I'll go and give it to my wife. She shall put it on, and you can go and talk to her, and see how beautiful it is in design."

"Hold your tongue, man. The pearls will do. How much?"

"Three hundred guineas, my lord. They are—"

"Bah! Robbery! I'll give you two hundred down. Do you think I want credit?"

"But, my lord, I should lose heavily."

"And a doosid good thing too, Barclay. You want bleeding. Am I to have them?"

"Two fifty, my lord, as you are so old a friend."

"Two hundred—in an instant. Yes, or no?"

"Well, yes, my lord."

"Give me another pinch of snuff, Barclay, and hold the pearls in your hand. Never mind the case. Thanks, that will do. Come for the money in the morning."

The exchange was ingeniously effected, but Colonel Mellersh saw it, and his lips tightened as he glanced at Richard Linnell.

"He's got the pearls, old woman," said Barclay, going back to his wife where she sat fanning herself, and alone.

"How much?"

"Two hundred guineas."

"Let's see; you gave the Hon. Mrs Bedam fifty for 'em, didn't you, Josiah?"

"Yes; but they're worth a hundred, honestly."

"And is he going to give 'em to Claire?"

"Don't know. Wait."

"Lady Drelincourt, Sir Matthew Bray, Colonel Lascelles," announced Isaac; and, before the small talk was half over, he shouted again: "Sir Harry Payne, Major Rockley, Mr Morton Denville."

Richard Linnell told himself that he was no spy, but he could not keep his eyes from the group, as the officers entered, and were received by Claire.

It was a crucial meeting, but she bore it well, bowing rather stiffly to Major Rockley as he advanced in a deprecating way; and he was evidently about to stay by her side, but Isaac announced:

"Mrs and Miss Dean."

There was a little buzz of excitement.

"Mrs Pontardent."

This lady meant to be before her *protégées*; but she was in time after all, and after a quiet, unaffected welcome from Claire, they formed a little group by themselves, about whom, like flies attracted by bright colours, the officers buzzed.

Mrs Pontardent was a tall, good-looking, lady-like woman, who patronised the Master of the Ceremonies when they spoke, and complimented him upon the appearance of "his little girl."

"You must bring her to one of my evenings, Denville."

He would have said "Impossible" had he dared. As it was, he said he should be charmed, and this set him thinking about how much money was won and lost there, when fresh arrivals took up his attention, and soon after Isaac announced:

"Mr and Mrs Frank Burnett."

Claire uttered a sigh of relief as she shook hands with her sister and brother-in-law, the latter pairing off directly with one of the officers.

"Well," said May eagerly, "is all right?"

"Yes, dear; but they want money, and I have none."

"Oh, dear, money again! Well, I'll see."

"But, May dear, you must do something more."

"What do you mean?"

"This task grows more difficult every day. You must really make some arrangements, or I shall be compromised."

"Well, how shall I be? do you want me to be compromised? I declare you have no more feeling than a stone."

"May—dear May!"

"It's quite true. I'm disgraced by my family at every turn. What with brothers turning common soldiers, and horrors in the house, and—"

"My dear Mrs Burnett, this is an unexpected pleasure," said Sir Harry Payne, coming up with Lord Carboro', who managed to cut in before Rockley, who was approaching Claire.

"Oh, what a wicked, wicked story-teller you are!" said May, with childish playfulness, as Sir Harry remained by her side, while Lord Carboro' led off Claire. "You knew I was coming."

"I did, I did," he whispered passionately.

"Hush! Don't go on like that. Everybody is watching us."

"Then when will you give me a chance to see you alone?"

"Oh, I couldn't think of such a thing."

"May! dearest May."

"Hush!"

The conversation was carried on in a low tone, and then May exclaimed:

"Oh, impossible!"

"It is not," he said eagerly. "It is simplicity itself."

He whispered again, and May Burnett shook her head.

"I implore you," he whispered. "You know all I feel, but you are as hard and cold as you are beautiful. There, I swear if you do not consent, I'll—"

"Pistols, or off the pier?" said May, with a provoking smile.

"Oh, you are maddening!" he exclaimed. "I believe you would like to see me lying dead."

"Oh, no; I don't like to see dead people," she said mockingly.

"All these weary months, and not one short interview. You are playing with me. Curse him!"

"Curse whom?" said May coolly.

"That husband of yours. I'll pick a quarrel with him next time we play cards and shoot him."

"Ha—ha—ha—ha—ha!"

It was a sweetly innocent sounding little trill of laughter as ever passed from a provoking pouting rosebud of a mouth; and Claire heard it, and turned paler than ordinary, as she saw in whose company her sister was.

"You will excuse me now, Lord Carboro'," she said. "I have my duties as hostess to attend to."

"One moment," he said, placing his back to the company, and gazing with a look of such reverence as he had not for long years felt for woman in the sweet face before him.

Claire looked up at him half wonderingly.

"I am a very old friend of your father, Miss Denville."

"Oh, yes, my lord. I remember you when I was quite a little child."

"And now," he said, "I am getting to be an old man, and you have grown into a beautiful woman. Will you—do not be alarmed; no one can see—will you accept this little offering from so old a friend, and wear it for his sake?"

He held out the lustrous necklace as he spoke, believing that they were quite unseen; but it was not so, for Colonel Mellersh said softly to Linnell:

"There, Dick, what did I tell you?"

"Lord Carboro'," said Claire, with quiet dignity, "I could only take so valuable a jewel from—from—"

"A very dear friend, my child. Let me be that friend."

She looked at him searchingly, and then dropped her eyes, saying nothing, but drawing back with a slight gesture that was unmistakable, and glided away.

"The mentor is not always right, Colonel Mellersh," said Richard Linnell quietly. "I feel as if I had been playing the spy, but I do not regret it, from the effect it must have on you."

"Egad, she's a very queen," said Lord Carboro', as he quietly took out his snuff-box, and dropped the necklet into his pocket. "By George, sir, I never thought there was such a woman in the world."

The conversation was at its height, and Claire twice over managed to intercept Sir Harry when he was approaching her sister, but only to be snubbed for her pains by May. She was conscious that Rockley was seeking an opportunity to approach her, but she gave him none, her position as hostess giving her plenty of chances for avoiding those she did not wish to meet, in attending and introducing others.

"Hang the girl! she's a regular sorceress," said Colonel Mellersh to himself. "She'll end by charming me. I want a game at cards, and if I leave Dick, he'll be hanging on to her strings directly."

"Well, mother, are you satisfied?" said Cora, as the evening went by.

"Satisfied? Oh, I don't mind, my dear, so long as you get on. And you are, you know, sitting here among the big people, I say, Cory, I am proud of you."

"That's right, mother."

"But I say, what did Colonel Mellersh say to you as he went to the card-table?"

"Asked me, as any gentleman would, whether he should take me down to have some refreshment."

"Well, that was kind and neighbourly. I rather like him, but I do wish you wouldn't encourage that young Linnell so."

"Mother!"

"There, I've done. I won't say another word. Don't fly out at me here. Now, that is a man to admire."

"What, Mr Richard Linnell?"

"No: stuff, Cory. You know who I mean—that Major Rockley. I couldn't hear a word he said to you. I wouldn't, for I don't like to stand in your way. I say, Cory, he'll be a Colonel and a General some day. Why not him?"

"Would you like to know what he said to me, mother?"

"Yes; he did quite make love to you, didn't he?"

"Yes."

"Hah, I thought so."

Mrs Dean's rings crackled as she rubbed her hands, and metaphorically hugged herself.

"That comes of getting into good society, Cora. Ladies drop into engagements without having to look after the gentlemen. You see, they are so brought together like. That Denville puts a sort of stamp on you like, and then you're in society, and handsome Majors come and throw themselves at your feet."

"Yes," said Cora, speaking through her teeth, "and insult you, and dare to speak to you as if you were some beautiful toy brought and set up for their amusement."

"Cory!"

"I tell you that every word he spoke to me in his mocking gallant way was an insult, and made my fingers tingle and my face burn. Mother, I've found out that there are two classes of men in the world."

"Oh, my gracious! now she's off again," sighed Mrs Dean.

"There are those who naturally honour and respect woman with all the manly chivalry of their nature, and those who look upon her as a being several degrees lower than themselves. Mother, that man made me feel to-night as if I could kill him."

"Oh dear; oh dear!" sighed Mrs Dean in a whisper to her daughter, "if this is coming into society, and you are going on talking in that savage way, we had better stop at home. I expect you snubbed the Major in that orty way of yours, and he has gone after that chit of Denville's."

"Where? Has he mother?" cried Cora, in an excited whisper.

"Yes; he is bending over her and making big eyes at her. I say, he is a handsome man, Cory, and if I know anything, he's regularly took with her."

"Are you sure, mother?"

"Sure? Just as if I couldn't tell in a moment. You might get him away from her if you liked, I dare say. Look at that."

She drew back a little that her child might see where Rockley was speaking in a markedly deferential manner to Claire; and Cora's colour went and came, and her bosom heaved in unison.

"Bless your 'art, Cory, I ain't lived to my age without picking up a little. Why, since I've been sitting here to-night I've picked up no end, and if I was a scandalous old woman I could make any amount of mischief."

Cora did not answer, for just then Lord Carboro' came up.

"Let me take you down to have a jelly, Miss Dean," he said.

Cora looked up at him and was about to refuse; but there was such a quiet, respectful look in the old man's eyes that she took his arm.

"I'll come and fetch you afterwards, Mrs Dean," he said and they crossed the room.

"There," said Mrs Dean. "Now I'm a happy woman. It might be after all. Countess—not a Shakespeare countess or duchess for six nights only, as it says in the bills, but altogether. Hah, I paid for this party, and I don't grudge the money, and Denville's made himself a friend. I was going to say to my gal: there's that Sir Matthew Bray making up to old Lady Drelincourt, and that Sir Harry Payne to Mrs Burnett, and Major Rockley to Claire Denville, and young Linnell as jealous as can be. And now, to top off with and finish the scene, Lord Carboro' comes and takes off my Cora. Well, we're in society at last."

"Look here, old woman, this bracelet case is banging against my leg horribly, and if I have two things old Drelincourt will hesitate between them and take neither. If I've only one she may take it. I think I can get her alone now. Here, slip this into your pocket."

"Oh, but Jo-si-ah, I can't."

"Yes, you can, stupid; you've got lots of room. Here, I want to clear my expenses to-night."

"Why, you have, Jo-si-ah."

"Pooh! That's nothing. Here, catch hold."

He slipped the case into his wife's hand, and she took it and passed it under a fold of her satin dress.

Barclay strolled away to try and get hold of Lady Drelincourt, and just then Denville came up.

"My dear Mrs Barclay," he said, "you have been sitting all alone so long, and I could not get to you, and poor Claire is so busy."

"Oh, don't you mind me, Mr Denville. I'm nobody."

"But you must be faint."

"Well, since you put it like that, Mr Denville, I really have got such a dreadful feeling of sinking inside me that if it was only a sangwidge and a glass of sherry, I'd say bless you."

"Come then, my dear madam," said Denville. "This way."

She rose and took the offered arm, and Lord Carboro' smiled as the florid little woman went by him. Then he drew back by a curtain, and began taking snuff and watching Claire, as she now stood still, and he saw her meet Linnell's eyes just as Rockley, who had been watching his opportunity, was going up to her.

Linnell looked at her with eyes that said, "May I come?" and he read that long, calm, trustful gaze to say "Yes."

"Very nicely done. In a sweet maidenly way," said Lord Carboro'. "How cleverly a woman can do that sort of thing, making one man a shield against another. By George! she is a queen—a woman of whom a man might be proud."

Rockley went scowling back, and threw himself on the seat where Mrs Barclay had been; and from where he stood Lord Carboro' looked at him sneeringly.

"Old, worn out, withered as I am, handsome Rockley, if Claire Denville became my wife, I shouldn't care a snap for you. Ugh! why, I must be standing just where old Teigne was smothered. How horrible! Pish, what matters! Why should I care, when her dear sister is laughing and showing her false teeth there just where the foot of the bedstead used to be. Sweet girlish creature; she's ogling that fat dragoon, and she'll marry him if she can."

He took another pinch of snuff.

"Hallo!" he muttered, "Payne after that little strawberry cream of a woman. We shall have a scandal there, as sure as fate, and—good girl, she sees through her and cuts the enemy out. Claire, my dear, you are indeed a little queen among women. I've never given you half the credit you deserve, and—damme!—never!—yes—no—yes!—the scoundrel! Well, that comes of reckless play. Curse it all, there must not be such a scandal as this. Where's Denville?"

He looked round, but the Master of the Ceremonies had not returned with Mrs Barclay.

Everybody was fully engaged, laughing, flirting, or card-playing. Assignations were being made; money was changing hands, and the candles were burning down and guttering at the sides, as Lord Carboro' exclaimed:

"Hang it! I did not think he could stoop to be such a scoundrel as that!"

# Chapter Thirteen
# Major Rockley's Mistake

"Now, Barclay, you are a wicked flatterer," said Lady Drelincourt, as she sat out in the balcony, with the money-lender leaning over her after leading her there and placing a chair.

"I shall risk being rude in my rough way," said Barclay in a low voice, "and repeat my words. I said those lustrous diamonds would look perfect on your ladyship's beautiful throat."

"Now, you don't mean it, Barclay. I am not so young as I was, and my throat is not beautiful now."

"There, I'm a plain man," said Barclay; "I've no time for fine sayings and polished phrases, and what I say is this: I know your ladyship must be forty."

"Yes, Barclay, I am," said Lady Drelincourt, with a sigh.

"I'm fifty-five," he said, "and what I say is, how a woman with a skin like yours can utter such deprecatory sentiments is a puzzle. Why, half the women here would be proud of such a skin. Look how they paint. Pah!"

"They do, Barclay; they do. Are the diamonds of good water?"

"Look," he said, holding them before him.

"No, no; some one in the room will see."

"I'll take care of that, my lady. Look at them. I daren't tell you whom they once belonged to, but they came to me through accidents at the gaming-table. They are perfect in match and size. Lady Drelincourt, you would not be doing yourself justice if you did not buy them. I wish I dare clasp them on."

"No, no; not now. How much did you say?"

"I am giving them away at four hundred guineas, Lady Drelincourt."

"Oh, but that's a terrible price, Barclay!"

"They will be worth more in a year or two, Lady Drelincourt."

"Oh, but I could not spare so much money."

"Pooh! what of that! If your ladyship likes the diamonds—"

"I do like them, Barclay."

"I should be happy to give your ladyship what credit you require."

"Really, this is very naughty of me, Barclay; it is, indeed, but I suppose I must have them. There, slip them into my hand. You can send me the case to-morrow."

"I will, my lady. You'll never regret the purchase, and I am delighted that they will be worn by the queen of Saltinville society."

"Go away, flatterer, and tell Sir Matthew Bray to bring me my salts. I left them on the chimney-piece."

"I fly," said Barclay; and he went through the rooms to perform his commission, Sir Matthew hurrying to get to her ladyship's side, while Barclay turned to meet his wife who was just returning with their host.

"Hallo!"

"Oh, I am so much better now, Jo-si-ah. I was so faint."

"Ah, Denville, I want a word with you," said Lord Carboro', coming up box in hand.

"I say, old lady," whispered Barclay, "got that bracelet safe?"

"Oh, yes, that's all right; but you can't have it."

"Why not?"

"Because it's right down at the very bottom of my pocket, where there's no getting at it at all. But you don't want it now?"

"No. I've sold the diamond necklace."

"No!"

"I have, to that old hag, Drelincourt."

"Did she pay you?"

"No; but we've got deeds worth four times as much, and I shall charge her interest until she pays."

"Then you've had a splendid night, Jo-si-ah."

"Glorious!" he said, rubbing his hands.

"Then I want a rubber of whist, and I shall see if I can't win a few guineas myself."

"All right. I'll get you to a table."

"Denville, old fellow," said Lord Carboro', chatting with his host and taking snuff from the box given by the Prince, "I've a bad habit of seeing everything that goes on around me."

"Your lordship is most observant."

"I'm sorry to say I am; and whether we become relatives or not, Denville, I take an interest in you and your belongings."

The Master of the Ceremonies looked up in alarm.

"Take a bit of good advice, Denville."

"My lord!"

"And keep a tighter rein over your daughter."

"Your lordship's opinions seem to change easily," said Denville bitterly. "The other day my daughter Claire—"

"Pooh! Absurd, man! Stop. She is perfect. A princess could not have been a more charming hostess. I did not mean her. Look there!"

"Mrs Burnett with Sir Harry Payne?"

"Yes; the fellow's a blackguard. The little woman married a fool—"

"My lord!"

"Who neglects her for drink and play. Don't be offended, Denville. I am your friend. You have had scandal enough in your family; you must have no more."

Denville drew a long breath.

"Your lordship is right; but you must not misunderstand my dear child."

"Pretty, sweet, young, and most impressionable, Denville. Constant dropping will wear a stone. Don't let the water drop on it any more."

"My lord, you may trust me."

"Stop, Denville. Another thing in confidence. You must get it back, treating it all as an error."

"My lord, you alarm me. Get *it* back?"

"I can't help it, Denville. Do you know that sometimes dashing fellows, ruined by play, have gone on the road mounted and masked, and, pistol in hand, have robbed?"

"Yes, my lord. But we have no highwaymen here."

"Don't be too sure. Did you know that Barclay, at my wish, brought some jewellery?"

"Yes, but not at my wish, my lord! I felt aggrieved—insulted."

"Forgive him and me. It was at my request. I wanted to make an offering—a string of pearls—to your daughter; and, like the sweet true lady she is, she has refused to accept them."

Denville flushed and turned pale as he glanced proudly at his child, where she stood talking to Colonel Mellersh.

"I saw Barclay give his wife a case with a diamond bracelet in it, to hold while he went to old Drelincourt."

"Yes, my lord. What of that?"

"Mrs Barclay did not put it in her pocket, but let it slip down on the carpet."

"Where was she seated, my lord?"

"Never mind; the diamond bracelet was found."

"Thank goodness!" gasped Denville.

"By Major Rockley."

"Who gave it back?"

"No; who has pocketed it, and will keep it; while Barclay will most likely credit you."

"Impossible, my lord!"

"Possible, Denville. I tell you there must be no more robberies here. Hang it, man, stand up."

"A sudden giddiness, my lord. I am better now. I will get the jewels back. But, one moment, my lord, are you really quite sure?"

"I am certain."

"But Major Rockley may mean—"

"Hush, Denville. What do you know of handsome Rockley? Do you think he will give the jewels back if he can get them away? Act; at once."

"Suppose he is wrong," said Denville to himself, as he went off on his painful task. "What an insult to an officer—the Prince's friend."

"I dare not do it," he said after a pause. "It must be some mistake. Such an act would be the work of a common thief. He must be wrong."

He shrank from his task, but he felt that it must be done, for how could he let it go forth that there had been another diamond robbery from his house. It was impossible.

As he hesitated he caught sight of Lord Carboro' watching him. Barclay too was there, evidently about to speak to him, and he felt that he must. Better to offend Major Rockley than have another scandal.

He mingled among his guests with a word here and there, sending some downstairs, and interfering in a *tête-à-tête* between May and Sir Harry Payne, who had at last won a promise from the giddy little creature to whom he was paying court. He then went up to Rockley, snuff-box in hand, and addressed him as he was leaning against the chimney-piece.

"I'm afraid our little reunion has no charms for you, Major Rockley," he said.

"On the contrary, my dear Denville, I am delighted."

"But you have had no refreshment. Pray come down."

"Without a lady?"

"Yes, without a lady. Or, no, I will speak now, and you can go afterwards. A little mistake, Major Rockley. You'll pardon me; a little mistake."

His heart sank as he spoke, and he trembled almost guiltily at the task he had in hand.

The Major's dark eyes flashed as he scowled at him.

"If you mean, sir, that by addressing—"

"No, no, Major Rockley; a little mistake. You thought you dropped your snuff-box."

"I thought I dropped my snuff-box, sir? Are you mad?"

"You'll pardon me, Major Rockley, no. You made a mistake; it is my duty to see the matter right. You imagined that you dropped your snuff-box, and you picked it up, when you were seated a little while ago."

"Well, sir?"

If Lord Carboro' had made a mistake, how dare he meet that man again?

"You do not seem to understand me, Major Rockley. The case you picked up was not a snuff-box, but contained jewels belonging to one of my guests."

"I did not know your guests carried their jewels in cases, Mr Denville," said the Major, with a forced laugh. "They seem to be wearing them."

"It is so easy to make a mistake, Major Rockley," continued the MC, on finding that it was more simple to attack than he had expected.

"I never make mistakes, sir," said the Major haughtily.

"I should not have spoken to you like this, sir, if the act had not been seen," said Denville, angrily now.

"Act? Seen? Good heavens, sir! Do you take me for a thief?" said Rockley, in a hoarse whisper. "Do you think—why—confound! I am astounded!"

He had been angrily thrusting a hand into first one and then another pocket, bringing out a snuff-box, then a handkerchief, and lastly the little morocco case.

"That must be it, Major Rockley," said the MC coldly; and their eyes met with a curiously long stare.

"As you say, Mr Denville, mistakes are so easily made. I am in your debt for this—I shall never forget it. You will excuse me now, I am sure. The little matter has agitated me more than I should care to own."

The MC bowed.

"Seen, you said, I think? Was it you who saw me pick up that case—by accident?"

"No, sir."

"Would you oblige me with the name of the person?"

"It is not necessary," said Denville. "I am master of the ceremonies, sir, of my own house. This affair, I may tell you, will be kept private by us both."

Major Rockley bowed and turned to gaze round the room, to see if he could select Denville's informant; but there was no one whom he felt ready to blame but Richard Linnell—Barclay he knew it could not be—or was it that handsome Cora Dean?

He turned again close by the door, and tried to catch Claire Denville's eyes; but she was talking gravely to Linnell, so, half bowing to Denville, he said quietly:

"Thank you for excusing me. Of course, I rely upon the discretion of yourself and friend. Adieu."

"*Adieu,*" and he left with curses and deadly threats in his breast.

"Had man ever such luck!" he hissed, as he strode by the house, glancing up at the well-lit balcony and drawing-room, from which he turned with an involuntary shudder. "Curse the old idiot, but I'll serve him out for this presently. I wonder whether the old dancing-master cares for his girl and boy? Well," he added, with a peculiar smile, "we shall soon see."

# Chapter Fourteen
# At the Card-Table

"Friends?" Richard Linnell was saying, as he stood looking earnestly at Claire. "Nothing more?"

"No," she said, in a low, sad voice; "always, come what may, your grateful friend."

She turned to her sister, who was watching her, and met her with:

"Claire dear, you're going mad. That man hasn't a penny."

"Well?" said Claire gravely. "And you are encouraging him."

"As you are encouraging Sir Harry Payne? No, May; you are mistaken."

"I declare if you are going to insult me I will not stay," cried May, turning scarlet. "It is disgraceful. It is cruel. If I could only find Frank—"

Just then a loud burst of angry voices came from one of the card-tables. It was eleven o'clock; there had been refreshments; the room was very hot, and the play, for ladies, high; and now the voice of the Master of the Ceremonies was heard in protest.

"Ladies—ladies—I beg—I must request—"

"Order my carriage directly, Sir Matthew. It serves me right for coming to such a place," cried Lady Drelincourt.

"Yes; you had no business here," cried Mrs Barclay.

"And mixing with such low people," cried Lady Drelincourt.

"Low people? Better be low than not honest."

"Oh! oh!—Denville, are you going to allow this insult to my face—from such a woman as that?" cried Lady Drelincourt.

"Hush, ladies! Pray—pray!" cried Denville.

"Hold your tongue and come away, old lady," said Barclay, in a croaking whisper.

"I won't, Jo-si-ah; not till she pays me my four guineas, I declare," cried Mrs Barclay aloud. "She's been doing nothing but cheat and rook ever since I sat down to play."

"Sir Matthew Bray, my carriage."

"And gone on shameful, and pretending it was all mistakes. I declare it's abominable."

"Ladies—ladies!"

"Will you be quiet, old girl? Hold your tongue."

"I will not, Josiah," cried Mrs Barclay, who, like many good-tempered, amiable women, took a great deal to make her angry, but when she was really excited, was not to be suppressed. "What I say is—"

"Oh—oh—oh—oh!"

A series of wild, hysterical cries from a couch in the front room, and Claire ran gladly from the painful scene to where her sister was in a violent hysterical fit, which, with the exit of Lady Drelincourt on Sir Matthew Bray's arm, after a withering glance round, quite stopped Mrs Barclay's vituperative attack.

"Think of that now," cried the latter lady. "Me again. I ought not to come out."

"That you oughtn't," growled Barclay. "Next thing will be you've lost that bracelet."

"Nonsense, Josiah. Let me help you, Claire dear. I am so sorry, but that wretched cheating old woman was either kicking me under the table in mistake for that Sir Matthew Bray, or else cheating. I am so—so sorry. It's 'sterricks, that's what it is."

"Yes, that's what it is," said Mrs Dean; "and if I might say a word, I should tell Mr Denville that he couldn't do better than behave like Lady Macbeth."

"Oh, mother!" whispered Cora impatiently.

"Now what's the good of you 'oh mothering' me, my dear? What could be better than for Mr Denville to say to his guests, 'Don't be on the order of your going, but go at once'?"

"Miss Dean," said Sir Harry, "your mamma speaks the words of wisdom. It is the wisest thing. Come, gentlemen, we can be of no service here. By Jove, she does it to perfection."

Mrs Dean's words broke up the party, and the visitors had nearly all gone, when, in answer to cold bathing and smelling-salts, Mrs Burnett began to recover; and just then Frank Burnett, who had been, no one but Isaac knew where, came up to make a fresh scene as he threw himself upon his knees beside the couch, imploring in maudlin tones his darling May to speak and tell him what it was.

"Oh, my head, my head!" sobbed the stricken wife. "My head, my head!"

"You'd better let her be, Mr Burnett, sir," said Mrs Barclay. "It's my belief that quiet's the thing."

"Yes, and we'll go," said Mrs Dean. "Good-night, Miss Denville. Good-night, Mr Denville, and thank you so much. Come, Cora, love."

Cora Dean glanced at Richard Linnell and Mellersh as she advanced to say good-night; for they were going to the same house, and it was possible, as the distance was short, that they would see them home.

"Good-night, Mr Denville," she said.

"We will say good-night too," said Mellersh, "unless we can be of any use."

"Oh, no," said their host. "She will soon be better—a mere trifle."

"Yes, please let me be," said Mrs Burnett. "I shall soon be better now."

"Good-night," said Cora, holding out her hand to the woman she told herself she hated with all her heart.

But it was in a spirit of triumph, for Richard Linnell was going to walk home with her.

"Good-night," said Claire, smiling in her face with a calm ingenuous look. "I am glad we have met."

How it came about they neither of them knew, but it was Claire's seeking; she was suffering so from that heart hunger—that painful searching for the love and sympathy of some woman of her age, while Cora Dean's handsome face was so near to her, and she kissed her as one sister might another.

"Well, I never," muttered Mrs Dean as she went down the stairs. "Think of that, and you as don't like her."

The next minute Cora Dean and her mother were walking along the Parade with Linnell and Mellersh on either side, chatting about the evening.

"One cigar, Dick, before we go to bed," said Mellersh, when they had been sitting together in his room for some time, after parting from their upstairs neighbours.

"I'm willing," said Linnell, "for I feel as if I could not sleep."

They lit their cigars, let themselves out, strolled down to the edge of the water, walked along by it in front of the Parade, and went upon the cliff again, to go back silently along the path till they neared the house where they had passed the evening, walking very slowly, and ending by stopping to lean over the cliff rails and gaze out to sea.

How long this had lasted they did not know, but all at once, as Mellersh turned, he gripped Richard Linnell by the arm and pointed.

Linnell saw it at the same moment: the figure of a man climbing over a balcony; and as they watched they could just see the gleam of one of the windows as it was evidently opened and he passed in.

"Dick!" whispered Mellersh; "what does that mean?" "The same as the night that poor old woman was slain. Quick! Come on!"

"Stop!" said Mellersh. "Here's another!"

# Chapter Fifteen
# Mrs Burnett's Seizure

"I think we had better go too," said Mrs Barclay at last. "But are you quite sure we can do no good?"

"No: indeed no, Mrs Barclay; and I am so much obliged to you for staying," replied Claire.

"It was the least I could do, my dear, after making all that miserable rumpus about a few paltry guineas. Your papa will never forgive me."

"Indeed, there is nothing to forgive, my dear Mrs Barclay. It was natural that you should be indignant," said Denville politely.

"Thank you very much for saying so, but it's always the way if I go out, and I shouldn't be at all surprised if there's something else wrong," cried Mrs Barclay piteously. "I'm a most unfortunate creature."

"There, put on your things and let's go," said Barclay huffily. "Give me that case. I'll carry it now, or you'll lose that."

Mrs Barclay began to thrust her hand into her pocket, and Denville was talking to his son-in-law at the other end of the room, while Claire bent over and kissed her sister.

"Are you better now, dear?"

"No-o! Oh, my head!—my head!"

"My darling!" cried Burnett, coming back and bringing with him a strong smell of cigars and bad wine.

"Don't, Frank. Don't you see how ill I am?"

"Yes, yes, my own, but the carriage is waiting. Let me help you down, and let's go home."

"Oh! My gracious! Oh!" shrieked Mrs Barclay.

"Oh!—oh!—oh!—oh!" sobbed May Burnett, again in a worse fit than before.

"Now you've done it again," cried Barclay angrily. "There never was such a woman. Here, come along home."

"The case—the bracelet, Jo-si-ah!"

"Well. What about it?"

"I knew something would happen. I felt it coming."

"Stop! Where's that diamond bracelet, woman?"

"It's gone, Jo-si-ah. I've lost it. It's gone."

"A two hundred pound bracelet, and gone!" roared Barclay. "Eh, what? Thank ye, Denville. How did you come by it?"

Denville, who was standing in a graceful attitude, smilingly offering the case, explained that Mrs Barclay had let it fall beneath the seat when she thought that she was placing it in her pocket.

"Oh, Mr Denville," cried Mrs Barclay, "you *are* a dear good man!"

"Denville! Thank ye!" said Barclay, shaking hands. "You might have stuck to that, and I should have been no wiser. I shan't forget this. Good-night, old man, good-night."

"Coarse, but very kindly," said Denville, after Mrs Barclay had made Claire's face wet with tears and kisses, and he had seen the pair to the door.

"Yes," said Burnett; "they're a rough couple. Come, May, no nonsense. Get up. I'm not going to have my horses kept waiting all night."

May made an effort to rise, but sank back, sobbing hysterically:

"My head!—my head!"

"Here, give her some brandy, Claire," cried Burnett.

"No, no, no. It makes it worse."

"Well, it will be better to-morrow. Come along."

"No, no, I cannot bear it. Oh, my head!—my head!"

"Let me bathe it with the eau de Cologne," said Claire tenderly.

"No, no. I cannot bear it."

"Then come home," cried Burnett.

"No, no," moaned his wife. "I'm so ill—so ill. Papa—couldn't I stay here to-night—my own old little room?"

"Yes, yes, my darling," said Denville tenderly.

"I am so ill, papa. My head throbs so if I move it."

"Let her stay, Frank," said Claire sympathisingly.

"Not I. What! go home without her? I'll be hanged if I do!" cried Burnett pettishly. "She'll be all right as soon as she gets out into the air. Now, May, jump up."

He caught her by the arm, but May uttered a wail.

"Frank, dear, you are cruel," said Claire.

"You mind your own business," said the irritable little fellow sharply. "She has got to come home with me."

"I—I—I can't, Frank. I am so ill."

"Nonsense! Sick headache. I often have them. You've taken too much wine."

"She has not had any, Frank," said Claire indignantly.

"Then she ought to have had some. That's the reason. You hold your tongue. Now, madam, jump up."

The MC had stood looking on, with his face working, but saying no word till now that Burnett caught his wife roughly by both hands and tried to pull her to her feet.

"Stop!" he cried firmly. "Really, Frank Burnett, you are ungentle in the extreme."

"Here, I know what I'm doing," he retorted. "She's my wife."

"And she's my daughter, sir," cried Denville haughtily; "and while I am by no half-tipsy man shall insult her."

"Half-tipsy? Who's half-tipsy? This is the result of coming here, sir."

"Where I have been on thorns for the last two hours, lest my guests should see what a state you were in."

"State? What do you mean?"

"I will not expose you more before your young wife," said Denville quietly. "We are both angry, and had better say good-night. May, do you feel well enough to go home?"

"No; oh no, papa."

"You hear, Frank Burnett. Claire, you can easily get her bedroom ready."

"Look here, I shan't stay," cried Burnett. "I shan't stay here."

"Well, go home then. We will take care of her, you may depend."

"It's all nonsense. She shall come home."

"My child is not well enough to go home," retorted Denville.

"Frank dear, don't be obstinate, for May's sake," said Claire. "There, go home, dear. I'll get her to bed soon, and she'll be better in the morning."

Burnett looked from one to the other with his teeth set, and was about to burst out into an angry tirade; but he met the firm, cold gaze of his father-in-law fixed upon him, and it was irresistible. It literally looked him down; and, with an impatient curse, he left the house and banged the door.

Directly after they heard the rattle of carriage-wheels, and May uttered a sigh of relief as she watched the MC walk round the room extinguishing the candles.

"Oh, papa dear," she sobbed, "he does behave so badly to me!"

"My child!" said Denville sadly, as he bent down and kissed her. "You are weary and excited to-night. Pray say no more."

He left the room, and went downstairs to bid the servants leave everything till morning, and go to bed; and as the door closed Claire knelt down beside her sister, and laid her hand upon her burning forehead.

"That's nice," sighed May; and then she sat up suddenly, glanced round, and flung her arms round Claire's neck to hide her face in her breast, and burst into a passionate fit of sobbing.

"Oh, hush, hush, May, my darling," whispered Claire tenderly, as she kissed and caressed the pretty little head, which was jerked up again in an angry, spasmodic way.

"You saw—you heard," she cried, with her face flushed and her eyes flashing, as she talked in a quick, low, excited manner. "You blamed me for loving poor Louis. Why, he was all that was gentle and kind. He loved me in his fierce Italian way, and he was so jealous that he would have killed me if I had given him cause. But so tender and loving; while this nasty, hateful little Frank—"

"May: oh, hush!"

"I won't hush. I hate him. I despise him. A mean, shabby, spiteful little wretch! You saw him to-night. He pinched me, and wrung my wrists. He often hurts me."

"May!—May!"

"It's true. He strikes me, too; and I tell you I hate him."

"May! Your husband, whom you have sworn to honour and love!"

"And I don't either, and I never shall," cried May sharply.

"You must, you must, May, my darling. There, there; you are flushed and excited with your head being so bad, and Frank was not so gentle as he might have been. He was vexed because you had turned ill."

"Nasty, fretful wretch!"

"May!"

"I don't care; he is," cried the little foolish thing, looking wonderfully like an angry child as she spoke.

"Hush! I will not let you speak of your husband like that, May."

"Husband! A contemptible little tipsy wretch who bought me of papa because I was pretty. I loathe him, I tell you. Papa ought to have been ashamed of himself for selling me as he did."

"May! May! little sister!" said Claire, weeping silently as she drew her baby head to her bosom, and tried to stay the flow of bitter words that came.

"Horses and carriages, and servants and dresses, and nothing else but misery. I tell you—I don't care! If he ever beats me again I'll run away from him, that I will."

"No, no, little passionate, tender heart," said Claire lovingly. "You are ill and troubled to-night. There, there. You shall sleep quietly to-night under the old roof. Why, May dear, it seems like the dear old times, and you are the little girl again whom I am going to undress and put to bed. There, you are better now."

"Old times? What, of misery and poverty and wretchedness, and having servants that you cannot pay, and struggling to keep up appearances, and all for what?"

"Oh, hush, hush, little May!" said Claire, holding her to her breast, and half sadly, half playfully, rocking herself to and fro.

"You don't know what trouble is. You don't know what it is to have your tenderest feelings torn. You never knew what it was to suffer as I have. I hate him."

She could not see Claire's ghastly face, nor the agonised twitching of the nerves about her lips which her sister was striving to master.

"No one knows what I have had to suffer," she went on; "and it's too hard—it's too hard to bear. No one loves me, no one cares for me. It's all misery and wretchedness, and—and I wish I was dead."

"No, no, no, darling," said Claire, as she drew the sobbing little thing closer to her breast; "don't say that. I love you dearly, my own sister, and it breaks my heart to see you unhappy. But there, there, you are so weary and ill to-night that it makes everything look so black. I suffer too, darling, for your sake—for all our sakes, and now I will not scold you."

"Scold me?" cried May, in affright.

"No, not one word; only pray to you to be careful of your dear, sweet little self. My darling, I am so proud of my beautiful little sister. You will not be frivolous again, and give me so much pain?"

"N-no," sighed May, with her face buried in her sister's breast.

"Frank—"

"Don't—don't speak of him."

"Yes, yes; he is your husband, and you must try to win him over to you by gentleness, instead of being a little angry tyrant."

"Clairy!"

"Yes, but you can be," said Claire playfully, as she pressed her lips upon the soft, flossy hair. "I can remember how these little hands used to beat at me, and the little tearful eyes flash anger at me in the old times."

Just then Denville entered the room softly, with a weary, dissatisfied air; but, as he stood in the doorway unnoticed, his whole aspect changed, and the tears stood in his eyes.

"God bless them!" he said fervently; and then, as he saw May raise her head, and look excitedly in her sister's face, he stepped forward.

"Well, little bird," he said, bending down to kiss May's forehead, "back once more in the old nest?"

Claire looked searchingly at him as she rose from her knees; and then she sighed as she saw May fling herself into her father's arms.

"There, there, I shall make the head ache again," he said, with a calm, restful smile upon his lips, such as Claire had not seen for months.

"How he loves her!" she thought; and then another idea flashed through her breast. Suppose May knew!

"Claire, my child, is her room ready?"

"Yes; Morton's room is prepared in case he came back. She will sleep there unless—May, will you come to me?"

"Yes, yes," cried the little girlish thing, in a quick excited way. "No, no; I'll be alone. Let me go now—at once."

Claire fetched and gave her a lighted candle, finding her clinging passionately to her father, looking, as it seemed to the thoughtful woman, like some frightened child.

She kissed him hastily, and seemed to snatch the candle from her sister's hand.

"Good-night, Claire," she cried, holding up her face, and clinging tightly to her sister's arm.

"I am going with you, dear—as I used to in the old times," said Claire, smiling; and they left the room together.

"Without one word to me," said Denville, as he stood with clasped hands gazing at the door. "Well, why should I be surprised? What must I be in her sight? Her father! Yes, but a monster without pity—utterly vile."

He heaved a piteous sigh, as he sank into a chair.

"No," he said to himself, "I will not influence her in any way. I will not stir. It would be too cruel. But if—if she should lean towards him—who knows?—women have accepted the wealth and position such as he offers. No, I will not stir."

He sighed again, walked to the drawing-room window to see that the bar was across the shutter; and, this done, he turned hastily and gazed back into the room that had been Lady Teigne's chamber, and as he did so the dew stood upon his forehead, for he seemed to see the bed with its dragged curtains, the empty casket on the floor, and by it the knife that he had picked up and hidden in his breast.

Yes, there it all was, and Claire standing gazing at him with that horrified look of suspicion in her beautiful face, as the thought came which had placed an icy barrier between them ever since. Yes, there she was, staring at him so wildly, and it was like a horrible nightmare, and—

"Father—are you ill?"

"Claire! Is it you? No, no; nothing the matter. Tired; wearied out. So long and anxious an evening. Good-night!"

She had come in to find him staring back into that room in a half cataleptic state; and the sight of his ghastly face brought all back to her. For a few moments she could not move, but at last, by an effort, she spoke, and he seemed to be snatched back by her voice into life and action.

"Good-night, father," she said, trembling as she read the agonies of a conscious-stricken soul in his countenance, and she was moving towards the door, when, with an agonised cry, he turned to her.

"Claire, my child, must it be always so?" he cried, as he clasped his hands towards her as if in prayer.

"Father!" she said, in a voice almost inaudible from emotion.

"Claire, my child," he moaned, as he sank upon his knees before her: "you do not know the burden I have to bear."

She did what she had not done for months, as she stood trembling before him; laid one hand upon his head, while her lips parted as if to speak, but they only quivered and no words came.

At last, with a sobbing cry, she flung herself upon his neck, and he clasped her in his arms.

"Not to me, father," she sobbed, "not to me; I am not your judge."

"No," he said softly, as he reverently kissed her brow; "you are not my judge."

His lips parted to speak again, but he shook his head, while a sad smile came into and brightened his countenance.

"The load is lighter, Claire," he said softly. "No, you are not my judge. If you were you would not condemn me unheard, and I cannot—dare not speak."

He led her towards the door, and stood watching her as she passed upstairs and out of sight, turning her face to him once before she closed the door.

"The sweet pure angel and good genius of my home," he said softly, with bent head, and with a calmer, more restful look in his countenance he went slowly to his own room.

All was soon dark and silent in the house so lately busy with the noise and buzz of many guests. Five minutes had not elapsed when the door was softly pushed open, and a slight little figure entered, and crossed to the window.

The noise made was very slight, as the swinging bar across the shutters was lifted and lowered, one of the shutters folded back, the fastening raised, and the window pushed ajar.

The figure stood in the semi-darkness in the attitude of one listening, and then drew back with a peculiar sigh as of one drawing in breath.

A couple of minutes passed, and then there was a scraping, rustling noise outside, the semi-darkness was deepened by a figure in the balcony, the window was drawn outwards, and a man passed in, whispering:

"May—sweet—are you there?"

A faintly uttered sigh was the response, and quick as thought the French window was closed, a step or two taken into the silent drawing-room, and May Burnett was tightly clasped in the arms of the nocturnal intruder.

"My darling!"

"No, no. Now one word, and you must go," she whispered quickly. "I have done as I promised; now keep your word—to stay only one minute—say one word and go."

"And I will keep it," he cried, "my beautiful little love, my—Damnation!"

May started from his arms, for at that moment there was a thundering knock at the front door, and a violent drag at the bell.

# Chapter Sixteen
## For her Sister's Sake

"Oh, go—go quickly," cried May excitedly. "It is my husband come back; what shall I do?"

"Stop!" cried Sir Harry. "Listen!"

"No, no; they are knocking again. My father will hear."

"But—"

"No, no, you must not stay. Go," she panted, and as she spoke, in her hurry and alarm, she pushed him towards the window.

"Confound it all!" he muttered, as he opened it softly. "Pray, pray be quick," she cried. "Oh, do—do go."

"Impossible!" he whispered back. "They would see. Hide me."

"I can't—I can't."

"You must. Somewhere here."

"No, no! You must go. Oh, what shall I do? I am lost—undone."

"Hush, little woman! Be calm," he said in a hoarse whisper. "I don't know much about this house. Here, I will go downstairs."

"But you cannot; the footman will see you."

"Then, curse it all, hide me upstairs," cried Sir Harry impatiently.

"My father—my sister—what shall I do!—Oh!"

That was all the visitor heard, and the faint cry that ended the sentence was drowned in a second tremendous peal at knocker and bell.

"Confound her! she's gone. May! hist!—May!—Don't leave me like this!"

He felt about for the door, but could not find it in his dread and confusion. Only one part of the room could he make out, and that was the window, by which flight was impossible without being seen.

"Little wretch!" he muttered. "What a fool I am! Where is the cursed door? There were three here somewhere. What the devil am I to do? Curse—"

He kicked against a chair, and nearly knocked it over, and then stumbled against a couch.

"The door must be here somewhere," he muttered. "Yes, there."

It was plain enough where the door was now, for a light shone beneath it, and the sides looked light, showing its shape, just as another peal came from knocker and bell.

He had just time to drop down behind the sofa when the door opened, and the Master of the Ceremonies appeared in his long dressing-gown, candle in hand, crossed the drawing-room, and, opening the farther door, went through, and it swung to, leaving the intruder once more in darkness.

He started up again as he heard the rattle of locks and bolts below, and made for the window, meaning to escape by it as soon as those who had alarmed the house had entered.

"Curse him! Mellersh left to watch," he muttered, as voices were heard from below—loud and angry voices—mingled with those of remonstrance.

"I tell you we saw a man climb up and enter by the balcony," came up; and in his alarm and horror the intruder knocked over an ornament now, as he made for the door that led to the bedrooms—his last chance of escaping unseen.

"Ah, there she is," he said beneath his breath, as the door was made visible once more by the rays of light all round.

"Come up, then, and I will search the place," came from below.

"Don't be alarmed: I'm going to see," said a voice outside the door leading to the upper staircase; and the next moment the door opened, and Claire, in her white dressing-gown, entered candle in hand.

"Sir Harry Payne!" she cried, as the light fell on the figure of the visitor.

"Hush! For heaven's sake, quick! Hide me somewhere. Quick! Before it is too late."

He had caught her by the arm and laid one hand upon her lips; and as she was trying to release herself, the other door opened, and Denville entered, closely followed by Frank Burnett and Richard Linnell.

"Claire! Sir Harry Payne!" cried the Master of the Ceremonies.

"Oh, that's it, is it?" said Burnett, with a grin. "No murder this time, except reputation. I had made up my mind to come and stop to-night, as my wife's here; but, after this, the sooner she's out of this place the better. Here, call her, some of you. Where's her room?"

Claire did not speak, but stood there, as if turned to stone, her eyes fixed upon the cold, stern face of Richard Linnell, as he stood back by the door.

"Sir Harry Payne, speak, I insist," cried Denville fiercely. "What does this mean?"

"Hush, sir! Hush! pray, gentlemen. A little bit of gallantry, nothing more."

"Sir!" cried Denville.

"Hush, sir, pray!" cried Sir Harry, who was white and trembling with dread. "No noise—the neighbours—the scandal. Perfectly innocent, I assure you. An assignation. I came to see Miss Denville here."

Claire turned her eyes slowly from Richard Linnell, whose look seemed to wither her, and fixed them on the despicable scoundrel, who was screening her sister before her husband, but who would not meet her stern gaze.

"I thought as much," said Burnett, with a sneer. "I tell you what—"

"Silence!" hissed a voice in his ear, and a broad, strong hand came down on his shoulder with a grip like a vice.

Claire saw it—the brave, true effort to defend her in her disgrace, and she lifted her eyes once more to Linnell's. Then she let them close, and stood there silent, with the sweet little girlish innocent-looking face of her sister before her, as she stayed listening to the condemnation of husband and father—little May, her father's darling—in her place. One word would save her, would clear her in the sight of the man who loved her, and of the father who stood sternly there; but she must condemn May to save herself, and she stood there as if convicted of the shameful act.

For she spoke no word, and her sister's fame was saved.

# Chapter Seventeen
# A Staunch Friend

"No, Miss Clode; I can be angry, and I can speak my own mind, but I'm not going to be so mean and shabby as to take my custom somewhere else, though it is so tempting; but what I say is this—don't you never say a word to me again about that young lady, or I shall fly out."

"I'm very sorry, ma'am, I'm sure, and you and Mr Barclay are such good customers, besides being my landlord and landlady."

"Oh, there's nothing in that, Miss Clode. You pay your rent to the day, and, as Mr Barclay says, it's a business transaction."

"Of course, it's very painful to me, Mrs Barclay, and I shouldn't have told you what I did, only you know you came and asked me what people were saying."

"Well, so I did. Yes, you're right, I did. But it isn't true, Miss Clode. Miss Claire Denville is as good as gold, and people tell most horrible stories, and where you get to know so much I can't think. But does everybody talk about it?"

"Yes, ma'am, everybody; and Mr and Mrs Burnett haven't been there since."

"I don't care: I won't believe it. And is it a fact that she goes regularly to Fisherman Miggles's to see that little girl?"

"Yes, ma'am, regularly."

"Then she has a good reason for it. There!"

"It's a terrible blow for Mr Denville, of course, ma'am; and they say the young gentleman who has only just joined the dragoons is horribly put out, and challenged Sir Harry Payne, only the Colonel would not let them fight."

"Dear—dear—dear! Poor Denville! he has nothing but misfortunes. I am sorry for him; I am indeed. Well, I must go; but mind this, Miss Clode: Claire Denville is a particular friend of mine, and no one shall say ill of her in my presence."

There was a very strong resemblance to a ruffled hen, whose chickens had been looked at by a strange cat, in Mrs Barclay's aspect as she left Miss Clode's, while, at her aunt's command, Annie, the bun-faced, moved a Berlin wool pattern on one side in the window so that she could command a view of the Parade from the bulging panes, and after watching there for a few minutes she said:

"She's gone by, auntie."

"Ah, with all her fuss, she daren't keep up the acquaintance."

"She has turned back and gone in, auntie."

"Oh, very well, just as she likes; it is no business of mine."

Annie, the innocent, was quite right, for Mrs Barclay had walked by the Denvilles', and then stopped short, indignant with herself; turned back and given a good bold rap at the door, to which Isaac, who looked discontented and strange, replied, and said, before he was asked:

"Not at home."

"Now don't you talk nonsense to me, young man," said Mrs Barclay, "because—"

"My master and mistress are—not—at—"

Isaac began to drag his works towards the last, for Mrs Barclay was rummaging in her reticule for a half-crown, but could only find a good old-fashioned crown, which she slipped into the footman's hand.

To a man-servant who was beginning to look upon his arrears of wages as doubtful, a crown-piece was a coin not to be despised, and he took it and smiled.

"Mr Denville is out, I suppose, isn't he?"

"Yes, ma'am."

"Well, I don't want to see him, but just you go and ask Miss Claire to see me, and if she says no, you say I must see her. There!"

The result was that Mrs Barclay was shown into the drawing-room, where Claire rose to meet her with cold dignity, and pointed to a chair.

Instead of taking it, Mrs Barclay caught the girl in her arms, and gave her rapidly some half-dozen hearty kisses.

"There, my dear," she said, "if every bit as I've heard was quite true, I should have come all the same; but as I don't believe one single synnable of the pack o' lies, I've come to see you. There!"

That *there* came like an expiration of the breath as she plumped herself down, and the next minute Claire was upon her knees, her arms round the wide waist, and her face buried in the extensive bosom, sobbing violently, and relieving herself in tears of the pressure that had been crushing her down ever since the troubles of that terrible night.

"That's right, my darling: you cry—cry hard. A good cup o' tea and a good cry's the greatest blessings o' Providence for us poor suffering women. No, no: you needn't put a hankychy between. My Jo-si-ah never stints me in dresses, and you may spoil a dozen of 'em if that'll do you any good."

"Mrs Barclay—Mrs Barclay!"

"No, no, no: you're going to take and try and explain and a lot more of it; but I won't hear a word. I tell you I don't believe nothing of what's about. I said if Miss Claire Denville did this or that, she had good reason, being like the mother of that family, as even manages her poor father, so I don't want to hear no lying scandal."

"Heaven bless you!" sobbed Claire, kissing her.

"Ah, that's nice," said Mrs Barclay, smiling. "My little girl died, my dear, as would have been as old as you. Not like you, of course, but it seems as if she might have kissed me like that. I'm a very vulgar sort of woman, I know, my dear, well enough: and if I didn't I soon should, with people sneering at me as they do. You ain't sorry I came?"

"Sorry? I can never say how it has touched me."

"I'm very glad of it, for I don't want to know. And now, not another word about all that, for I know everything, and how all the people are cutting you and your poor pa. But never you mind, my dear. Lots of the people you knew were very fine-weather friends, such as run away as soon as a storm blows. You've got a clear conscience, so don't you take on about it, but live it down."

"I shall try to," said Claire, with a smile—the first that had been seen on her face for days.

"It's what I often say to my Jo-si-ah, though I haven't got a clear conscience through Barclay's money transactions, which ought to be on his, but as I keep his books, and know everything, they trouble me all the same. So everybody's cutting you, eh?"

"Yes," said Claire sadly.

"Then you cut them till they beg your pardon. And now, my dear, just one word from a simple plain woman, whose heart's in the right place. If you want some one to confide in, or you want help of any kind, you know where

Betsey Barclay lives, and that's where there's help, whether it's a kind word, a cup o' tea, or some one that you can put your arms round and cry upon, and whose purse is open to you, if you'll excuse me for mentioning it."

"Miss Dean, ma'am," said Isaac, opening the door.

"Not at—"

"Which I thought you were receiving, ma'am," said Isaac in defence.

Mrs Barclay rose to go, but Claire laid a hand upon her arm, and she resumed her seat as Cora Dean entered, elaborately dressed, and exchanged a most formal courtesy as the visitor rose once more.

Cora could not have explained her visit, even to herself. She hated Claire: she loved her. She was triumphant over her fall: she was sorry for her. She was certain that she would no longer find in her a rival, and in spite of this, she felt a curious sensation of soreness of heart.

She who had for a couple of years past been slighted by the fashionable folk of Saltinville, while Claire had been received everywhere, felt in the new flush of the success she had won a kind of triumph over an unfortunate sister, who would now, she knew, be socially ostracised; and in the plenitude of her own wealth of position she had told herself that she could afford to go and call upon the fallen rival, and, under the guise of politeness, see for herself how she bore her trouble, and assume a consolatory *rôle* that she told herself she did not feel.

But Cora Dean, ill-educated and badly brought up, violent in her passions and quick to dislike a rival, had a very kindly woman's heart within her breast; and as soon as she had formally saluted Mrs Barclay, and had seen the sad, grave face that met hers, ready to suffer insult if it were offered in the guise of friendship, a change came over her, the tender heart leaped, and in full remembrance of their last parting, she advanced quickly and kissed Claire warmly.

There was no disguising the tears in her eyes, and they were infectious, for Mrs Barclay, whose feathers had been rising fast and her tongue sharpening into a point, heaved a tremendous sigh as she jumped up and exclaimed:

"It's very little I know of you, Miss Dean, and—I'm a plain woman—I never thought I should like you; but if you wouldn't mind, my dear!"

It was a kiss of peace, and Mrs Barclay added another that was very loud and very warm.

"And her saying that she had no friends," she exclaimed. "Pooh!"

Claire darted a grateful look at both, and then began to wince and shrink as Mrs Barclay, in all well-meaning, went on talking from one to the other with the most voluble of tongues.

"I declare," she cried, "as I said to my Jo-si-ah, there's no end to the nasty scandals talked in this miserable town."

"Pray say no more, Mrs Barclay," cried Claire; "I am so grateful to you both for coming here, but—"

"I won't say much, my dear, but I must tell Miss Dean, or I shan't be able to bear myself. What we want here is a great high tide to come all over the place and wash it clean."

"Why, we should be drowned, too, Mrs Barclay," said Cora, laughing.

"I hope not, my dear, for I'm no lover of scandal; but do you know, they actually have had the impudence to say that my dear Claire here has been seen at her back door talking to a common soldier."

Claire tried to control herself, but her eyes would stray to Cora Dean's and rest there as if fascinated.

"When the reason is," continued the visitor, as Claire was asking herself should she not boldly avow her connection, "the reason is that she has been seen talking to her brother, who is not a common soldier, but an officer. What do you think of that?"

Cora turned to her, smiled, and said:

"I can believe in the Saltinville people saying anything ill-natured for the sake of petty gossip. We had much to contend against when we came."

"Of course, you had, my dear. Look at me, too: just because my poor Jo-si-ah does money business with some of the spendthrifts, and, of course, lets 'em pay for it, I'm made out to be the most greedy, miserly, wicked, drinking woman that ever breathed. I'm bad enough, I dare say, and between ourselves I do like a glass of hot port wine negus with plenty of nutmeg; but I am not so bad as they say, am I, my dear?"

"You are one of the truest-hearted women I know," said Claire, taking her hand.

"There's a character for me, my dear," said Mrs Barclay, turning to Cora and nodding her head and laughing. "Ah, I must tell you that too," she cried as the recollection came, "just because—"

"Mrs Barclay," said Claire, rising, "pray spare me. I am not well; I have not been well lately, and—and—I know you will forgive me."

"Forgive you, my dear?" cried Mrs Barclay. "Why, of course. It's horribly thoughtless of me. There, good-bye. Are you coming, Miss Dean?"

Cora rose, feeling that she could not stay longer, and after a warm leave-taking, during which the two younger women mentally asked themselves whether they were friends or bitter enemies, Claire's visitors withdrew and walked together along the parade.

The slightest touch set Mrs Barclay's tongue going, and before they had gone far Cora was in full possession of the newly-retailed story about Claire's visits to the fishermen's huts.

"And do you believe this of her?" said Cora, with an eagerness that she could not conceal.

"Now, we're just become friendly, my dear, and I should be sorry to say anything nasty, but I ask you do I look as if I believed it?"

"You look as if you were Claire Denville's best friend," said Cora diplomatically.

"And so I am," replied Mrs Barclay proudly. "I can't help people talking scandal. They glory in it. And, look here, my dear, it isn't far from here, and if you don't mind, we'll go along the cliff to the very house and call."

"Call!" said Cora in amaze.

"Yes; it's at a fisherman's, you know—Fisherman Dick's—and we can get a pint or two of s'rimps for tea."

The consequence was that Cora did walk along the cliff to Fisherman Dick's cottage, and when Mrs Barclay reached her house an hour later her reticule bag was bulging so that the strings could not be drawn close, and the reason why was—shrimps.

On the other hand, Cora Dean had not filled her reticule with shrimps, but her mind with unpleasant little thoughts that made it bulge. Curious thoughts they were, too, and, like Mrs Barclay's shrimps, all jumbled together, heads and tails, ups and downs. She felt then that she could not arrange them, but that there was a great sensation of triumph in her breast, and what she wanted to do most was to sit down and think—no easy task, for her brain was in a whirl.

# Chapter Eighteen
# A Stormy Scene

"I've never dared to write to you before, Clairy. Frank watches me so; but, though I don't come, I think lots about you, and I shall never forget what a dear, good thing you were that night. Good-bye. We must be separate for a bit, till that bother's all forgotten, but don't you fidget; I'm going to be so good now."

Claire was reading the note that had come to her, she knew not how, for the second time, wondering how a woman—her sister—could be so utterly heartless; and, after leaving her to bear the brunt of Sir Harry Payne's shameless accusation, treat it all as such a mere trifle.

Claire held the letter in her hand, with her spirits very low, and a bitter, despairing look was in her eyes as she sat gazing before her, thinking that no greater trouble could come to her now.

Richard Linnell had just passed the house, and though ever since the night of the "At Home," she had shrunk away and rigidly kept from noticing him, the one pleasure she had longed for was to see the grave, wistful look he was in the habit of directing at the window. Now, he had gone by without raising his eyes.

It was the most cruel pang of all. He might have had faith in her, even if she had rejected his suit, and told him that it was hopeless in the extreme.

Her cheeks burned as she thought of Cora Dean with her Juno-like face and her manifest liking for Richard Linnell.

"What is it to me?" she said to herself; and her tears fell fast upon the letter she held in her hand, and she did not hear her father enter the drawing-room, nor see him glance quickly from her in the flesh to the sweetly innocent face of his favourite child, smiling down upon him from the young Italian artist's canvas.

Then he caught sight of the letter, and saw that she was weeping.

An angry flash came into his eyes; the mincing dandyism gave place to a sharp angular rigidity, and stepping quickly across the intervening space that separated him from his child, he was about to take the note from her hands.

Claire uttered a faint cry of alarm, started from the sofa, and hastily thrust the folded paper into her pocket.

"That letter," he said, stamping his foot, "give me that letter."

"No, no, I cannot, father," she cried, with a look of terror at his worn and excited face.

"I insist," he cried. "I will not allow these clandestine correspondences to be carried on. Give me the letter."

"Father, I cannot," she said firmly.

"Am I to take it from you by force?" he cried. "Am I, a gentleman who has struggled all these years to make himself the model from which society is to take its stand, who has striven so hard for his children, to be disgraced by you?"

No answer.

"Heaven knows how I have struggled, and it seems that two of my children must have been born with some base blood in their veins, and to be for ever my disgrace."

Claire raised her eyes to his full of pitying wonder.

"See how your—no, God help me!" he cried wildly, "I dare not utter his name. See how you have disgraced your married sister—lowered me in the eyes of society. I am almost ruined, and just at a time when I had succeeded in placing your brother well. And now, see here—see here!"

He tore a note from his breast, and held it out rustling in his trembling hand.

"Here—I will not punish you more by reading it aloud," he said; "but it is from my own son."

"From Fred?"

"Silence, woman!" cried Denville, with a wild look of agony in his eyes, and a ghastly pallor taking the place of the two feverish spots that had stood in his cheeks. "I have no such son. He is an outcast. I forbid you to mention his name again."

He stood quivering with a curious passion, his lips moving, his eyes staring wildly, and he beat one hand with the open letter he held in the other.

"Here!" he exclaimed at last, "from Morton—to say that, under the circumstances, he feels bound—for the sake of his own dignity and position in his regiment, to hold aloof from his home. The regiment will soon change quarters, and in time all this, he hopes, will be forgotten. Till then, all is to be at an end between us. This—from my own son."

He began to pace the room nervously, thrusting back the letter; and then he turned upon Claire again.

"Not content, you still go on. Clandestine correspondence. Let me see who wrote that."

"I cannot, father."

"But I insist. Here, just when I had had your hand asked in marriage by one who is wealthy and noble, you disgrace us all by that shameless meeting. Give me the letter, I say."

In his rage he caught her by the arms, and she struggled with him and fell upon her knees at his feet.

"Am I to use force?" he cried.

"For your own sake, no. Father, the letter is not what you think. For your own peace of mind, let it stay."

His hands dropped to his sides at his daughter's wild appeal, and the convulsed angry look once more gave place to the one of dread, as he drew back a step.

"Tell me," he cried, still hesitating, "is it from that libertine, Sir Harry Payne?"

"No, no!"

"From Rockley?"

"No, father. How can you think me so degraded—so low!"

"Then—then—"

"Father, for pity's sake!" she cried, as she crept to his knees and embraced them. "Can you not see how I am willing to bear everything to save you pain? Has there not been agony and suffering enough in this house? You cannot think—you cannot believe. Is it not better that we should let this rest?"

He raised his trembling hands to his lips in a nervous, excited way, looking searchingly and furtively by turns in his child's piteous face. The rage in his own had died out, to give place to the look of terror; and, as Claire clung to him, he now and again glanced at the door, as if he would flee from her presence.

"No, no," he said at last. "I was wrong. I will not see the letter. You have your secrets: I have mine. Claire, my child, there is a veil, drawn down by you, over that night's work. I dare not lift it, I dare not look."

"Once more, father," she said, "had we not better let it rest? I am content; I make no murmur against my fate."

"No," he said, flashing out again into anger; "but—hush!—stop!—I must not," he whispered hoarsely. "These strange fits. I cannot bear them."

He threw back and shook his head excitedly.

"I should go mad—I should go mad."

"Father!"

"There, I am calm again, my child. I am not myself sometimes. There—there—it is past."

He bent over and raised her to his breast, where she laid her head, uttering a piteous sigh.

"Stricken," he whispered; "stricken, my child. The workings of a terrible fate. Don't reproach—don't think ill of me, Claire. Some day the light may come—no, no," he cried wildly; "better the darkness. I am so weak—so torn by the agony I have endured. So weak, so pitiful a man; but, with all this wretched vanity and struggle for place, my miserable heart has been so full of love for you all—for my little May."

Claire shivered.

"No, no," he cried excitedly. "Claire, my child, don't speak. Hush! listen, my child. There have been cases where, in self-abnegation—the sins of others—have been borne—by the innocent—the innocent! Oh, my child, my child!"

His head dropped upon his daughter's shoulder, and he burst into a fit of sobbing, the outpourings of a flood of anguish that he fought vainly to restrain.

"Father, dear father!" she whispered, as her arms tightened around him.

"Claire, my child—my child!"

"Yes," she said, as she seemed to be growing stronger and more firm; "your child—not your judge. Father, I see my duty clearly now. Your help and comfort to the end."

# Chapter Nineteen
# Peace and Sympathy

"And I thought that there would be no more rest and comfort here, my child. Claire, one night—"

"No, no, dearest," she cried, as she laid her soft white hand upon his lips; "the past cannot be recalled."

"Only this little revelation," he said, as he kissed the soft hand and held it to his cheek, "then the past shall be as dead with us. One night—since that night—I said to myself that I could bear no more, and I locked myself in my room; but something seemed to stay my hand—a something seemed to bid me live on, even in my pitiful, degraded state; and always—I cannot tell you how—your face seemed to be before my eyes. I tried to put it from me, but it was there. I fought against it, for I was enraged with you one minute, trembling with dread of what I dare not see the next; but still your face seemed to be there, my child, and I said at last that I would live it down or face it, if the dread time that haunts me always, as if lying in my path, should at last leap out."

"Father!"

"My child! There, there; we do not know how much we can bear until the burden is laid upon us; and now let us cleave together like soldiers in the battle of life. Claire, child, we must live."

She sat holding his hand in hers, with her brow knit, and a far-off look in her eyes.

"I am so old and broken," he said musingly; "so helpless. For so many years my miserable energies have been bent solely to this pitiful life, or I would say let us leave here at once, and go where we are not known, to live in some simple fashion; but—I know nothing. I cannot work."

"But I can, father," she said, with a look of elation in her eyes. "I am young and strong, and I will work for you as you have worked for me. Let us go."

"Where, my child?" he said, as he kissed her hand tenderly. "What work would you do—you, so beautiful, so unfit for the rough toil of life?"

"As a teacher—a governess," she cried; but he shook his head, and began to tremble and draw her closer to him.

"No, no," he said excitedly; "that would mean separation; and Claire," he whispered, "I am so weak—so broken—that I must have your young spirit to sustain me. I cannot live without you. Left alone—no, no, no, I dare not be left alone."

"Hush, dear!" she said, laying her cheek upon his shoulder, and drawing him to her breast, to soothe the agony of dread from which he suffered. "I will not leave you, then, father, I will be your help and stay. Nothing shall separate us now."

"No, no." He whispered the words. "I could not live without you, Claire, and I dare not die. My miserable, useless life may prove useful yet. Yes, my child, I feel it—I know it. My work is not yet done. Claire, my course is marked out for me; we must stay here till then."

"Till then, father?"

"Yes; and live it down. Yes, I am wanted here. You will help me?"

"Father, I am your child."

"Yes, yes," he cried, resuming his old flippant air so suddenly that Claire, who did not realise the reaction that had set in, gazed at him tremblingly. "I shall live it down as of old. We must begin again, my dear, and those miserable, brainless butterflies will soon forget, and come to me for my help and introductions. We must not leave here, and the old fees will come once more."

Claire sighed.

"Yes, child, it would have been a happier life to have gone; but it is braver to stay. Let your sweet face show in its dignity how lightly you treat all slander and scandal. Some day, after all, you shall marry well."

She did not reply, and he went on excitedly:

"Now let me see what friends we have left. The Barclays stand firm as rocks. Those Deans, too—so vulgar, but quite as friendly as before. Mrs Pontardent."

"Mrs Pontardent, father?"

"Yes, my dear, yes. Among so few, we must not be choosers. Remember old Hobson, you know. I know nothing against her but her tables. They gamble high; but where do they not? She has arranged for an evening, and I have promised her to go and take the management, and help her to receive her visitors—and—er—and—"

"She has asked you to bring me?"

"Yes. How did you know?"

"I could read it in your eyes, father," said Claire. "Oh, it is impossible."

"I will not press you, my child; but it is almost life to me, and it would be giving us a stepping-stone to recover our lost ground."

"Do you wish me to go, father?"

"If—if—you would not mind very much, my dear," he said hesitatingly. "It would be helping me."

He kissed her hand and left her to her own thoughts. The tears flowed for a while, and then, with a sigh, Claire rose with a look of resignation on her countenance, as if she accepted her fate.

# Chapter Twenty
# Private Instructions

"Look here, Bell," said Major Rockley, as he stood in his quarters, with his regimental servant before him; "you were drunk again last night?"

"Yes, sir."

"Then you are not ashamed of it?"

"Yes, sir, very much ashamed of it. It's my weakness, sir."

"Weakness, you scoundrel? It's your blackguardly conduct. You have been under arrest so many times for this disgraceful behaviour, and I have such a black list against you, that if I lay it before Colonel Lascelles he will have you flogged."

"But you won't do that, sir."

"Yes, I will, you scoundrel. No: I'll give you another chance."

"Thank you, sir; I was sure you would," said the young man, flushing slightly, and with a strange look in his face.

"By the way, what time did Mr Denville come back to his quarters?"

"Two o'clock, sir."

"With whom had he been?"

"Sir Matthew Bray, sir. Lady Drelincourt's, I think."

"Humph! Now, look here; can I trust you, Bell?"

"Yes, sir."

"Then I'm going to give you a delicate bit of business to do for me."

"Yes, sir."

"If you do it well, I shall give you a clean slate to begin again, and wipe off that last report."

"Thankye, sir."

"I cannot—at least I do not wish to—be seen in the business preparations, so I trust to you."

"Yes, sir."

"Go directly then, to Moggridge's, and arrange for a post-chaise and four to be at Prince's Road to-night at—say eleven—no; half-past ten."

"Yes, sir."

"Pick good fast horses. Pack a light valise with a change; put my pistols in the pockets of the carriage, and you will be there ready to see me off. You understand?"

"Yes, sir."

"There's—well, to be plain with you—a lady in the case."

"I see, sir."

"And, mind this; after we have started, you stay behind, and if there is any inquiry directly after, you volunteer information, and say we have taken the London Road. You understand?"

"Quite, sir."

"There's a sovereign for you. No: you'll get drunk if I give it you now. I'll give you five when I come back."

"Very good, sir."

"And mind, if I am wanted, I am unwell in bed. I want a good start."

"I see, sir. You may depend on me. But what house, sir, in Prince's Road?"

"You'll see, blockhead. The one that is lighted up. Mrs Pontardent's."

Major Rockley's regimental servant saluted, turned upon his heel, and went out muttering "Scoundrel!" between his teeth. "I wonder who the lady is?"

"I wouldn't change places with you, my fine fellow," he muttered, as he went across the parade ground; and, turning a corner, he came suddenly upon Sir Harry Payne, Sir Matthew Bray, and the new cornet, who flushed scarlet, as he saw the dragoon.

James Bell saluted, and was passing, but Sir Harry Payne stopped him, and Cornet Denville said hastily:

"I've left my cigar-case. Join you directly."

He went away quickly, and Sir Harry Payne said:

"Where are you going, Bell?"

"Major's washerwoman, sir," said the dragoon promptly.

"Then you can call at River's for me. Half a dozen pairs of white kid gloves. He knows my size. Shall he get you some, Matt?"

"No; not going."

"Isn't she going?"

"No."

"Never mind; you'd better come. Denville's pretty sister will be there."

"Phew! Will she?" said Sir Matthew, whistling. "I say, mind what you're about. There may be a row."

"Not there. I shan't notice her; and if I did, Denville's all right. We're the best of friends now."

"But are you sure she's coming?"

"Pontardent told me herself. She came round the old man."

"Then I will come. Order me some gloves, Harry. I've no change."

"You never do have any. Here! Tell them to send half a dozen pairs for Sir Matthew, and put them down to me. What's the matter with your lip?"

"My lip, sir?"

"Yes; it's bleeding."

"Cracked, sir."

"Yes: fevered. Drink too much. That will do. Nines, or tens—the gloves?"

"No, no: eights," cried Sir Matthew; and the dragoon went on out of the barrack gates, with his face growing grey.

"This is being a soldier," he muttered. "The scoundrel! If I thrash him till he can't move, they'll shoot me. But no, it can't be. She's too good a girl. Impossible. Besides, I shall be there."

He went straight to the livery-stable keeper, and arranged for the best four horses he had, and gave the man a hint.

"Very private, you know."

"Right, my lad. I know what the Major is. Here's half-a-crown for you to get a glass."

"Thank ye."

James Bell pocketed the coin, and went off back to pack his master's valise, and load the case of pistols ready to take to the chaise in the evening, after which he went to have one half-pint of ale, for he was suffering from a severe sensation of thirst, one that he often felt come on.

"Just one glass," he said. "That's all."

James Bell partook of his one glass, but it was not all. Then he went back to see to the horses in his charge in a stable near the barracks—two belonging to the Major, and one of the Colonel's.

The helper was there, and as the extra work would fall to his share that night, there was an excuse for giving him a glass of ale, of which he partook, nothing loth.

The message of Sir Harry Payne had been given, the clothes were packed up, the pistols ready. Yes, every thing had been done; and at last, when it was getting dark, James Bell, looking very stern and determined, and with a tendency to walk extremely straight, as if he were aiming at something right ahead, went off to Moggridge's, placed the packed valise under the seat of the post-chaise, the pistols in the pockets, and then had a chat with the postboys, and—a glass of ale.

There was an hour yet to the time, so he strolled to the end of the yard, and thought he would just go as far as the stables to see if the helper had properly bedded down the horses; and this proving to be the case, and a shilling still remaining unspent of that half-crown, the dragoon suggested that a pot of the best ale should be fetched, and that they should drink it before he went.

The helper was worthy of his title, and fetched the ale, and then, one seated on a truss of straw, the other upon the corn-bin, the two men finished the ale between them, and just at the time that James Bell should have been at Mrs Pontardent's gate, he was fast asleep in the stable.

That afternoon Mr Barclay was busy with his partner, when a visitor was announced, and as it was probably a call relating to money matters, Mrs Barclay left the room.

"Oh, it's you, Moggridge," said Barclay gruffly. "You don't want money, I'm sure."

"Thank ye, no, Mr Barclay, sir," said the visitor, a closely shaven, sharp-faced man, with bow legs. "Things is moving, sir. I'm doing tidy;" and he went on chewing a piece of clover hay, which he had between his lips.

"What do you want then?"

"Well, you know what you said, sir, after the Hon. Tom Badgley went off that night, and dodged the sheriff's officers; and you know what I promised you."

"Who's going now?"

"Major Rockley, sir."

"The deuce! Alone?"

"No, sir. I think there's a lady in the case."

"Who?"

"Don't know, sir. Take up at Mrs Pontardent's party; half arter ten."

"Thank ye, Moggridge. What'll you take?"

"Well, sir, champagne's a thing as don't often come in my way, and—"

"Come along," said Barclay, and Mr Moggridge's desires were satisfied.

"Not a bolt!" said Barclay to himself. "Who's the woman? Well, I don't want him to go. If he goes off he won't meet my bill. He must be stopped, but how?"

He stood thinking for a few minutes, and then sat down and wrote a letter which he took out, and picking a boy from the idlers on the cliff, sent it to its destination.

# Chapter Twenty One
# A Walk and a Drive

Richard Linnell found a good deal of relief in his restless state of mind in taking long country walks, telling himself that he got away from his thoughts; but, on the contrary, he thought the more, and enjoyed his misery as some young men do whose love affairs go crooked.

He was about nine miles away from Saltinville on the day of Mrs Pontardent's party, and rapidly increasing the distance, when he suddenly became aware of the sound of wheels behind in the road, and looking round as he gave place to the driver, he found that Cora Dean was checking her ponies.

"Confound her! she has followed me," he said to himself, as she drew up by his side, quite alone, for the little seat generally occupied by the boy-groom was turned over and closed.

"This is unexpected, Mr Linnell," she said, holding out her gloved hand. "I thought you were at home."

"I felt sure you were," he said, smiling.

"Why?"

The question was accompanied by a half resentful, half tender look, the first intended, the latter not.

"I expected that you would be busy with hair-dressers and dressmakers, preparing for to-night's battle."

"To-night's battle?"

"Yes," he said, in a bantering, reckless way that was new to him, "the battle with the beaux whom you are going to slay."

He felt as if he could have bitten his tongue off the next moment, as he saw the look of pain she gave him.

"What have I done?" she said in a soft, low, half-passionate tone.

"Done! What do you mean?"

"Why do you take pleasure in laughing at me and mocking me?"

"Oh, nonsense!" he cried. "I was only speaking lightly."

"Why should you speak lightly to me?" she said. "We have lived in the same house now for over a year, and, instead of being neighbours and friends, there always seems to be a great gap between us."

"Why, what a sentimental view you take of things," he said. "We shake hands when we meet. We smile at one another, and nod and chat."

"Yes," she said sadly, "we shake hands, we smile at each other, we nod and chat, but—"

She stopped and seemed to try and command herself; and, to his great relief, she spoke lightly as she said:

"I shall see you to-night, of course?"

"No; I thought you were going to a party."

"Yes, but you will be there?"

"No," he said gravely; "I am not going."

"Not going!" she cried. "Why, you were asked."

"How do you know?"

She turned crimson, and avoided his searching look.

"Did Mrs Pontardent tell you?"

"Yes, and you will go?"

"No," he said; "I declined. Why was I asked—do you know?"

She darted an appealing look at him; and the haughty, self-assertive woman seemed to be completely changed.

"Don't—don't be angry with me," she said. "I—I thought it would be so pleasant if you were going to be there."

"You never asked that woman to invite me, Miss Dean?"

She did not speak, but her face began to work, her hands dropped in her lap, her head drooped upon her chest, and she wept bitterly.

"Oh, Miss Dean, for heaven's sake don't do that," he said. "I hate to see a woman cry. I can't bear it. Pray forgive me if I spoke harshly. I could not help feeling annoyed that you should have done this."

"You ought to be grateful," she cried passionately. "The woman you love so dearly will be there with gay Major Rockley—oh, Mr Linnell—Richard—for heaven's sake forgive me. What have I said—what have I done?"

In her alarm at the start he gave, and at his ghastly face, she let fall the reins and caught at his arm, when the ponies, feeling their heads free, dashed off; but this brought Linnell back to the present, and with one bound he reached the rein, hung on to it, and was dragged along for a few yards, turning the ponies' heads towards a steep bank by the side of the narrow unfrequented road. The result would have been that he would have been crushed between the chaise and the bank, but for Cora's presence of mind in seizing the other rein and dragging at it with all her might.

As it was, he received a violent kick which turned him sick and faint, and when he came to, the ponies' reins were secured to a tree in the hedge, and he was lying upon the grass, with Cora's arm supporting his head, and her frightened face bending over him.

"What is it?" he cried sharply. "Are you hurt?"

"No," she said softly. "Don't move. How brave you are!"

He looked at her wonderingly, and then flushing once more, he recalled the whole scene, and what led to it.

"I was afraid you were hurt," he said, trying to rise; but the giddy feeling came back, and he sank down again.

"You are hurt," she cried. "What shall I do? Richard—dear Richard! He's dying. Oh, my love—my love!"

"Hush!" he cried huskily, as she was raising his head in her arms; "for God's sake don't speak to me like that. There—there—you see I am better. The pony kicked me. It made my head swim. There," he cried, rising to his knees, "you see it is all right. I quite frightened you."

He stood up now and offered her his hand to rise; but she did not take it, for she covered her face with her hands and crouched lower and lower on her knees, sobbing wildly in a passion of grief, for his words had been as cold and distant as if they had been strangers.

"Miss Dean—Miss Dean—pray let me help you to your carriage," he said; but she shrank from him.

"Don't touch me!" she cried bitterly; "you made me love you—you made me disgrace myself like this, and now I am to be your laughing-stock and scorn." She looked up at him with her eyes full of rage, which died out on the instant as she cried to him wildly, "I wish you had let me drown!"

He stood looking at her for a few moments, and then glanced along the winding lane; but they were quite alone. Then, taking her hand, he made her rise, for she submitted to his will without a trace of resistance.

"I am very sorry," he said at last simply.

"Sorry!" she cried angrily. "Oh, why am I such a mad fool? Why did I betray myself like this?"

"Hush!" he said softly, as he held her hand between both of his; "listen to me. Do you think I have not seen for long enough that you are beautiful, and that—"

"How dare you?" she cried fiercely. "It is not true."

"You must hear me," he said; "and forgive my awkwardness for speaking as I do. You know my story so well: have I not always been steadfast to that love?"

She sobbed violently and tried to snatch away her hand, but he held it firmly.

"I have always tried to be to you as a friend. Heaven knows I would not have wounded you like this."

"Yes," she sobbed bitterly, "Heaven knows."

"Why did you stab me with those cruel words?" he cried resentfully.

"I don't know," she wailed. "I was mad. It makes me mad to see you go on worshipping her as you do. Does she make you love and hate her too, as she does me?"

"Hush—hush!" he said quickly. "I want to like and respect you, Cora Dean."

"Like! Respect!" she cried, with a flash of her former rage. "Why have I degraded myself like this?"

"Do you not trust me?" he said gently, as he looked in her eyes. "Do you think I should be such a despicable coward as ever to whisper word of this to a soul? Come," he said, with a frank smile, "we have both been unfortunate. Let us be friends."

"Friends?" she cried. "No; a woman never forgives a slight like this. Do you think I could?"

"Yes," he said, after a few moments' pause. "You hate me, and are bitter against me now; but when you have grown calm you will respect me, I am sure. Cora," he cried, with an outburst as excited as her own, "there is no such thing as love or truth on earth. I—Bah! What am I saying?" he cried, checking himself. "Come, we are friends. Let me help you to your place again."

He offered his hand once more, but she struck it aside, and went to the ponies' heads while he tried to forestall her, but had to catch at the side of the chaise to save himself a fall.

Her anger was gone on the instant as she saw his face contract with pain, and in a moment she was by his side.

"It is my turn to triumph," she said in a deep, low tone. "Richard Linnell, you must trust to the woman you despise I shall have to drive you home."

He tried to master the pain, but he could not; and, with a deprecating smile, he had to confess his weakness, and accept a seat back to Saltinville, for it was impossible to walk.

It was a triumph, Cora Dean saw, as she sat up proud and stately beside him; and she felt her heart glow as they reached the town, and scores of promenaders noted him seated by her side; but it was not a pleasant drive home, all the same.

# Chapter Twenty Two
# Linnell Changes his Mind

"Getting cured then, Dick?" said Colonel Mellersh grimly, as Richard limped into the room after finding a note in his own place, which his father said had been brought by a boy.

"Cured? Look, I am quite lame. One of Miss Dean's ponies kicked me; but it will only be a bruise."

"Humph! How convenient!" said the Colonel, with a grim look.

"Don't laugh at me," said Linnell quickly. "I could not help myself."

"That's what we all say when we fall victims to fascination."

"Mellersh, pray stop this banter. You refused Mrs Pontardent's invitation for yourself and me?"

"I did."

"I want you to ask her pardon, and get the invitations for us. I must get there to-night."

"Because Miss Cora Dean, your beautiful charioteer, will be there?"

"No!" fiercely.

"Why, then, most impressionable youth?"

"Because—must I tell you?"

"Yes, if you wish me to act," said the Colonel sternly.

"Because Claire Denville will be there."

"Good heavens! that old fop is never going to take that girl?"

"He is."

"Pooh! What am I saying?" cried the Colonel, half laughingly. "Well, what of it? Why do you want to go?"

"Look."

Linnell held out the note he had found in his room, and Mellersh read it.

"Rockley—post-horses—for the London Road. Who sent this, Dick?"

"I don't know."

"It may be a trick."

"Who would trick me like that? And what for?"

Mellersh remained silent for a few minutes, and then he said gravely:

"Well, Dick, suppose it is so. Surely you are going to awake from this madness now?"

"What do you mean?"

"What does this letter mean? It is plain enough. Constant sapping has carried the fortress, and the lady has consented."

"Don't talk like that, Mellersh. For heaven's sake, don't take that cynical tone."

"Why not, madman? I have heard tell that women often say no when they mean yes. A lady we know must have meant yes. Hang it, boy, what more proof do you want that the woman is unworthy of your love?"

"None," said Linnell bitterly; "none, but I love her all the same."

"Nonsense! Be a man."

"I am a man," cried Linnell furiously, "too much of a man to see the woman I love suffer for her weakness when I can stretch out a hand to save her. That hand I can stretch out, and I will. Now, will you help me?"

"To the death, Dick. I abhor your folly, but there is so much true chivalry in it that I'll help you with all my heart."

"I knew you would," cried Linnell excitedly. "Write at once and get the invitations."

"Pish!" said Mellersh contemptuously. "Don't trouble yourself, my boy. I have only to walk in at Madame Pontardent's door with any friend I like to take. Ah, I wonder how many hundred pounds I have won in that house!"

Linnell was walking up and down the room when the strains of music heard across the hall ceased; and directly after old Mr Linnell's pleasant, grave head was thrust into the room.

"Another letter for you, Dick, my son. Just come."

He held it out, nodded to both, and went back to his room, when the violin was heard again.

"Strange hand," said Richard, opening it quickly.

"Good God!"

"What's the matter?" cried Richard, as he heard his friend's exclamation—saw his start.

"What has Miss Clode to say to you?" said Mellersh huskily.

"Miss Clode? This is not from Miss Clode. Look—no, I cannot show you," cried Richard excitedly. "Yes, I will; I keep nothing from you."

Mellersh glanced at the note which had been delivered by hand. It was anonymous, and only contained these words:

"If Mr Richard Linnell wishes for further proof of the unworthiness of a certain lady, let him visit Mrs Pontardent's to-night."

"That cannot be from Miss Clode," said Richard, as he saw his friend's face resume its cynical calm.

"Possibly not. Of course not. Why should she write to you? Well, Dick, we'll go and see the affair to-night; but what do you mean to do?"

"Act according to circumstances. At any rate stop this wretched business."

"Good," said Mellersh. "I'm with you, Dick; but if it comes to a meeting this time, let me take the initiative. I should like to stand in front of Rockley some morning. The man irritates me, and I am in his debt."

"What, money?"

"No; I want to pay back a few insults thrown at me over the tables now and then."

# Chapter Twenty Three
## An Exacting Guest

Mrs Pontardent was a lady of a class who prospered well in the days when George the Third was king, and fashionable men considered it the correct thing to ruin themselves at cards wherever the tables were opened for the purpose. If you go to an auction sale now, in out-of-the-way places, there are sure to be card-tables in the catalogue; but if you furnish newly, your eyes rarely light upon green baize-lined tables exhibited for sale.

There were several at Mrs Pontardent's handsomely-furnished detached house in Prince's Road, where it stood back in fairly extensive grounds. In fact, it was, after Lord Carboro's, one of the best houses close to Saltinville.

There were plenty of carriages waiting about in the road that night—so many along by the garden wall that Major Rockley found it necessary to alter his plans, for a post-chaise and four was likely to attract attention, and its postboys might be the objects of a good deal of ribald jest if they were close up with the servants of the private carriages.

To meet this difficulty, not being able to find his servant, he went round himself to the livery-stables, feed the postboys, and gave them instructions to wait in the back lane close by the door in the wall at the north side of the garden.

That door was only unlocked when the gardener was receiving fresh soil, plants or pots, or found it necessary to go out for a quiet refresher in the heat of the day; but after an interview and the offer of a golden key, the gardener thought it possible that the door might be left open that night.

Mrs Pontardent lived in style, and her rooms deserved the title of saloons, draped as they were with amber satin, and bright with wax candles, whose light was reflected from many girandoles.

The drawing-room windows opened on to a well-kept lawn; there were bosky walks; a terrace from which the glittering sea was visible; and in the saloons and about the garden a large and brilliant company was assembled.

The Barclays were there, for Barclay was everybody's banker, and a necessity. The Deans arrived early, and Cora looked handsomer than ever.

In fact, the officers of the dragoon regiment, as they saw her go up and speak to Claire, declared that they were the most perfect blonde and brunette that the world had ever seen. But then Mrs Pontardent's wines were excellent, and it was acknowledged that it was a guest's own fault if he did not have enough.

Tea, coffee, ices, and sandwiches at various buffets were spread as a matter of course, but the servants who waited there had a light time compared with that of the butler and his aid.

The Master of the Ceremonies had arrived early with his daughter, whom Mrs Pontardent kissed affectionately, and called "My dear child," and then her father was obliged to leave her, as he had so many duties to perform, receiving guests and introducing them to the hostess as if it were a royal ball; getting couples ready for the dances that went on to the strains of a string band in a very languid way, and finding places for elderly ladies at the card-tables, as opportunity served.

As soon as she could, Claire found a refuge by the side of Mrs Barclay; but her hand was much sought after by dancers brought up from time to time by her father, and every time she trembled lest one of those present should offer himself as a partner.

But, though Major Rockley was there, and had spoken to her gravely once, and bowed on two other occasions as he passed her, he had made no other advance; and when Richard Linnell arrived he did not attempt to speak, but passed her arm-in-arm with Colonel Mellersh, bowing coldly, and giving her one stern, severe look that made her draw her breath once with a catch, and then feel a glow of resentment.

Cora came and sat down once by her side, to be by turns loving and spiteful, as if her temper was not under command; but they were soon separated, for Cora's hand was also much sought after for the various dances.

The evening was less trying than Claire had anticipated. She had come prepared to meet with several slights from the ladies present, but, somehow, the only one who openly treated her with discourtesy was Lady Drelincourt, who gave her the cut direct in a most offensive way, as she passed on Morton Denville's arm.

That was the unkindest act of all, for the boy had seen her, and was about to nod and smile, forgetful in the elation produced by several glasses of wine, of the cause of offence between them; but, taking his cue from the lady on his arm, he drew himself up stiffly and passed on.

The tears rose to Claire's eyes, but she mastered her emotion, as she saw Major Rockley on the other side of the room, keenly observant of all that had passed; and to hide her grief she went on talking to the gentleman who had just solicited her hand for the next dance.

Richard Linnell passed her soon afterwards with Cora upon his arm, and a jealous pang shot through her; but it passed away, and she resigned herself to her position, as if she had suffered so many pangs of late that her senses were growing blunted, and suffering was becoming easier to her.

Morton Denville was dismissed soon after in favour of Sir Matthew Bray; and, in his boy-like excitement, looked elated one moment as the half-fledged officer of dragoons, annoyed and self-conscious the next, as he kept seeing his father bowing and mincing about the rooms, or caught sight of his sister, whom he shunned.

It was a miserable evening, he thought, and he wished he had not come.

Then he wondered whether he looked well, for he fancied that the Adjutant had smiled at him.

A minute later he was thinking that he was thoroughly enjoying himself, and this enjoyment he found in a glass of Mrs Pontardent's champagne.

The dancing went on; so did the flirting in the saloons and in the garden, which was brilliant in front of the windows, deliciously dark and love-inspiring down the shady walks, for there the strains of the band came in a sweetly subdued murmur that the young officers declared was intoxicating, a charge that was misapplied.

The play grew higher as the night wore on, the conversation and laughter louder, the dancing more spirited, and the party was at its height when Mrs Pontardent, in obedience to an oft-repeated look from Major Rockley, walked up to him slowly, and took his arm.

"My dear Major: what a look!" she said banteringly. "You met the handsome youth, and you shot him. After that you ought to be friends, whereas I saw you exchange a look with poor Mr Linnell that was only excelled by the one you gave Colonel Mellersh."

"Damn Colonel Mellersh!" said Rockley savagely.

"By all means," said the lady mockingly; "but not in my presence, please."

"Don't talk twaddle," exclaimed Rockley, as they passed out of the drawing-room window and across the lawn.

It so happened that Cora Dean had been dancing with a handsome young resident of the place, and, after the dance, he had begged her to take a stroll with him out in the grounds.

"No, no," she said, amused by the impression made upon his susceptible nature; "that means taking cold."

"I assure you, no," he exclaimed rather thickly. "It's warm and delightful outside. Just one walk round."

She was about to decline, when she caught Richard Linnell's eyes fixed upon her and her companion, and, urged by a feeling of coquetry, and a desire to try and move him to speak to her, if it were only to reproach, she took the offered arm, and, throwing a lace scarf over her head, allowed her partner to lead where he would, and that was naturally down one of the darkest grass alleys of the grounds.

"Do you know, Miss Dean," he began thickly, "I never saw a girl in all my life who—"

"Can we see the sea from the grounds here?" said Cora.

"Yes; lovely view," he said. "Down here;" and he led her farther from the house. "There, you can see the sea from here, but who would wish to see the sea when he could gaze into the lovely eyes of the most—"

"Is not that an arbour?" said Cora, as they stood now in one of the darkest parts of the garden.

"Yes. Let's sit down and have a talk, and—"

"Will you lead the way?" said Cora.

"Yes; give me your hand—eh—why—what dooce! She's given me the slip. Oh, 'pon my soul, I'll pay her for that."

He started back towards the house, passing close by Cora, who had merely stepped behind a laurustinus, and who now went in the other direction, along a grass path at the back of the lawn.

Her white satin slippers made not the slightest sound, and she was about to walk straight across the lawn and out into the light, when a low, deep murmur reached her ear, and she recognised the voice.

"Major Rockley," she said to herself. "Who is he with?"

Her jealous heart at once whispered "Claire!"

"If I could but bring Richard face to face with them now!" she thought, "he would turn to me after all."

She hesitated, for the thought of the act being dishonourable struck her; but in her mental state, and with her defective education, she was not disposed to yield to fine notions of social honour; and, with her heart beating fast, she hurried softly along the grass, to find herself well within hearing of the speakers.

The words she heard were not those of love, for they were uttered more in anger. It was at times quite a quarrel changing to the tone of ordinary conversation.

Cora glanced behind her, to see the brightly lit-up house and hear the strains of music and the sounds of laughter and lively remark, while, by contrast with the glow in that direction, the bushes amid which she stood and into which she peered seemed to be the more obscure.

There was a pause, and then a woman's voice said quickly:

"No, no; I cannot. You must not ask me, indeed."

A curious feeling of disappointment came over Cora, for her plan was crushed on the instant. What were other people's love affairs to her?

She was turning away with disgust, when the deep voice of the Major said quickly, and in a menacing way which rooted the listener to the spot:

"But I say you shall. One word from me, and you might have to leave Saltinville for good. I mean for your own good."

"Oh, Rockley!"

"I don't care; you make me mad. Here have I done you endless little services, helped you to live in the style you do; and the first little favour I ask of you, I am met with a flat refusal."

"I don't like to refuse you, but the girl is—"

"Well, you know what the girl is. Hang it all, Pont, should I ask you if it were not as I say—unless it were that rich heiress I am to carry off some day."

"And the sooner the better."

"Yes, yes; but time's going. It's now eleven, and I must strike while the iron's hot."

"But, Rockley—"

"More opposition? What the devil do you mean?"

"I don't like to be mixed up with such an affair."

"You will not be mixed up with it. No one will know but our two selves."

"My conscience goes against such a trap."

"Your conscience!" he hissed angrily.

"Well, and do you suppose I have none? The girl is too good. I like her. It is a shame, Rockley."

Cora Dean's heart beat as if it would suffocate her, while her mouth felt dry and her hands moist. She could hardly have moved to save her life. She knew what it was, she felt sure. It was a plot against Claire, and if it were—

Cora Dean did not finish her thought, but listened as Rockley spoke again.

# Chapter Twenty Four
## Too Late

"How long has the fair Pontardent taken to the nursing up of scruples?"

"Do you suppose a woman is all evil?" was the retort. "You men make us bad enough, but you cannot kill all the good. I say it is a shame."

"A shame!" said Rockley derisively. "Ha, ha, ha! What a woman you are! You don't know what has taken place. I tell you this; she is mine. All she wants is the excuse and opportunity that she finds to-night with me. The old man watches her like a hawk."

"Is this really so, Rockley?"

"On my honour. I should not have done what I have if she were not willing. I've a chaise and four waiting outside the lower gate behind here."

"You have?"

"It has been there this half hour, and we are only waiting for our opportunity. Now then, will you help me?"

"Well," said Mrs Pontardent hesitating, "if it is that—"

"It is like that, I tell you; but she wants it to appear that she had no hand in it, to keep up the fiction. You see?"

"Yes," said the woman, rather hoarsely; "but I don't like it, Rockley."

"Friends or enemies?—one word?" he said sternly.

"Friends," she said quickly. "What am I to do?"

"Go back at once, and get hold of young Denville. He's half-tipsy somewhere."

"Yes."

"Tell him he has shamefully neglected his sister, and that he is to take her out in the garden for a walk straight down the broad grass path, and beg her pardon."

"But—"

"Not a word. Do what I say. The boy will obey you like a sheep dog."

"And then?"

"What then? That is all."

"But, Rockley, no violence."

"Bah! Rubbish! Do as I bid you. I shall push the boy into a bush; that's all."

There was a dead silence.

"Must I do this, Rockley?"

"Yes, you must. Go at once. You shall not be mixed in the affair at all. No one can blame you, for the boy is too tipsy to recollect anything to-morrow. Now go."

There was a rustle of a dress, and Cora had just time to draw out of sight as Mrs Pontardent passed her.

Cora heard her voice as she went by. It was almost like a sigh, but the words were articulate, and they were:

"God forgive me! It is too bad."

What to do?

Cora stood motionless, her pulses beating furiously, and the blood surging to her brain, and seeming to keep her from thinking out some plan.

Major Rockley—the cruel, insolent libertine—had a post-chaise waiting; by a trick Claire was to be got out, and down the broad walk, led like a sheep to the slaughter by her weak, half-tipsy brother, and then carried off. The plan seemed to Cora devilish in its cunning, and the flush of her ardent blood intoxicated her with a strange feeling of excitement—a wild kind of joy.

It was all for her. Claire away—carried off, or eloped with Rockley, Richard Linnell would rage for a week, and then forget her. Poor fellow! How he had struggled to hide that limp, and how handsome he looked. How she loved him—her idol—who had saved her life. He would be hers now, hers alone, and there would be no handsome, sweet-voiced rival in the way to win him to think always of her soft, grey, loving eyes—so gentle, so appealing in their gaze, that they seemed to be looking out of the darkness at her now.

Yes, there they were so firm and true—so softly appealing, and yet so full of womanly dignity that, as she hated her, so at the same time she loved.

"And in perhaps half an hour she would be away—on the road to London—in the Major's arms."

"And Richard Linnell will be free to love me, and me alone?"

She said it aloud, and then tore at her throat, for a thought came that made the blood surge up and nearly suffocate her.

"Why, he would curse me if he knew, and loathe me to his dying day."

She took a few hasty steps forward, and then staggered and stopped short.

"I must have been mad!" she panted. "Am I so bad as that?"

She hurried towards the house, and narrowly missed her late partner as she reached one of the windows.

Thank heaven! she was not too late. There sat Claire where she had left her. No: it was some other lady.

She hurried in as quickly as she could without exciting notice.

Where was Claire?

She went from room to room, but she was not visible.

Where was Richard Linnell?

Nowhere to be seen.

If she could find Colonel Mellersh, or Mr Barclay—but no; there was not a soul she knew, and from different parts of the room men were approaching her, evidently to ask her to dance.

She escaped into another saloon, and there was Denville.

She took a few steps towards him, but he hurried away as if to attend to a call from their hostess, who was smiling at the end of the room. The next moment Cora saw her take the arm of the Master of the Ceremonies and go through a farther door.

Impossible to speak to him now. It was as if Mrs Pontardent had divined the reason of her coming, and was fighting against her with all her might.

Another gentleman approached, but she shrank away nervously, expecting each moment to see again her companion of the dark walk.

All at once, to her great joy, she caught sight of Mrs Barclay, looking in colour like a full-blown cabbage-rose, and exhaling scent.

She hurried up to the plump pink dame, to be saluted with:

"Ah, my dear, how handsome you do look to-night!"

"Where's Claire Denville?" cried Cora huskily.

"Claire, my dear? Oh, she was with me ever so long, but she has just gone down the grounds."

A spasm seemed to shoot through Cora Dean as she said to herself: "Too late!"

# Chapter Twenty Five
# Mellersh is Convinced

"Well, Dick," said Mellersh, as he sought Linnell out, after a stroll round the rooms in search of Cora Dean, "how long are you going to keep yourself on the gridiron?"

"I don't understand you."

"Then I shall not try to explain."

"Have you seen anything?"

"N-no."

"Don't hesitate, man; you have?"

"No, Dick, no. Of course, I've seen a certain young lady, and I've seen Rockley hanging about."

"Well, that proves nothing, does it?"

"My dear Dick, why should I waste my breath on a man in your condition?"

"My condition, you wretched old cynic? You never knew what it was to love."

"Wrong. I have loved, and I am in love now."

"You? You?"

"Yes, my boy, and with a woman who cares for somebody else; but I don't go stalking about like a tragedy hero, and rolling my eyes and cursing the whole world. If I cannot have the moon, I shall not cry for it."

"Hist! There goes Rockley."

"Well, let him go."

Richard Linnell made no reply, but quietly followed the Major.

"I mustn't let them meet without me there," thought Mellersh. "The scoundrel might hit him badly next time."

He strode off after Richard Linnell, but missed him, and it was quite half an hour before they met again.

"I have been about the gate," said Richard hoarsely. "There is no post-chaise there."

"Then it is a hoax."

"No; I cannot think that it is. Rockley is yonder, and he is watching about in a curious, restless way that means something."

"Where is he?"

"Over there by the saloon window."

"Oh, my dear Dick, I am hungry for a good hand at whist, and to win a little Philistine gold, and here you keep me hanging about after you, looking for a mare's nest."

"I can't stop," said Linnell. "Where shall I find you if I want you?"

"Here, on this seat, under this bush, smoking a cigar. No; I'll stick by you, my lad."

They went off together, and, going straight up to the window pointed out by Linnell, found that Rockley was not there.

"I left him there, I'll swear," said Linnell savagely. "No, don't let us separate; I may want you."

"Quite right; and I may want you," replied Mellersh.

They walked hastily round, looking in at window after window, but there was no sign of Rockley. The throng of guests were dancing, playing, or conversing, and the scene was very brilliant; but the tall, dark officer of the dragoons was the only one of his party that they could not see.

"Mellersh," exclaimed Linnell suddenly, "with all my watchfulness, I seem to have failed."

"Why do you say that?"

"Claire!"

"Claire? Why, I saw her seated on that rout-chair five minutes ago."

"Yes; but she has gone."

"Quick, then—down to the gate! We must see them there."

"Unless they have passed through," said Linnell, with a groan. "I ought not to have left the entrance."

"Don't talk," said Mellersh, almost savagely now, he seemed so moved from his ordinary calm. "I don't want to think you are right, Dick, but I begin to be suspicious at last."

They hurried down to the gate, where a knot of servants were chatting, the lights from the carriage-lamps glistening in polished panels and windows, and throwing up the gay liveries of the belaced footmen waiting.

"Has any one passed through here lately?" said Mellersh sharply.

"No, sir," was chorused.

"Not a lady and gentleman?"

"No, sir—yes, about half an hour ago Colonel Lascelles and the doctor at the barracks went out together."

"But no lady and gentleman separately or together?"

"No, sir."

"No carriage?"

"No, sir," said the footman who had acted as spokesman.

"Only wish they would," grumbled a coachman from his box close by the gate.

"We are in time," said Mellersh, and Linnell breathed more freely as he took up a position in the shade of a great clump of evergreens just inside the gate.

"Have you any plan?" said Mellersh, after a few minutes' waiting, during which time the servants, gathered in a knot, were at first quiet, as if resenting the presence of the two gentlemen. Then their conversation began again, and the watchers were forgotten.

"Plan? Yes," said Linnell. "I shall take her from him, and not leave her until she is in her father's care."

"Humph! That means mischief, Dick."

"Yes; for him, Mellersh. I shall end by killing that man."

Mellersh was silent, and the minutes glided by.

"I can't bear this," said Linnell at last. "I feel as if there is something wrong—that he has succeeded in getting her away. Mellersh! man! why don't you speak? Here, come this way."

Mellersh followed as his companion walked to the gate.

"Is there a servant of Mrs Pontardent's here?"

"Yes, sir," said a man holding a lantern, "I am."

"Is there any other entrance to these grounds?"

"No, sir," said the man sharply, and Linnell's heart beat with joy. "Leastwise, sir, only the garden gate."

"Garden gate?"

"Yes, sir; at the bottom of the broad walk."

"Here—which way?"

"Right up through the grounds, sir; or along outside here, till you come to the lane that goes round by the back. But it's always kept locked."

"Stop here, Mellersh, while I go round and see," whispered Linnell. "If I shout, come to me."

"Yes; go on. It is not likely."

They went outside together, past the wondering group of servants, and then separating, Linnell was starting off when Mellersh ran to him.

"No blows, Dick," he whispered, "Be content with separating them."

Linnell nodded, and was starting again when a man ran up out of the darkness, and caught Mellersh hastily by the arm.

"Seen a post-chaise about here, sir?"

"Post-chaise, my man?"

"Yes, sir—four horses—was to have been waiting hereabouts. Lower down. Haven't heard one pass?"

"No," said Linnell quickly; "but what post-chaise? Whose? Speak man!"

"Who are you?" said the man roughly.

"Never mind who I am," cried Linnell. "Tell me who was that post-chaise waiting for?"

The man shook him off with an oath, and was starting again on his search, when about fifty yards away there was the tramp of horses, the rattle and bump of wheels; and then, as by one consent, the three men ran towards the spot, they caught a faint glimpse of a yellow chaise turning into the main road; then there was the cracking of the postboys' whips, and away it went over the hard road at a canter.

"Too late!" groaned the man, as he ran on, closely followed by Linnell and Mellersh.

"Too late!" groaned Linnell; but he ran on, passing the man, who raced after him, though, and for about a quarter of a mile they kept almost together, till, panting with breathlessness and despair, and feeling the utter hopelessness of overtaking the chaise on foot, Linnell turned fiercely on the runner and grasped him by the throat.

"You scoundrel!" he panted. "You knew of this. Who's in that chaise?"

"Curse you! don't stop me. Can't you see I'm too late?" cried the man savagely.

"Linnell! Are you mad?" cried Mellersh, coming up.

"Linnell!—are you Linnell?—Richard Linnell?" panted the man, ceasing his struggles.

"Yes. Who are you?"

"Don't waste time, man," groaned the other. "We must stop them at any cost. Did you see them go? Who is it Major Rockley has got there?"

"A lady we know," said Mellersh quickly. "Who are you?"

"The drunken fool and idiot who wanted to stop it," groaned Bell. "Here, Linnell," he said, "what are you going to do?"

"The man's drunk, and fooling us, Mellersh," cried Linnell excitedly. "Quick! Into the town and let's get a post-chaise. They are certain to take the London Road."

"No," cried Bell excitedly; "he would make for Weymouth. Tell me this, though, gentlemen," he cried, clinging to Linnell's arm. "I am drunk, but I know what I am saying. For God's sake, speak: is it Claire Denville?"

"Who are you?" cried Mellersh sharply. "Stand off, or I'll knock you down. It is the Major's man, Dick, and he's keeping us back to gain time. I didn't know him at first."

"No: I swear I'm not," cried the dragoon, in a voice so full of anguish, that they felt his words were true. "Tell me, is it Miss Denville?"

"Yes."

"Curse him! I'll have his life," cried the man savagely. "This way, quick!"

"What are you going to do?" cried Linnell, as Bell set off at a sharp run towards the main street of the town.

"Come with me and see."

"No: I shall get a post-chaise and four."

"And give them an hour's start," cried the dragoon. "Horses, man, horses."

"Where can we get them quickly?"

"In Major Rockley's stable, curse him!" was the reply.

In five minutes they were at the stable, and the dragoon threw open the door.

"Can you saddle a horse?" he panted, as they entered the place, dimly lit by a tallow candle in a swinging horn lantern.

"Yes—yes," was the reply.

"Quick then. Everything's ready."

Each ran to a horse, the head-stalls were cast loose, and the order of the well-appointed stable stood them in such good stead that, everything being at hand, in five minutes the three horses were saddled and bridled, and being led out, champing their bits.

"We've no spurs. Where are the whips?"

"They want no whips," cried the dragoon excitedly; "a shake of the rein and a touch of the heel. They're chargers, gentlemen. Can you ride, Mr Linnell?"

"Yes," was the answer; and as it was given Linnell's foot was painfully raised to the stirrup.

He stopped though, and laid his hand upon the dragoon's shoulder.

"The London Road?" he said, looking him full in the eyes.

"The Weymouth Road, I tell you."

Another half minute and they were mounted and clattering down the lane to turn into the main street, up which the three sleek creatures pressed, hanging close together, and snorting, and rattling their bits as they increased their stride.

"Steady—steady—a carriage," cried Mellersh; and they opened out to ride on either side of a chariot with flashing lamps, and as they passed they had a glimpse of Lady Drelincourt being escorted home from the party by Sir Matthew Bray.

"Steady!" cried Mellersh again, as they came in sight of the cluster of lamps and carriages by Mrs Pontardent's gates; and but for his insistance there would have been a collision, for another carriage came out and passed them, the wheel just brushing Linnell's leg in the road narrowed by a string of carriages drawn up to the path.

"Now we're clear," said Mellersh; and they cantered by the wall, past the lane in which the chaise had been waiting, past a few more houses and the ragged outskirts, always mounting, and then bearing off to the left as the way curved, till there it lay, the broad chalk western road, open, hard, and ready to ring to their horses' beating hoofs.

"Now then, forward!" cried the dragoon hoarsely.

"At a trot!" shouted Mellersh.

"No, no; gallop!" roared the dragoon, and his horse darted ahead.

"Halt!" shouted Mellersh in a ringing voice, for he had not forgotten old field-practice; and the three horses stopped short.

"Listen!" he continued, in a voice of authority; "they've half an hour's start nearly, and we shall not overtake them this stage. We must not blow our horses at the beginning. A steady trot for the first few miles, and then forward at a canter. It will be a long race."

"Right, sir," cried the dragoon. "He's right, Mr Linnell. Take the lead, sir; my head's on fire."

"Forward!" cried the Colonel; and away they went through the dark night, but with the chalky road making their way clear.

After a mile or two the rapid swinging trot of the chargers grew into a regular military canter, and that, by an imperceptible change, into a rapid gallop that was now kept up, for the excitement of the chase told upon Mellersh, and his ideas of prudence as to husbanding the horses' powers were swept away as if by the keen wind that dashed by their ears.

"I ought to check him," said Mellersh, as he toned down his excitement for the minute; and then—"No, I cannot, for I must take that scoundrel by the throat."

# Chapter Twenty Six
# The End of the Race

Colonel Mellersh was the only one who was likely to ride with a cool head: the others were for racing at the top of the horses' speed. And so it was that before long, as Richard Linnell sat well down and gave his horse its head, James Bell, whom the ride was gradually sobering in one sense, but also making far more excited as he realised clearly the position of his sister, shook his reins, pressed his horse's flanks with his heels, and the brave beast began to almost fly. Naturally enough, the Colonel's steed pressed more heavily upon its bit, refusing, after the fashion of a cavalry horse, to be left behind, and forcing itself between the other two, till the riders were knee to knee, and tearing along as if in a desperate charge.

"We're distressing the horses, Dick," said Mellersh, turning his head to his right; but Bell heard him.

"I'm sorry for the horses, sir; but they are his. Let them be distressed."

"We must overtake them," said Linnell between his teeth.

"Right, sir, right," cried Bell. "Forward, Colonel. Please don't draw rein."

Fortunately for them, the night grew a little lighter, and along the treeless Down road they thundered. Every now and then one of the horses snorted as the dust flew, but mile after mile was spurned beneath their heels and they showed no sign of distress, but seemed to rejoice in the long night gallop and the music of their clattering hoofs.

The road was singularly silent and deserted; not so much as a foot-passenger was on the way, not a vehicle was seen.

A gate at last came in view as they were breathing the horses up a hill, after riding for some distance without a word, the very silence telling the intensity of the men's feelings.

Here was a check, for the gate was closed, and no light visible, but Bell rode close up and kicked hard at the panel, till the door in the gatekeeper's hut was opened.

"Now, then, quick!" cried Bell. "How long is it since a chaise and four passed?"

"Chaise and four?" said the man surlily.

"Yes, chaise and four. Has a chaise and four passed?"

"What, to-night?"

"Yes, to-night. Answer; quick, or—"

He caught the man by the collar, and the evasion he was about to utter did not pass his lips.

"Yes," he growled; "one went by."

"How long ago?" said the Colonel.

"How long?"

"Yes, yes. Quick, man, quick! and here's a crown for the toll. Keep the change."

This seemed to enliven the surly fellow's faculties, and he took the money and rubbed his head as he began to unfasten the gate.

"Well, how long?" cried the Colonel.

"Long? Well a good bit ago, sir."

"Yes, yes, but what do you mean by a good bit?"

"Mebbe two hours—mebbe hour and a half. I've been asleep since."

"Come along," cried the Colonel, who was as excited now as his companions. "There's nothing more to be got from this lout."

They left the man leaning on the gate, having gained nothing whatever by the colloquy but a short breathing space for their horses, and these continued their gallop the moment they were through.

They passed a side road now and then, and at the first Linnell turned in his saddle.

"Is it likely that they will leave the main road?" he said.

"No," was the prompt answer given by Bell, without waiting for the Colonel to speak. "They're going west—far enough, I dare say—and they must change their horses now and then. We shall hear of them at Cheldon."

Bell was right, for, when, at the end of another quarter of an hour, they cantered into the little post town, there was a light still burning in a lantern in the inn yard, and an ostler proved to be a little more communicative.

Yes, a post-chaise—a yellow one—came in half an hour ago, and changed horses and went on. Their horses were all in a muck sweat, and here was one of the boys.

A postboy came out of the tap, and stood staring.

He knew nothing, he said, only that he and his mate had brought a party from Saltinville.

"A lady and gentleman?" said Linnell sharply.

"I d'know," said the postboy. "I didn't ride the wheeler; I was on one of the leaders."

"But you must have seen?" cried Linnell angrily.

"No; I didn't see nothing. I'd enough to do to look after my horses. Bad road and precious hilly 'bout here, sir."

"Come along," cried Linnell angrily.

"Walk your horses for a few minutes," said Mellersh quietly; and as Linnell and Bell went on he dismounted and thrust his hand into his pocket. "Just tighten these girths for me a little, will you, my man?" he said, turning to the postboy, and slipping a guinea into his hand.

"Cert'ny, sir. Get a bit slack they do after a few miles canter. Steady, my lad. Nice horse, sir, that he is," continued the postboy, who was smooth civility itself. "Must be a pleasure to ride him."

"Yes," said Mellersh, as the man went on talking and buckling with his head supporting the saddle-flap. "You don't get such a nag as that for a leader, eh?"

"No, sir, not likely. Fifteen pounders is about our cut. That one's worth a hundred. All of a sweat he is, and yet not a bit blown. You've come fast, sir."

"Yes; at a good rattling gallop nearly all the ten miles."

"'Leven, sir, a good 'leven, and a bad road."

"Is it, though?" said Mellersh quietly, as he prepared to mount again.

"All that, sir."

"Postboys' miles, eh?"

"No, sir; honest miles. We'd charge twelve. Wouldn't you like them stirrups shortened two or three holes?" said the man eagerly.

"No, thanks; no. I'm an old soldier, and we always ride with a long stirrup. Matter of use. Shall we catch them, do you think?"

"What, with them horses, sir? Yes, easy. They've got a shocking bad team. They never have a decent change here. Lookye here, sir. You put on a decent canter, and you'll be up to them before they get to Drumley. The road's awful for wheels for about six miles; but when you get about a mile on from here, you can turn off the road on the off-side, and there's five miles of good, close turf for you where a chaise couldn't go, but there's plenty of room for a horse. Good-night, sir; thankye, sir. Good luck to you."

Mellersh said "good-night" and cantered off after his companions, his steed needing no urging to join its fellows.

"Anyone would think that a guinea dissolved into golden oil and made a man's temper and his tongue run easily. I can't prove it, but I should not be surprised if that was one of Rockley's own guineas. Odd. Running him down with his own horses, and his own coin. Well, he deserves it all."

"We're on the track right enough, Dick," he cried, as he overtook Linnell; Bell, in his impatience, being a couple of hundred yards ahead.

"Are you sure? I don't understand this fellow. Why should he be so eager to overtake that scoundrel?"

"Can't say. Puzzled me," replied Mellersh drily.

"Is he leading us wrong?"

"No. We are well on our way, and shall overtake them by the time they reach the next posting house. Forward."

Mellersh did not feel quite sure, but his confidence increased as he found the postboy's words correct about the badness of the road, and the smooth turf at the side, on to which they turned, and cantered along easily for mile after mile.

Every now and then Bell burst forth with some fierce expletive, as if he could not contain his rage; and they gathered that at times it was against himself, at others against Rockley. As fierce a rage, too, burned in Linnell's breast, compounded of bitter hatred, jealousy, and misery.

He could not talk to Mellersh, many of whose remarks fell upon unheeding ears, while Linnell asked himself why he was doing all this to save from misery and shame a woman who did not deserve his sympathy.

But, when he reasoned thus, it seemed as if Claire's pure, sad face looked up into his reproachfully, and the thoughts her gentle loving eyes engendered made him press his horse's flanks, and send him along faster as he said to himself:

"It is a mystery. I cannot understand it; and were she everything that is bad, I should be compelled to fight for her and try to save her to the end."

Mile after mile was passed, and though the dull thudding of their horses' hoofs upon the soft turf gave them opportunities for hearing the rattle of wheels and the trampling on the rough road, no sound greeted their ears.

"We shall never catch them, gentlemen, like this," cried Bell at last. "Curse the horses! Push on. If we kill the poor brutes we must overtake that chaise."

"Forward then," said Mellersh eagerly, for there was that in the young man's voice that cleared away the last shadow of doubt and suspicion.

They had been on the grass waste beside the road for quite five miles when, all at once, the way seemed to narrow; and they were about to turn on to the road, but Linnell drew rein suddenly.

"Stop!" he cried. "Listen!"

There was no doubt about it. As soon as they drew up, with their mounts breathing hard, and snorting or champing their bits, there came on the night air the *beat, beat* of trotting horses, and the rattle of wheels.

"There," cried Mellersh, "that settles it. Forward, again!"

The horses seemed almost to divine that they had only to put on a final spurt and finish their task, for they went off at a free gallop, and before long there was the rattle of the wheels plainly heard, though for the most part it was drowned by the sound of the trampling hoofs, for the pursuers were now upon the hard, chalky road.

A quarter of an hour's hard riding and they were well in view, in spite of the darkness of the night and the cloud of dust churned up by the team in the chaise. It was evident that the postboys were being urged to do their best; and as they had put their wretched horses to a gallop, the pursuers could see the chaise sway from side to side when the wheels jolted in and out of the ruts worn in the neglected road.

Had any doubt remained as to the occupants of the chaise, they would soon have been at an end; for, as Linnell pushed on taking one side, and Mellersh the other, Rockley's voice could be heard shouting from the front of the chaise, and bidding the postboys whip and spur.

It was the work of minutes, then of moments, when Linnell, who was now leading in a break-neck gallop, yelled to the postboys to stop.

"Go on, you scoundrels! Gallop!" roared Rockley from the front window. "Go on, or I fire."

The man on the wheeler half turned in his saddle and made as if to pull up, but there was the flash of a pistol, the quick report, and as a bullet whistled over his head, the postboy uttered a cry of fear, and bent down till his face almost touched the horse's mane, while his companion on the leader did the same, and they whipped and spurred their jaded horses frantically.

"Stop!" shouted Linnell again. "Stop!"

"Go on! Gallop!" roared Rockley, "or I'll blow out your brains."

The men crouched lower. Their horses tore on; the chaise leaped and rocked and seemed about to go over, and all was rush and excitement, noise and dust.

Linnell was well abreast of the chaise door now, and pushing on to get to the postboy who rode the leader, when the glass on his side was dashed down, and, pistol-in-hand, Rockley leaned out.

"Back!" he said hoarsely, "or I fire."

"You scoundrel!" roared Linnell. "Cowardly dog! but you are caught."

"Stop, or I fire," shouted Rockley again, fuming with rage and vexation at being overtaken in the hour of his triumph.

"Fire if you dare!" cried Linnell excitedly, as he pressed on.

*Crack!*

There was a second flash and report, and the horse Linnell rode made a spring forward as if it had been hit.

The thought flashed across Linnell's brain that in another few moments the brave beast he bestrode would stagger and fall beneath him, and that then the cowardly scoundrel who had fired would escape with the woman he was ready to give his life to save. A curious mist seemed to float before his eyes, the hot blood of rage to surge into his brain, lights danced before him, and for the moment he felt hardly accountable for his actions.

All he knew was that he was abreast of the wheeler, with the man whipping and spurring with all his might; that the horses were snorting and tearing along in a wild race, and that Rockley was leaning out of the window yelling to the men to gallop or he would fire again.

Linnell had a misty notion Mellersh was somewhere on the other side, and that Bell was galloping behind, but he did not call to them for help. He did not even see that Mellersh was pushing forward and had reached out to catch the off-leader's rein. All he did realise was that Claire Denville, the woman he loved, was in peril; that her whole future depended upon him; and that he must save her at any cost.

He was galloping now a little in advance of the postboy. Their knees had touched for an instant; then his leg was in front, and he was leaning forward.

"Touch that rein, and I fire," roared Rockley.

Then there was once more a flash cutting the darkness; and as the bullet from Rockley's pistol sped on its errand, the horse made one plunge forward, and then pitched upon its head. There was a tremendous crash of breaking glass and woodwork, and beside the road the wreck of a chaise with two horses down, and the leaders tangled in their harness and kicking furiously till they had broken free.

# Chapter Twenty Seven
# Richard Linnell thinks he has been a Fool

For a few moments, in the suddenness of the catastrophe, every one was too much astounded to take any steps. Linnell was the first to recover himself, and, leaping from his horse, he threw the rein to Bell.

Mellersh followed his example, joining Linnell as he tried to drag open the door of the chaise, which was over upon its side with the off-wheeler kicking in the front, as it lay there upon its companion in a tangle of harness.

The framework was so wrenched that for a minute or two the door would not yield, and the utter silence within sent a chill of horror through Linnell.

"Let me come, Dick," whispered Mellersh, the catastrophe that had so suddenly befallen them forcing him to speak in subdued tones; "let me come, Dick. I'm stronger, perhaps."

"Pish!" was the angry reply, as Linnell strained at the door, which suddenly yielded and flew open, the glass falling out with a tinkling noise.

Just at the same time the man with the leaders trotted back with his frightened horses, the broken traces dragging behind.

"Hurt, Jack?" he cried to his fellow.

"No, not much," was the answer, as the postboy who rode the wheeler dragged his leg from beneath his horse, and immediately stepped round and held down the head of the animal, which was kicking and struggling to rise. "Woa! will yer. Hold still, Captain!"

With the customary feeling of helplessness that comes over a horse as soon as its head is pressed down, the poor animal ceased its frantic efforts, uttered a piteous sigh that was like that of a human being, and lay perfectly still.

"Old Spavin's a dead 'un, mate," said the man.

"Dead?" said the second postboy.

"Dead as a nit, mate. There'll be something to pay for to-night's job."

"Anyone killed?" said the second man in a whisper.

"I d'know, and I don't care," grumbled the man; "my leg's bruzz horrid. Shutin' like that! It's as bad as highwaymen. Here, come and help cut some of this harness. They'll stand now. Take out your knife, mate, and use it. They'll have to pay. I can't sit on this 'oss's head all night."

"There's some of 'em got it," whispered the second man in a low voice, as he dismounted and stood beside his comrade watching while Linnell lifted out the insensible figure of one of the occupants of the chaise, and bore her, tangled in a thick cloak, to the roadside, where he laid her reverently upon the turf.

"With you directly, Dick," said Mellersh, still in the subdued voice, as he climbed into the chaise, and, exerting all his strength, raised Rockley and half thrust, half lifted him out, to drag him to the other side of the road.

"Is she much hurt, sir?" said Bell hoarsely. "I can't leave the horses."

"I can't say. I don't know yet," panted Linnell, who was trying to lay open the folds of the cloak, which he at last succeeded in doing, so that the air blew freely on the insensible woman's face.

Linnell's pulse beat madly, as he half closed his eyes, and kept his head averted while he knelt there in the semi-darkness, and placed his hand upon the woman's breast.

Then he snatched his hand away and felt giddy. But a throb of joy ran through him. Her heart was beating, and he felt sure she was only fainting from the fright.

"Why don't you speak, sir?" cried Bell angrily. "Is she much hurt?"

"I think not, my man, only fainting," said Linnell.

"Well?"

This to Mellersh, who came to him from where he had laid Rockley.

"I don't know," was the answer to the abrupt query. "Only stunned, I think. Head cut with the broken glass."

"Not killed then?" said Linnell bitterly.

"No. Such as he generally come off easily," replied Mellersh. "What's to be done?"

"Better send our man back for a fresh post-chaise," said Linnell quickly. "Will you attend to Miss Denville?" he whispered. "I think I'll take one of the horses and ride back myself for the chaise."

"Why not let me go, Dick?"

"No," said Linnell in sombre tones. "I've stopped this wretched flight. My part's done. Mellersh, I trust to you to place her once more under her father's charge."

"Will not you do it?"

"I? No. I have done. We'll send this man for the chaise, though. That scoundrel Rockley may come to again and be troublesome."

"Lookye here, gents," said the man who had ridden the wheeler, "we want to know who's going to pay for this night's job. My leg's bad; my 'oss is dead; and the chay's all to pieces."

"Wait and see, my man," said Mellersh sternly. "You will be recompensed."

"But fine words butter no parsnips, you know, sir. I want to know—"

"Hold your tongue, fellow! I am Colonel Mellersh, of Saltinville. That man you were driving is Major Rockley, of the —th Dragoons. Of course everything will be paid for, and you will be recompensed. Now then, which of you can ride back for a fresh chaise?"

"Well, sir, I—"

"Damn it, man, don't talk. Five guineas if a chaise is here within an hour."

"Ah, that's business, sir. Come on, mate. We'll be back before then."

The man seemed to forget his bruised leg, and with the help of his comrade the girths were unbuckled, and the saddle dragged off the dead horse, placed upon the other, and they were about to start when the first postboy asked whether it would be safe to leave the injured chaise where it was.

As it happened, in the struggle it had been dragged off the road on to the grass border, and lay there, so that there was ample room for passers-by; and, satisfied with this, the postboys were off at a rapid trot.

"Rather an awkward position if that fellow is seriously injured," said Linnell grimly.

"Pooh! man; it was an accident, and he was engaged in an unlawful act," said Mellersh coolly, but with a peculiar meaning in his tone.

Linnell winced, for the mental pang was sharp. His old friend suggested that Claire might have been a willing partner in that night's adventure.

He made no reply. He dared not, for fear that it should be an angry retort; and content that he had certainly for the present frustrated Rockley's machinations, he walked to his side, and, seeing that his temple was bleeding, he knelt down by him, took out his handkerchief, and bound up the cut, furtively watching Mellersh the while as he stood by the other prostrate figure on the turf.

Linnell longed to go to her and kneel there, holding her little hand in his, but he was too heartsore; and, telling himself that there was more dignity in keeping aloof and playing the manly part of ceasing to care for one whom he believed to be unworthy of his love, even if he rendered help when there was need, he contented himself with deputing the care he would gladly have bestowed to another.

It had grown darker during the past few minutes, a thicker cloud having veiled the sky, when, as Linnell rose from where he knelt, he heard a sigh which went through him.

"She is coming round," he muttered. "Poor girl! Poor, weak, foolish girl! I—"

"Why, Dick!" cried Mellersh in a sharp, angry voice. "Come here!"

"What is it? There is no danger, is there?" cried Linnell, hastening across the road.

"Danger? No," cried Mellersh angrily. "Whom do you suppose we have stopped here?"

"Whom? Miss Denville, of course, and—Good Heavens!—Miss Dean!"

"What is it? Where am I? You—Mr Linnell!—Colonel Mellersh!" said Cora confusedly, as she struggled up into a sitting position.

"At your service, madam," said Mellersh, with a peculiar bitterness in his voice.

"What has happened?" cried Cora, holding her hand to her head, and staring wildly round till her eyes lighted upon the broken chaise. "Oh!"

She said no more, but struggled to her feet, turned giddy, and would have fallen, had not Mellersh caught her arm and supported her.

It was evident that she had realised her position in that one glance, and she seemed to shudder slightly. At the end of a few minutes, though, she recovered, and, shrinking from Mellersh, she looked round.

"Give me that cloak," she said calmly. "It is cold."

Linnell, who was half-stunned by the discovery, hurriedly stooped and picked up the cloak, spreading it rather clumsily and placing it upon her shoulders.

"Thank you," she said coldly; and there was an awkward pause, during which Mellersh walked to and fro with the look of a caged wild beast.

"Well?" said Cora suddenly. "Why are we waiting, Colonel Mellersh? Will you kindly see me home?"

"See you home?" he replied.

"Where is that man—Major Rockley?" cried Cora hastily.

"I am afraid he is incapacitated for further service, Miss Dean," said Mellersh coldly. "The accident has prevented him from carrying out—shall I say your wishes?"

"What?" she replied. "Do you think I—! Pah!"

She turned her back upon him angrily.

"Mr Linnell," she said, "you will not insult me if I ask you to see me safely home, even if I do not enter into any explanations. Let us go at once."

There was a strange resentful hauteur in her tone, and Linnell offered her his arm.

"We will walk a little way if you wish it, Miss Dean," he said; "but we ought hardly to leave Major Rockley in this state. My friend Colonel Mellersh—"

"Don't mind me, Dick," said the latter. "I'll play hospital nurse, if Miss Dean will trust me with the care of the Major."

Cora did not condescend to reply, but stepped forward as if to walk back.

"We are many miles from Saltinville, Miss Dean," said Linnell, "and a post-chaise will be here soon."

Further conversation was prevented by James Bell whispering hurriedly:

"It's all a mistake, Mr Linnell, and the consequences will be terrible if I am found to have taken the Major's horses. Can you do without me?"

"Yes," said Linnell quickly; "but your master?"

"I can't think of him, sir," said Bell hastily. "I must think of myself. Gentlemen, I thought we were chasing another lady whom I would have given my life to save. I stood by you; will you stand by me?"

"Yes," said Mellersh quickly. "Take the horses back. I'll stay by your master till help comes."

"And you will not tell upon me about the horses, gentlemen?"

"No," said Mellersh shortly. "Go."

"And you, Mr Linnell?"

"You may trust me," was the reply.

Bell went off with the horses on the instant, and a tedious time of waiting ensued, the end of which was that it was arranged when the fresh post-chaise came that Mellersh should ride with Cora and the injured man back to the posting house, Linnell walking by the side of the chaise.

On reaching the inn, Rockley was placed in the landlord's care, with instructions to fetch a medical man, and the three afterwards had a perfectly silent ride back to Saltinville, where Mrs Dean was found sitting up in a high state of excitement, and ready to greet her daughter:

"Lor! Bet—Cora—you have give me a turn. I thought it was a real elopement, and now you've come back."

"Well, Dick," said Mellersh grimly, as they stood together in the latter's room. "What do you think of it now?"

"I think I've been a fool," said Linnell shortly; "but I can't quite make it out."

"Neither can I," responded Mellersh, after a pause.

# Chapter Twenty Eight
## Under a Thick Cloak

"You'll be so glad to hear, my dear," prattled on Mrs Barclay, who was exceedingly warm and happy. "There's quite a reconciliation, my dear."

"Reconciliation?"

"Yes, dear. Young Cornet Denville has just fetched her to take her round the grounds, which is just as it should be, you know. I'd have gone with them, but I'm afraid of the night air, and catching a bad cold, you see, and so I think it's better not to risk taking a chill, and—"

"Who fetched her—Cornet Denville?"

"Yes, my dear, her brother; and I've been thinking—"

"Don't talk, Mrs Barclay," cried Cora quickly—"don't talk, pray, only tell me which way she went."

"Through that door, my dear, and on to the lawn. You'll catch 'em if you make haste. Bless us and save us, what is the matter with her? Any one would think poor Claire had run off with her young man. Dear, dear! what a blessing to be sure," sighed Mrs Barclay complacently, as she fanned herself, "to have one's own Jo-si-ah, and no troubles of that kind now."

Cora was gone—out through the window and on to the grass. There were couples here and there in the dim light, but not those she wished to see, as she stood passing her large lace scarf over her head.

"What shall I do?" she moaned; and in frantic haste she ran down the first path she came to, feeling more and more sure that she was wrong; but directly after she found that this crossed a broad grass path at right angles; and as she reached it she uttered a gasp, for there was a couple coming down towards her, and she felt rather than saw that it was those she sought.

They were close upon her, coming between the bushes, and Morton was talking loudly, with the thick utterance of one nearly inebriated, while Claire was answering in a troubled way.

"Very sorry," he said slowly, "sorry, little sis. Love you too much not to 'pologise, but—man's position—as officer and a gentleman—"

"Yes, yes, dear, you've said so before."

"And I must say you—Hallo! Who's thish?"

"Claire!" cried Cora, in a low whisper. "Back to the house—quick!"

"Miss Dean!"

"Yes. Quick! For heaven's sake. Go. Your father."

Cora did not know it, but she had touched the right chord.

Claire had seemed startled at first, and had hesitated as they stood together in the darkness with Morton holding the new-comer's arm; but as Cora exclaimed, as the place of safety Claire was to seek, "your father!" the thought flashed through Claire's brain that he had had some terrible seizure—or, worse, that horror of which he was in dread had come upon him, and in an instant, she had turned and run back towards the house.

"Why, what the dickensh—I say, what's matter?" stammered Morton. "Here, Miss Dean, I know you—you know—bu'ful Miss Dean. Proud of your company. Officer and a gentleman—and take my—"

It was so cleverly done that Cora was taken by surprise. She was about, as the simplest way out of the difficulty, to take the lad's arm, and walk back with him to the house, when there was a slight rustle behind her, the sound of a blow or fall, and the latter muffled and strange, for a great cavalry cloak was thrown over her head, twisted tightly round her, binding her arms to her side, and stifling the cry she uttered; and as she struggled fiercely for her liberty she was lifted from her feet and borne away.

It was all done so quickly that she was staggered, and she had not recovered from her confusion when she felt herself forced into a carriage— the chaise, evidently, of which she had heard. Then came the banging of a door as she was held back by two strong arms, the swaying and jerking of the chaise as it went over rough ground and ruts. Then she realised that it swayed more than ever as they turned on to a hard road, and she could hear the dull, smothered rattle of the wheels and the tramp of horses' feet.

She was a woman of plenty of strength of mind; but, for the time being, the fact of having fallen into this trap laid for Claire stunned her, and she felt a depressing dread. But by degrees this gave place to her returning courage, and she struggled furiously, but found that she was tightly held, and a deep voice she knew kept on bidding her to be patient—not to be alarmed—and the like.

In the midst of her excitement she ceased struggling and lay back in the corner of the chaise thinking, for the adventure had now assumed a ludicrous aspect. It was dramatic—a scene that might have happened in a play, and she laughed as she thought of Major Rockley's rage and disappointment when he realised his mistake.

"I'm not afraid of him," she thought, "and I hate him with all my heart. It is only waiting till we stop, and then the tables will be turned."

"Ah, that's more sensible," came through the thick cloak. "Promise to be patient and not call out, and I will take off the cloak."

It was very hot. She could hardly breathe, but she dreaded having it removed till she recalled how dark it was; that it must be even darker, shut up in the chaise, and that she had on her large lace mantilla, with which she could well cover her face.

"Shall I take off the cloak?" was said, after they had stopped and changed horses; and, feeling that she must have air, she made a gesture with her hands, passing them up towards her face as she felt the great cloth-covering partly removed, and, as it was drawn away, carefully covering her face and neck with the scarf.

"At last!" exclaimed her companion, trying to pass his arm round her, but she struck at him so fiercely that he desisted, and just then the chaise slackened speed.

"What is it?" he cried, gripping his prisoner's arm with one hand, as he leaned forward and let down a front window.

"Like us to go on as fast as this, Captain? Road's getting a bit hilly."

"Yes, and faster, you fools. On, quick! What's that?"

"Sounds like horses, sir, coming on behind."

"Oh, not after us, but go on as fast as you can."

The chaise rumbled on as the window was drawn up, and the sound of the horses deadened; but Rockley let down the window on his side of the vehicle and thrust out his head.

As he did so Cora listened intently, and made out the beating of horses' hoofs behind, now dying out, now louder, now dying out again, but always heard; and her heart gave a joyful bound as the thought came that an alarm might have been given by Morton Denville, and these be friends in pursuit— Richard Linnell perhaps.

Her heart sank like lead. No; she was not afraid of Major Rockley, and she did not care a fig for the opinion of Saltinville society. She had been carried off against her will, and the sneers would be those against Rockley, not against her.

The chaise might go on for hours—all night, if the Major liked. The longer it was before he discovered his mistake the greater his rage would be. What was there to fear? If she shrieked the postboys must come to her help, or she could command help at the next stopping-place.

And the horsemen coming on?

Yes, they were evidently gaining ground, but it was not to overtake her. He was trying to save the woman he loved—he, Richard Linnell—and her heart sank lower and lower still.

Then it gave a bound, for there was the click-click of a pistol, just as before now she had heard it on the stage, and Rockley said:

"That's right. I'm glad you are quiet. I've got you, and, by Jove, I'll shoot the man who tries to get you away as I would a dog."

# Chapter Twenty Nine
## A Little Gossip

That hat which the Master of the Ceremonies raised so frequently to the various visitors looked in its solidity as if it might very well become an heirloom, and descend to his son, should he in more mature life take to his father's duties.

Stuart Denville had just replaced it for about the twentieth time that morning, when he encountered Lady Drelincourt in her chair.

Her ladyship had been very cold since her visit to the Denvilles, but this particular morning she was all smiles and good humour.

"Now, here you are, Denville, and you'll tell me all about it. You were there?"

"Yes, dear Lady Drelincourt," said Denville, with his best smile, as he thought of Morton and his possible future. "I was there. At—er—"

"Pontardent's, yes. Now, tell me, there's a good man, all about it. Is the Major much hurt? Now, how tiresome! What do you want, Bray? You are always hunting me about with that wicked boy."

"No, no," said Sir Matthew, in his ponderous fashion. "Drawn, Lady Drelincourt, drawn. Attracted, eh, Payne?"

Sir Harry Payne—"that wicked boy," as he was termed by her ladyship—declared upon his reputation that Sir Matthew Bray was quite right. It was attraction.

"I felt it myself, demme, that I did, horribly, madam; but I said I would be true to my friend Bray, here, and I fled from temptation like a man."

"I'm afraid I can't believe you—either of you," said her ladyship, simpering. "But, now, do tell me—no, no, don't go, Denville; I want to talk to you. Sir Harry, now was Major Rockley, that dreadful Mephistopheles, half killed?"

Sir Harry Payne screwed up his face, shook his head, took snuff loudly, and, raising his hat, walked away.

"How tantalising!" cried Lady Drelincourt. "Now, Bray, do tell me. Is it true that he was carrying off that Miss Dean, and her mother sent Colonel Mellersh and Mr Linnell to fetch them back?"

"Mustn't tell. Can't say a word, dear Lady Drelincourt. Brother-officer, you see. But—"

Sir Matthew Bray blew out his cheeks, frowned, rolled his eyes, pursed up his lips, and looked as if he were fully charged with important information which honour forbade him to part with, ending by shaking his head at her ladyship, and then giving it a solemn nod.

"I knew I was right," said her ladyship triumphantly. "Now, didn't you hear the same version, Denville?"

"Well, I—must confess, your ladyship—that I—er—did."

"Of course. That's it. Well, Rockley's a very, very wicked man, and I don't think I shall ever speak to him again. I've quite done with him. Yes, you may stay a little while, Bray, but not long. People are so scandalous. Good-bye, Denville. Is your little girl quite well?"

Denville declared that she was in the best of health; and, as Lady Drelincourt was wheeled away in one direction, so much fashionable lumber, the Master of the Ceremonies went mincing in the other.

Saltinville boasted of about a dozen versions of the scandal, one of the most popular being that which was picked up at Miss Clode's. In this version Cora Dean had no part, but Claire Denville had.

For a whole week these various accounts were bandied about and garbled and told, till the result of the mixture was very singular, and it would have puzzled an expert to work out the simple truth. Then something fresh sprang up, and the elopement or abduction—nobody at last knew which, or who were the principals—was forgotten, especially as Rockley was seen about as usual, and the proprietor of the chaise and the killed horse was fully recompensed by the Major. How he obtained the money, he and Josiah Barclay best knew.

But Stuart Denville was disappointed with respect to his daughter's prospects. It was sheer pleasure to her to be able to stay quietly at home; but her father bitterly regretted the absence of invitation cards, while he, for one, remained strangely in ignorance that it was his own child who was nearly carried off that night.

# Chapter Thirty
# A Terrible Resurrection

"A gentleman to see you, ma'am."

"To see me, Isaac?" said Claire, starting in terror, and with a strange foreboding of ill. "Who is it? Did he give his name?"

"No, miss; he would not give any name. Said it was on important business. He asked for Miss May first."

"For Miss May?"

"Yes, ma'am; and I told him she was married, and did not live here now; and he smiled, and said 'Of course.' Then he said he would see you."

Claire had risen, and she stood listening to the man, clutching the chair tightly, and striving hard to seem composed.

"Where is he, Isaac?" she asked, hardly knowing what fell from her lips.

"In the dining-room, ma'am."

"I will come down."

Isaac left the room, and Claire drew a long breath.

Who could it be? Some one who had forgotten that May was married, and then recalled it! What did it mean?

She stood with her hands tightly clasped, gazing straight before her, and then walked quickly to the door, and down into the dining-room, so quietly that the short, slight man gazing out of the window did not hear her entrance.

Claire was puzzled while for the moment she gazed at the attitude of her visitor, whose long black hair fell over the collar of his tightly-buttoned surtout, as he stood with one hand resting upon his hip, the other holding his hat and tasselled cane.

She drew a breath of relief. It was no one she knew, of that she felt sure. Perhaps it was no fresh trouble after all.

As if divining the presence of some one in the room, the visitor just then turned quickly, displaying handsome aquiline features, with the olive skin and dark eyes of a young man of about thirty, who threw down his hat and cane and advanced smiling.

"My dear Miss Denville—my dear Claire!" he exclaimed, speaking with a foreign accent.

Claire stood as if frozen, gazing at him in horror.

"M. Gravani!" she cried at last in a hoarse whisper.

"Say Louis," he said eagerly, taking her hands and kissing them. "Why not? Surely my dear May told you—that she is my wife. No, no, do not be angry with me. It was wrong, I know. But you—you were always so sweet and good and kind, dear Claire!"

He kissed her hands again, and she stood as if in a dream while he went on—speaking fervidly.

"You, so tender, and who loved dear May so much. You will forgive me. We were so young—I was so poor—I dared not speak. What would the Signore Denville have said? That I was mad. May must have told you—she did tell you we were married?"

"Yes—yes," said Claire slowly, "she told me."

"That is well. And the old man—the good father, she told him, too!"

"No," said Claire, still in the same slow, dreamy way, as she strove to listen to her visitor, and at the same time work out in her own mind the meaning of the horrible situation in which her sister was placed.

"She did not tell him? She promised me she would. But the servant told me he knew that May was married."

"Yes," stammered Claire; "he knew."

"I ought to have spoken, but I dared not. I was younger then and so poor. I was obliged to go back to my Italia to try if I could not win fame there and fortune for my little flower of beauty—my May-bud. Claire—dear sister—no, no, you frown—you must forgive us, for we were so young, and we loved so much. Ah, you are not well. I frighten you. I came here so sudden. But my news is so good. I have succeeded so in my art, and I have possessions too. My poor father is dead. I am not a rich man—what you English call rich; but I have enough, and you will forgive me. But, May? She is not here?"

"No, no," said Claire, with her lips turning ashy pale.

"She is not far away?"

"Not far away," said Claire, "but Louis, Monsieur Gravani—"

"No, no, not Monsieur—not Signore. I am Louis, your fratello, your brother. Now tell me. My heart beats to be with her once again. She is not changed, I know. The same little angel face that Raffaello painted, and that I have had ever in my heart."

"No, she is not changed," sighed Claire.

"No, she could not change. La mia fiorella!"

"But Louis—"

"Yes? What? Why do you look at me so? She is ill!"

He raised his voice to a wild cry, and his handsome face grew convulsed as he seized Claire's hands.

"No, no," she cried. "No, no; she is quite well."

"Then take me to her now. I can wait no longer. I must see her now."

"No, no, you cannot. It is impossible," cried Claire.

"Then there is something that you do not tell me. Speak; you are killing me."

"She—she—my poor sister—she thought—she heard—she had news, Louis—that you were dead."

"Dead?—I?—dead? Oh, my poor little flower!" he cried, with a ring of tender pity in his voice, but changing to a fierce burst of anger on the instant. "But who told her? Who sent her those lies?"

"I don't know—I never knew. But she grieved for you, Louis—because you were dead."

"My little tender flower! Oh! oh! it is too cruel. But I am here—here, waiting to press her to my heart once more. You shall take me to her now."

"It would be impossible. I could not. It would kill her. No, you must wait till to-morrow."

"No, no; I could not wait," he cried excitedly. "I love her. I am here. I must see her now."

Claire felt beside herself, and her hands dropped helplessly to her side, as if she despaired of averting the catastrophe that was to come. What was she to do?—say something to deceive this man and keep him waiting until she had seen and prepared her sister?

The task was hateful to her in the extreme; and it seemed as if her life was to be made up of subterfuges and concealments, all of which caused reflections upon her.

Z"Addio, cara mia!" he said, as he bent over and tenderly kissed her hands, and then her cheek. "Addio, sweet sister, I am dying till I once more hold her in these arms."

Claire led him to the door, as if she were in a dream; and, as she listened to his departing steps, her hands involuntarily clasped her throbbing head, and Isaac confided to his fellow-servants the information that there were strange goings-on in that house, and that when he liked to speak—well, they would see.

"What shall I do?"

# Chapter Thirty One
## Claire Takes Steps: so does May

"What shall I do?"

The low wild cry of agony that escaped from Claire Denville's breast was heard by none, as she stood motionless, listening to Louis Gravani's steps till they died away.

Then, trembling violently in an agony of terror and despair, she rushed up to her bedroom, and threw herself upon her knees, with her hands still clasping her temples.

What should she do? To whom could she go for help and counsel? Mrs Barclay? Impossible! Cora Dean! No, no: she could not tell her! Her father? She shivered at the thought. It would nearly kill him. He believed so in poor, weak, childish May. She could not—she dared not tell him.

If she had only gone to him at once and shared her secret with him when May had confessed her marriage, and told her about the little child, how easy all this would have been now!

No! Would it? The complication was too dreadful.

Claire knelt there with her brain swimming, and the confusion in her mind growing moment by moment worse.

She wanted to think clearly—to plan out some way of averting a horrible exposure from their family; and, as she strove, the thought came upon her with crushing force that she was sinking into a miserable schemer—one who was growing lower in the sight of all she knew.

She pressed her hands over her eyes, but she could not shut out Richard Linnell's face, and his stern, grave looks, that seemed to read her through and through, keeping her back from acting some fresh deceit, when something was spurring her on to try and save poor weak May.

The horror of Lady Teigne's death: the suspicion of her having made an assignation with Sir Harry Payne; the supposed elopement with Major Rockley—all these clinging to her and lowering her in the sight of the world. There were those, too, who had noted her visits to the fisherman's cottage.

It was terrible—one hideous confusion, to which this fresh trouble had come; and she asked herself, in the agony of her spirit, whether it would not be better to wait till the dark, soft night had fallen, and the tide was flowing, lapping, and whispering amongst the piles at the end of the pier. She had but to walk quietly down unseen—to descend those steps, and let the cool, soft wave take her to its breast and bear her away, lulling her to the easy, sweet rest of oblivion.

And May?

She started to her feet at the thought.

And Richard Linnell?

He would go on believing ill of her, and she would never stand up before him, listening as he asked her forgiveness for every doubt, never to be her husband, but ready then to look up to her as all that was pure and true.

May! She must save May. How, she knew not, but she must go to her. Something must be done.

Hurriedly dressing, she went out, and walked swiftly to her brother-in-law's house, where the servant admitted her with no great show of respect, and she was shown into the drawing-room.

"I'll tell my mistress you are here," said the footman; and he went out, closing the door behind him rather loudly.

The effect was to make a little man jump up from the couch where he had been sleeping, with a loud exclamation.

"What is it? Who the—. Oh, it's you, is it? Well, what do you want?"

"I came—I called to see May, Frank dear," said Claire, trembling.

"Well, then, I just wish you wouldn't," he said testily. "It's bad enough to have to bear the relationship, without having you come here."

"Frank!—dear Frank!"

"There, don't 'dear Frank' me. I should have thought, after what had occurred, you would have been ashamed to show your face here again."

"Frank dear, we are brother and sister; for pity's sake, spare me. Is it the duty of a gentleman to speak to me like this?"

She looked at him with a pitying dread in her eyes, as she thought of the horror hanging over his house. His allusions were keen enough, but they were blunt arrows compared to the bolts that threatened to fall upon his home; and, in her desire to shield him and his wife, if possible, from some of the suffering that must come, she scarcely felt their points.

"Gentleman, eh? You behave like a lady, don't you? Nice position we hold in society through you and the old man, don't we? I'll be off abroad, that's what I'll do, and take May away from the old connection."

"Yes, do!" cried Claire excitedly. "Do, Frank, at once. No, no; you must not do that.—Heaven help me! What am I saying?" she sighed to herself.

"Best thing to do," said Burnett. "Shouldn't have you always coming in then."

"Frank dear," said Claire deprecatingly, "I have not been to see May since—"

"You disgraced yourself on the night of the party," he said brutally.

"Frank!"

"Oh, come: it's of no use to ride the high horse with me, my lady. I'm not a fool. I repeat it: you haven't been since the night you disgraced us by inviting that little blackguard, Harry Payne, to see you; and it would have been better if you had not come now."

Claire winced as if she were being lashed, but she uttered no word of complaint. It was her fate, she told herself, to suffer for others, and she was ready to play the social martyr's part, and save May and Burnett if she could.

As she debated in her mind whether Burnett had not proposed the solution of the difficulty in taking her sister away, the thought was crushed by the recollection that May was Gravani's wife, and that she would be saved and made happier could she leave with him.

Then the feeling came that all this was madness, and the position hopeless, and she said imploringly:

"Let me see May, Frank."

"What do you want with her? To beg for more money? You've kept her short enough lately."

"Frank! indeed—"

"No lies, please," he cried. "I know you've had at least a guinea a week from her for long enough past."

It was true, but the money was for Gravani's child; and Claire's face grew hollow and old-looking as she felt that she dared not defend herself.

"I suppose you have come for more money, haven't you?" said Burnett spitefully.

"No—indeed no!" cried Claire.

"I do not believe you," he said brutally; "and—"

"Ah, Claire, you here!" said May, rustling into the room, all silk, and scent, and flowers.

"Yes, she's here," said Burnett; "and the sooner she's gone the better. I'm going out."

"Very well, dear," said May. "But don't pout and frown like that at his little frightened wife."

"Get out!" said Burnett, "and don't be a fool before people."

He shook her off as he said this, and strutted towards the door, where he turned with a sneering grin upon his face.

"I say," he cried, "I didn't give you any money when you asked me this morning."

"No, dear, you didn't. Give me some now, before you go. Don't go out and leave me without."

"Not a shilling!" he cried, with an unpleasant cackling laugh.

May stood with the pretty smile upon her face, a strange contrast to the pained classic sorrow upon her sister's better-formed features, amid perfect silence, till the front door closed, and Frank Burnett's strutting step was heard on the shingle walk leading to the gate, when a change came over the bright, flower-like countenance, which was convulsed with anger in miniature.

"Ugh! Little contemptible wretch!" she exclaimed. "How I do hate you! Claire, I shall end by running away from the little miserable ape, if I don't make up my mind to kill him. Ah!"

She ended with an ejaculation full of pain, and turned a wondering, childish look of reproach on her sister, for Claire had crossed to her, and suddenly grasped her wrist.

"Silence, May!" she cried.

"Oh, don't!" said May, wresting herself free, and stamping her foot like a fretful, angry child. "And if you've come here to do nothing but scold me and find fault, you'd better go."

"May—May! Listen to me."

"No, I won't. I'll go up to my own room and cry my eyes out. You don't know; you can't imagine what a little wretch he is. I wish you were married to him instead of me."

"May!"

"I won't listen," cried the foolish little woman, stopping her ears. "You bully me for caring for Sir Harry Payne, who is all that is tender and loving; and I'm tied to that hateful little wretch for life, and he makes my very existence a curse."

"May, will you listen?"

"I can see you are scolding me, but I can't hear a word you say, and I won't listen. Oh, I do wish you were married to him instead of me."

"I wish to heaven I were!" cried Claire solemnly.

"What?" cried May, the stopping of whose ears seemed now to be very ineffective. "You wish you were married to the little mean-spirited, insignificant wretch?"

"Yes," said Claire excitedly, "for then you would be free."

"What do you mean by that, Claire?"

"Did you not tell me that Louis Gravani was dead?"

"Yes, of course I did."

"Why did you tell me that?"

"Because he went to Rome or Florence—I am not sure which—and caught a fever and died."

"Are you sure?"

"Well, dear, he never wrote and told me he was dead, of course," said May with a little laugh, "but he told me he had caught the fever, and he never wrote to me any more, so, of course, he died."

"And, without knowing for certain, you married Frank Burnett?"

"Don't talk in that way, dear. It's just like the actress at Drury Lane, where Frank took me. You would make a fortune on the stage. What do you mean, looking at me so tragically?"

"May, prepare yourself for terrible news."

"Oh, Claire! Is poor, dear papa dead?"

"May, Louis Gravani is alive."

"Alive? Oh, I am so glad!" she cried, clapping her hands. "Poor, dear little Louis! How he did love me! Then he isn't dead, after all, and I'm his wife, and not Frank's. Oh, what fun!"

Claire caught at the back of a chair, and stood gazing wildly at her sister, utterly stunned by her childish unthinking manner.

"May—May!" she cried bitterly; "your sin is finding you out."

"Sin? How absurd you are! Why, what sin have I committed?"

"That clandestine marriage, May."

"Now what nonsense, dear. It wasn't my fault, as I told you before. You don't know what love is. I do, and I loved poor, dear little Louis. I couldn't help it, and he made me marry him."

"Oh, May, May!"

"I tell you, I was obliged to marry him. One can't do as one likes, when one loves. You'll know that some day. But, I am glad."

"May!" cried Claire reproachfully.

"So I am. Why, he'll come and fetch me away from my miserable tyrant, and we can have little pet blossom away from Fisherman Dick's, and take a cottage somewhere, and then I can sing and play to baby, while dear old Louis reads the Italian poets to me, and goes on with his painting."

A piteous sigh escaped from Claire Denville's lips as she fervently breathed in wild appeal:

"My God, help me!" And then—"It is too hard—too hard. What shall I do?"

A change came over the scene. The picture May Burnett had painted dissolved in the thin air, and she turned quickly upon her sister.

"How do you know this, Claire? Has Louis written to you?"

"No. He is here."

"Here! In Saltinville?"

"Yes, here in Saltinville. He would have been at this house, only I prevailed upon him to stay till I had seen you—to prepare you."

"Oh, Claire! Does he know I am married?"

"No; he believes you have been as faithful to him as he to you."

"Oh!"

It was a wild cry; and a look of frightened horror came over the pretty baby face, as its owner caught Claire round the waist, and clung to her.

"Claire, Claire!" she cried. "Save me! What shall I do? Louis is an Italian, and he is all love and passion and jealousy. I dare not see him. He would kill me, if he knew. What shall I do? What can I do? Oh, this is terrible, Claire!" she cried. "Claire!" and she shook her sister passionately. "Why don't you speak? What shall I do?"

Claire remained silent.

"Why don't you speak, I say?" cried May with childish petulance.

"I am praying for help and guidance, sister, for I do not know."

May let herself sink down upon the carpet with her hands clasped, as she gazed straight at her sister, looking to her for advice and help, while Claire remained with her eyes fixed, deeply pondering upon their terrible position.

"I can only think of one thing," she said at last. "I must see Louis Gravani, and tell him all."

"No, no; I tell you he will kill me."

"He loves you, May; and I must appeal to him to act like a gentleman in this terrible strait."

"Don't I tell you that he is a passionate Italian, and that he would kill me. He always used to say that he felt as if he could stab anybody who came between us. Oh, Claire, what shall I do? My poor life's full of miserable troubles. I wish I were dead."

"Hush, May, and try and help me, instead of acting in this childish way."

"There, now you turn against me."

"No, no, my poor sister. I want to help you, and give you strength."

"Then you will help me, Claire?"

"Help you!" said Claire reproachfully. "Did I spare my poor reputation for your sake?"

"Oh, don't talk of that now, only tell me, what shall I do?"

"You must come with me."

"With you, dear? Where?"

"Home, to your father's roof; and we must tell him all. He will protect you."

"Come—home—tell poor papa? No—no—no, I cannot—I dare not."

"You must, May. It were a shame and disgrace to stay here, now that you know your husband is alive."

"My first husband, Claire dear," said May pitifully.

"Oh, hush, May; you'll drive me mad. There, go and dress yourself, and come home."

"I will not—I daren't," cried May; "and, besides, this is my home."

"And Louis? Am I to tell him where you are?"

"No, no. I tell you he would kill me. I must have time to think. Didn't you tell me he was going to wait, Claire? Look here, I dare not see him. No, everything is over between us. You must see him, dear."

"See him?" said Claire.

"Yes, dear, yes. Oh, Claire, Claire!" she cried wildly, going upon her knees to her sister, "pray—pray, save me. Tell Louis I am not married to Frank. Tell him he must go away, and not come back till I write to him."

"May, how can you be so childish?" cried Claire piteously.

"I am not childish. This is not childish. I know—I know—tell him this, and he will go away."

"Tell him this?"

"Yes, yes; don't you understand? He is very stupid; tell him I am dead."

"May!"

"Stop a moment; you said he was going to wait."

"Till I can give him news of you."

"Yes; then you must keep him quiet for a day or two, till I have had time to think."

"There is no time."

"Give me till to-morrow, Claire. Don't you see I am all confused, and mad with grief?"

"Till to-morrow?" said Claire, gazing at her, for it was like a respite to her as well, in her horrible doubt and confusion of intellect.

"Yes, till to-morrow. I will shut myself up in my room till then, and try and think out what will be best. There, go now. I can't talk to you; I can't think; I can't do anything till you are gone; and I must have time."

Claire left her at last unwillingly, but with the understanding that May was to stay in her own room till the next day, and await her return.

"It will all come right at last, Claire," said May, at parting. "It always does, dear. There, don't fidget. It's very tiresome of him to come now; but I don't know: perhaps it's all for the best."

She kissed Claire affectionately at parting; and the latter sighed as she hurried home, struggling with herself as to how she should make all this known to her father.

"He must know," she said; and she entered the dining-room at once, to find that he was absent, though he had been home while she was away.

"Master said he had some business to transact, ma'am, and would have a chop at the Assembly Rooms. You were not to wait dinner."

Claire went to her own room to think.

May had, in accordance with her promise, gone to hers; then she had written a brief note, ordered the carriage, and gone for a drive, closely veiled. One of her calls was at Miss Clode's, where she entrusted her note, not to some volume to be sold, but to Miss Clode's round-eyed, plump-cheeked niece, who promised to deliver it at once.

# VOLUME THREE

## Chapter One
## Miss Clode is Mysterious

Richard Linnell had left his quiet, patient-looking father busily copying a sheet of music, and joined Colonel Mellersh, who was waiting at the door ready for a stroll.

Cora Dean's ponies were in the road, and that lady was just about to start for a drive.

Somehow, her door opened, and she came rustling down, closing her ears to a petulant call from her mother, and—perhaps it was an accident—so timed her descent that it would be impossible for the gentlemen to avoid offering to hand her to the carriage.

They both raised their hats as they stood upon the step, and she smiled and looked at Richard Linnell, but he did not stir.

"Come, Dick," said Mellersh, with a half-sneer; "have you forgotten your manners?"

Linnell started, offered his arm, which was taken, and he led Cora down to the little carriage, the ponies beginning to stamp as the groom held their bits, while the bright, smiling look of their mistress passed away.

"The ponies look rather fresh," said Richard Linnell, trying to be agreeable. "I should have their bearing reins tightened a little."

"Why?" said Cora sharply, and with a glance full of resentment: and, at the same moment, she noted that Mellersh was leaning against the door-post, looking on.

"Why?" repeated Linnell, smiling in her face—but it was not the smile she wished to see—"for fear of another accident, of course."

"What would you care?" she said in a low whisper. "I wish there would be another accident. Why didn't you let me drown? I wish I were dead."

She gave her ponies a sharp lash, the groom leaped aside, caught the back of the carriage, and swung himself up into his seat, and away they dashed at a gallop, while Linnell stood gazing after them, till Mellersh laid a hand upon his shoulder.

"Dick, Dick," he said banteringly, "what a fierce wooer you are! You have been saying something to offend the fair Cora. Come along."

"Does it give you pleasure to banter me like this?"

"Banter, man? I was in earnest."

They walked along the parade in silence, and had not gone far before they met the Master of the Ceremonies, who raised his hat stiffly, in response to their salutes, and passed on.

"Oh, man, man, why don't you take the good the gods provide you, instead of sighing after what you cannot have."

"Mellersh," said Richard, as if he had not heard him, "if I make up my mind to leave Saltinville, will you pay a good deal of attention to the old man?"

"Leave—Saltinville?"

"Yes; I am sick of the place. I must go right away."

"Stop a moment! Hold your tongue! There is that scoundrel, Rockley, with his gang."

In effect, a group of officers came along in the opposite direction, and, but for the disposition shown them to avoid a quarrel, their offensive monopolisation of the whole of the path would have resulted in an altercation.

"I shall have to cripple that fellow," said Mellersh, as they walked on, after turning out into the road in passing the group. "I wonder young Denville does not shoot him for his goings on with his sister."

"Mellersh!"

"I can't help it, Dick; I must speak out. Rockley is indefatigable there. The fellow is bewitched with her, and is always after her."

"It's a lie!" exclaimed Linnell.

"Call me a liar if you like, Dick, my lad. I shan't send you a challenge. Plenty of people will satisfy you as to the truth of what I say, and I speak thus plainly because I am weary of seeing you so infatuated with Claire Denville."

Linnell tried to draw his arm away, but the Colonel retained it.

"No, no, my dear boy, we cannot quarrel," he said. "It is impossible. But about this going away. Right. I would go. It will cure you."

"Cure me?" said Linnell bitterly.

"Yes, cure you. Dick, my boy, it makes me mad to see you so blind—to see you let a woman who looks guileless lead you—Well, I'll say no more. I cannot believe in Claire Denville any more than I can in her little innocent-looking jade of a sister."

Linnell uttered an impatient ejaculation.

"She goes about with a face as round-eyed as a baby's, and as smooth; while all the time I know—"

Linnell turned to him a look so full of agony that he ceased on the instant, but began again.

"I cannot help it, Dick," he said. "It worries me to see you growing so listless over a passion for a woman who does not care a straw for you."

"If I could believe that," said Linnell, "I could bear it; but I am tortured by doubts, and every friend I have seems to be bent upon blackening the reputation of a woman who has been cruelly maligned."

Mellersh began to whistle softly, and then said, sharply:

"What! going in here?"

"Yes; will you come?"

"No," said Mellersh, giving him a curious look. "Expect a letter? Tut-tut, man, don't eat me. You would not be the first man who made a post-office of Miss Clode's circulating library. What is it, then—fiddle-strings?"

Linnell nodded.

"Go in, then; you can join me presently. I shall be on the pier. I say, Dick, the fair directress of this establishment ought to put up on her sign, 'Dealer in heart-strings and fiddle-strings.' There, good-bye for the present."

The Colonel went on, keeping a sharp look-out for Cora Dean's pony-carriage; but it did not meet his eyes; and Richard Linnell turned into the library, meeting Lady Drelincourt, who smiled and simpered as she passed out, thrusting a book into her reticule.

Miss Clode was just disappearing into the inner room, leaving round-eyed Annie in charge; but as soon as that young lady caught sight of Linnell, she darted back to whisper loudly:

"Auntie, auntie: here's Mr Richard Linnell."

The latter saw no reason why little Miss Clode should flush and turn pale, and then look up at him in a wistful manner, almost with reproach in her eyes.

"Why, it's quite a month since I've seen you, Mr Linnell," she said, "and—and you look quite pale and thin."

"Do I, Miss Clode?" he said, smiling. "Ah, well, it's a healthy sign—of robust health, you know. I want some—"

"But you don't look well, Mr Linnell," she said hastily. "Annie, my dear, take this book to Mrs Barclay's, and make haste back."

"Yes, auntie," said the girl, in an ill-used tone.

"And make haste," cried Miss Clode. "Will you excuse me a minute, Mr Linnell?"

"Oh, of course," said the young man listlessly. "Give me the case with the violin strings, and I'll select some."

Miss Clode did not appear as if she heard him, but went to the back of the shop to hurry her niece away, to that young lady's great disgust, for she wanted to stare at Richard, whom she greatly admired, and hear what was said. Consequently, he was left turning over the books for a few minutes before Miss Clode returned, and, to his surprise, stood gazing up at him wistfully.

"Well, Miss Clode," he said with forced gaiety, "suppose somebody were waiting for me to join in a sonata?"

"I—I beg your pardon," she cried, flushing, and turning her back, she obtained the tin case that held the transparent rings, and placed it before him with a deep sigh.

"Not well, Miss Clode?" said Richard cheerfully.

To his astonishment she caught his hand in hers, and burst into tears.

"No, no, no," she cried, sobbing violently, "I am ill—heart-sick. Mr Linnell, please, pray come in, I want to speak to you."

"Why, Miss Clode!" he exclaimed.

"Yes, you are surprised," she exclaimed, "greatly surprised. You, so young and handsome, an independent gentleman, are astonished that a poor insignificant woman in my humble position should be always anxious about you—should—should—there, I can keep it back no longer," she cried passionately, as she held with both hands tightly that which he tried to withdraw. "I must speak—I must tell you, or you will wreck and ruin your dear life. Mr Linnell—Richard—I love you. I love you so that I cannot bear to see and hear what I do—you are breaking my heart."

"Miss Clode!" cried Richard Linnell, amazed, filled with contempt, sorrow, pity, all in one. "Think of what you are saying. Why, what madness is this?"

"The madness of a wretched, unhappy woman, who has known you so long, and whose love for you is a hundred times stronger than you can believe. But hush! Come in here. Some one may call at any moment, and I could not bear for them to see."

She loosed his hand, made a quick movement towards the little door at the end of the counter, and held it open for him to pass in.

It was a painful position for one so full of chivalrous respect for women, and the young man stood trying to think of what to say to release himself in the best way from a situation that he would have looked upon as ludicrous, only that it was so full of pain.

"You are shrinking from me!" she exclaimed. "Pray, pray, don't do that, Mr Linnell. Have I not suffered enough? Come in; let me talk to you. Let me try and explain."

"It is impossible," he said at last sternly. "Miss Clode, believe me that I will never breathe a syllable about this to a soul, but—"

"Oh, you foolish, foolish boy!" she exclaimed, bursting into an hysterical fit of laughter. "How could you think such a thing as that? Is there no love a poor, weak, elderly woman like I am, could bear for one she has known from a boy, but such as filled your mind just then? There, there!" she cried, wiping her eyes quickly. "I have spoken wildly to you. Forgive me. I am a poor lonely woman, who fixed her affection upon you, Richard Linnell, farther back than you can imagine. Listen, and let me tell you," she said in a soft, low voice, as she came round to the front of the counter, and laid her little thin hand upon his arm. "You lost your mother long ago, and have never known what it was to have a mother's love; but, for years past, your every movement has been watched by me; I have suffered when you have been in pain; I have rejoiced when I knew that you were happy."

"My dear Miss Clode!" he exclaimed, in a half-wondering, half-pitying tone.

"Yes—yes," she panted; "speak to me like that. You pay me for much suffering and misery; but don't—pray don't despise me for all this."

"Despise you? No!" he said warmly; "but you do surprise me, Miss Clode. I know you have always spoken very kindly to me."

"And you have always thought it almost an impertinence," she said sadly. "It has been. This is impertinent of me, you think, too, but I shall not presume. Mr Linnell, I have something to say to you, and when that is said, I shall keep my distance again, and it will be a secret between us."

"Why, Miss Clode," said Richard, trying to smile cheerfully, "you are making up quite a romance out of one of your own books."

"Yes," she said, looking wistfully in his eyes, "quite a romance, only it is all true, my dear. Now, will you come in?"

He hesitated for a moment, and then walked right in to the parlour, and she followed him, wiping her red eyes with her handkerchief.

"You will sit down?" she said, drawing forward an elbow-chair.

He took it from her and placed it so that she could sit down, while he took another.

"No," she said softly, "I will stand. Mr Linnell, please sit down."

He smiled and looked at her, full of expectancy, while she stood wringing her handkerchief, and puckering up her forehead, her lips parted, and an eager look of pride in her eyes as she gazed at him.

"It is very good of you to come," she faltered. "I will say what I have to say directly, but I am very weak, my dear—I—I beg your pardon, Mr Linnell. Don't—don't think me too familiar. You are not angry with me for loving you?"

"How can I be angry?" he said quickly. "I am surprised."

"You need not be," she said. "You would not be, if you knew more of human nature than you do. Mr Richard Linnell, it is in a woman's nature to desire to cling to and love something. Why should you be surprised that a poor lonely woman like me should love—as a son—the handsomest and truest gentleman we have in Saltinville?"

"It is fortunate for me that we meet but seldom, Miss Clode," said Richard, smiling, "if you hold me in such estimation as this."

"I do not see why," she said gravely. "You are handsome. You are brave. Do you think I do not know how you fought that duel below the cliff?"

"Oh, tut-tut," he said quickly; "let that rest."

"Or how bravely you followed that Major Rockley the night when he carried off Miss Dean?"

"My dear Miss Clode," said Richard quickly, "we shall be drifting into scandal directly."

She looked at him pityingly, as she saw the flush upon his cheeks, and it seemed to be reflected in hers, as she spoke out now eagerly and quickly, as if she thought there was a risk of his taking offence and hurrying away.

"I will not talk scandal," she said, standing before him with her hands clasped; "I only want to talk of you—of your future, and to try and stop you before you go wrong."

"Miss Clode!" he exclaimed warmly.

"Yes," she said; "be angry with me. I expect it, and I'll bear it; I'll bear anything to see you happy. If I had seen you taking the downward course— gambling, or drinking, or intriguing, I should have tried to stop you—tried fiercely, and braved your anger, as I do now. For I must—I will speak."

"I have neither been gambling, drinking, nor intriguing, Miss Clode," said Richard laughingly, "so I have not deserved your wrath."

"You are mocking at me, boy," she said, with spirit.

"You think me a foolish, eccentric little woman—half mad, perhaps. Think so," she cried, "and, maybe, you are right; but, with all my weakness and folly, I love you, Richard Linnell, as a mother loves her offspring, and it is to save you from future misery that I have nerved myself to risk your displeasure, and perhaps your future notice, for I am not so vain as to think I can ever be looked upon by you as anything but what I am."

There was such warmth and sincerity in her words that Richard hastily took her hands.

"Forgive me," he said; "I am serious, and respect you for all this, Miss Clode."

She bent down quickly and kissed his hands, making him start, and then look down on her pityingly, his wonder increasing as he saw how moved she was, her tears having fallen on the hands she kissed.

"There," she cried, "I will not keep you, but I must say what I have on my mind, even if I offend you and make you angry as I did before."

Richard Linnell looked at her sharply, with his eyes kindling; but, without speaking, she joined her hands together and stood before him as if pleading.

# Chapter Two
# Miss Clode Feels that she has done Right

"The woman is mad," said Richard Linnell, with a pitying look, and he made a movement as if to leave, but she caught his hand.

"Pray—pray stay," she whispered, "and let me—let me speak."

"Well, speak," he said, in a low, angry voice, "but be careful of what you say."

"It is for your sake," she whispered. "You do not know what I do. It is my lot to hear and see so much. I only want to take the veil from before your eyes."

"If it is to blacken some one whom I respect—"

"Whom you love, boy, with a foolish, insensate love. It is to save you from misery that I speak."

"To tell me some vile scandal that I will not hear," he cried.

"That you shall hear, if I die for telling you, boy," she cried, catching his wrist with both her hands. "Strike me if you like. Crush me if you will, but you shall hear the truth."

"The truth—what truth, woman?" cried Richard indignantly.

"The truth about—"

"Hush! you shall not speak her name," cried Richard furiously.

"It is enough that you know," said little Miss Clode quickly. "Boy, boy, place your affection elsewhere, and not upon a woman who is about to elope to-night."

"It is not true," he cried furiously, "and I am a weak fool to stay and listen to such calumnies."

"It is true," said Miss Clode; "and it was to save you from the misery of discovering all this that I made up my mind to tell you."

"To have the pleasure of retailing this wretched scandal," he retorted scornfully. "Woman, you disgrace your sex by calumniating a sweet, pure woman."

"It was to save you agony and despair," she said piteously. "You might never have known of this. People work so slyly, and in such secrecy; and if you only knew how jealous I am of your future, you would not speak and look at me so cruelly as you do."

"Stop!" cried Richard fiercely. "It was you sent me that wretched anonymous letter once?"

"Yes," she said humbly—"to save you from misery—to open your eyes to the truth."

"To open my eyes to a lie," he cried. "Miss Clode, enough of this. I promised you that I would look upon this as our secret: let it remain so, and we know each other no more."

He moved towards the door, but she clung to his wrist.

"That was a mistake," she panted; "but this time I am sure."

"I will not listen," he cried. "Loose my wrist, woman."

"You shall listen," she cried. "Richard Linnell, the post-horses are ordered, and Claire Denville leaves her home to-night with—"

He did not hear the rest, for he had reached the shop, and hurried away, nearly overturning Annie, as she came in to find her aunt in tears.

"Oh, auntie, what is the matter?" she cried.

"Look here," whispered Miss Clode, "are you sure there was no mistake in what you told me to-day?"

"Quite sure, aunt dear. Jane Moggridge told me that there were post-horses ordered for Major Rockley, and for Sir Harry Payne, and for Sir Matthew Bray."

"That will do," said Miss Clode quickly. "Now go right away."

Annie looked wider-eyed and rounder-faced than ever in her disappointment as she obeyed her aunt, while Miss Clode stood with her hands clasped to her side, gazing straight before her.

"Have I done right?" she said to herself; "have I done wrong? It maddens me to see him so deceived—so blind. It was my duty to awaken him from his miserable infatuation, but suppose mischief should come after it?"

She turned ghastly pale, and clutched at a chair.

"No, no," she cried, as she battled with her fears; "he is too brave and strong, and he will have Mellersh on his side. I have done right, I am sure. It is half breaking his heart, poor fellow; but better the sharp pain now than one that would last for life."

# Chapter Three
# Mr Barclay is Busy

Josiah Barclay sat at his writing-table, looking about the most uncompromising specimen of humanity possible, when the door was softly opened, and his man-servant came in.

"And nine's seventy-three," muttered Barclay, making an entry. "Hang the woman! I wish she'd come down and go on with these accounts. Well, Joseph?"

"Lady Drelincourt, sir."

"Humph! Bless her! Let her wait. Seen that monkey again, Joseph?"

"Isaac, sir? Denville's Isaac?"

"Yes, him. Dropped any more hints?"

"Saw him last night, sir, at the Blue Posts."

"Well?"

"Went on dropping hints again, sir, as soon as he had had a glass or two. 'Fraid he's a fool, sir."

"Nothing to be afraid of in a fool, Joseph, so long as you keep him at a distance. So he chatters, eh?"

"Yes, sir. Professes to have a mystery. He could speak if he liked, and there's a deal he could say if he pleased, and lays his finger on the side of his nose, and all that sort of thing, sir. That's been going on for months, and it's what he calls confiding in me; but it never goes any further."

"And what do you think of it, Joseph?"

"Nothing, sir," said Barclay's confidential man drily. "I believe it's all to make him seem important. Lived a long while in an artificial soil, sir, and goes in for shams."

Barclay chuckled.

"Don't give him up, Joseph. I think he does know something, and it may be worth hearing. I find we can't know too much. Does he confide in anyone else?"

"No, sir, I think not."

"Well, don't give him up. Now you can show Lady Drelincourt in: and while she is here run on to Moggridge's. He has sent me a hint that a chaise or two are ordered for to-night. Find out who are going."

Joseph nodded and went out, while Barclay was muttering to himself that he liked to make sure none of his sheep were going astray, when Lady Drelincourt was shown in.

"Humph! I must send for my wife," said Barclay to himself. "It is dangerous when Venus invades one's home;" and he looked gravely at the overdressed, painted-up old woman, with his thoughts dwelling upon her likeness to Lady Teigne—the murder, the missing jewels—and Isaac's mysterious communications to his servant when they met at the Blue Posts to smoke a pipe.

"Ah, doctor," cried her ladyship playfully, "I've come to let you feel my pulse."

"Your pulse, Lady Drelincourt?" said Barclay. "Surely your ladyship's circulation is not low?"

"Horribly, Barclay. I am fainting for want of the circulating medium."

"But your ladyship's lawyers?"

"Oh, I can't go to them again, and be bothered about deeds."

"Your ladyship wants acts, eh?"

"To be sure, and at once, Barclay. I want five hundred pounds."

"A large sum, my lady," said Barclay warily.

"Stuff! A trifle. Just enough to take me on the Continent and back."

"Humph!" said Barclay aloud; and to himself: "One of the post-chaises."

"Now, no nonsense, Barclay, or I shall be compelled to whip you severely with my fan."

"That ought to be a pleasure, madam," said Barclay politely. "But what security do you offer for five hundred pounds?"

"Security! and from me, you wicked ogre!" said her ladyship playfully. "Why, you ought to feel honoured."

"I do, my lady, greatly; but—"

"There, I don't want to waste my time listening to stuff. I know what a close-fisted, miserly old wretch you are, and so I came prepared."

"Prepared, Lady Drelincourt?"

"Of course. I only want a temporary loan, and here are my diamonds."

She drew a morocco case from the large reticule hanging on her arm, and passed it across the table.

Barclay opened the case, took out a glittering necklet, breathed upon it, glanced at the rest of the contents of the case, replaced the necklet, and closed it.

"Well, monster," said her ladyship playfully, "will that do?"

"Admirably, my lady," said Barclay, taking a cash-box from a drawer, and counting out, with deft fingers, a number of notes. "Four fifty-five," he muttered, as he passed the rustling bundle across to his visitor, and slipped the case and cash-box back.

"I must have no nonsense about those diamonds, Barclay," said her ladyship, "when I want them back."

"Your ladyship has only to sign this paper," replied Barclay, "and hand me 600 pounds, and the gems come back to their owner."

"Ah, Barclay, you are a dreadful ogre," she sighed, as she slipped the notes into her reticule. "You are quite as bad as a highwayman."

"Only more useful, my lady," chuckled Barclay. "Well, Joseph?"

The servant bent down and whispered:

"Lord Carboro'."

"Humph!" ejaculated Barclay. "Would your ladyship object to meet Lord Carboro'?"

"Yes. Horrors!" exclaimed her ladyship. "Or no, never mind; let him come up. I have called to inspect some of your china—these Sèvres jars."

Barclay nodded to his man, who left the room; and, in support of her ladyship's suggestion, the money-lender was saying: "It's an opportunity, my dear madam, that does not often occur; the workmanship is unique," when Lord Carboro' was shown in, and his keen eyes glittered as he took in the situation at a glance.

"Ah, Lady Drelincourt, you here!"

"Yes, I'm here," she said, "but I've not come to borrow money; have you?"

"Yes," said his lordship sharply. "Barclay, a word with you."

The money-lender bowed.

"Don't change countenance," said his lordship, "and talk about money. Get out your cash-box, and make believe to give me some."

Lady Drelincourt walked to the window with a small vase, and took out her great, square, gold-rimmed eye-glass.

"Money's very tight just now, my lord," said Barclay aloud.

"That's right," said his lordship, in a low tone. "Look here, Barclay. I'd have waited till that old cat had gone, but time's precious. Look here. I've had a nasty hint that hits me very hard. You'll call me an old fool. Well, I am; but never mind. I shall never have her, but I love that girl of Denville's, and, damme, sir, I can't see her go to the bad without stretching out a hand."

"What have you heard, my lord?" said Barclay, rattling his keys and opening his cash-box.

"There's some cursed plan afloat—elopement, or that sort of thing—to-night, I think; and we must stop it."

"We, my lord!" said Barclay, jingling some coin.

"Yes, we. You're an old friend of Denville's. I can't go to him."

"Who's the man?" said Barclay.

"Rockley, I think; curse him! Curse all these young, handsome men! Damme, sir, if I were forty years younger I'd be proud to marry her, for she's a good girl—yes, sir, a good girl."

Barclay nodded.

"But of course I can't expect her to take to a toothless, gouty old imbecile like me, poor child."

"What do you know, my lord?"

"Oh, only a garbled set-out. I'm not quite sure how things are; and sometimes it seems that it's Sir Harry Payne, sometimes it seems to be Rockley. Now, look here, Barclay. Will you try with me to stop it? I couldn't bear it to come off. If the girl were going to the church with some true-hearted fellow, I should feel a twinge, but I'd settle a thousand or two on her, and say, 'God bless her!' like a man; but I can't see her go to the bad without making an effort to save her. Barclay, you old scoundrel, you're laughing at me, and calling me an idiot for taking you into my confidence like this."

"You don't think so, my lord," said Barclay sternly; "and you give me credit for being an honest man, or you would not talk to me in this way."

"Honest?"

"Yes," said Barclay sharply. "Am I dishonest for making all the profit I can out of a set of profligates and fools?"

"Barclay," said his lordship, "if that old cat were not here I'd shake hands with you; as it is, that kick under the table means it. Yes, I do trust you, and your good-hearted wife, too. Will you help me?"

"In every way I can," said Barclay. "Between ourselves, Lord Carboro', I've had a hint or two of an elopement to-night, and I'm going to see what it means."

"You have had a hint?" said Lord Carboro' eagerly.

"Yes, my lord. I must have twenty-five per cent. The risk is too great," added Barclay aloud. "Drelincourt's looking," he said in a low tone. "I'm not sure who it is yet, or what it means; but there's something on the way, and I'll help your lordship all I can."

"That's right, Barclay. I know you have wires all over the place, and can pull them. You started Moggridge, and I suppose, if the truth's known, you could arrange for a post-chaise to break down anywhere you pleased."

"Your lordship gives me credit for being quite a magician," said Barclay drily. "However, I'll promise you this: Claire Denville shan't come to harm if Josiah Barclay can save her."

"Thank you, Barclay," said Lord Carboro' softly. "I've not forgotten how she refused those pearls."

"And cheated me out of a score of good jewel transactions with your lordship," said Barclay, handing him a slip of paper and a pen, which the old nobleman took and signed in Lady Drelincourt's full view. "You trust to me, my lord. I'll make all the inquiries necessary, and communicate with you to-night."

There was a little mock exchange of papers, and then, pocket-book in hand, Lord Carboro' turned to Lady Drelincourt.

"I have finished my business," he said. "Shall I attend you down to your chair?"

As the couple went out of the room with her ladyship mincing and simpering, and giving herself airs, Barclay uttered a low growl.

"I believe that old woman would make love to a mummy or a stone statue if she couldn't meet with a man. How I do hate the old wretch to be sure!"

"Now look here, Jo-si-ah," exclaimed Mrs Barclay, entering the room. "I won't have it, though I don't believe it's true."

"Don't believe what's true?"

"That when anyone is by himself and talking aloud, he is holding a conversation with—there I won't say whom."

"Pish!" ejaculated Barclay angrily. "There, sit down, woman, and make an entry about Lady Drelincourt's diamonds and the money I've lent on them. Set 'em down in the jewel book and then lock them up in the case. It wouldn't do to lose them."

"Like her sister's were lost," said Mrs Barclay. "I wonder what became of them, Jo-si-ah."

She opened the case, examined the jewels, and then opened a cabinet and an iron safe within, where she deposited the valuables, afterwards making an entry in a book kept for the purpose, and another in the big ledger.

"That's done," she said with a sigh of content. "Why, Jo-si-ah, what a rich man you are getting."

"Stuff! Don't talk nonsense."

"I say, dear," she said, "I wonder how it is that Claire Denville hasn't been here for so long. It seems strange. Here's somebody else."

The visitors proved to be Sir Harry Payne with Sir Matthew Bray, Mrs Barclay hurrying out to leave them with her husband.

"Well, gentlemen?" said Barclay drily.

"No, Barclay, it isn't well," cried Sir Harry, "nor will it be till I've got a couple of hundred pounds out of you."

"And I one hundred," said Sir Matthew pompously.

"My turn first," said Sir Harry, laughing. "Now, Barclay, two hundred, and no nonsense."

Barclay shook his head, but his money was safe with Sir Harry, for he already held certain deeds that would cover principal and his large interest.

"Now, Matt," said Sir Harry, "your turn."

He thrust a sheaf of notes into his pocket laughingly, and Sir Matthew rolled up.

"Now, Mr Barclay," he said, taking his friend's seat, while that gentleman began inspecting china and bronzes, "I want only a hundred."

"Which you can't have, Sir Matthew," said Barclay shortly. "You've got to the end of your tether, and I shall have to put you in my lawyer's hands."

"What, just now, when I have only to go on to be a rich man?"

"My dear Sir Matthew, for two years past I've supplied your wants, and you've been for ever dangling before my eyes the bait of a rich marriage, when you would pay me back. No more money, sir, from me."

"Barclay, my dear fellow, don't be a fool."

"I've just told you that I do not mean to be," said Barclay shortly. "No hundred from me, Sir Matthew."

"What, not if the matter were settled, and it was a case of post-horses, Dover, Continent, and a wedding abroad?"

"With some penniless girl," growled Barclay.

"With a lady of property and title, sir. Hush! be quiet—On my soul, Barclay. It's all right and settled. A rich marriage."

"Stuff, sir! If it were a rich marriage you would not need money."

"Preliminary expenses, dear boy. I can't ask her to pay the postboys."

Barclay looked at him keenly.

"Is this a fact?"

"Yes; to-night, sir. Honour bright. Don't spoil sport, Barclay."

The money-lender pursed up his lips and twisted a pen in his fingers for a few moments.

"Well, Sir Matthew," he said at last, "I'll give you this chance. If it does not come off your commission is mine. You'll have to sell out."

"And I will, Barclay. But there's no fear. The game's won, sir. After a long siege the lady has at last surrendered."

"A young and pretty woman, eh, Sir Matthew?"

"Well—er—not too young," said the great dragoon. "I don't care for bread-and-butter misses."

"Drelincourt, sure enough," said Barclay to himself, as he wrote out the customary form on a bill stamp. "Well, let the old fool marry him. He'll make her pay for it pretty sharply, I'll be bound. I shall get my money back, and he'll save his commission, which will go for future loans."

"There, Sir Matthew, sign that, please," he said aloud.

"Barclay, you're a gentleman. I'm a made man, and you shall have all the other bills taken up."

He scratched his name across the bill, passed it back, and Barclay counted out some notes and gave them in exchange.

"That's your sort," cried Sir Matthew, counting the notes. "Why, Barclay, the bill was for a hundred. Here are only notes for sixty."

"Quite right, Sir Matthew: the other is for the discount."

"Oh, but—"

"My dear Sir Matthew, if you are dissatisfied, pray give me the notes, and I'll tear up the bill. You forget the risk. Those are my terms."

"Oh, but, Barclay."

"What's he making you smart, Matt?" cried Sir Harry, joining them. "Just his way."

"I've offered to cancel the bill, if Sir Matthew likes," said Barclay.

"Have you got any money at all, Matt?"

"Yes, some, but—"

"Hang it! Come along then, man; we've no time to lose. Come on and chance it."

Sir Harry took his friend's arm, and hurried him out, and Barclay was nodding his head thoughtfully as the door closed, but only for another to open, and Mrs Barclay to enter and sit down, making the entries of his two transactions as a matter of course.

"Old woman," said Barclay quietly.

"Jo-si-ah!" she said, turning to him quickly, and laying her hand upon his.

"I try to think Claire Denville a good girl."

"I'm sure she is," cried Mrs Barclay. "Oh, Josiah, why do you talk like that?"

"Because things look ugly, old lady, and I shall be very sorry if you've been deceived."

"Oh, but, my dear," panted Mrs Barclay, "I'm sure."

"One can't be sure of anything with a pretty well-flattered woman. You know what you said about that row at Denville's, when Sir Harry Payne was found with Claire that night."

"Yes: I said it was May, and I'm sure of it."

"You're not sure, old lady—you can't be. Suppose it was Claire after all."

"I say it was May. Claire Denville couldn't do such a thing."

"I don't know. I hope not," said Barclay. "I want to believe in her. Well, Joseph?"

"Two chaises to-night, sir, Moggridge says. Sir Harry Payne and Sir Matthew Bray."

"That will do. Well, old lady?"

"It can't be for Claire, Jo-si-ah, I'm sure," cried Mrs Barclay. "She wouldn't look at that miserable fop."

"Suppose he is jackal for Rockley, old lady?"

"Oh, Jo-si-ah, don't. It must be for her sister May."

"No, I think not. She and Burnett have got on all right lately, and Payne hasn't been near her, that I know. Look here, old woman, I won't believe it if I can help it, but it looks very much as if Claire is really going off to-night."

"Then she shan't," cried Mrs Barclay, beginning to cry. "If the poor girl has been worked upon just when she was poor and miserable, and has been weak enough to consent, she shall find she has got a friend who will stand by her, and give her good advice, and stop her. Jo-si-ah, I love that girl as if she was my own child—and—"

"Well?"

"I shall go down to their house and see her and talk to her, and I shall stop with her till I know she's safe. That is, mind, if it's true. But it ain't."

"Well," said Barclay, "you shall do so, for I don't want her to go wrong. Only mind this, it is suspicious that she has not been near you lately."

"Not it," said Mrs Barclay, "bless her! She's had some reason, and— there, that's her knock, I'll swear."

She ran out of the room, and came back directly with Claire, looking more pale and troubled than ever, leaning upon her arm.

Mrs Barclay darted a triumphant look at her husband, and Barclay took Claire's hand in a grave distant manner that made the visitor wince.

# Chapter Four
# Mrs Barclay has her Turn

Claire winced again, and involuntarily glanced at the door, repenting that she had come, as she saw Mrs Barclay frown and make a series of grimaces at her lord, all of which were peculiar enough to a stranger, but which simply meant to the initiated: "Go away and leave us together: I can manage her better than I could if you stayed here."

Barclay comprehended from old experience all that his wife meant to signify, and, making some excuse, he shortly left the room.

"There, that's right, my dear," said Mrs Barclay warmly. "Men are such a nuisance when you want to have a nice cosy chat. Why dear, dear, dear, how white you look. Your bonny face oughtn't to be like that. You've been wherriting yourself over something. It isn't money, is it?"

"No, Mrs Barclay, we seem to have been a little better off lately."

"But you are in trouble, my darling? Now don't say you aren't, but speak out plain to me. Oh, I wish I could make you believe that I am a very, very true friend, and that I want to help you. There, I know: you've been falling out with Cora Dean."

Mrs Barclay prided herself on this as being a master stroke of policy to draw Claire out and make her ready to confide in her; but Claire shook her head and smiled sadly.

"No," she said dreamily, "I am not in trouble about that. I thought I would call and see you to-day. There, I must go now."

"Is that all?" said Mrs Barclay in a disappointed tone. "Why, I was in hopes that you were over head and ears in trouble, and had come to me for help."

"Mrs Barclay!" exclaimed Claire.

"No, no, no, my dear. What a stupid old woman I am! I didn't mean that, but if you were in trouble, I hoped that, seeing how much you are alone, you had come to me for help and advice."

Claire's face worked and her lips quivered. She vainly tried to speak, and finally, utterly broken-down with the agony of her encounters on the previous day with Louis and her sister, with the following sleepless night and the despair of the present day, during which she had been vainly striving to see some way out of the difficulty, she threw herself upon the breast offered to receive her troubles and sobbed aloud.

"I knew—I knew," whispered Mrs Barclay, soothing and caressing the poor girl by turns. "I knew as well as if some one had told me that you were in trouble and wanted help. There, there, cry away, my darling. Have a good long patient one, and don't hurry yourself. You'll be a world better afterwards; and if you like then to tell me about it, why, you see, you can, and if you don't like to, why, there's no harm done."

Even if the amiable plump old soul had said nothing more than the first sympathising words, Claire's emotion, so long pent up, would now have had its vent, the tears seeming to relieve her overburdened brain as she clung to her hostess, listening, and yet only half hearing her whispered words.

It was perhaps as well, for with all its true-heartedness there was a comic side to Mrs Barclay's well-meant sympathy; and some of her adjurations to "cry away," and not to "stop it," and the like, would have provoked a smile from anyone who had been present at the scene.

"There, there, there, then, that's better," cried Mrs Barclay, beaming in Claire's face and kissing her tenderly. "Now you'll be comfortable again; and now, my dear child, we're all alone, and if you like to make a confidant of me, you shall find you can trust me as much as my Jo-si-ah can. But don't you think I'm a scandal-loving old busybody, my dear, for I don't ask you to tell me anything."

"You are always so good to me, Mrs Barclay," sighed Claire, clinging to the ample breast.

"Oh, nonsense, my dear. I only offer to be your confidant, so as to help you in your trouble. For you are in trouble, my dear—dreadful trouble, and it hurts me to see you so—hurts me, my dear, more than you think for, so what I say is—If it does you good to come and sit with me and be comforted by having a good cry over me, just as if you were my little girl, why you shall, and I shan't ask you a single question; but if you think such a silly stout old woman can do you any good by giving you advice, or—now don't be offended—finding you money; or by asking my Jo-si-ah what to do—"

"Mrs Barclay!" cried Claire in tones of dismay, and with her cheeks flushing.

"Ah, that's the way of the world, my dear," said Mrs Barclay with a quiet contented smile, as she drew Claire's head back upon her shoulder, and stroked and patted her cheek. "You don't know my Jo-si-ah. He seems a rough harsh-spoken old money-grubber, but he's the tenderest-hearted, most generous man that ever lived. There, there, you needn't speak. I was only going to finish and say Claire Denville has two true friends here in this house; and as for me, here I am, ready to help you in any way, for I believe in you, my dear, in spite of everything that has been said, as being as good a girl as ever breathed."

"Heaven bless you!" exclaimed Claire, nestling to her; "you are a true friend, and I will tell you all my trouble."

"That's right, my dear, so you shall, and two heads are better than one. Shall I help you?"

"Oh, yes, yes, Mrs Barclay, if you can. I am so helpless, so weak with this new trouble, I don't know what to do."

"No; and you'll be driving yourself half crazy, my dear," whispered Mrs Barclay. "Why, I know as well as can be what it is."

"You know, Mrs Barclay?"

"To be sure I do, my dear. Now, why not let me ask him here some day, and just talk the matter quietly over with him?"

"Yes, yes," cried Claire; "but he is so impetuous, and the situation is so horrible."

"Not a bit of it, my dear. Of course, he is impetuous. Enough, to make him, hearing such things as he does; but just you let me get him here some day and have a chat with him, and then you see him, and try and understand each other. Never mind about the money, my dear: be poor and happy. Love's better than riches; and the happiness enjoyed by two good people who really care for each other is—well, I don't want to be single."

"Mrs Barclay! What do you mean?"

"Why, that with all his doubts and distances, Richard Linnell worships you as much as you love him."

"Oh, hush, hush, hush!" cried Claire piteously. "Don't talk about that, Mrs Barclay. It is impossible."

"It isn't, my dear, and that's flat. You're being cruel to him, and more cruel to your own dear self. Come, now, try and be advised."

"Mrs Barclay," cried Claire wildly, "you don't know. My trouble now is far greater than anything about self;" and, clinging to the only friend she seemed to have, she told her all.

Mrs Barclay sat with wide-open eyes to the very end, and then, in the midst of the terrible silence, she took out a violently-scented pocket-handkerchief, and wiped the dew from her brow, as she said softly:

"Oh, my gracious me!"

"It has driven me nearly mad," cried Claire, wringing her hands, "and while I stay here something terrible may have happened. I must go—I must go."

"No, no; sit still, my dear," cried Mrs Barclay, drawing her back to her side, and speaking in a quick, businesslike way. "I was quite knocked over by what you said. My poor, dear child! Is there to be no end to your troubles? But there, we mustn't talk nonsense, but act sensibly. This is like a smash—a sort of bankruptcy, only it's what Jo-si-ah would call social and not monetary. There, there, it's a terrible business, but I'm glad you've had the courage to tell me. Oh, my dear, I've always said to Jo-si-ah that she was a wicked little thing who was getting you into trouble. But let that go. Now, then, what to do first? Your poor father don't know a word?"

"I have not dared to tell him."

"No, and you've been screening her, and taking care of that little one, and—dear—dear—what a world this is! Tut—tut—tut! I am doing nothing but talk. Now, look here, Claire; the first thing that strikes me is that she must be got away—right away—for the present."

"Yes, yes; but how?" cried Claire.

"Jo-si-ah shall settle that."

"Mr Barclay!" cried Claire in terror.

"To be sure, my dear. We want a strong man to act in a case like this. Your sister must be got away somewhere, and you must go with her. You had both better go to-night. No one shall know where you are but Jo-si-ah and me, and you can take care of her until Jo-si-ah has told your father all about it."

"Yes," sighed Claire, as her companion's calm, businesslike manner impressed her.

"If we tell him first he will do no good, poor man, only be horribly upset, and there'll be no end of scenes, and no business done."

Claire acquiesced with a look.

"Then Jo-si-ah can settle it all with your father and Mr Burnett, and this Mr Gravani, what is to be done in a businesslike way. There, there, let me finish. The weak little thing has got herself into this dreadful tangle, and what we have to do is to get her out the best way we can. It's of no use to be sentimental and sit down and cry; we must act like women."

Claire looked at her in admiration, astounded by her friend's calm, businesslike manner.

"Now, perhaps, my dear, my Jo-si-ah may upset all my plans by proposing something better; but, as far as I see it now, you had better go straight off to your sister May—it will soon be dusk—and bring her here. I'll be ready and waiting, and I'll go with you both to the coach. You had better put on veils, and we'll go right away to London. It's the best place to hide, as my Jo-si-ah knows with the people who don't pay him. Yes, that's best. I'll go with you."

"You will go with us, Mrs Barclay?"

"Of course, I shall, my dear, and stay with you till you're out of your trouble, and Jo-si-ah has finished the business. Did you think I was a fine-weather friend?"

Claire could not speak; her kisses and clinging arms spoke her thanks.

"Yes, that's as far as I can see it, and we must be quick."

She rose to go to the bell.

"What are you going to do?" cried Claire, in alarm.

"Ring for Jo-si-ah, and to send our Joseph to book three seats for the coach."

"But Mr Barclay? Must you tell him—now?" faltered Claire.

"Why, of course, my dear, or we may be too late. Do you know that some one else is evidently making plans?"

"What do you mean?" cried Claire excitedly.

"We know a great deal here, my dear. My husband has to keep an eye upon the slippery people who borrow money of him; and there was a hint brought here to-day that a certain gentleman was going to elope to-night with a certain lady, and the idea was that you were the lady. We know it was Sir Harry Payne."

Claire caught at her friend's arm as she went on.

"But I said 'No;' it is only a miserable scandal, based upon that wretched business at your house. 'It's Mrs Burnett,' I said, 'if it's anyone.' Claire, my dear, she is in this dreadful fix, and she is going off to-night with that fop to escape from it."

Claire's lips parted as she looked at the speaker in horror, realising it all now, and reading May's excuse to gain time.

For a moment the deceit and cruelty of the act seemed too horrible; but she was now thoroughly realising the nature of her sister, and was so agitated that she felt almost paralysed as she stood gazing straight before her.

"I cannot believe it, Mrs Barclay," she said at last. "It is too terrible. My poor sister would never be so base."

"Go at once, my dear. Stand no nonsense with the little thing. I'll settle it all with my Jo-si-ah. You bring her here."

Claire was white as ashes now, as she caught Mrs Barclay's hands and kissed them.

"No, no, my dear; not my hands. There, go, and heaven bless you. We'll help you through it, never fear."

She folded Claire in her arms for a moment, and then hurried with her downstairs, and let her out.

"One moment, my dear," she whispered, detaining her, to thrust her purse in her hand. "Stop for nothing. Bring her here; drag her if she says she will not come. Say anything, but bring her here."

"Ah!" sighed Mrs Barclay, as she watched Claire disappear down the street, and then closed the door. "Now for Jo-si-ah."

# Chapter Five
# The Master of the Ceremonies is Stung

Josiah Barclay was in his business room when his wife returned, panting and wiping her eyes, and he gave her one of his grim looks.

"Well, old woman, I was right, wasn't I?"

"No, Jo-si-ah."

"Then you didn't get it all out of her?"

"Oh, yes, everything, dear. She told me all, and it is that wicked—wicked little woman, May."

She told him all that had passed, and he stood and stared at her, blowing out his cheeks, and then looking his hardest.

"Let me see," he said, when she had done speaking. "May Burnett is, of course, my own child by my first wife."

"Jo-si-ah! Why, you never had no first wife."

"Nonsense, woman."

"Nonsense, Jo-si-ah! Do you mean to tell me—now, how can you? Why, we've been married over thirty years, and that wicked little hussy isn't above twenty. How can you talk such stuff?"

"You set me going," he said grimly. "You talked as if May Burnett must be my own flesh and blood."

"I didn't, Jo-si-ah. What do you mean?"

"Why you want me to mix myself up in this miserable scandal over a wretched, frivolous, heartless wench, spend my hard-earned money, and let you go off on a sort of wild goose chase with her and Claire Denville. I thought you had found out that she really was my own flesh and blood."

Mrs Barclay wiped her eyes, and indulged in one of her laughs—a blancmange sort of laugh—as she sat back in the chair vibrating and undulating all over, while her husband watched her with the most uncompromising of aspects till she rose.

"What a man you are," she said at last. "But there, don't let's waste time. You will help us, dear, won't you?"

"Us?"

"Yes; *us*, Josiah. Don't you think what I have proposed is the best?"

"Well, yes," he said slowly. "I do not think I could suggest anything better."

"I *am* glad," she said. "Then send Joseph at once, and take three seats for London."

"You mean to go, then?"

"Yes, dear, of course."

"And what's to become of me?"

"You will stop and see Mr Burnett, and this Mr Gravani, and poor Mr Denville, and settle the matter the best way you can."

"For May Burnett's sake?"

"No, dear: for mine and poor Claire Denville's; and look here, Jo-si-ah, you just beg her pardon, sir."

"If I do I'll be—"

"Hush! Stop, sir. I don't mean to her. Now, just you own that you have misjudged her."

"Humph! Well, perhaps I have."

"That's right, dear; and you will do your best now, won't you?"

"I tell you what, woman; I've read about men being fooled by their wives and turned round the thumb; but the way you turn me round beats everything I ever did read."

"Yes," she said, nestling to his side. "I like turning you round my thumb, dear; and let's always go on to the end just the same, Jo-si-ah; and you'll let me try to do some good."

"Humph!" ejaculated Barclay, in his grimmest manner. "But, don't you see, old lady, that this May Burnett is a worthless sort of baggage?"

"I can't see anything, dear, only that poor Claire Denville, whom I love very much, is in great trouble, and that we are wasting time."

"Wasting love, you mean," cried Barclay. "If you've got so much love to spare, why don't you pour it on my devoted head, to wash away some of the hate which people bestow upon me?"

"Jo-si-ah dear! Please."

"All right," he said grimly. "I'll do it, old lady. Let's see; the coach goes at half-past eleven. You've plenty of time. I'll send Joseph. But tell me, where are you going?"

"To the Bell, in Holborn, dear, for the first day. Then I shall take apartments somewhere till it is all settled."

"But the expense, woman?"

"I've plenty of jewels, dear. Shall I sell something?"

"Yes, you'd better!" he said grimly. "There, I suppose you must do as you like."

She nodded and kissed him affectionately, while he seemed to look less firm in the pleasant light shed by her eyes as he handed her the keys of his cash-box.

"Now then, dear," she said, "business. Bless us! Who's that?"

There was a sharp rolling knock at the door, and they stood listening.

"I hope we're not too late, dear," whispered Mrs Barclay excitedly.

"Denville's voice for a guinea," cried Barclay.

"Then you can tell him all, and you two can go and stop any attempt the silly little woman may make to run away."

"Mr Denville, sir," said Joseph, ushering in the Master of the Ceremonies, very pale and careworn under his smiling guise, as he minced into the room, hat in one hand, snuff-box in the other, and his cane hanging by its silken cord and tassels from his wrist.

"My dear Mrs Barclay, your very humble servant. My dear Barclay, yours. It seems an age since we met."

"Oh, poor dear man!" sighed Mrs Barclay to herself. "He can't know a word."

She exchanged glances with Barclay, who gave her a nod.

"You will excuse me, Mr Denville," she said. "A little business to attend to. I'll come back and see you before you go."

"I should apologise," said Denville, smiling and bowing as he hastened to open the door for her to pass out; and as he closed it he groaned as he said to himself:

"She does not ask after my children."

"Sit down, Denville," said Barclay; "you've come to pay me some money, eh?"

"Well—er—the fact is—no, Barclay, not just at present. I must ask you to give me a little more time. Morton, my son, you see, is only just launched. He is getting on, but at present I must ask a little forbearance. Interest, of course, but you will wait a little longer?"

"Humph! Well, I suppose I must, and—come, Denville, out with it. What's the matter, man? Some fresh trouble?"

Denville had been playing uneasily with his snuff-box, and taking up and setting down his hat, glancing nervously about the room. As Barclay spoke in this abrupt way to him, he started and stared wildly at the speaker.

"Oh! nothing, nothing," he said, smiling. "I was only coming this way. Ha—ha—ha! my dear Barclay, you thought I wanted a little accommodation. No, no, not this time. The fact is, I understood that my daughter, Miss Denville, had come on here. I expected to find her with Mrs Barclay—a lady I esteem—a lady of whom my daughter always speaks most warmly. Has she—er—has she called here this evening?"

"Miss Denville was here a short time since."

"And has gone?" said Denville nervously. "She—she—is coming back here?"

"I think so. Yes, I believe my wife said she was; but, hang it, Denville, why don't you speak out, man? What's the matter? Perhaps I can help you."

"Help me?" faltered the miserable man. "No; it is not a case where money could assist me."

"Money, sir! I offered the help of a friend," said Barclay warmly. "Come, speak out. You are in trouble."

Denville looked at him hesitatingly, but did not speak.

"I don't ask for your confidence," said Barclay, "but you have done me more than one good turn, Denville, and I want to help you if I can."

Still the old man hesitated; but at last he seemed to master his hesitation, and, catching the other's sleeve, he whispered:

"A scandalous place, my dear Barclay. I used to smile at these things, but of late my troubles have a good deal broken me down. I am changed. I know everybody, but I have no friends, and—there, I confess it, I came to speak to your wife, to ask her advice and help, for at times I feel as if the kindly words and interest of some true woman would make my load easier to bear." "Nothing like a good friend," said Barclay gruffly.

"Yes—exactly. You'll pardon me, Barclay; you have been very kind, but your manner does not invite confidence. I feel that I cannot speak to you as I could wish."

"Try," said Barclay, taking his hand. "Come, you are in trouble about your daughter."

"Yes," cried Denville quickly. "How did you know?"

"Never mind how I know. Now then, speak out, what do *you* know?"

"Only that there is some fresh gossip afloat, mixing up my daughter's name with that of one of the reckless fops of this place."

"Claire Denville's?"

"Yes, my dear sir. It is most cruel. These people do not think of the agony it causes those who love their children. I heard that my child had come here—ah, here is Mrs Barclay back. My dear madam, I came to bear my daughter company home, to stay with her, and to show these wretched scandal-mongers that there is no truth in the story that has been put about."

"Have you told him, Jo-si-ah?"

"No, madam," cried Denville; "there was no need. Some cruel enemy contrived that I should hear of it—this wretched scandal. But you'll pardon me—the lies, the contemptible falsehoods of the miserable idlers who find pleasure in such stories. My daughter Claire has been maligned before. She can bear it again, and by her sweet truthfulness live down all such falsities."

"But, Mr Denville!" cried Mrs Barclay.

"Hush, ma'am, pray. A father's feelings. You'll pardon me. We can scorn these wretched attacks. My child Claire is above them. I shall take no notice; I wished, however, to be by her side. She will return here, you say?"

"Yes, yes, my dear good man," cried Mrs Barclay; "but you are blinding yourself to the truth."

"No, ma'am, you'll pardon me. My eyes have long been open to the truth. I know. They say that my dear child Claire is to elope to-night with Sir Harry Payne. I had a letter from some busybody to that effect; but it is not true. I say it is not true."

"No, Mr Denville, it is not true," cried Mrs Barclay warmly. "Our dear Claire—your dear Claire—is too good a girl, and the wretches who put this about ought to be punished. It is not dear Claire who is believed to be going to-night, but—"

"You'll pardon me," cried Denville, turning greyer, and with a curious sunken look about his eyes. "Not a word, please. The scandal is against some one else? I will not hear it, ma'am. Mrs Barclay, I will not know. Life is too short to mix ourselves up with these miserable scandals. I will not wait, Barclay. It is growing late. I shall probably meet my daughter, and take her back. If I do not, and she should come here, might I ask you to see her home?"

"Yes, Denville, yes; but, look here, we have something to tell you. Wife, it is more a woman's work. You can do it more kindly than I."

"You'll pardon me," said Denville, looking from one to the other, and smiling feebly. "Some fresh story about my daughter? Is it not so, Mrs Barclay?"

"Yes, yes, Mr Denville," she whispered; "and you ought to know, though I was going to leave my Jo-si-ah to tell you."

"Always good and kind to me and my family, dear Mrs Barclay," said Denville, smiling, and bending over the plump hand he took, to kiss it, with chivalrous respect. "But no—no more tales, my dear madam; the chronicles of Saltinville are too full of scandals. No, no, my dear Mrs Barclay; my unfortunate house can live it down."

He drew himself up, took a pinch of snuff with all the refined style and air of the greatest buck of the time, and handed his box to Barclay, who took it, mechanically helped himself noisily, and handed it back.

"The old man's half mad," he muttered, as he looked at him.

"But Mr Denville," cried Mrs Barclay pleadingly; "you ought to know— you must know."

"Nonsense, madam, nonsense!" cried Denville, with his most artificial manner reigning supreme, as he flicked away a tiny speck of dust from his frill. "We can laugh at these things—we elderly people, and treat them as they deserve."

"But, Mr Denville—"

"No, dear madam, no; I protest," he continued, almost playfully.

"Jo-si-ah, time's flying," cried Mrs Barclay, in a pathetic manner that was absolutely comic. "What *am* I to say to this man?"

"Tell him," said Barclay sternly.

"Ah!" ejaculated Mrs Barclay, with a long sigh, as if she shrank from her task. "It must be done. Dear Mr Denville, I don't like telling you, but Mrs Burnett—"

Denville reeled, and caught at Barclay's arm.

"Hold up, old fellow! Be a man," cried the money-lender, supporting him.

The old man recovered himself, and stood up very erect, turning for a moment resentfully on Barclay, as if angry that he should have dared to touch him. Then, looking fiercely at Mrs Barclay:

"Hush, ma'am!" he cried. "Shame, shame! How can you—you who are so true and tender-hearted—let yourself be the mouthpiece of this wretched crew?"

"But indeed, Mr Denville—"

"Oh, hush, ma'am, hush! You, who know the people so well. Mrs Burnett—my dear sweet child, May—the idol of my very life—to be made the butt now at which these wretches shoot their venomous shafts. Scandals, madam; scandals, Barclay. Coinages from the very pit. A true, sweet lady, sir. Bright as a bird. Sweet as some opening flower. And they dare to malign her with her bright, merry, innocent ways—that sweet young girl wife. Oh, shame! Shame upon them! Shame!"

"Oh, Denville, Denville," said Barclay softly, as he laid his hand upon the old man's shoulder.

"Ah!" he cried, "even you pity me for this. Dear Mrs Barclay, I ought to be angry with you: but no, I will not. You mean so well. But it is all I have—in a life so full of pain and suffering that I wonder how I live—the love of my daughters—them to defend against the world. Madam, you are mistaken. My daughter—an English lady—as pure as heaven. But I thank you—I am not angry—you mean well. Always kind and helpful to my dear child, Claire. Ha, ha, ha!"

It was a curious laugh, full of affectation; and he took snuff again with all the old ceremony; but he did not close the box with a loud snap, and as his hand fell to his side, the brown powder dropped in patches and flakes here and there upon the carpet.

"Ha, ha, ha!" he laughed again. "Calumnies, madam—I say it as I take my leave—the calumnies of false fribbles and envious women. Busy again with my dear children's names. But we must live it down. Elopement! Pshaw! The coxcombs! The Jezebels! My child! Oh, I cannot mention her sweet, spring-flower name in connection with such a horror. It is atrocious."

"Denville," said Barclay, in answer to an appealing look from his wife.

"No, no! Not a word, sir, not a word," cried Denville, raising his hand. "It is too absurd—too villainous. Madam, it is from your good heart that this warning comes. I thank you, ma'am, you meant to put me on my guard.

Barclay, adieu, my good friend. You'll shake hands. You'll take no notice of this slight emotion—this display of a father's indignation on hearing such a charge. Mrs Barclay, if I have spoken harshly, you'll forgive me. I don't blame you, dear madam. *Au revoir*! No, no; don't ring, I beg. I pray you will not come down. You'll banish all this—from your thoughts—"

He stopped short and reeled again, dropping snuff-box, hat, and cane as he clasped his hands to his head, staring wildly before him. The feeble affected babble ceased suddenly, and it was another voice that seemed to come from his lips as he exclaimed loudly in hot anger:

"It is a lie! You—May! The girl I've loved so well—you! When my cup of suffering is brimming over. A lie—a lie, I say. Ah!"

His manner changed again; and now it was soft and full of wild appeal, as he cried:

"May—May! My darling! God help me, poor broken dotard that I am! Shall I be in time?"

He made a dash for the door, but staggered, and would have fallen had not Barclay caught him and helped him to a chair, where he sat gazing before him as if at some scene passing before his eyes.

"Blood," he whispered at last, "to the head. Help me, Barclay, or I shall be too late."

"No, stay here. I'll go and do all I can."

"No!" cried Denville fiercely. "I am her father, Barclay; we may save her—if I go too."

He rose with nervous energy now, and gripping the money-lender's arm they went together out into the dark street, where, indignantly refusing further help, the old man strode off, leaving Barclay watching him.

"I don't hardly know what to do," he said musingly. "Ah! who are you?"

"His lordship's man, sir," said a livery servant. "Lord Carboro' says could you make it convenient to come to him directly?"

"No, I'm busy. Well, yes, I will. Is he at home?"

"No, sir; at the reading-room."

"Go on, then," said Barclay. "Tell his lordship I'll be there directly."

The man went off, and Barclay hurried indoors to speak with his wife, and came out five minutes later to join the old nobleman at the reading-room that answered the purpose of a club.

# Chapter Six
# On the Downs

High up on the Downs behind the town lay a patch of wood, dwarfed and stunted in its growth by the sharp breezes that came off the sea. The soil in which they grew, too, was exceedingly shallow; and, as the chalk beneath was not very generous in its supply of nutriment, the trees sent their roots along the surface, and their low-spreading branches inland, with a few shabby twigs seaward to meet the cutting blasts.

Right through this patch of thick low wood ran the London Road, and across it the coast road, going west, while a tall finger-post that had once been painted stood with outstretched arms, bending over a little old grey milestone, as if it were blessing it for being so humble and so small.

It was along this road that Richard Linnell, Mellersh, and James Bell had cantered, and then turned off at the cross, on the night of their pursuit, and the chalky way looked much the same beneath twinkling stars on the night succeeding the day when Louis Gravani had had his interview with Claire, as on that of Mrs Pontardent's party.

The similarity was increased by the presence of a yellow post-chaise; but it was not drawn up at the back of Mrs Pontardent's garden, but here on the short turf close up to the trees and opposite the finger-post.

The chaise, an old yellow weather-beaten affair, seemed to be misty, and the horses indistinct in the darkness, looking quite the ghost of a vehicle that might be expected to fade away like a trick of the imagination, everything was so still. The very horses were asleep, standing bent of knee and with pendent heads. One of the wheelers, however, uttered a sigh now and then as if unhappy in its dreams, for it was suffering not from nightmare, a trouble that might have befallen any horse, but from the weight of the sleeping postboy on its back. The man evidently believed in his steed as an old friend, and had lain forward over the pommel of his saddle, half clasping the horse's neck, and was sleeping heavily, while his companion, who rode one of the leaders, had dismounted and seated himself upon the turf where the road was cut down through the chalk, so that his legs were in the channel and his back against a steep bank.

They had been asleep quite an hour, when a quick step was heard, a misty-looking figure in a long grey wrapper, and closely-veiled, came along the road, stopped short by the postboys, retreated and whispered softly as the turf opposite was reached:

"Hist! Are you there? Oh, gracious! What a wicked girl I am! He has not come."

The figure seemed to take courage and approached the chaise again.

"He may be inside," she said softly, and going on tip-toe to the door her hand was raised to the fastening, when one of the wheelers snorted and half roused the mounted postboy.

"Hullo, then, old gal," he muttered loudly. "Yo—yo—yo—yo—yo! Gate—gate."

"What shall I do?" exclaimed the veiled figure, and she seized one of the spokes of the wheel and clung to it as the other postboy, slightly roused by his companion, took up his cry and shouted drowsily:

"Yo—yo—yo—yo—yo! Gate—gate!"

The horses sighed, and the men subsided into their nap, a long ride on the previous evening having made them particularly drowsy.

"Talking in their sleep," said the veiled figure, raising herself and trying the handle of the chaise door, opening it, and reaching in to make sure whether it was tenanted or no.

"Not come," she sighed. "He must be late, or else I've missed him. He is looking for me. Oh, what a wicked girl I am! What's that?"

She turned sharply round, darting behind the chaise and among the trees as a faint sound was heard; and this directly after took the form of footsteps, a short slight man approaching on the other side of the road, stopping to gaze at the chaise and then backing slowly into the low bush-like trees, which effectually hid him from sight.

There was utter stillness again for a few moments, when the dull sound of steps was once more heard, and another short slight figure approached armed with a stout cane.

He kept to the grass and walked straight up to the sleeping postboys, examined them, and then stood listening.

"Just in time," he said to himself. "Drowsy dogs! Ha—ha—ha! I wish Dick Linnell were here. I should like the fool to see her go. Hang it! I'd have given Harry Payne fifty to help him on the road if he had asked me. Get rid of her for good, curse her! I'm sick of the whole lot. Eh! What, the devil—"

"What are you doing here, Burnett?" said Richard Linnell, crossing the road from the Downs in company with Mellersh.

"What am I doing? Taking the air. Did you think I was going to elope in a post-chaise. Hist! don't speak aloud or you'll wake the boys. But, I say— hang it all—have I been humbugged? Was it you then who were going off with Claire, and not Sir Harry Payne?"

"Do you want me to horsewhip you, Burnett?" cried Linnell in a low, passionate voice.

"Not I. There, don't be cross. I can't help it, if she is going."

Linnell turned from him impatiently, but Burnett followed.

"Let her go, man. What's the good of worrying about her? Better for both of us."

"Come aside," said Mellersh softly. "Here they are."

Linnell seemed disposed to stand fast, but Mellersh took his arm.

"Look here, my dear boy," he whispered. "You don't want to interfere. Let her go."

Linnell turned upon him fiercely, but he yielded to his companion's touch, and they walked on some twenty yards, followed by Burnett, who was laughing to himself and nibbing his hands.

"Lucky I heard," he said to himself. "I only want to be satisfied."

The steps approaching were not those of a lady and gentleman, but of Lord Carboro' and Barclay, who, in utter ignorance of anyone but the postboys being at hand, stood for a few minutes listening.

"Yes, Barclay," said the former. "I could not bear for the poor girl to go without making a step to save her. I'm an old fool, I know, but not the first of my kind. I tell you, asking nothing, expecting nothing, I'd give ten thousand pounds to feel that I had not been deceived in her."

"Pay up then, my lord, for I tell you that you have been deceived. Once more: the lady is May Burnett, her sister."

"I'm assured that it is Claire Denville, and if it is, Barclay, I'll save her, damme, I will, if I shoot the man."

"But, my lord—"

"Don't talk to me, sir. I tell you if I saw her going to the church with a fellow like young Linnell I'd give her a handsome present; but I can't bear for such a girl as that to be going wrong."

"Unless it was with you, my lord," said Barclay abruptly.

"You confounded rascal! How dare you!" snarled Lord Carboro'. "Do you think I have no good feeling in me? There, you wouldn't believe in my disinterestedness, any more than I would in yours. Don't talk. What shall we do? Pay the postboys and send them off?"

"No, my lord: stand aside, and make sure that we have made no mistake."

"If *you* have made no mistake," said his lordship quickly; and he and his companion had hardly drawn aside into the convenient wood to swell the circle gathering round the intending evaders, when Richard Linnell made a step from his concealment and was arrested by Mellersh, as Burnett whispered:

"What are they here for?"

Just then one of the postboys yawned and stretched himself, making noise sufficient to awaken his fellow, who rose from the bank and flicked his whip.

"How long have we been here?" said the man on the horse.

"Hours, and not a soul come. My ticker's been asleep as well," he muttered, after pulling out his watch. "I believe the 'osses have been having a nap too. I say, I'm getting sick of this."

"Think they'll come?"

"Hang me if I know. Guv'nor seems to have been about right."

"Why, what did he say?"

"You was there and heard him."

"No: I was in the stable."

"Said two po'chays was ordered, and he'd only horses for one. That it was certain as it was a 'lopement, that both parties wouldn't come, and perhaps neither of 'em. If they did, Sir Matthy Bray and Sir Harry Payne had better fight it out, and the gals go home. Hist! Is that them?"

The two men listened attentively as steps were heard, and the listeners in the wood were all on the *qui vive*.

Directly after, Sir Harry Payne came up.

"Seen a lady, my lads?"

"No, sir. Been on the watch ever since we come, and no one's been near," said the first postboy.

"Humph! Past time. Horses fresh?"

"Fresh as daisies, Sir Harry. Don't you be afraid. No one'll catch us."

"Are you sure you've both been watching? Not been asleep, have you?"

"Sleep a-top of a horse, Sir Harry? Not we."

"Mount!" cried Sir Harry to the second man. "Here she comes."

What followed was the business of a few moments. A slight little veiled figure came panting up, and was caught in Sir Harry's arms.

"At last!" he cried. "This way, little pet—curse the woman! What are you doing here?"

Claire Denville's cloak dropped from her shoulders as, panting and utterly exhausted with the chase after her sister, she flung her arms about her and held her fast.

"May!" she panted. "Sister, are you mad?"

"You'll make me in a moment," cried Sir Harry. "Curse you! Why do you interfere?"

"May!" cried Claire again. "For pity's sake—for the sake of your husband, do not do this wicked thing. Come back with me; come back. No one shall know. Sister, dear sister, before it is too late."

"Nay, it is too late," whispered Sir Harry. "Choose; will you go back to misery and disgrace?"

At the edge of the wood the scene was just visible, but the words were inaudible. Burnett had not at first recognised his wife; but Claire's voice rang out clear, and with a sneer he turned to Richard Linnell:

"There!" he said. "What did I say? What are you going to do now?"

"Try and save your foolish wife, idiot, if you are not man enough to interfere."

He sprang out of the wood as he spoke, but ere he could reach the group, Sir Harry Payne, by a brutal exercise of his strength, swung Claire away from her sister; and as she staggered on the turf she would have fallen but for the quick way in which Richard Linnell caught her in his arms.

She clung to him wildly, as she strove to recover herself.

"Help! Mr Linnell! Quick! my sister!" she panted, as Sir Harry Payne hurriedly threw open the door of the chaise.

"In with you—no nonsense, now," he cried to May. "Be ready, my lads—gallop hard. I'll pay!"

He was leaning towards the postboys as he spoke, but as the words left his lips they were half drowned by a piercing shriek that rang out upon the night, sending a thrill through every bystander. It was no hysterical cry, but the agony and dread-born appeal for aid from one in mortal peril.

Sir Harry held the door open, and stood as if paralysed by the cry, for as if instantaneously, a dark lithe figure had glided out from beneath the chaise, caught May's arm, and, as the word "*Perfida!*" seemed hissed in her ear, there was a flash as of steel, and a sharp blow was delivered like lightning, twice over.

"Curse you!" cried Sir Harry. "Cowardly dog!" He seized May's assailant by the throat, but only to utter a low cry of pain, and stagger back from the effect of the heavy blow he received in the shoulder.

To the startled spectators at hand it was all like some scene in the half-light of a drama. No sooner had the dark figure rid himself of Payne than he glided rapidly beneath the chaise again, and before those who ran up to arrest him could reach the farther side of the vehicle, he had darted into the wood and was gone. Just then a voice cried: "Help! for heaven's sake, or she'll bleed to death."

# Chapter Seven
## "Too Late! Too Late!"

The words uttered by the first to run to May Burnett's help seemed to paralyse the party instead of evoking aid, while in the horror and confusion there was no attempt made to pursue, so stunned were all by the rapidity with which one event had succeeded the other.

Lord Carboro' was the first to recover himself.

"This is no place for you, Miss Denville," he said. "Will you place yourself under my protection? Or, no," he added hastily; "Mr Barclay, take Miss Denville home."

Barclay took a step towards Claire, who stood as if turned to stone, staring wildly at where her sister lay upon the turf, with Mellersh kneeling beside her, while Sir Harry Payne also lay without motion.

"Who was that man who struck Mrs Burnett?" said Lord Carboro' sharply, but no one answered. "Mr Burnett," he continued to that individual, as he stood aloof looking on, but speechless with mortification and rage. "Will no one speak? Who is this? You, Mellersh?"

"Yes," was the reply, in a low, pained voice. "This is a terrible business, Lord Carboro'."

"It generally is when a lady tries to elope and is stopped. Curse me, though, what a coward that Burnett was to set some one to strike her."

"Did he?" said Mellersh, in a curious tone.

"Yes; didn't you see? Is she fainting?"

"Yes," said Mellersh. "Here, Linnell, help Miss Denville into the chaise, and she can support her sister."

"No; I forbid it," cried Lord Carboro' sharply. "I—"

"Hush, my lord!" whispered Mellersh. "Do you not see? The wretched woman is stabbed."

"Stabbed!"

"Claire! Claire! Help! Claire!" wailed May faintly. At her sister's wild cry a spasm seemed to shoot through Claire's frame, and she wrested herself from Linnell, and threw herself beside the wretched little woman where she lay.

"May—sister," she whispered.

"Take me—take me home," said May, in a feeble, piteous voice. "Did you see him? I was frightened. I was going and he—he stabbed me."

"Help! A doctor! For heaven's sake, help!" cried Claire. "May, May, speak to me—dear sister."

She raised the frail little figure in her arms as she spoke, till the pretty baby head rested upon her bosom, and Linnell shuddered as, in the dim light, he saw the stains that marked her dress and Claire's hands.

"Miss Denville," he whispered, "let Colonel Mellersh place her in the chaise. She must be got home at once."

"Yes," said Mellersh solemnly. "I can do no more."

As he spoke he gave a final knot to the handkerchief with which he had bound the slight little arm.

"Who did this?" cried Lord Carboro' quickly. "Mr Burnett, do you know?"

Burnett did not speak, and the answer came from May, in a feeble, dreamy voice.

"It was poor Louis," she said. "I saw him this evening—watching me—he must have followed. Ah!"

"Quick! Get in first, Miss Denville," cried Mellersh. "Draw her away, Dick, for God's sake! The poor little thing will bleed to death. Good heavens!"

The last words were uttered in a low tone, as from out of the darkness a tall gaunt figure staggered up and sank down beside the injured girl.

"Too late! Too late! May! my child! Blood! She is dead—my darling. She is dead!"

"Hush, sir! She has fainted," cried Linnell. "Mr Denville! For heaven's sake, sir, be firm. Command yourself. A terrible mishap. Mrs Burnett must be got back to the town at once. Can you act calmly?"

"Certainly. I'll try," groaned the Master of the Ceremonies; and then, "Too late—too late!"

He rose, holding one little hand in his as Claire tottered into the carriage, and May was lifted to her side.

"Now, Mr Denville. In—quick!" cried Linnell. "Straight home. The postboys shall warn a doctor as they pass."

The door was banged to, the orders given, and the next minute the horses were going at a canter, on no flight to London, but back to the Parade.

Richard Linnell stood gazing after the departing post-chaise for a few moments, to start as a hand was placed upon his shoulder.

"Is she hurt badly, Mellersh?" he whispered.

"Badly? Yes," was the reply. "I'm afraid it is the last ride she will take— but one."

"For heaven's sake, gentlemen, lend a hand here," cried Lord Carboro' impatiently; and they turned to where Barclay was now kneeling by Sir Harry Payne, that worthy having just struggled back from a fit of fainting.

"Cursed cowardly blow," he said in a shrill voice. "Who was it— Burnett? Why couldn't he call me out?"

"Don't talk, man," cried Lord Carboro'. "Here, Mellersh, the fellow's bleeding like a pig."

"Am I?" cried Sir Harry faintly. "Damn it. A surgeon. The post-chaise."

"A knife," said Mellersh shortly, as he made as rapid an examination as he could in the darkness.

A pocket-knife was handed to him by Barclay, and he ripped up the coat and threw it aside.

"Is—is it dangerous?" faltered Sir Harry.

"Dangerous enough for you to be more silent," said Mellersh. "Another handkerchief, please. That'll do. Yes. I'll use both. There, Sir Harry," he said, as he bound up the prostrate man's arm, "we are only a mile from the barracks. You must contrive to walk."

"Sick as a dog," muttered Sir Harry; but he struggled to his feet with a little help. "Don't—don't let that little beast Burnett come near me. Mellersh, your arm."

There was no need for his desire to be attended to, for Burnett had stood looking on for a few minutes, and then gone off, to be slowly followed by the others, the wounded man being compelled by faintness to halt from time to time till the barrack gate was reached.

Half an hour later Lord Carboro' was in consultation with Barclay, Mellersh, and Linnell outside the Denvilles' house.

"Gravani?" said Lord Carboro', "to be sure—Louis Gravani. I gave him some painting to do when he was here. Italian—and the knife—a former lover, of course?"

"Mrs Barclay tells me, my lord," said Barclay, gravely, "that he was really Mrs Burnett's husband."

"Dick," said Mellersh, as they were walking slowly back, "of what are you thinking?"

"Of Claire."

Mellersh said no more, but when they reached home sat musing over the fact that there was a light in Cora's window, and that she was looking out. But it was not for him.

# Chapter Eight
# The Friend in Need

There was quite a meeting at little Miss Clode's the next morning, after a heavy storm that had set in during the night; but, though the ordinary atmosphere was fresh, clear, cool and bright after the heavy rain, the social atmosphere grew more dense and lurid, hour by hour, as the callers rolled the news snow-ball on till Annie Clode's eyes looked as if they would never close again, and her mouth formed a veritable round O.

Miss Clode herself was in a state of nervous prostration, but she forced herself to be in the shop and listen, gathering scraps of information which she sifted, casting aside the rubbish and retaining only what was good, so as to piece together afterwards, and lay before herself what was the whole truth.

The accounts were sufficiently alarming; and among others it was current that Sir Harry Payne was eloping with Claire Denville, when Mrs Burnett followed to stop them, and Frank Burnett in a fit of rage and jealousy, stabbed her and Sir Harry.

Another account stated that it was Sir Matthew Bray who had stabbed Mrs Burnett, and that he had been seized and put in prison for the deed, while Lady Drelincourt had gone mad from love and misery, and had been found by Fisherman Dick and a couple of friends six miles inland, lost on the Downs, drenched with rain, and raving so that she had had to be held down in the cart that the fishermen had been using to carry mackerel.

Everybody smiled at the word mackerel, and thought of French brandy for some reason or another.

This last business was as much canvassed as May Burnett's injury, for subsequent inquiry proved that Lady Drelincourt really had been brought home by Fisherman Dick, and that she was delirious and attended by two doctors.

Sir Matthew Bray, too, was certainly in prison, and nobody troubled him or herself to discriminate between an arrest for debt set about next day by Josiah Barclay, and one for some criminal offence.

The whole affair was like a godsend, just when scandal was starving for want of sustenance, and Saltinville at its lowest ebb.

Some one had seen the postboys, and knew that Lord Carboro' was up at the cross-roads, where he had gone to fight a duel with Colonel Mellersh over a card-table quarrel, and they happened to be just in time to help May Burnett when her sister stabbed Sir Harry Payne.

Some one else quarrelled indignantly with this version, for she knew from Lady Drelincourt's maid that it was her ladyship herself, who in a fit of indignant jealousy had stabbed Claire Denville and Sir Matthew Bray, whom everyone knew she loved desperately, and that she had afterwards gone distracted because she had nearly killed Sir Matthew.

This narrator went off in high dudgeon on being openly contradicted, and told that she was entirely wrong, for the fact was that young Cornet Morton Denville, who saved Lady Drelincourt's pet dog, and for whom her ladyship had bought a commission, had challenged Sir Matthew Bray to fight with swords at the cross-roads. They had met, but Lady Drelincourt, in alarm, had gone and told Morton Denville's sisters, and they had all three gone up together in a post-chaise with Sir Harry Payne on horseback. They had come up just in the heat of the fight, and Sir Harry and Mrs Burnett had rushed between them, and both been wounded; and in her horror at being the cause of such bloodshed, Lady Drelincourt had exclaimed, "I would give my diamonds and everything I possess to be able to undo this terrible night's work."

Such minute knowledge carried all before it, and for quite an hour this was the accepted version.

Somehow, Louis Gravani, save with three or four of the witnesses of the tragedy, dropped entirely out of the affair, going as suddenly as he had come, though he seemed always present in the little bedchamber on the Parade, where May lay almost at the point of death, muttering feebly, and appealing to him not to be so cruel as to kill her, because she always thought that he was dead.

The surgeon had done all that was possible, and he had consulted with the principal physician as to the course to be pursued; and then, in the face of two grave wounds in the neck and breast of the frail, childish little creature, they had left her to the wild delirium that had set in—one whose fever was burning away rapidly the flickering life that was left.

The window was wide open, and the soft, low rush of the water upon the shingle floated in like soft, murmurous music through the flowers that it had always been Claire's pleasure to tend. Then a faint, querulous cry, oft repeated, came from seaward, where the soft grey-plumaged gulls swept here and there, and dipped down at the shelly shoals laid bare as the tide ebbed and flowed. It was a weird, uneasy sound, that accorded well with the painful scene in the chamber given up to the sick girl, by whose side stood Claire, pale and anxious, ready to fan the burning face, or rearrange the bedclothes tossed uneasily away.

Near the foot of the bed sat the Master of the Ceremonies, grey, hollow-cheeked, and with a wild look of despairing horror in his eyes, as he gazed at his little fallen idol, for whom he had fought and schemed, and whom he had so obstinately held aloft in his own heart, to the disparagement of her patient, forbearing sister.

"Is it true, Claire?" he murmured at last; "is it true, or some dreadful dream? My child! My child!"

Then his face grew convulsed with horror, as May turned her face towards him, and began speaking rapidly:

"Don't, Louis—pray: don't.—No: I am afraid.—Take me away quickly, dear.—No one will know, and I hate him so.—Little mean wretch!—They made me marry him, and I hate him more and more.—Hush!"

Denville groaned, and, as his head drooped upon his breast, Claire heard him murmur:

"Is it a judgment—is it a judgment for the past?"

She shivered as she listened to his words, but a quick movement and a low cry of pain made her bend over her sister again.

"Take me away," she said, after a few moments; and her pinched face bore a look of terror that stabbed those who watched with an agonising pain. "I tell you I hate Frank, and I dare not meet poor Louis now. It is not he, but something from the dead. Claire—Claire—hold me. Sister, help! Don't let me go. Am I going to die?"

"May, May!" whispered Claire soothingly, as she laid her cheek against the burning face; and the sick girl sighed, and made an effort to cling to her, but her feeble arm dropped heavily upon the coverlid.

"Don't let Louis come now. Is that Frank? Is that—"

She wandered off, muttering quickly and incoherently as she threw her head from side to side for a time; and then, utterly exhausted, seemed to sleep.

"Has—has Frank Burnett been?" whispered her father, looking timidly at Claire.

She shook her head sadly.

"No," said Denville; "he will not come. He would not even if she were to die. She must get better; and we will do as you have often said: go right away, where we are not known, and where we shall be safe."

In spite of herself, Claire darted at him a horrified look, which he saw and winced at, as he rose feebly, and began to pace the room, stopping at length before the window to gaze out at the sunlit sea.

"Strange!" he murmured; "the world so beautiful, and my life one dreary course of agony and pain. Claire, what do the doctors really think—that she will live?"

"I pray God they do!" said Claire solemnly.

"Yes; she must live and repent. There is pardon for those who suffer and repent, my child. Don't look at me like that; you do not know. Claire, is this my punishment? Surely no worse suffering can befall me now."

"Dear father," whispered Claire; "let the past be dead."

"Hush!" he cried, grasping her hand; "Don't talk of death, girl—here. She must live, and we will go away before—before it is too late. Has Morton been?"

Claire shook her head mournfully.

"No; he would not come. He must not come," said the old man quickly. "He is well placed, and he must not come near such pariahs as we are. No, no; don't look like that," he whispered passionately. "Why should he drag himself down? It is too much to ask of the boy."

He went on tip-toe to the bed, and took the little feverish hand that lay outside the coverlid, and kissed and stroked it as he muttered to himself:

"Poor little wandering lamb! So weak and timid, and ready to go astray; but you are safe here with me. Oh, how wrong everything is!"

Claire glanced at him, half stunned by this new trouble; and, as her father talked of punishment, and the impossibility of a greater trouble than this befalling them, a cold hand seemed to clutch her heart, and a vague, black shadow of another horror came back with double force, she shuddered, and devoted herself more and more to her task of attending the sister sick apparently unto death.

As she sat there, with the shadow of death impending, after the first shock, it seemed to lose its terrors, and she found herself looking upon it as less dreadful than she had been wont to do. There was rest in it, and a cessation from the pain and suffering that had so long been her portion;

and, as the hours rolled on, her throbbing brain grew dull and heavy, her own suffering lighter, and she seemed better able to attend to the sufferer at her side.

Towards noon there was a soft knock at the front door, and Isaac—who had been planning with Eliza an immediate flight from the grief-stricken house, on the ground that, even if they lost their wages, it was no longer a place for them to stay at—opened it, and told the visitor that Miss Denville could see no one.

"But me, young man," said the caller, quietly entering. "You need not say I'm here. I shall go up soon, and you have got to go on to my house for another basket like this, only bigger."

She patted the one she carried—one which she had crammed with such things as she thought would be useful at such a time.

Isaac gave way, allowed Mrs Barclay to go up to the drawing-room, and directly after called Eliza into his pantry to tell her that his mind was made up, and that they must go at once.

Mrs Barclay did not hesitate for a moment, but went softly up to the bedroom, tapped gently, and turned the handle to enter on tip-toe.

"I've only come to help, my dear," she said softly, as she clasped Claire in her arms. "We weren't quick enough, my dear," she whispered, "or we might have saved all this."

There was no reply, and after a time, in respect to Claire's wishes, Mrs Barclay went downstairs.

"I shall be there if you want me, my dear. Don't you go and think that you are left alone."

Mrs Barclay had hardly seated herself in the dining-room, and taken some rather grubby work from her pocket, when she heard a peculiar noise, and the bump of something being placed heavily upon the floor.

She listened, and heard some one ascend the stairs again, and there was a whispering, which ceased as the whisperers ascended, and then there was silence, and Mrs Barclay took a stitch, and thought and wondered whether Cora Dean would come, or whether the Denvilles would be cut by everyone now.

Then she took another stitch, and nibbed her nose, which itched.

"Poor little soul!" she said to herself, "it's come home to her at last. I never thought any good of her, but I'm not one to go on punishing those who've done wrong."

Mrs Barclay took another stitch and began to think again.

"Jo-si-ah says if they catch the little Italian fellow, he'll be transported for life, and if poor little Mrs Burnett dies, they'll hang him. Well, I don't hold with hanging people, so I hope she won't die."

She took another stitch and drew the thread through very slowly.

"Jo-si-ah says Sir Harry isn't very bad, and the constable and a magistrate have been to see him, but he says he knows nothing hardly about it. Poor Claire! What a house this is! What trouble!"

She took another stitch.

"I wonder whether Richard Linnell will come. I shall begin to hate him if he doesn't stand by the poor girl in her distress. He's a poor shilly-shally sort of a fellow, or he'd believe in her as I do."

There was quite a vicious stitch here.

"Perhaps, it isn't his fault. She kept him at a distance terribly, and no wonder with the troubles she's had; but of course he can't understand all that, being impetuous, like my Jo-si-ah was, and I dessay it will all come right at last. Now, what are they lumping down the stairs, making a noise, and that poor child so ill?"

She threw her work on the table, got up softly, and, just as there was a fresh bump and a whispering, she opened the door to find Isaac and Eliza standing over a box which they had just set down in the passage beside another, while Isaac in plain clothes and Eliza with her bonnet in her hand started at seeing the visitor.

"Why, highty-tighty, who's going away?" cried Mrs Barclay wonderingly.

Eliza glanced at Isaac, who cleared his throat.

"The fact is, ma'am, this young person and I have come to the conclusion that seeing how we suffered from arrears, and what goings on there are here, Mr Denville's isn't the service in which we care to stop any longer."

"Oh," said Mrs Barclay; "and have you told Mr Denville you are going?"

"Well, ma'am; no, ma'am. We have thought it is not necessary under the circumstances, and—"

"Nor yet, Miss Claire?"

"No, ma'am; she is too busy."

"Then just you take those boxes up again, young man, and take off that finery, and put on your livery," said Mrs Barclay in a low angry voice. "Now, no words. You do as I say—there take those boxes up."

The tone of voice, manner, and a hint about the wages had their effect. Isaac and Eliza glanced at each other, and took the boxes away without a word, Isaac coming back in livery a quarter of an hour later to tell Mrs Barclay that "that soldier" was at the back door.

Mrs Barclay started and followed Isaac, to stare in wonder at the fine soldierly young fellow, who eagerly asked her a score of questions about Claire and May, and, declining to be questioned in turn, hurried away with troubled mien.

# Chapter Nine
# May Begins to See

"Claire."

It was the faintest whisper of a call, but she to whom it was addressed heard it, and leaned over the bed to lay a cool hand upon the little wistful face looking up from the pillow.

"How long have I been lying here, Claire?"

"Hush, dear; don't talk," said Claire tenderly, "you are still so weak."

"Yes, but I must know. If you do not answer my questions, I shall fret and die sooner than I should do if you told me."

"Six weeks, dear."

"Six weeks!" sighed May; "and it seems like a dream. Since I seemed to wake up the day before yesterday, I have been thinking about it all, and I recollect everything now."

She spoke with perfect calmness, and as she went on, Claire's brow wrinkled.

"Poor old dad! How fond he is of me, and how ready to forgive me," she went on quietly. "Has Frank Burnett been?"

Claire shook her head.

"Not once?"

"No."

"Ah, well, I suppose he would not come. He felt that I was not his wife, and he was glad to cut himself clear from such an unhappy family. Has Sir Harry sent?"

"May! dear May!"

"I only wanted to know, Claire," said May quietly. "Don't be angry with me, dear. It's all over now. Is he better?"

"I believe so. He has gone away."

"Thank God!" said May fervently.

Claire turned upon her with wondering eyes.

"Yes," she said again. "Thank God! I should not have liked to see him again, nor to know that he had been to ask for me. I am so weak, Claire. I always—I was so different to you."

Claire sighed, and bent down and kissed the white forehead, beneath which the large eyes look unnaturally bright.

"That's nice," said May, with a sigh of content. "I wish I had been born such a girl as you. Always so calm and grave. I was so different. I used to feel, and I am sure of it now, that I was like one of the pretty little boats out there at sea, with the great white sails, that are blown over sometimes for want of ballast. I never had any ballast, Claire, and that made me giddy."

"Had you not better be silent now, May dear?" whispered Claire.

"No. Perhaps I may not be able to talk to you again, and I should like to tell you everything that is in my mind."

"May, dear!" cried Claire, kissing her lovingly.

"You forgive me, then?" sighed May. "I'm glad of that, for I want a deal of forgiving—here—and there," she added, after a pause.

"Which may come the easier, dear, for a life spent in repenting what is past."

"Yes; that would be easy, Claire, easy enough; but it is better as it is with me. I should be so weak and foolish again if I got well.—Claire."

"Yes, dear."

"Has poor Louis been seen again?"

"No: not since that night."

May lay silent for a few minutes, and then said softly:

"It seems very cruel of him to strike me like that, but he had been true to me, Claire, and I was so weak I couldn't be true to him, and he is not like us; he is foreign, and loves and hates so passionately. It made him angry and mad against me. As soon as I saw him in the street, after I had written to ask Sir Harry to take me away, I knew there was danger, and I tried so hard to escape. I felt obliged then. Sir Harry had often before begged me to go, but I never would."

"Hush! May, I beg of you."

"No: I must talk," said May. "I will speak softly so that it shall not hurt me much; but I want to be made happy by telling you everything and getting you to freely forgive me."

"I do—I do freely forgive you, everything, May, dear sister," whispered Claire, "and you must get well quickly, so that we may go far away from here, and begin life afresh."

"Yes," said May, with a peculiar smile, "far away, and begin life afresh."

Claire saw her peculiar look, and held her tightly to her breast.

"Yes," said May softly, "it means that, dear. I've always been like a spoiled child. Poor papa has made me his idol, and I've been so weak and foolish. I can see it all now, since I have been ill. Claire, I hope they will not take poor Louis and punish him for this."

"No, no, dear; he has gone far away; but pray, pray, say no more."

"I must," she said smiling. "I have wasted so much time that I cannot spare a moment now. Ah, Claire, if I had been like you!"

"I wish you had been happier than ever I have been," said Claire sadly. "Now try and sleep."

"I want to talk to you about baby, Claire dear," continued May, without heeding her sister's words.

She laughed softly, and her sister gazed at her in wonder, thinking that she was wandering again, as in the days of her long delirium.

"I was laughing about baby," she said. "Such a droll little soft thing. I laughed when I saw it first, for we both seemed to be such bits of girls, and it seemed such nonsense for me to be the poor little tot's mother. I have never been like a mother to it, though, leaving it always to strangers; but you, Claire, you will see to it, and be a better mother to her than ever I could."

"You shall get better, May, and make your little one a blessing to you when we are far away from here."

"Yes," said May with the same peculiar look, "far away from here. Poor little baby! Does my father know?"

"Yes: everything now, dear."

"Oh, yes, I had forgotten: he kissed me as if he did, and forgave his weak, wilful child."

"How is she?" whispered Denville, entering the room softly a few minutes later.

"Asleep," said Claire in the same tone.

"Is she—do you think she—"

He trailed off in his speech, and ended by looking imploringly in his daughter's face.

"I dare not say," said Claire mournfully. "Father, she is very ill."

"Then you must nurse her, Claire," said the old man excitedly, as he caught her hand to hold it tightly. "You must get her well, so that we can go—all go—far away—where we are not known. We cannot stay here in misery and debt and disgrace. Everything is against us now. My old position is gone. I dare not walk to the Assembly-Room, for fear of some insult or slight. I am the Master of the Ceremonies only in name. I am disgraced."

"Then we will go," said Claire sadly; "but it cannot be yet. Have patience, dear."

She laid her hand upon the old man's shoulder, and bent forward and kissed his cheek.

He caught her in his arms.

"You do not shrink from me?" he said bitterly.

"Shrink? No, father; I am your child. Now, tell me—about money—what are we to do?"

Denville shook his head.

"There is only one way out of the difficulty, Claire."

"A way, father?"

"Yes; Lord Carboro' spoke to me again this morning on the Parade. He came up to me like the gentleman he is, and just as I had been openly cut by townsman after townsman. He shook hands with me and took my arm, Claire, and—and—I told him he might come here—to-day—and speak to you."

"Oh, father, what have you done? You have not taken money from him?"

"No—no—no!" cried the old man indignantly. "I have not sunk so low as that; but it was tempting. That man Isaac has grown insolent, and has twice come home intoxicated. Claire, I am the fellow's slave while I am in his debt. I want to send him away, but I cannot. Hush!"

There was a double knock at the door, and Denville went softly down, leaving Claire with a fresh agony to battle against, for, few as had been her father's words, they had been sufficiently plain to make her ask herself whether it was not her duty to give up everything—to sell herself, as it were, to this old nobleman, that her father might be saved from penury, and her sister placed beyond the reach of want; for her home must in future be with them.

"Have we not at last reached the very dregs of bitterness?" she said wildly. "Heaven help me in this cruel strait!"

The door opened softly, and Denville signed to Claire to come to him on the landing.

"It is Lord Carboro'," he whispered. "You must speak to him."

Claire shrank back for a moment, but her firmness returned, and she closed the door and followed her father to take his hand.

"I would do everything, now, father, even to this," she said solemnly; "but it is impossible. Ask yourself."

"Yes," he said sadly, "it is impossible. But it is very hard—to see wealth and prosperity for you, my child, and to have to say *no*. But it is impossible. Speak gently to the old man. He has been a good friend to me."

It seemed as if a mist was about her as Claire Denville entered the drawing-room, beyond which she could dimly see Lord Carboro', looking almost grotesque in his quaint costume and careful get-up, fresh from the hands of his valet. He had been labouring hard to appear forty; but anxiety and the inexorable truth made him look at least seventy, as he rose, bowed, and placed a chair for the pale, graceful girl, and then took one near her.

The old man had prepared a set speech of a very florid nature, for, matter-of-fact worldling as he was, he had felt himself weak and helpless before the woman for whom he had quite a doting affection. But the sight of Claire's grief-stricken face and the recollection of the suffering and mental care through which she must have passed, drove away all thought of his prepared words, and he felt more like a simple-hearted old man full of pity than he had ever been before.

He took her hand, which was given up unresistingly, and after a thoughtful look in the calm clear eyes that met his, he said slowly:

"My dear Miss Denville, I came here to-day, a vain weak man, full of the desire to appear young; but you have driven away all this shallow pretence, for I feel that you can see me clearly as what I am, an old fellow of seventy. Hush! don't speak my dear child till I have done. I have always admired you as a beautiful girl: I now love you as the sweet, patient, suffering woman who has devoted herself to others."

"Lord Carboro'—"

"No, no; let me try and finish, my dear. I will be very brief. It would be a mockery to speak flattering follies to such a one as you. Tell me first—Did your father give you to understand that I was coming?"

Claire bent her head.

"Then let me say simply, my child, that if you will be my wife and give me such love as your sweet dutiful heart will teach you to give to the doting old man who asks you, I will try all I can to make your young life happy, and place it in your power to make a pleasant home somewhere for poor old Denville, and your sister. We must bring her round. A trip abroad with your father, and—and—dear me—dear me, my child, I am rambling strangely, and hardly know what I say, only that I ask you to be my wife, and in return you shall be mistress of all I possess. I know the difference in our ages, and what the world will say; but I could afford to laugh at the world for the few years I should be likely to stay in it, and afterwards, my child, you would be free and rich, and with no duty left but to think kindly of the old man who was gone."

Claire listened to the old man's words with a strange swelling sensation in her breast. The tears gathered slowly in her eyes as she gazed wistfully at him, wondering at the tender respect he paid her, and one by one they brimmed over and trickled down.

She could not speak, but at last in the gratitude of her heart, as she thought of the sacrifice he made in offering her rank and riches, after the miserable scandals of which she had been the victim, she raised his withered hand slowly to her lips.

"No, no," he cried, "not that. You consent then?"

"No, my lord," said Claire firmly. "It is impossible."

"Then—then," he cried testily. "You do love someone else."

Claire bowed her head, and her eyes looked resentment for a moment. Then in a low sweet voice she said:

"Even if I could say to you, Lord Carboro' my heart is free, and I will try to be your loving, dutiful wife, there are reasons which make it impossible."

"These troubles—that I will not name. I know, I know," he said hastily; "but they are miserable family troubles, not yours."

"Troubles that are mine, Lord Carboro', and which I must share. Forgive me if I give you pain, but I could never be your wife."

The old man dropped the hand he held, and his face was full of resentment as he replied:

"Do you know what you are throwing away?" Then, checking himself, "No, no, I spoke angrily—like a thoughtless boy. Don't take any notice of my words, but think—pray think of your father—of your sister. How you could help them in the position you would hold."

"Lord Carboro'," said Claire, "I am weak, heart-sick and worn with watching. I can hardly find words to thank you, and I want you to think me grateful, but what you ask is impossible. It can never be."

The old man rose angrily and took a turn or two about the room, as he strove hard to fight down his bitter mortification.

Twice over he stopped before her, and his lips parted to speak, but he resumed his hurried walk, ending by catching her hands and kissing them.

"Good-bye," he said abruptly. "I shall try to be your friend, and—and I never loved you half so much as I do now."

He left the room, and Claire heard his footsteps on the path, and then, in spite of herself, she stole towards the window from which she saw him go slowly along the Parade, looking bent, and as if his coming had aged him ten years at least.

The opening of the drawing-room door roused Claire, and turning, she saw that her father had entered, and that he was trembling as he gazed at her with a curiously wistful look that was one long question.

Claire shook her head slowly as she returned his gaze, with her thoughts reverting to the night when she sank fainting where she stood, and the notes of the serenade floated in at the window.

"No, father," she said softly; "it would be impossible."

"Yes," he said feebly; "impossible!"

# Chapter Ten
# The Storm-Cloud Bursts

That night, as Claire sat by the open window of her bedroom, where May lay sleeping, and the flowers that she had tended so carefully in the past for the most part withered and dry, her thoughts went back to the morning's interview with Lord Carboro', and there was a feeling of regret in her breast as she thought of the old man's chivalrous devotion.

Then her heart seemed to stand still, and again beat with a wild tumult as she told herself that the silent reproach she had felt was not justified; that it was her own doing, that Richard Linnell was not at her side. For that was his step, and she knew that he would stop opposite to her darkened window and gaze upwards before passing on.

There was pleasure and yet pain in the thought, for she felt that though it was impossible that they could ever even be friends, he must believe in her and she must dwell in his heart.

How often might he not have passed like that, and looked up, thinking of her!

It was a pleasant thought, but one that she dismissed at once, as if it were a temptation.

Trying to stop her ears to the sounds, she crept back from the window, and bent over May, who seemed to be sleeping more easily; and a feeling of hope began to lighten the darkness in her heart, and the black shadow of dread that so oppressed her was forgotten, till, all at once, it came back, blacker, more impenetrable than ever, as the sound of voices loud in altercation rose from below.

Claire's heart stood still, and she held on by a chair-back, listening with her lips apart, and wondering whether this was the bolt fallen at last—the blow she was always dreading, and that she felt must one day come.

She crept to the door, passed out and listened, closing it after her that the noise might not awaken May, to whom sleep meant life.

Angry voices rose, and then there were the sounds of blows struck apparently with a cane. Then there was a scuffling noise, and the front door was driven back.

"Leave the house, scoundrel! leave my house, insolent dog!" came up sharp and clear in her father's voice, quivering with anger, and the scuffle was renewed.

"You pay me my wages; you pay me what you owe me, or I don't stir a step."

The voice that uttered these last words was thick and husky, and full of menace. It was a familiar voice, though, that Claire recognised, and her cheeks burned with shame as she felt that passers-by, perhaps Richard Linnell, would hear the degrading words that were uttered.

Her sister lying there sick, and this pitiful disturbance that was increasing in loudness, and must be heard by any one who happened to be upon the Parade!

She hurried down to find that the scuffling sounds had been renewed, and as she reached the passage it was to find that her father was trying to drag Isaac to the door, and force him into the road, where quite a little crowd was collecting.

"Leave this house, sir, directly."

"I shan't for you," cried Isaac, resisting stoutly. "I want my wages. I want my box."

"Leave this house, you drunken insolent scoundrel!"

"Father! for pity's sake," cried Claire, trying to interfere.

"No, no; stand back, my child," cried the old man angrily. "He has come back again to-night tipsy. He has insulted me once more, and he shall not stay here—I can turn him out, and I will."

"Not you, and I shan't go," hiccupped Isaac, seizing the plinth at the bottom of the balusters and holding on. "I don't go from here 'thout my money—every penny of it, so now, old Denville."

"Pray, pray let me pass, father, and shut the door," cried Claire.

"No, my dear," said the old man, whose blood was now up. "He shall leave this house at once."

"No, I shan't leave neither without my box."

The struggle went on, and the lamp would have been knocked off the bracket but for Claire's hand. The contending parties swayed here and there, but it was evident that the footman was far the stronger, while Denville's forces were failing moment by moment.

"Can I be of any assistance, Mr Denville?" said a voice that thrilled Claire through and through, but which made her shrink back up a few stairs to avoid being seen.

"Who's that?—Mr Linnell? Yes," panted Denville. "My servant, sir—my lacquey. This is the fourth time he has come back from being absent without leave, intoxicated, sir. Tipsy. Not fit to come into a gentleman's presence."

"Ha, ha, ha!" laughed Isaac—"Gentleman's presence! I don't call you a gentleman. Why, you're all that's mean and shabby and poor. Just you pay me my wages in arrears."

"Come to-morrow, scoundrel," said Denville loftily. "Mr Linnell, if you would kindly send one of the people outside for a constable. He will find one by the Assembly-Room. Let him say that the man is wanted at Mr Denville's—at the Master of the Ceremonies', and he will come on directly."

Linnell glanced up at where Claire was turning back in shame and distress of mind, little thinking that in a few minutes she would be bravely standing at her father's side.

"Fetch a constable!" cried Isaac defiantly. "Do, if you dare. What do I care for a constable?"

"Why don't you pay the man his wages?" said a voice at the door.

"Ah, to be sure," cried Isaac, with a tipsy laugh. "Why don't you pay the man his wages? 'Cause you can't. Beggarly old upstart."

"Silence, you scoundrel!" cried Linnell fiercely, "or I'll drag you out and throw you over the cliff for your insolence."

"Do it—do it!" cried Isaac fiercely. "Who's afraid?"

"Silence, dog!" cried Denville, catching up his cane.

"Don't strike him, Mr Denville," said Linnell. "Some one there fetch a constable. Five shillings for the first man who brings one here."

"Don't you, m'lads," cried Isaac. "He daren't send for a constable. I tell you he daren't—not for me. Send for one for himself."

Claire trembled and shuddered at those words; and, had it been possible, she would have ended the scene at any cost, but she was helpless.

For a moment Linnell had thought of seizing and dragging out the tipsy servant; but on second consideration he felt that it might just as well be done by some one in authority, so, hurrying out, he despatched one of the crowd in another direction to that taken by the two or three who had hurried off on the promise of a reward, and then turned back to see if he could be of any further service.

"Cons'able for me!" said Isaac, with tipsy gravity. "I like that. I like that—much. Let him come. Make him pay me *my* wages. Then I'll go. Not before, if all the old Masters o' Ceremonies in England wanted me to go."

"The insolent scoundrel!" panted Denville; "after all I've done for him since he came to me a boy."

"Done for me! Ha-ha-ha!" laughed Isaac; "kept me on short commons, and didn't pay my wages. Now, then, are you going to pay my money?"

"Here he is." "Here's one," rose in chorus, and way was made for the fussy-looking individual who occupied the post of chief constable of Saltinville.

"Now, then, what's this?" he said.

"Tipsy servant," chorussed half—a—dozen voices. "Drunk."

"My servant, Mr Cordy," said Denville importantly. "He has misconducted himself again and again. You see the condition he is in."

"Yes, I see," said the constable. "Come along."

"Wait till he pays my wages," hiccupped Isaac.

"You can talk about that another time," said the constable importantly. "Come along."

He seized the footman, gave him a shake which wrenched his fingers from their hold upon the bottom of the balusters, and with another shake jerked him upon his feet.

But Isaac was not going to be dragged off like that without making a scene, and he shouted out:

"Stop!"

"Well, what is it?" said the constable.

"Does he give me into custody, cons'ble?"

"Yes. Come along."

"Then I give him into custody—do you hear?—custody—for murder. I won't go alone."

"There, come along, fool," cried the constable.

"No—not without him," cried Isaac. "Murder!"

"Silence!" cried Denville excitedly, as Claire rushed down the stairs and caught her father's arm.

"Shan't silence!" yelled the man, who now threw off his half-tipsy, contemptuous manner, and seemed stung by the treatment he had received into a fit of furious passion. "I give him into custody—for murder."

"Nonsense! Hold your tongue, and come along," cried the constable; while Linnell seized the man on the other side, and hurriedly tried to force him out.

But it is not easy to get a man along a narrow passage if he resists fiercely; and so they found, for, setting his feet against the edge of the dining-room door, Isaac thrust himself back, and yelled to the throng at the door:

"Do you hear? For murder! I charge this man—Denville—with killing old Lady Teigne."

"Silence, villain!" hissed Linnell in his ear, as he darted an agonised glance at where Claire was half supporting her father, while the black cloud she had seen impending so long seemed to have fallen at last.

"Silence? When there's murder?" shouted Isaac. "I tell you I heard a noise, and got up, and then I saw him go to Lady Teigne's room, the night she was murdered. Ask him there who did it, and see what he'll say."

"Father, come away!" panted Claire, as she threw herself before him, as if to defend him against this terrible charge.

"What's that?" cried the constable. "Oh, nonsense! Come along."

"I tell you it's true," cried Isaac, with drunken fierceness; "it's true. I saw him go to her room. Let him deny it if he can."

Denville stood up, holding tightly by Claire's arm, and looking wildly from one to the other as a strange murmur rose amongst the fast-augmenting crowd. Then, as if it were vain to fight against the charge, he made a lurch forward, recovered himself, and sank into a chair, Richard Linnell catching sight of his ghastly countenance before he covered it with his hands.

"It is a false charge, constable," cried Linnell hastily. "Take that man away."

"It's all true," snarled Isaac, with drunken triumph. "Look at him. Let him say he didn't do it if he dare!"

As every eye was fixed upon him, the Master of the Ceremonies did not move; he made no bold defiance, but seemed half paralysed by the bolt that had fallen—one from which his child had failed to screen him, though she had thrown herself upon his breast.

# Chapter Eleven
# After the Storm

Matters ran their course rapidly during the following days. The black cloud that had so long been threatening had come down lower and nearer, and had at last poured forth its storm upon Denville's devoted head. And now, as he sat thinking, all that had passed seemed misty and dreamlike, and yet he knew that it was true.

There was the finish of that terrible night, when, forced by the direct charge of his servant, the constable had taken steps against him. He had been arrested; there had been magisterial examinations, and appeals to him to declare his innocency; he, the magistrates' respected townsman, charged with this horrible crime by a drunken servant!

But he had made no denial, only listened with a strange apathy, as if stunned, and ready to give up everything as hopeless. In fact, so willing did he seem to accept his position that, after examination and adjournment—one of which was really to give the broken-down, prostrate man an opportunity for making some defence—the magistrates had had no option but to commit the prisoner for trial.

All Saltinville had been greatly concerned, and thus taken off the scent of the previous trouble at the Master of the Ceremonies' house. The departure of Frank Burnett from the town, and the state of his wife's health, became exceedingly secondary matters. Sir Harry Payne's wound was of no more importance than Lady Drelincourt's rheumatic fever, brought on by exposure on the Downs at her age. People forgot, too, to notice that Sir Matthew Bray was clear of his arrest, and to heed the rumour floating about at Miss Clode's, that Lady Drelincourt had paid Sir Matthew's debts, her affection for the big heavy dragoon having received a strong accession from the fact that her love was no longer divided, her overfed dog having died, evidently from plethora.

Ordinary affairs were in abeyance, and everyone talked of Lady Teigne's murder, and metaphorically dug the old belle up again to investigate the affair, and, so to speak, hold a general inquest without the coroner's help.

Lord Carboro' took the matter down on the pier with him and sat at the end to watch Fisherman Dick shrimping; and as he watched him he did not think of the sturdy Spanish-looking fellow, but of Lady Teigne's jewels, and as he thought he tried to undo this knot.

"If Denville killed the old woman for her diamonds, how is it he remained so poor?"

"Thinking, Lord Carboro'?" said a voice.

The old beau looked up quickly and encountered the dark eyes of Major Rockley, who had also been intently watching Dick Miggles, using an opera-glass, so as to see him empty the shrimps into his creel.

"Yes: thinking," said Lord Carboro' in a short, sharp way. "Like to know what I was thinking?"

The Major shrugged his shoulders.

"Of the sea, perhaps, or the vessels passing, or Lady Drelincourt's illness."

"No, sir," said Lord Carboro' shortly. "I was thinking of Lady Teigne's jewels."

Rockley raised his eyebrows, and looked at the old man curiously.

"Of Lady Teigne's jewels?"

"Yes, sir; and it seems a strange thing to me that if Denville killed the old woman for her diamonds, he has not become rich."

"To be sure," said Rockley; "it does seem strange."

"It's all strange, sir, deuced strange," said the old man. "Took me aback, for I never suspected Denville, and I don't suspect him now."

They stood looking at each other for a few minutes, and then Rockley said quietly:

"A great many people seem to believe him innocent. Do you think they will get him off?"

"Yes, of course—of course, sir. It would be an abominable thing to bring such a charge home to the poor old fellow. Why, I suppose, sir, that even you would not wish that."

"I should be deeply grieved, my lord," said Rockley. "Good morning."

"The scoundrel's still thinking about Claire," said the old beau, as he sat gazing after the handsome cavalry officer. "Well, it's of no use to sit here. I'll go up to Clode's, and see if there is any news."

He trudged slowly along the pier and the Parade, stopping now and then to take a pinch of snuff.

He was indulging in a very big pinch, standing by the edge of the path, when there was the trampling of hoofs, and Cora Dean's pony-carriage was drawn up by his side.

"Let me drive you there," said Cora's deep, rich voice.

"Drive me! Where?" said the old man.

"Where you ought to be going; to the prison to see poor Mr Denville, and get him out. I haven't patience with you people leaving the poor old man there—you who professed to be his friends."

"Hah! Yes! No, I don't think I'll trouble you, my dear Miss Dean," said the old man, recovering his balance, and speaking in his old sarcastic tone. "You are such a female Jehu."

"Such a what?" said Cora.

"Female Jehu, my dear. You drive furiously, but you can't control your steeds. I don't want to be brought ashore in triumph. It's all very well for you to come on to the beach like a goddess in your car, but to me it means rheumatism and pain. So, no thanks."

"And you are going to leave Mr Denville in trouble?"

"Perhaps," said his lordship drily. "We're a heartless lot down here, and I'm one of the worst."

"And you think that poor old man killed Lady Teigne."

"No, I don't, my dear Miss Dean; but even if he had done so I don't think he ought to be punished. It was a meritorious action."

"Oh, Lord Carboro'!"

"It was, my dear madam; and if some enterprising party would come and kill off Lady Drelincourt and your humble servant, and a few more of that stamp, it would be a blessing to society. What do you think?"

"I think that a poor old man is lying in prison," said Cora Dean, tightening her reins; "that his broken-hearted child is tending a sick sister, and that the world of society talks about it all as if it were stuff sent on purpose to supply them with news. Lord Carboro', I used to wish I were well in society. I don't wish it now. Good morning."

"One moment," said the old man hastily. "You'll shake hands?"

He held out his, but Cora gave it a tap with her whip handle, and her ponies went off at a canter, leaving his lordship hat in hand.

"And looking dooced ridiculous," he said angrily. And then, "Confound the jade!" he muttered. "How dare she!"

Then his wrinkled countenance changed, and a pleasant smile took the place of the angry look.

"Confound her! What a dig to give me with her sharp tongue. Well, it's true enough, and I like her for it. Does she like Claire, or does she hate her and pretend to feel all this? Who can say? The more you know of a woman, the greater mystery she seems. Poor old Denville! The place doesn't seem natural without him and his snuff-box. I miss him horribly. Now I wonder whether they'd miss me if I were to go—as I shall go—soon."

He walked thoughtfully on.

"Yes; they'd miss me, and talk about me as if I were a confounded old curiosity, and make jocular remarks about my donkey—by George, how my corns shoot, I wish he were here. But no one will care when I'm gone—not one; and no one will be the better for my having lived."

He walked on slowly, thinking of the last time he had seen Claire, and of the troubles that had fallen to her share, and then he muttered:

"Yes! something must be done."

# Chapter Twelve
# From Parade to Prison

Sunken of eye, hollow of cheek, with the silvery stubble of many days' growth upon his chin, glistening in the bar of light that came through the grated window, Stuart Denville, Master of the Ceremonies at Saltinville, high-priest to the votaries of fashion who worshipped at that seaside shrine, sat upon his truckle bed, his head down upon his hands, his elbows on his knees, gazing apparently at the dancing motes in the well-defined ray of sunshine that illumined his cell.

It seemed as if he saw in those tiny motes that danced and rose and fell, the fashionable people who had so influenced his career; but hour after hour, as he sat there motionless, thinking of his arrest, his examination, the fashionable world was to him something that had never existed: he could see only the terminative.

On first picturing that terrible end, when, with hideous exactness, the scaffold, the hangman, and the chaplain whispering words of hope and comfort to the thin, grey-haired, pinioned figure moving on in the slow procession had loomed up before him in all their terrible minutiae, he had shivered and shrunk away; but, after a few repetitions of this horrible waking dream, he had grown so accustomed to it that he found himself conjuring up the scene, and gazing at it mentally with a curious kind of interest that gradually became fascination.

As to the final stage, it would not be so painful as many pangs, mental and bodily, which he had suffered; and, as to the future, that troubled him but little. He saw no terrors there, only a long restful sleep, freed from the cares and sufferings that had for long past fallen to his lot.

There were no shudders now, but only a sad wistful smile and a sigh almost of content, the rest of the future seemed so welcome.

"Yes," he said at last, as he pressed his trembling white hands to his lips, and left his seat to pace the cell, falling for the moment involuntarily into his old mincing pace, but stopping short and gazing up at the little patch of blue sky he could see; "yes—rest—sleep—Oh, God, I am so weary. Let it end!"

He stood with his hands clasped before him, and now a cloud came over his countenance, almost the only cloud that troubled him now. Claire; if she only could know—if he could tell her all—his temptations—his struggles—the long fight he had passed through.

Then he thought over his past—the mistakes of his life. How much happier he might have been if he had chosen differently. How piteous had been all this sham and pretence, what a weary existence it had been—what insults he had suffered for the sake of keeping up his miserable position, and obtaining a few guineas.

May!

The thought of his child—his favoured one, with her pretty innocent rosebud of a face and its appealing, trusting eyes. How he had worshipped that girl! How she had been his idol. How he had believed in her and sacrificed everything for her sake; and now—he lay in prison, one whom the world called murderer; and she, his idol, to whom he had sacrificed so long, for aught he knew, passing away, and everyone turned from him and his family as if they were lepers.

Well, he was a social leper. He had made no defence. This man had charged him with the crime, and he had not denied it. What wonder that people shrank from him as if he were unclean, and kept away. It was his fate. The world turned from him—son—daughter. They feared the contamination of the gaol.

No suffering that the executioner even could inflict would equal the agony of mind through which he had passed.

He clasped his hands more tightly and gazed fixedly before him, his lips moving at last, as he said in a low husky whisper:

"All forsake me now. The Master of the Ceremonies must prepare for the great ceremony of the law. Oh, that it were over, and the rest were come!"

He was at the lowest ebb of his misery amid his meditations and thoughts of home and the social wreck that was there with her thin baby face, when there was the distant sound of bolts being shot. Then there were steps and the rustle of a dress, the rattle of a great key in the door. Next the bolts of this were shot at top and bottom with a noisy jar; the door was thrust open, and the gaoler ushered in a veiled figure in black. Then the door was closed, the locks and bolts rattled; the heavy steps of the gaoler sounded upon the stone floor, and then the farther door opened and closed.

There was a moment's silence before, with a quick rustling sound, veil and cloak were thrown aside upon the bed, and Claire's soft arms clasped the wasted, trembling form, drawing the grey careworn face down upon her breast as she sobbed out:

"Father—father, has it come to this?" Denville remained silent for a few moments, and then with an exceeding bitter cry:

"My child! my child!" he wailed. "I said you had forsaken me in my sore need."

"Forsaken you, dear? Oh, no, no, no!" whispered Claire, fondling him as if he had been a child, and gently drawing him to the bed, upon which she sank, while he fell upon his knees before her, utterly weak and helpless now, as he yielded to the caresses she lavished upon him, and she whispered words that seemed full of comfort—forerunners of the rest he had prayed for so short a tune before.

"Forsaken you?" she whispered. "Oh, my dear, dear father! How could you think it of your child!"

"The world says I am a murderer, and I am in prison."

"Hush!" she cried, laying her hand upon his lips. "It was only this morning I could get permission to see you."

She laid her soft white hand upon his lips as she spoke, and then, seeming to make an effort and check her own emotion, she drew him closer to her.

"Ah!" he sighed as he clung to her; "and I always acted so unfairly to you, my child. But tell me—May?"

"She does not know," said Claire earnestly. "In her weak state it might kill her."

"Perhaps better it did," said Denville solemnly. "Poor, weak, erring girl!"

"Hush! Don't!" cried Claire. "Father, there is hope—there is forgiveness for us all if we show that we are indeed repentant. May is not like others. Always weak and wilful and easily turned aside from what was right. No: we must not despond. I must take you both far, far away, dear. I have come for that now. You must advise with me and help me," she said quickly. "Tell me what I am to do—what I am to set about. Come, father, quick!"

"What you are to do?" he said sadly. "Trust in heaven, my child: we cannot shape our own paths in life, and when we do try the end is wreck."

"Father," she cried impetuously, "do you think I was speaking of myself? I want you to tell me whom to ask for help."

"Help, my child?"

"Yes: for money. May I ask the Barclays? They have always been so kind. Surely they will help us now."

"Help us—money?" he said vacantly.

"Yes, for your defence. We must have counsel, father. You shall be saved—saved that we may go far from here. Father, I cannot bear it. You must be saved."

He was startled by the wildness of her manner and the fierce energy she threw into her words.

"You do not speak," she cried imperiously, and she laid her hands upon his shoulders and gazed into his eyes. "You must not, you shall not give up and let yourself drift to destruction. Why do you not tell me? I am only a woman. Father, what shall I do?"

"What shall you do?" he said mournfully.

"Yes, yes. Forgive me for what I say—I, your child, who love you most dearly now that you are in this terrible trouble. Father, we must go away together to some distant place where, in a life of contrition and prayer, we may appeal daily for the forgiveness that is given to those who seek."

He gazed in her eyes with his lip quivering, and a terrible look of despair in his face.

"Forgiveness for those who seek?"

"Yes, from a merciful God. Oh, father, if I wring your heart in what I say it is because I love you as your child."

"Ah!"

A piteous sigh escaped his lips, and his head sank down upon his breast.

"You are silent," she cried reproachfully, "silent, when the time is so short. I shall be dragged from your side directly, and you have not advised me what to do. I must have money. I must get counsel for you and advice."

He drew a long breath and raised his head, his lips parting but uttering no sound.

"Yes!" she cried, "yes! Speak, father. Shall I go to Mr Barclay?"

"No."

"Then tell me what I shall do, dear. Pray rouse yourself from this despair. Speak—tell me. What shall I do first?"

"Nothing."

"Nothing? Oh, father!"

"They say I committed this murder—that I crushed out the life of that miserable old woman. So be it."

"Father!"

"I say—so be it," he repeated firmly. "The law says one life must answer for another. Well—I am ready."

Claire wrung her hands, as he rose from where he had knelt, and gazed at him in pitying wonder and awe.

"God is merciful," said the old man mournfully. "He readeth all our hearts. Claire, my child, I am not afraid to die. I am sick for the rest that is to come."

"But, father!" wailed Claire.

"My child, I know. I have thought of all. I have seen everything in the silence and darkness of this cell; but it is only a passing away from this weary life to one that is full of rest and peace. There is no injustice there."

"Father, you madden me," whispered Claire hoarsely. "You must not give up like this. Tell me what to do."

"Think me innocent, my child," he said softly—"innocent of that crime. And now let us talk of yourself and your brother Morton."

She noticed that he did not mention May's name.

"It is very bitter," he said. "I had hoped to provide for my child, but I was not able. But there, you are stronger of mind than I, and you will be protected. That woman, Mrs Barclay, loves you, my child. But Morton, he is a mere boy, and weak—weak and vain, like his father, my child—as I have been. Watch over him, Claire. Advise him when he is falling away."

"Oh, yes, yes, yes, father; but you—"

"I shall be at rest, my child," he said sadly. "Do not think of me. Then there is—"

He paused for a few moments with his lips quivering till he saw her inquiring eyes, and with a heavy sigh he went on.

"—There is May."

He paused again, to go on almost lightly, but she read the agony in his eyes, and clung to his arm and held it to her breast.

"This is like my will," he said, "the only one I shall make. There is May. I have not been fair, my dear. I have given her all my love—to your neglect. I have made her my idol, and—and—like her brother Morton, she is very weak. Such a pretty child, beautiful as an angel. Claire dearest, I loved her so well, and it has been my punishment for my injustice to you."

"Dearest father!"

"Yes, I was unjust to you, but that is past. I pray your forgiveness, my child, as I say to you, I leave you the legacy of that boy and girl—that child-wife. Claire, you must forgive her, as I pray Him to forgive me. Ignore the past, Claire, my child, and in every way you can be ready to step between her and the evil that she goes too near. You will do this?"

"Oh, father, yes. But you? What shall I do now?"

"Claire, only a few short weeks, and I shall be in my grave. Don't start, my child. To you, in your sweet spring of life, it is the black pit of horror. To me, in the bitter winter of my life, there is no horror there: it is but the calm, silent resting-place where tired nature sleeps and life's troubles end. There, there, my little one, to whose sweet virtues and truth I have been blind, I am almost content with my fate for the reason that you have awakened me from a trance into which I had fallen. Claire, my child, can you forgive this weak, vain, old man?"

She leaned forward and kissed his white forehead, and, as he drew her closer to him, she nestled in his breast, and clung to him, sobbing convulsively.

"Hah!" he sighed, "I did not know I could be so happy again. Think of me as an innocent—an injured man, my child, as of one whose lips are sealed. Pray for me as I shall pray for you."

"But, father, I may see Mr Barclay?"

He was silent for a few minutes.

"Yes," he said at last.

Claire uttered a sigh of relief.

"You shall ask him to come here. I will appeal to him to watch over you. He is rough, Claire, and his wife is vulgar—coarse; but, God help me! I wish I had had such a true and sterling heart. There, hush! I have made my will," he said, smiling. "It is done; I have but to seal it with my death, and I see its approach without a shade of fear."

"But, father! my dearest father!"

"My own," he said tenderly, as he kissed her and smiled down upon her. "Ah! you do not shrink from me now. Sweet, true woman. Oh, that I could have been so blind! You were going to ask me something."

"Yes, dearest," she whispered; "I want you to forgive—"

"May? Yes: she is forgiven. I forgive her, poor, weak child. Tell her that I had but tender words for her even now. I would send her messages, but of what avail would they be, even as the words of a dying man? No; she has not the stability. It is more her failing than her sin. You were asking me to forgive her."

"I knew you forgave her, dearest, but I want you to forgive poor Fred."

He started from her as if he had been stung.

"I saw him last night, and he begs and prays of you to forgive him and let him come. Father, he loves you in spite of all this estrangement."

"Silence!" cried the old man furiously. "Have I not said that I would not hear his name?"

"Father dearest, what have I done?" cried Claire, as she gazed in terror at the convulsed features, at the claw-like hands, extended, clutching, and opening and shutting as the old man gasped for air.

"Father! Oh, help!"

A terrible purple colour suffused his face; his knotted veins started upon his temples, and it seemed as if he were about to fall in a fit; but the paroxysm began to pass away. He caught at Claire's hand, and held by it while with his other he signed to her to be silent, for just then the clanking of bolts and locks was heard, and the door was thrown open to admit Richard Linnell and Mr Barclay.

# Chapter Thirteen
## Under Barclay's Shell

Denville grew composed at once, and taking Claire's hand, stood up facing his visitors with a slight trace of the old manner returning, as he bowed and pointed to the stool and bed.

"Poor accommodation for visitors, gentlemen," he said; "but it is the best I have to offer. Mr Barclay, Mr Linnell, will you be seated?"

"Couldn't get to you before, Denville," said the money-lender, shaking hands warmly. "Terrible business this. Miss Claire, my dear, the wife has gone to your house again. Taken some things with her; said she should stay."

"Mr Denville, I am truly grieved," said Linnell, offering his hand, after giving Claire a grave, sad look. "Mr Barclay and I have come to see of what service we can be to you."

"Yes, yes, of course, Denville," cried Barclay briskly. "Bad business, this, but—eh, Mr Linnell?"

"Miss Denville," said the latter, turning to Claire, "as we are about to discuss business matters about counsel and your father's defence, would you like to leave us?"

"No," said Denville quickly, as he drew Claire's hand through his arm, and shook his head. "You will pardon me, gentlemen, but in the little space of time I am allowed to see visitors, I should like to keep my child by my side. Gentlemen—Mr Barclay—Mr Linnell—half an hour ago I said that I had no friends. I was wrong—I thank you for coming. God bless you!"

"Why, of course you had friends, Denville," cried Barclay. "You don't suppose because a man's hard and fast over money matters, that he has no bowels of compassion, do you? But now, business. About counsel for your defence?"

"I had already discussed the matter with my daughter, gentlemen. Counsel! It is useless. I need none."

"Need none, Mr Denville?" cried Linnell quickly. "Pray think of what you are saying. You must have legal help."

Claire darted a grateful look at Linnell, and then drew back with pain depicted in her countenance, mingled with pride and mortification as she saw the coldness in his manner towards her.

"I must repeat what I said, Mr Linnell," said Denville in a low, pained voice. "I want no counsel. I will have none, but I thank you all the same, Mr Barclay. Claire, my child, you will pardon me. I must speak with Mr Barclay."

Claire shrank into one corner of the cell, her brow drawn with the pain inflicted upon her as her father kept reverting to his old displays of deportment and mincing ways—ways that had become so habitual that even now, incongruous as they were, he could not quite throw them off.

"You need not go, Mr Linnell," he continued, "that is if you will bear with the pain of listening to a dying man's request. We have never been friends, sir, but I am your debtor now for your kindly act. My dear Barclay, the little drama of my poor life is nearly over; the curtain is about to fall. You have known me long—my little ambitious hopes and disappointments. I cannot say to my child there is a home for her with her sister; will you help her when—you know what I would say?"

"Denville, old fellow, I don't know what to say to this," said Barclay quickly. "It's a mystery to me. Damn it, sir, I can't believe you killed that old woman even now. I want to get you counsel who will clear you, sir, and throw the deed on to whoever did it—some one unknown."

"Hush!—hush! Pray hush!" cried Denville, shuddering. "We are wasting time. Barclay—my daughter."

"My dear old fellow," said the money-lender quickly, "I told you that my wife had gone on to your place to see Miss Claire there. Don't you be afraid for her. She has a friend in Mrs B who will never fail her. Friend? She will prove a mother. Don't you trouble about Miss Claire. There's only one obstacle to her having a happy home, and that's me, and—"

He stopped short, for his voice had turned husky, and gripping Denville's hand very tightly, he held it for a few minutes.

"God bless her sweet face!" he whispered; "we never believed one of the miserable scandals about her, Denville. But now about yourself."

Denville turned away his face, took a couple of steps to the side, and stood with his back to them for a few minutes. Then, turning, with his face wearing a curious look of calm, he laid his hand upon Barclay's arm.

"You have taken away the bitterness of death, Barclay," he said in a low voice. "Heaven help me for the weakest of men. I never knew who were my friends."

"Then you will let us get counsel for you?"

"No, no! I forbid it," said Denville sternly. "Good-bye, Mr Linnell. I thank you. Barclay, God bless you!"

His voice trembled as he pressed the money-lender's hand, for the gaoler had opened the door, and was waiting to usher them out.

"Claire, my child," he whispered, taking her in his arms, "you will come again. Good-bye now. Good-bye."

She clung to him wildly for a few moments, and then, with a look of desolation in her eyes, slowly followed the gaoler and the other visitors along the echoing stone passages to the gate, where Linnell laid his hand upon her arm.

Before he could speak there was a rustle of a silk dress, a hurried panting as some one brushed by him, and a voluble voice exclaimed:

"They wouldn't let me in, my dear, and I've been waiting for you to come. There, there, there, you and May are coming home along with me, and—"

Her voice died away as Linnell stood there, feeling desolate and cold. There was an intense bitterness in his heart, as he told himself that his love for Claire was of a very poor type, that he had been ready to believe ill of her, and let that love become chilled. What had he done now that she was plunged into the very depths of despair? Almost held aloof when he would have given all he had—life itself—to save her from her pain.

"I am mad, jealous, weak, and contemptible," he cried to himself at last. "I will go to her and tell her I love her more than ever. It is not too late."

He had taken a step to follow, when a hand was laid upon his arm, and Barclay said huskily:

"There's a woman for you, Mr Linnell, sir. I often think she ought to have had a better husband. There, the best thing is to let them alone together. You wouldn't think it, Mr Linnell, with me, such a hard nut as I am, but this business has quit upset me. Good-day, sir, good-day."

"Good-day, Mr Barclay," said Linnell dreamily; and they were parting, when Barclay said in a low quick whisper:

"You may think of some way of helping the old fellow, Mr Linnell. If you do there's any amount of money ready for the lawyers, if you give me a hint. For he's an innocent man, sir. Kill that old woman? Pho! Pooh! Stuff! He couldn't kill a cat!"

# Chapter Fourteen
# Fred Denville Forward

"What do you say, my dear—another of those mad fits of excitement as soon as my name's mentioned? Oh, it's too bad. I don't think I've ever been rake enough to deserve it. Well, whether or no, I must go and see him. I can't stop away. I'm his eldest son, and a man's a man even if he is a common soldier, and has disgraced himself in the eyes of society."

"Fred dear, I'm broken-hearted," sobbed Claire, as she nestled close to her brother, and hid her face in his breast, neither seeing nor hearing Mr and Mrs Barclay open the door and cross the room, the latter making a sign to the dragoon not to take any notice of them, and as soon as she was alone with her husband, saying indignantly:

"The scandalous old hags, making out that the poor dear was carrying on with a common soldier. Lor'! Jo-si-ah, what a little wickedness there would seem to be in the world if everything was properly explained."

"Well, I don't know so much about that," replied Barclay. "Perhaps we should find out some of the very innocent ones were not so good as they seemed."

"I shall go on at once and see the old man," said Fred Denville, kissing his sister tenderly. "I can't stop away. The old fellow will be calmer perhaps to-day; and, Claire, my girl, I'm going to try and get my discharge, and start a new life. It's a strange thing if I can't keep a home for you and take care of you. I can't stand this soldiering any longer. Servant to that blackguard, Rockley! Has he spoken to you lately?"

"No, Fred," said Claire wearily. "No."

"I can't stand it, girl. It's a shame to talk of my beggarly troubles now, but it's precious hard to be meeting one's own brother—one's superior officer—and him not to know me. Has Morton been to see father?"

"N-no, dear; not yet."

"Curse him!"

"Fred!—dear Fred!"

"Well, no, I won't curse him. It's the boy's training, not his nature. He ought not to cut the poor old man, though, in his disgrace. Claire, damn it all; I don't believe father killed that old thing."

He looked at his sister with a quick intelligent gaze, full of conviction; but as he met her full in the eyes, and saw the change that came over her countenance, the conviction seemed blunted, and he shuddered.

"She believes it!" he muttered. Then aloud: "Why, Claire!"

"Hush—don't—don't speak to me—don't say anything," she panted. "Fred, shall I be dragged before the judge and be forced to answer questions—horrible questions?"

He was silent.

"You believe I shall. You think I shall," she panted. "Oh, Fred, Fred, I would sooner die."

He drew a long breath, and looked at her in a horrified way, while she seemed to be growing wild with dread.

"I could not bear it," she cried, "to go up before those people and condemn my own father. It would be too horrible. It would be against nature. I could not, I would not speak."

"Hush, little sister," said Fred tenderly. "You are growing wild. Perhaps you will not have to go. Perhaps they will find out the right man before the time—hush!—hush!"

Claire had uttered a piteous cry full of despair, as she buried her face in her hands.

"I cannot bear it—I cannot bear it," she cried. "There, go—go and see him," she said quickly. "You must go. It would be too cruel to stay away from him now he is so low in spirit. Be gentle with him, Fred, if he says hard things to you; and pray—pray don't resent them. You will bear everything for my sake—say that you will."

"Of course, of course."

"Trouble and misery have made him irritable, and so that he hardly knows what he says at times."

"Poor old fellow!" said the dragoon sadly. "Ah, Claire, my little girl, it did not want this trouble in our unhappy home."

He kissed her very tenderly, and then, as if moved by some sudden impulse, he took her in his arms again and held her to his breast, whilst she clung to him as if he were her only hope, and so they remained in silence for a time.

At last he loosed himself from her embrace, and stood over her as she crouched down upon the sofa.

"I'm going there now, Claire," he said, "but before I go, have you anything to say to me about that night of the murder? Is there anything I ought to know, so as to be able to talk to the old man about his defence? Will he tell me all he knows about the affair—why, Claire, child, what is the matter—are you going wild?"

He caught her two hands, and held her, startled by the change which had come over her, as she shrank from him in horror, with eyes dilated, face drawn and lips apart.

"There, my little girl," he said, with rough tenderness, "I ought to have known better than to talk to you about it. Perhaps all will come right yet after all."

Claire seemed to be so prostrated that it was some time before he attempted to leave her, and then it was upon her urging, for she seemed at last to rouse herself to action, and with feverish haste bade him go.

"It is your duty, Fred," she said agitatedly, "but—but don't question him—don't say a word to him. Only go to him as the son to the father in terrible distress. Let him speak to you if he will."

"But his defence, girl, his defence. Something must be done, and I am without a guinea in the world."

"Mr Barclay—Mr Linnell are arranging that without his knowledge," said Claire. "I had forgotten to tell you, Fred: my head seems confused and strange."

"No wonder, little one," he said. "Ah, I like that Barclay. One never knows who are our friends until trouble comes—and young Linnell. It isn't a time to talk about such things now, Clairy; but young Linnell's a good fellow, and he thinks a great deal of you."

Claire joined her hands as if begging him to be silent, and he once more kissed her, and after begging Mrs Barclay to watch over her, hurried away.

# Chapter Fifteen
# Father and Son

James Bell, dragoon, otherwise Fred Denville, the disgraced prodigal of the Master of the Ceremonies' home, had a couple of shillings in his pocket as he strode towards the prison; and as he was on his way, low-spirited and despondent at the troubles of his house, a great thirst came upon him, and he felt that he could never go through the scene he had to encounter without a stimulant in some form.

Then he thought of what a curse drink was to him, and how he could not take one glass without wanting another, and many others, and with this thought he manfully passed the first public-house.

But, as he passed, the door was swung open, and the hot, spiritous odour of strong drinks floated out and half maddened him.

"Just one glass would tighten me up," he muttered, "and I could go through with it better."

He thought of his last interview with his father, their struggle, and how he had nearly struck him, and he shrank from what was to come.

"I can't help it," he said. "I must have a drop. It will steady a fellow's nerves. Good God! how horrible to go and see that old man charged with murder."

He had thought a great deal about it before, but now the whole affair struck him as if in a new light, and the examinations, the trial, and the following of that trial came upon him with a terrible force that frightened him. It had never seemed so horrible before, and he burst out in a cold perspiration as in imagination he saw the white bared head of the old man, with wild eyes and ghastly face—saw him in the grey of some chilly morning, pinioned and with the white-robed priest by his side, walking towards—

It was too horrible! A curious feeling of blind terror made him shiver and hurry on, as something seemed to whisper in his ear, "He did murder that wretched old woman, and he must suffer for his crime."

"Curse me, I must have some brandy, or I shall never be able to face him," he gasped, as he strode on, no longer the stern, upright, well-built cavalry soldier, but a bent, trembling man, at whom more than one passer-by looked askance. He even reeled, and albeit perfectly sober, he evoked comments upon "these drunken soldiers" in the streets.

"It is too horrible," he said again. "I never saw it like this before;" and, hurrying on with unsteady step, he was making straight for a public-house he knew, when, on turning a corner, he suddenly encountered Major Rockley.

The meeting was so sudden that he had passed him before he remembered his duty to salute his superior; but the encounter brought with it a flood of recollections of the night of Mrs Pontardent's party, and the remembrance of his helplessness, and of the pangs he had suffered as he awoke to the fact, as he believed, that the sister he almost worshipped was in the power of a relentless scoundrel. This cleared the mental fumes that were obscuring his intellect, and, drawing himself up, he strode on straight past the public-house door and on to the prison gates.

"It's time I acted like a man," he said to himself, "and not like a cowardly brute."

He was provided with a pass, and, in ignorance of the fact that Rockley had turned and was watching him, following him, and standing at a distance till he saw him enter the gates, he rang, presented his paper, and was ushered along the blank stone passages of the prison till he reached the cell door.

"One minute," whispered Fred, wiping the drops from his forehead, as a sudden trembling fit came over him. Then, mastering it, and drawing himself up, he breathed heavily and nodded to the gaoler.

"I'm ready," he said hoarsely: "open."

The next minute he was standing in the whitewashed cell with the door closed behind him, locked in with the prisoner and half choked with emotion, gazing down at the bent grey head.

For the Master of Ceremonies was seated upon a low stool, his arms resting upon his knees, and his hands clasped between them, probably asleep. He had not heard the opening and closing of the door, and if not asleep, was so deaf to all but his own misery that Fred Denville felt that he must go and touch him before he would move.

The young man's breast swelled, and there was a catching in his breath as he looked down upon the crushed, despondent figure, and thought of the change that had taken place. The light from the barred window streamed down upon him alone, leaving the rest of the cell in shadow; and as Fred Denville gazed, he saw again the overdressed leader of the fashionable visitors mincing along the Parade, cane in one hand, snuff-box in the other, and the box changed to the hand holding the cane while a few specks of snuff were brushed from the lace of his shirt-front.

Then he looked back farther, and seemed to see the tall, important, aristocratic-looking gentleman, to whom people of quality talked, and of whom he always stood in such awe; and now, with this came the recollection of his boyish wonder how it was that his father should be so grand a man abroad while everything was so pinched and miserable at home.

Back flitted his thoughts as he stood there, looking down at the motionless figure, to the encounter when he had been surprised by his father with Claire. The terrible rage; the fit; the horrible hatred and dislike the old man had shown, and the unforgiving rancour he had displayed.

Fred Denville sighed as it all came back, but he felt no resentment now, for his breast was full of memories of acts of kindness that had been shown him as a boy, before he grew wild and resisted the paternal hand, preferring the reckless soldier's life to the irksome poverty and pretence of the place-seeker's home and its pinching and shams.

"Poor old dad!" he said to himself, as the tears stood in his eyes; "he is brought very low. Misery makes friends. God help him now!"

The stalwart dragoon, moved by his emotion, took a couple of quick steps forward and went down upon one knee by the old man's side, took his hands gently in both of his own, and held them in a firm, strong clasp, as he uttered the one word—

"Father!"

The touch and the voice seemed to galvanise the prisoner, who started upright, gazing wildly at his son, and then shrank back against the wall with his hands outstretched to keep him off.

There was a terrible silence for a space, during which Fred Denville remained upon his knee, then slowly joining his hands as he looked pleadingly in his father's face, he said slowly:

"Yes, I know I have been a bad son; I have disgraced you. But, father, can you not forgive me now?"

The old man did not speak, but shrank against the wall, looking upon him with loathing.

"Father," said Fred again, "you are in such trouble. It is so dreadful. I could not stay away. Let us be friends once more, and let me help you. I will try so hard. I am your son."

Again there was that terrible silence, during which the old man seemed to be gathering force, and the look of horror and loathing intensified as he glared at the man humbling himself there upon his knee.

"Do you not hear me?" cried Fred, piteously. "Father: I am your son."

"No!" exclaimed Denville, in a low, hoarse whisper that was terrible in its intensity. "No: you are no son of mine. Hypocrite, villain—how dare you come here to insult me in my misery?"

"Insult you, father!" said Fred softly. "No, no, you do not know me. You do not understand what brings me here."

"Not know?—not understand?" panted Denville, still in the same hoarse whisper, as if he dreaded to be heard. "I tell you I know all—I saw all. It was what I might have expected from your career."

"Father!"

"Silence, dog! Oh, that I had strength! I feel that as I gave you the life you dishonour, I should be doing a duty to take you by the throat, and crush it out from such a wretch."

"He's mad," thought the young man as he gazed on the wild distorted face.

"You thought that you were unseen—that your crime was known but to yourself; but such things cannot be hidden, such horrors are certain to be known. And now, wretch, hypocrite, coward, you have brought me to this, and you come with your pitiful canting words to ask me for pardon— me, the miserable old man whom you have dragged down even to this—a felon's cell from which I must go to the scaffold."

"No—no, father," panted Fred. "Don't—for God's sake, don't talk like this. I've been a great blackguard—a bad son; but surely you might forgive me—your own flesh and blood, when I come to you on my knees, in sorrow and repentance, to ask forgiveness, and to say let me try and help you in your distress. Come, father—my dear old father—give me your hand once more. Let the past be dead, for Claire's sake, I ask you. I am her brother— your boy."

"Silence! Wretch!" cried the old man. "Leave this place. Let me at least die in peace, and not be defiled by the presence of such a loathsome, cowardly thing as you."

"And you," said Fred softly, as he held out his hands; "you, I can remember it well, used to hold these hands together, father, and teach me to say, 'Forgive us our trespasses, as we forgive them that trespass against us.' Father, have I sinned so deeply as all this?"

"Sinned!" cried the old man starting forward, and catching his son by the throat. "Sinned? Blasphemer! coward! hypocrite! You dare to say this to me! Go, before I try to strangle you, for I cannot contain myself when you are here."

"Father!" cried Fred, kneeling unresisting as the old man clasped him tightly by the throat, "are you mad?"

"Would to God I were before I had lived to see this day," cried Denville, still in the same hoarse whisper. "But go—I have done ill enough in my wretched life without adding murder to the wrong. Go, and coward that you are, escape to some far-off land where your crime is not known, and there try and repent, if you can. No, there can be no repentance for the coward who destroys one wretched, helpless life, and then to save his own worthless body—he can have no soul—sends his poor, worn-out, broken father to the scaffold."

Fred did not move, but gazed pityingly in his father's face.

"You cannot be a man," continued Denville, "a man as other men. You do not speak—you do not speak. Fool! Murderer! Do you think that your crime was not known?"

Fred still remained silent, gazing in the convulsed face, with the veins in the temples throbbing, the eyes glaring wildly, and the grey hairs seeming to rise and move.

"Speak, since you have forced it upon me, though I would have gone to the scaffold without a word, praying that my sacrifice might expiate my own child's crime. Speak, I say: do you still think it was not known?"

Fred Denville remained upon his knees, but neither spoke nor resisted.

"I tell you that when I awoke to the horrors of that night, I said to myself, 'He is my own son—my own flesh and blood—I cannot speak. I will not speak. I will bear it.' And I have borne it—in silence. Wretch that you are—listen. I have, to screen you, borne all with my lips sealed, and let that sweet, pure-hearted girl shrink from me, believing—God help me!—that mine was the hand that crushed out yon poor old creature's life."

"Father, you are raving," cried Fred hoarsely.

"Raving! It is true. Claire, my own darling, has gone, too, with sealed lips, loathing me, and only out of pity and belief in her duty as a child borne with my presence—poor sweet suffering saint—believing me a murderer, and I dare not tell her I was innocent, and that it was the brother she loved, who had come in the night, serpent-like, to the room he knew so well, to murder, and to steal those wretched bits of glittering glass."

"My dear father!"

"Silence, wretch!" cried Denville. "I tell you, knowing all, I said that I could not speak, for I was only a broken old man, and that my son might repent; that I could not condemn him and be his judge. And, my God! it has come to this! I have borne all. I have suffered maddening agony as I have seen the loathing in my poor child's eyes. I have borne all uncomplaining, and when, as I dreaded, the exposure came, I unmurmuringly suffered myself to be taken, and I will go to the scaffold and die, a victim—an innocent victim for you, so that you may live; but let me die in peace. Free me from your presence, and I will wait till, in a better world, my darling can come and say, 'Forgive me, father; I was blind.'"

"Heaven help me! What shall I say?" muttered Fred. "Poor old fellow! It has turned his brain."

The old man was in the act of throwing him off and shrinking from him when Fred caught his hands.

"My dear old father," he said tenderly, "neither Claire nor I believe that you could commit this terrible crime. You must be cleared from all suspicion, and—come—come—let us be friends. You will forgive me, father—all the past?"

"Forgive you? No, I cannot. It is impossible. I have tried. Sitting here alone in this awful silence, with the shadow of the gallows falling across me, I have tried, but it is impossible. I will suffer for your crime. I have told you that I will, but upon one condition, that you never go near Claire again. She thinks me guilty, but she has fought hard and striven to forgive me. Do not pollute her with your presence, but go far away from here. Go at once, lest in the weakness of my nature I should be tempted to try and save myself from death by confessing all."

"Heaven help me!" said Fred again; "he is mad."

He had spoken aloud, shaping his thoughts unconsciously, and the old man took up his words.

"God help me! I wish I were," he said pitifully, "for the mad must be free from the agony which I have to bear."

Fred rose to his feet and looked at the old man aghast. Then, as if for the first time, he seemed to realise that his father was not wandering in his mind, and clasping the thin arms tightly, he pressed him back into a sitting position upon the bed, bending over him, and, in his great strength, holding him helplessly there, as he said quickly, and with a fierce ring in his voice:

"Why, father, do you know what you are saying? You do not think I killed Lady Teigne?"

"Hypocrite!" cried the old man fiercely.

"Speak out, man!" cried Fred, as fiercely now. "What do you mean? How dare you charge me with such a crime!"

"Hypocrite!" panted the old man again. "You cannot shield yourself now. It is a punishment for my weakness that day—that night. I would not have done it," he cried wildly, "but I was at my last gasp for money. Everything was against me. I had not a shilling, and there all that day the devil was dancing the jewels of that miserable old woman before my eyes."

"Father!" cried Fred, "for God's sake, don't tell me you killed her—for God's sake don't. No, no; it is not true."

"Silence! hypocrite! murderer!" cried the old man. "Listen. I tell you that all that day the devil was dancing those diamonds before my eyes. I saw them in the glittering waters of the sea. I turned to Claire, and her eyes shone like diamonds. The night came, and the sky was all studded with gems, and they were sparkling and reflected in the water. Diamonds—always diamonds; and above stairs, in that room, a casket with necklet and bracelets, all diamonds, and the devil always whispering in my ear that I had but to get two or three taken out and replaced with paste, while I pledged the real stones for a few months, and redeemed them as soon as I could turn myself round. Do you hear me?"

"Yes, I hear you," said Fred, with a strange look of horror intensifying in his face.

"I fought against the temptation. I struggled with it, as I said that I had always been a weak, foolish fashion-seeker, but an honest gentleman. I swore that I would not defile myself by such a crime; but there were my bills; there was the demand for money for a score of pressing necessities, and the fiend whispered to me that it would not be a crime, only taking them from that miserable old worldly creature as a loan."

"Go on," said Fred hoarsely; "go on." And he stared with horror in the old man's upturned face.

"Then the night came, and my children went to their beds innocent of the agony I suffered, for there was the temptation stronger than before. I went to my room, and looked out. The sea and sky were all diamonds; and I tore back the blind, and I said that I must have two or three of the wretched stones—that I would have them—borrow them for a time, and be free."

"Oh, father, father!" groaned Fred; and Denville went on excitedly.

"I said I would have them, and I waited till it would be safe to go. I knew that the old woman would have taken her sleeping-draught, and that it would be easy enough to go in and get her keys—I knew where she kept them—take out the diamond cross, get the stones changed, and replace it before she would miss it the next afternoon."

Fred groaned, and the old man went on, clutching him now by the arm as he spoke, gazing fiercely in his eyes the while.

"I waited till all were sleeping, and the time seemed to have come, and then, like a thief, I stole out of my room and along the passage, till I was outside the door where the old woman—poor old wreck of a woman—lay. It was only to borrow those diamonds for a time, and I meant to replace them, though I knew that I was little better than a thief—a cold-blooded, treacherous thief—to deal thus with the woman who trusted to my honour for her safety. But I was so sorely pressed for money, I said to myself; and keeping my creditors quiet meant placing Morton and Claire both well in life, and then my troubles would cease. Do you hear me?"

"Yes—I hear," groaned Fred.

"I stood there on the mat outside her door thinking that, and that it would be for Claire's sake; and as I thought that, I saw her sweet, pure face before me, as it were, her eyes looking into mine; and I said: 'How can I ever look into those eyes openly again?' I felt that I was still a gentleman, but that in a few minutes I should be a despicable thief. Then I raised my hand to open the door, always unfastened so that Claire might go in and out, but it dropped to my side, and I sank upon my knees and prayed for strength to resist temptation, and the strength I asked was given."

The old man paused, for there was a step outside in the stone passage, and it seemed that the gaoler was coming there; but he passed on, and Denville gripped his son's arm more tightly.

"I don't know how long I knelt there, but I was rising with the temptation crushed, and as I rose I was going back to my room."

"Hah!" ejaculated Fred excitedly, and he breathed more freely.

"Back to my room, boy, when I seemed to be roused from the stupor brought on by my agony of mind, for there was a sound in the countess's chamber. I listened, and there it was again. It was a confused sound, as if she were moving in her bed, and I thought she must be ill, and want Claire. I was about to go and rouse her, when there were other sounds; there was a loud crash, and I stood as if turned to ice."

"You heard sounds!" gasped Fred; and he looked horror-stricken and shrinking as his father seemed to grow in strength.

"Yes," whispered the old man fiercely, as he seemed to fix Fred Denville with his eye; "I heard sounds that froze me with horror, as I felt that my temptation had been in the shape of a warning of evil, and that another was at work in the poor old woman's room. For a few minutes I could not stir. Then, mastering my horror and fear, and calling myself coward, I hurried into the room, to find myself face to face with him who had entered before. I saw all at a glance, as a hoarse groan came from the bed—the curtain torn aside, and the murderer by the dressing-table, with the jewel-casket in his hand."

"You saw all this?" cried Fred, white as ashes now. "Father, you saw this?"

"Everything, as I dashed—old weak man as I was—at the wretch who had done this thing. It was only a momentary struggle, and I was thrown down, and saw him dart to the folding-doors and pass through. I staggered after him in time to hear him overturn a pot or two in the verandah, as he swung himself over and slid down the pillar. Then I was alone panting there in that chamber of death; for as I took the candle from the little stand, and drew aside the curtain, it was to gaze down upon the starting eyes of the strangled woman—dead in my house, under the protection of my roof; and, with the horrible thought upon me that only a brief while back I was nearly entering that chamber to play the part of thief, I gave no alarm, but shrank towards the door, and stole out trembling, bathed with sweat, to get back to my room, and try to think out what I should do."

Fred Denville groaned, and the old man's breath went and came with the sound of one who has been hunted till he stands at bay.

"I had not been there a minute before I heard steps; a light shone beneath my door, and I sat trembling, utterly prostrated, for I knew that it was Claire who had been alarmed. I wanted to go out and stop her, to set her on her guard; but I sat there as if suffering from nightmare, unable to move, even when she came at last and summoned me; and, like one in a dream, I listened to what she had to say, and followed her to the murdered woman's room. I could not stay her; I could do nothing. I dared not give the alarm; I dared not speak, but went with her, and saw all again in a dazed, confused way, till I noticed something on the floor, which I snatched up and hid from Claire; and then the confusion was gone—driven away by the agony I felt. My God, what agony, as I read in Claire's eyes that she believed I had done that deed!"

"She believed this of you?"

"Yes; and believes it still," groaned the prisoner.

"But—but," cried Fred excitedly, "what was it you snatched from the floor?"

"A knife; a knife I knew. One that I had seen before."

"But the murderer—you saw him?"

"Plainly as I see you."

"But you did not summon help."

"I could not."

"I knew you were innocent," cried Fred excitedly. "I swore you were."

"I am," said the old man coldly.

"Should you know the wretch again?" panted Fred.

"Yes; too well."

"But you did not say this at the inquest."

"My lips were closed."

"But, father, you do not—"

"Silence, hypocrite! Enough of this. I could not speak. I dare not tell the world the murderer was my own son."

Fred Denville drew himself erect. His father rose from the bed, and the two men stood gazing for some minutes in each other's eyes without a word.

It was the Master of the Ceremonies who broke the spell.

"Now," he said, "I have spoken. It is enough. Your secret is safe with me. Go. Repent, but do not ask me to forgive you. Ask that of Heaven. I am old and broken, and can die."

"But, father!" groaned Fred wildly, "it was not I."

"It was my eldest son. I saw him as he struggled with me—in his uniform, and I picked up afterwards from the floor his knife—his pocket-knife that had been used to wrench open the casket of jewels. The knife with 'RM' on the handle. It was given to my son by the fisherman, Miggles."

"Yes, Dick gave me that knife years ago," said Fred, speaking like one who has received a tremendous blow. "I have not seen it since that night."

"No," said the old man bitterly; "it lies far out beyond the end of the pier, buried deep in sand by now."

Fred Denville stood holding his hands pressed to his head, staring straight before him at the whitewashed wall, while neither spoke.

The silence was broken by the rattling of bolts and the turning of a key, when the gaoler threw open the door, and, without a word, the dragoon walked, or rather reeled, from the cell, as if he had taken strong drink till his senses were nearly gone.

# Chapter Sixteen
# Blow for Blow

Fred Denville went straight to Barclay's, and was admitted, Claire looking at him reproachfully as he threw himself into a chair.

"Oh, Fred!" she cried, "and at such a time!"

"Not been drinking," he said; "not been drinking. How's May?"

"Very ill, dear," said Claire sadly. "Here?"

"Yes, Mrs Barclay insisted upon her being brought, so that we could be together."

"God bless her," said Fred softly. Then, after a pause—"I've seen the old man."

"And you are friends, Fred?"

He shook his head, and sat staring down at the carpet. "But you tried to be, dear?"

"Yes; tried hard. I've been. I've done my duty—for once," he said with a strange laugh.

He did not speak again for a few minutes, and Claire sat holding his hand, looking at him doubtingly, his manner was so strange.

"You think I've been drinking," he cried fiercely. "Give a dog a bad name, and then hang him. I haven't touched a drop to-day."

He changed his manner to her directly, and his voice was low and tender as he took her to his breast and kissed her.

"Poor little Clairy," he said; "you've had a rough time. Never mind; brighter days coming. The old man will be found innocent."

"Innocent, Fred?" she faltered.

"Yes, innocent," he cried. "Wait: you will see. Clairy, look here. Tell me this. Did I ever talk about Lady Teigne's jewels when I came to see you?"

"I don't know, dear. Yes, I remember now, I think you did."

"Hah!" he ejaculated. "I must go now. Good-bye, little woman. I always loved my little sister, always. You know that, don't you, Clairy?"

"Yes, dear Fred, always."

"Bad as I was?"

"Oh, Fred, I never thought you bad," cried Claire piteously. "I only thought it was a pity you did not try to raise yourself, and—"

"Leave the drink alone. Quite right, Clairy. It was the drink. It makes a man stupid and mad. He doesn't know what he's about when he has taken too much. Remember that, my dear, it was the drink."

"Fred, how strangely you are talking."

"Strangely?" he said, clasping her to his breast, "strangely? Well, I meant to be kind and tender to my poor, suffering little sister. I've been a bad lot, but I always loved my little Claire."

She stood gazing wonderingly after him, he seemed so strange in his way, as, after straining her to his breast, he kissed her passionately again and again, and then turned and literally ran from the room, while, as she placed her hand against her face, she found that it was wet.

"Poor Fred," she said, "if I could only win him from his ways."

She said no more, for her thoughts were only too ready to turn to their usual theme—her father and his imprisonment, and she sat down to rest her aching head upon her hand, wondering what had passed during the interview within the prison walls.

Fred Denville found Mr and Mrs Barclay below, and in a quick, agitated way he caught Mrs Barclay's hand.

"It's very kind of you to let me call upon my sister," he said, "seeing what I am. I thank you. I am not coming again."

"Not coming again? Oh, I'm sure you're welcome enough, Mr Fred, for your sister's sake," said Mrs Barclay, "isn't he, Jo-si-ah?"

"Of course, of course."

"Thank you—both of you," cried Fred hastily. "You are very good, and that's why I say be kind to my poor sisters, and try and comfort both if anything happens."

"Oh, but we must not let anything happen," said Barclay. "The poor old gentleman must be saved."

"Yes, of course," said Fred dreamily; "he must be saved. He's innocent enough, poor old fellow. I did not mean that. You'll take care of the poor girls, won't you?"

"Why, of course we will, Mr Fred Denville; of course we will. There, don't you make yourself uneasy about them."

"I won't," said Fred, in his bluff, straightforward way. "I may be quite happy, then, about Claire?"

"To be sure you may."

"I shouldn't like her to suffer any more, and it would be terrible for those wretched dandy scoundrels to get hold of her and break her heart."

"Don't you fidget yourself about that, young man," said Mrs Barclay with quite a snort. "Your dear sister's too proud for any jack-a-dandy fellow to win her heart."

"You're a good woman," said Fred softly. "I'm not much account as a man, but I know a good woman when I meet one, and I wish I'd had such a one as you by me when I was a boy. If I had, I shouldn't have been a common soldier now. Good-bye, ma'am; good-bye, sir. Heaven bless you both."

He hurried out, afraid of showing his emotion, and Mrs Barclay turned round wiping her eyes.

"There, Jo-si-ah, you see everybody don't think ill of us, bad as we are."

"Humph! no," said Barclay thoughtfully; "but I don't understand that chap—he's so strange. Why, surely, old girl, he had no hand in that murder."

"Lor'! Jo-si-ah, don't! You give me the creeps all over. I do wish you wouldn't think about murders and that sort of thing. You give me quite a turn. I wouldn't have my dear Claire hear you for the world."

"All right! I won't say anything before her; but this young chap has set me thinking; he seemed so strange."

Other people thought Fred Denville strange, notably Major Rockley, who, in company with Sir Matthew Bray and Sir Harry Payne, was on the Parade, as, with brows knit and eyes bent down, the dragoon came along, walking swiftly.

The three officers were in undress uniform, having just left parade, and each carried his riding-whip.

Fred did not notice them, he was too deep in thought, and walking straight on he went right between them, unintentionally giving Sir Matthew Bray a rough thrust with his shoulder, for of course an officer could not give way to a private.

It was Fred Denville's duty, in the character of James Bell, private dragoon, to have saluted his officers and given them all the path, if necessary;

but at that moment he could see nothing but the grey white-faced old man in the cell at the gaol, in peril of his life and threatened with a felon's death.

"I must have been drunk," he was muttering to himself. "Yes: I remember, I was horribly drunk that night, and didn't know what I was doing. Poor old father! with all your faults you did not deserve this. Yes: I must have been drunk."

At this point he was brought from his musings to the present by a stinging cut from a riding-whip across the back, his tight uniform being so little protection that the sharp whalebone seemed to divide the flesh.

With a cry of rage he turned round, and flung out his fist, striking Sir Harry Payne, who had given the blow with the whip, full on the nose, and sending him backwards.

"You insolent dog!"

"You scoundrel!"

The epithets were delivered in a breath by Major Rockley and Sir Matthew Bray, just as Lord Carboro' approached, walking by Lady Drelincourt's bath-chair.

It was an opportunity for showing how an insolent drunken private should be treated; and as several loungers of society were coming up, the two officers accompanied their words with a couple of blows from their whips.

It is dangerous to play with edged tools, is proverbially said; and, in his then frame of mind, Fred Denville felt no longer that he was James Bell, the disciplined, kept-down servant and private. He felt as a man smarting from the blows he had received. The service, the penalty for striking an officer, were as nothing to him then; he saw only the big, pompous, insolent bully of his regiment, Sir Matthew Bray, and the man who had insulted him a thousand times, which he could have forgiven, and his sister again and again, which he could not forgive.

With one bound he was upon Sir Matthew Bray, whom he struck full in the chest, so that he staggered back, tripped his heels on the front wheel of Lady Drelincourt's bath-chair, and fell heavily into the road.

With another bound he was upon Rockley, who had followed and struck him again a sharp, stinging cut.

There was a momentary struggle, and then the whip was twisted out of Rockley's hand, his wrist half dislocated, and for a couple of minutes the thin scourge hissed and whistled through the air as, half mad with rage, Fred lashed the Major across shoulders, back, and legs, and finally dashed him down with a parting cut across the face.

"That for you, you horsewhipped cur and scoundrel! You disgrace the uniform you wear!"

There was a little crowd gathering, but only one man dared to seize upon the fierce-looking dragoon, and that one was Lord Carboro'.

"Loose my arm," roared Fred, turning upon him with uplifted whip; but, as he saw who held him, and that Bray and Payne were holding aloof, and helping Rockley to rise, he lowered his whip. "Loose my arm, my lord; you're an old man, I can't strive with you."

"You rascal! You have struck your superior officers."

"Superior!" raged out Fred. "I have horsewhipped a vile *roué* for the blow he struck me, and ten times as much for—Keep off!" he roared, as Colonel Mellersh and Linnell joined the group.

"I shall hold you till a picket comes from the barracks, sir, to take you in arrest," cried Lord Carboro' sternly.

Fred Denville did not attempt to wrest his arm away, but smiled half contemptuously at the padded, made-up old nobleman, and gave the whip a lash through the air as he stared hard at Rockley, who was white with rage, but talked to him who held his arm.

"Look here, my lord," he said, "is it amongst your set a social sin for a man to horsewhip the blackguard who insults his sister?"

"No," said Lord Carboro' stoutly; "but you have struck your superior officer."

"I have thrashed the scoundrel who would have dragged my sister in the mire could he have had his way. It was my last act as a free man, and thank God I have had the chance."

"James Bell," cried Sir Matthew Bray, "I arrest you. Give up that whip."

"Touch me if you dare," roared Fred. "Stand back, or I'll kill you."

"Private Bell—"

"Damn Private Bell!" cried the young man fiercely. "My name is Frederick Denville, and I am a gentleman."

Lord Carboro's hand dropped to his side, and as the young man faced him for a moment, it was anything but anger that flashed from the old nobleman's eyes as he muttered to himself:

"Damme, so he is; and he has Claire's very look."

Fred Denville strode right away along the Parade, followed at a distance by Linnell and Mellersh, till, to their surprise, they saw him enter their door, no attempt being made to arrest him then.

# Chapter Seventeen
## "Surrender!"

"No, Mr Denville, I am a soldier, and yours is a terrible crime against discipline, but I can't say a word in condemnation of your act."

"Thank you, Colonel. Will you give me a few words here with Mr Linnell?"

"Yes; but I should advise you to be quick," said Mellersh. "Hang it, man, they'll shoot you for this. What's to be done, Dick? Look here, Denville, can't you knock one of us down, take a suit of plain clothes and make off. There's twenty pounds on the chimney-piece yonder."

"Thank you, sir, thank you," said Fred, smiling sadly; "but I'm not going to run. I shall give myself up."

"No, no," cried Linnell excitedly. "For heaven's sake don't do that, man. There's trouble enough in your home. You'll break her heart."

Fred Denville swung round in an instant, and caught Linnell's hands in a strong grip.

"Then you do love her," he cried, his voice quivering. "My little true-hearted, suffering darling. Oh, man, man, man, don't let wretched shadows stand between you now. I know everything, and how you have been ready to believe all kinds of unhappy scandals about the best girl who ever lived. Look here—no, don't go, Colonel; you've heard the beginning, you may as well hear the rest. It came out like a flash. Stop now, and hear me, both of you. Ours is an unhappy family; I've been a wild, foolish scamp: my father lies in prison under a false charge; he is innocent. I know that such a family is not one that a gentleman would seek to enter, save under exceptional circumstances; but I've watched you, Richard Linnell, and I know you loved my sister, and I know that she never had a thought save for you."

Linnell clenched his hands, compressed his lips, and began to pace the room.

"You, Colonel Mellersh, are a bit of a cynic; you don't believe in women, but you are mistaken here."

"What do you wish me to do?" said Linnell hoarsely.

"To do? She is almost friendless, broken-hearted, and has not a strong true hand to take hers, a loyal heart who will stand by her against the world. Richard Linnell, my poor sister is suffering and in pain, and a great trouble is coming upon her that will not balance the joyful news she will soon hear."

"Then, why not make a dash for it, man, while you have time?" cried Mellersh.

"Because I shall give myself up to the civil authorities, sir; that is all. Mr Linnell, remember what I have said. Good-bye."

"Too late!" cried Mellersh, as a tramping was heard, and Sir Matthew Bray, a sergeant, and half a dozen dragoons marched quickly up.

Fred Denville's whole manner had changed.

He dashed to the front. There was no escape there, and the soldiers were already in the hall.

Rushing to the back window he threw it up, but it moved stiffly, and before he had it well raised, the picket was in the room.

"Surrender!" cried the sergeant. "Halt, or I fire."

For answer Fred Denville rose on the sill and leaped down into the garden, a good dozen feet, and ran swiftly for the wall at the bottom.

"Halt!" roared Sir Matthew; but the fugitive paid no heed, and in response to rapid orders four carbines were raised, there was a ringing little volley, and, to Linnell's horror, Fred Denville made a bound, and fell upon his face.

"Oh, this is too bad, sir!" roared Mellersh fiercely.

"Mind your own affairs, sir," said Sir Matthew sharply. "Saved him from being shot after a court-martial."

In a few minutes the wounded man was borne in and laid in the hall, where Cora Dean was one of the first to fetch restoratives, while her mother brought a pillow and placed beneath his head, for a couple of the dragoons had been sent to fetch the means to transport him to the barracks.

It seemed at first that the one bullet which had struck him had been aimed too truly; but after a few minutes the poor fellow opened his eyes, looked wildly round, and then recognised Linnell.

"Ah!" he ejaculated, "you! Look here. I was on the way—to give myself up—civil authorities—my father—in prison—innocent—Lady Teigne—murder—in a fit of drunkenness—I climbed up—to get the diamonds—save the poor old man—I—I—did the deed."

# Chapter Eighteen
# Morton Denville Becomes a Man

"You here, Morton?"

"Yes. Don't look at me like that, Claire, pray don't. You can't think what I've suffered."

"What you've suffered?" said Claire coldly, as she recalled how she had taken a mother's place to this boy for so many years till he had obtained his advancement in life, when he had turned from her. He had made some amends on the night of Mrs Pontardent's party; but after that he had heard some whispered scandal, and had kept aloof more and more till the great trouble had fallen, and their father had been arrested, when he had stayed away and made no sign.

It had seemed so hard. When a few words on paper would have been so consolatory and have helped Claire in her agony and distress, Morton had not even written; and now he came to her at last to tell her she did not know what he had suffered.

"You don't know," he continued, with the tears in his eyes. "It was bad enough to be in the regiment with Payne and Bray, always ready to chaff me and begin imitating the old man, and that beast Rockley sneering at me; but when people began to talk as they did about you, Clairy—"

"Silence!" cried Claire, flashing up as she rose from her seat, and darted an indignant glance at the boy. "If you have come only to insult your sister—go."

"Don't talk like that, Clairy dear," cried the boy. "Don't be so hard upon a fellow. I suffered horribly, for they did talk about you shamefully, and I was very nearly calling Sir Harry out, only the Colonel wouldn't let me fight. I'm sure I behaved well enough. Every one said I did."

"Why have you come this morning?" said Claire coldly.

"Why have I come? Hark at her!" said Morton piteously. "Oh, dear, I wish I were a boy again, instead of an officer and a gentleman, and could go down and catch dabs with Dick Miggles off the pier."

"Officer—gentleman? Morton, is it the act of a gentleman to side with the wretched people who made sport of your sister's fame? To stand aloof when she is almost alone and unfriended, and this dreadful calamity has befallen us? Oh, Morton, are you my brother to act like this? Is it your manliness of which you made a point?"

"Claire—sis—dear sis," he cried, throwing himself on his knees, and clasping her waist as he burst into a boyish fit of passionate weeping. "Don't be so cruel to me. I have fought so hard. I have struggled against the pride, and shame, and misery of it all. You don't know what a position mine has been, and I know now I ought to have taken your part and my father's part against all the world. But I've been a coward—a miserable, pitiful, weak coward, and it's a punishment to me. You, even you, hate me for it, and—and I wish I were dead."

Claire's face softened as she looked down upon the lad in his misery and abasement, and after a momentary struggle to free herself from him she stood with her hands stretched out over the head that was buried in the folds of her dress, and a tender yearning look took the place of the hard angry glance that she had directed at him.

"I have fought, God knows how hard," he went on between his sobs, "but I'm only a boy after all, sis, and I hadn't the strength and manliness to stand up against the fellows at the mess. I've shut myself up because I've been ashamed to be seen, and I've felt sometimes as if I could run right away and go somewhere, so that I could be where I should not be known."

Claire's hands trembled as they were very near his head now—as if they longed to clasp the lad's neck and hold him to her breast.

"I've been coming to you a hundred times, but my cursed cowardice has kept me back, and everything has been against me. There has been your trouble."

Claire's hands shrank from him again.

"Then it was bad enough about father without this horrible charge."

Claire's face grew hard and cold, and in a moment she seemed ten years older.

"Then there was poor Fred: Rockley's servant in my regiment. You don't know what a position mine has been."

Claire made no movement now. Her heart seemed to be hardening against the lad, and she shrank from him a little, but he clung to her tightly with his face hidden, and went on in the same piteous, boyish wail.

"I've been half mad sometimes about you and your troubles—"

Claire's hands began to rise again and tremble over his head.

"Sometimes about myself, and I've felt as if I was the most unlucky fellow in the world."

There was a pause here, broken by the lad's passionate sobs.

"There: you hear me," he said. "I'm only a boy blubbering like this, but I feel pain as a man. I tell you, Clairy, dear sis, it has driven me nearly mad to know that this false charge was hanging over my father, and that he was in prison. The fellows at the mess have seemed to shrink from me, all but the Colonel, but whenever he has said a kind word to me I've known it was because the old man was in prison, and it has been like a knife going into me. I couldn't bear it. I hated myself, and I fought, I tell you, to do what was right, but I couldn't. It was as if the devil were dragging at me to draw me away, till this came, and then I felt that I could be a man, and now," he cried, raising himself, and shaking his hair back, as he threw up his head proudly, "forgive me, sis, or no—Damn my commission! Damn the regiment! Damn the whole world! I'm going down to the prison to stand by my poor old father, come what may."

"My darling!"

Claire's arms were round his neck, and for the space of a few minutes she sobbed hysterically, as she strained him to her breast.

"What, sis? You forgive me?" he cried, as her kisses were rained upon his face.

"Forgive you, my own brave, true brother? Yes," she cried. "Of course I know what you have suffered. I know it all. It was a bitter struggle, dear, but you have conquered, and I never felt so proud of you as I feel now."

"Sis!"

The tears that stole down from Claire's eyes seemed to give her the relief her throbbing brain had yearned for all these painful days, and her face lit up with a look of joy to which it had been a stranger for months.

"You will go to him then, dear?" she whispered, with the bright aspect fading out again, to give place to a cold, ashy look of dread, as the horror of their position came back, and the shadow of what seemed to Claire to be inevitable now crossed her spirit.

"Yes, I'm going. Poor old fellow! It will be a horrible shock to him about Fred."

"About Fred?"

"Yes. Had I better tell him?"

"Tell him?" faltered Claire.

"Yes. I thought not. He has enough to bear. I thought," said the lad bitterly, "that I was doing a brave thing when they brought him in. I said he was my poor brother: but I found that they all knew. Claire! Sis!"

She had staggered from him, and would have fallen had he not held on to her hand.

"Speak—tell me!" she cried. "No, no! I can't bear it! Don't tell me there is some new trouble come."

"What! Didn't you know?"

She shook her head wildly, and wrung her hands and tried to speak, while he held her and whispered softly:

"Oh, sis—sis—dear sis!"

"Something has happened to Fred," she panted at last. "Tell me: I can bear it now. Anything. I am used to trouble, dear."

"My poor sis!" he whispered.

"Why do you not tell me?" she cried wildly. "Do you not see how you are torturing me? Speak—tell me. What of Fred?"

Her imperious, insistent manner seemed to force the lad to speak, and he said, slowly and unwillingly:

"He was going along the Parade, and ran up against Rockley, and Payne, and Bray; poor chap, he did not salute them, I believe, and Rockley gave him a cut with his whip."

"Major Rockley!" cried Claire, with ashy lips.

"Yes; and he knocked over Bray and that puppy Payne. Curse them! they were like skittles to him. Fred's full of pluck; and, sis," cried Morton excitedly, as his eyes flashed with pleasure, "he took hold of that black-muzzled, blackguard Rockley, snatched his whip from him, and thrashed him till he couldn't stand."

"Fred beat Major Rockley?" cried Claire, with a horrified look, as she realised the consequences forgotten for the moment by the boy.

"Yes; thrashed the blackguard soundly; but they followed him with a sergeant and a file or two of men to take him."

"Yes. Go on."

"They found him at Linnell's, talking to Richard Linnell and—"

Morton stopped with white face, and repented that he had said so much.

"I must know all," cried Claire, trembling. "I am sure to hear."

"I can't tell you," he said hoarsely.

"Is it not better that it should come from you than from a stranger?"

"It is too horrible, sis," said the lad.

"Tell me, Morton, at once."

Her words were cold and strange, and she laid her hands upon his shoulders, and gazed into his eyes.

The boy winced and hung his head as he said slowly:

"They called upon him to surrender, but—"

The lad raised his head, and tossing it back, his eyes flashed as he cried in a different tone:

"I can't help being proud of him—he was so full of pluck, sis. He wouldn't surrender, but made a bold leap out of the window, and made a run for it; but that beast Bray gave the order, and they shot him down."

"Shot him down!"

"Yes; but he's not dead, sis—only wounded; but—"

"But what? Why do you keep anything from me now?" cried Claire piteously.

"It's court-martial, and—it's court-martial for striking your officer, Claire, and he knows it; and, poor fellow, in a desperate fit, so as to get into the hands of the magistrates instead of the officers, to be condemned to death, he—he—Claire, I can't speak if you look at me in that wild way."

"Go on!" she said hoarsely.

"He said—that it was not father—who killed Lady Teigne—but it was he."

# Chapter Nineteen
# Morton Bears the News Further

"Do all you can to comfort them, Mrs Barclay, please," said Morton, as he left the house. "It's all so shocking, I don't know what to say or do."

"You've done quite right in coming here, my dear," said Mrs Barclay, whose eyes were red with weeping.

"I'm afraid I've done more harm than good," said Morton dolefully. "Poor Claire, she's half crazy with what she has to bear."

"You told her, then, about your brother Fred?" said Mrs Barclay, in a whisper.

The lad nodded.

"It was quite right; she would have heard of it, and it was better it should come from you, my dear. Are you—are you going to see your poor father in prison?"

"Yes," said Morton firmly. "I've got an order to see him, and I'm going at once."

He turned round sharply, for he had received a hearty clap on the shoulder, and found that Barclay had approached him unperceived; and he now took the young fellow's hand and shook it warmly.

"Good lad!" he exclaimed. "That's brave. Go and see him; and if you like you may tell him that Mr Linnell and I have got the best lawyer in London to defend him."

"You have, Mr Barclay?"

"Yes; we have. There, don't stare at me like that. Your father once did me a good turn; and do you suppose a money-lender has no bowels? You tell him—no, don't tell him. He is in a queer, obstinate way just now, and you've got your work cut out to tell him about your brother's trouble. That's enough for one day, but you may give him a bit of comfort about your sisters. You can tell him that my stupid, obstinate old wife has got 'em in hand, and that as long as there's a roof over Mrs Barclay's head, and anything to eat, Miss Denville will share them. No, no; don't shake hands with me. I've nothing to do with it. It's all her doing."

Morton could not speak, but gripped the money-lender's hand tightly before turning to Mrs Barclay. He held out his hand and took hers, his lips trembling as he gazed in the plump, motherly face. Then, with something like a sob of a very unmanly nature, he threw his arms round her and kissed her twice.

"God bless you!" he cried; and he turned and ran out of the room.

Barclay's face puckered up as his wife sank down in a chair sobbing, with her handkerchief to her eyes, and rocking herself to and fro, but only to start up in alarm as Barclay dashed to the fireplace, and caught up the poker, before running towards the door.

"Jo-si-ah!" she cried, catching his arm.

"Just got away in time, a scoundrel—and before my very face! You suffered it, too, madam."

"Oh—oh—oh—oh!" sobbed Mrs Barclay hysterically, as she took the poker away, and replaced it in the fender before throwing herself on her husband's breast. "My own dear old man! I won't ever say a word again about money. The best and dearest fellow that ever lived!"

Barclay drew her close to him and played the elderly lover very pleasantly and well, leading his plump wife to a sofa, and sitting down by her with her head resting upon his shoulder.

"Hush, old lady, don't cry so," he whispered. "What's the good of having money if you don't try and do some good with it? I like little Claire; she's about as near an angel as we find them in Saltinville; and as for poor old Denville, he has been the most unlucky of men. He's not a bad fellow at heart, and as for that affair about old Lady Teigne—well, there's no knowing what a man may do when tempted by poverty and with a lot of jewels twinkling before his eyes."

"Oh, hush, Jo-si-ah, you don't think—you can't think—"

"Hush, old girl! we must not think it of him aloud. We must get him off, but I'm very much afraid."

"Oh, Jo-si-ah, don't say it, dear."

"Only to you, my gal. I'm afraid the poor old fellow was trying to—well, say borrow a few diamonds, and what happened afterwards was an accident."

"Oh, my dear! my dear!"

"It looks sadly like it."

"But this Fred Denville says he did it."

"Yes, poor lad, to get clear of his officers, and to save his father's life. That will go for nothing. Soldiers often charge themselves with crimes to get out of the army. That story will never be believed."

Morton Denville shivered as he approached the prison, and felt half disposed to turn back as he encountered a couple of men of his regiment; but he mastered his nervousness and walked boldly up to the gate and was admitted.

He found his father in much the same despondent attitude as he had occupied when Fred Denville came to the prison, and Morton stood with his lip quivering and breast heaving, looking down for some minutes at the wasted form.

"Father," he said at last, but there was no reply, and when the lad went and laid a hand upon his shoulder, the old man did not start, but raised his head in a dazed manner, as if he did not quite realise who it was.

Then, recognising him, he rose from his stool, smiling sadly.

"You, Morton!" he said. "You have come!"

Morton did not answer for a few moments, struggling as he was with intense emotion, and the Master of the Ceremonies looked at him keenly now. His face changed directly, though, as Morton threw his arms round him and stood with his head bowed down upon the old man's shoulder.

"I'm glad: very glad. Egad, Morton, my son," said Denville, trying to assume his old parade manner, but with his piping voice quavering, and sounding forced and strained, "you make me feel very proud of you. It is, of course—yes, egad—of course—a very painful thing for a gentleman—an officer—to have to visit—a relative in prison—a man situated as I am—to a man in your position, it is a terrible thing—and—and you'll pardon me— my son—I could not have felt—er—surprised if you had—stayed away; but—but—you have come; and—God bless you, my boy—my boy."

The old man would have sunk upon his seat quivering with emotion, but Morton held him in his clasp.

"No, no, father," he said with spirit, "you must not give way. We must meet this trouble like men. You must advise with me. I've been playing the boy too long. There, sit down and let's talk. What shall I do about your trial?"

Denville took his son's hand, and looked at him proudly, but he shook his head.

"What do you mean, father?" cried Morton, the lad flushing and looking manly as he spoke. "This is no time for indecision. I have seen Mr Barclay and Mr Linnell. They have engaged counsel, and what we want now is your help over your defence."

Denville smiled sadly, and again shook his head,

"No, my boy, no," he said, "you can do nothing. It is very brave and true of you."

"But, father—"

"Hush, my son! Let me speak and act as my knowledge and experience dictate. I am glad you have come, for you have been much in my mind; and I want to get you as free as I can from this horrible disgrace."

"My dear old father, don't think of me," pleaded Morton, "but of yourself."

"Of myself, my boy? No, I am only an old worn-out stock, and I am quite resigned to my fate—to my duty. I am old; you are young. There is your future to think of, and your sister's. Look here—"

"But, my dear father," cried Morton, "I must insist. I am only a mere boy, I know, but I am forced to take command."

"Not yet, Morton; I have not resigned. You'll pardon me, my son— wounded, but not unfit to command—as yet. Morton, my boy, Lord Carboro' has always been my friend. Go to him, my son, and ask him to use his influence to get you an exchange into some other regiment. Try foreign service, my boy, for a few years. It will be taking you clear of the stain upon our name. Claire has friends, I have no fear for her—good, true woman. It is about you I am concerned. You must exchange and get right away from here. Go at once. Carboro' will see the necessity, and advise and help you."

"And leave you here in prison—in peril of your life; charged with a crime you did not commit? Father, you don't know me yet."

The old man's lip quivered, and he grasped his son's hand firmly.

"It is my wish, my boy. For your sake and for your sister's," he said firmly. "You must go at once."

"And leave you here—like this, father?"

"Yes, my boy—it is my fate," said the old man sadly. "I can bear it. You must go."

"And leave Fred in his trouble?"

"Silence! Don't name him. Don't let me hear his name again," said the old man, firing up.

But it was only a flash of the old fire which died out at once, and he grew pale and weak again, his head sinking upon his breast.

"Father!" cried Morton, "I can't bear this. You are too bitter against poor Fred, and it seems doubly hard now."

"Hush! Say no more, my boy. You do not know," cried the old man angrily. "You do not know."

"It is you who do not know, father. You have not heard that he has been shot down."

"Fred—my son—shot?"

"Yes, while attempting to escape from arrest, father. He is dangerously wounded. Forgive me for telling you at such a time, but you seem so hard upon him."

"Hard, my boy? You do not know."

"I know he is dangerously wounded, and that he is your son."

"My God!" muttered Denville, with his lip quivering—"a judgment—a judgment upon him for his crime."

"And that in his misery and pain he raised his voice bravely to try and save you, father, by charging himself with the murder of Lady Teigne."

"What?" cried the old man excitedly. "Fred—my son—charged himself with this crime?"

"Yes; he boldly avowed himself as the murderer."

"Where—where is he?" cried Denville excitedly.

"In the infirmary; weak with his wound. Father, you will forgive the past, and try to be friends with him when—when you meet again."

The Master of the Ceremonies looked up sadly in his son's face and bowed his head slowly.

"Yes," he said sadly; "I will try—when we meet again. But tell me, my boy," he cried agitatedly; "they do not believe what he says—this—this charge against himself?"

"No; they look upon it as what it is—a brave piece of self-denial to save his father from this terrible position. Oh, father! you did not think he could be so staunch and true."

"They don't believe it," muttered Denville. "No; they would not. It does not alter the situation in the least. I shall suffer, and he will be set free."

"You shall not suffer, father," cried Morton impetuously. "Surely there is justice to be had in England. No, I will not have you give way in this weak, imbecile manner. There: no more now; I must go, and I shall consult with your friends."

"No; I forbid it," cried the old man sternly. "You will not be disobedient to me now that I am helpless, Morton, my son. You cannot see it all as I see it."

"No, father; I hope I see it more clearly."

"Rash boy! you are blind, while it is my eyes that are opened. Morton, one of us must die for this crime. I tell you I could not live, knowing that I did so at the expense of your brother who had gone, young in years and unrepentant, to his account."

"Unrepentant, father?"

"Hush, hush, my boy! No more. I can bear no more."

"Time, sir," said the voice of the gaoler, and Morton went sadly back to join his sisters.

# Chapter Twenty
# Under Pressure

"Father, I am nearly mad with grief and horror. I come to you for help — for comfort. What shall I do?" cried Claire, sinking upon her knees before him on her next visit to the prison.

"What comfort can I give you, child?"

"Oh, father, dear father, were not our sufferings enough that this other trouble should come upon us? Fred—"

"Yes, tell me of him," cried the old man excitedly. "Is he very bad?"

"Dangerously wounded, father. And this story of his! They believe it, father; what shall I do?"

"Do, my child?"

"They will take him and punish him for the crime. I fear they will, for he persists that it was he."

"And you would save him and let me die," said the old man bitterly.

"No, no. Don't, pray don't, speak like that, father. Think of what I must feel. I'd lay down my life to save you both, but it seems so horrible that my brother should die for that of which he is innocent."

The old man wrested himself from her grasp, and paced the cell like some caged wild creature, seeking to be free.

"I cannot bear it," he exclaimed. "Heaven help me for a wretched weak man. Why has this complication come to tempt me? Claire, I would have died — without a murmur, without a word, but this dangling before me the means of escape is too much. Yesterday, I did not fear death. To-day, I am a coward. I see before me the hideous beam, the noosed rope, the executioner, and the hooting crowd, hungry to see me strangled to death, and I fear it, I tell you, for the hope of life has begun to burn strongly again now that Fred has spoken as he has."

"Father!"

"Yes; you shrink from me, but you do not know. Claire, I speak to you as I could speak to none else, for you have known so much from the beginning. You know how I have suffered."

"Yes, yes," she said mournfully.

"You know how I have shrunk and writhed in spirit to see you loathe me as you have, and look upon me as something unutterably base and vile. Have I not suffered a very martyrdom?"

"Yes, father, yes," sighed Claire.

"And heaven knows I would not have spoken. I would have gone boldly to the scaffold, and died, a sacrifice for another's crime. But now that he has confessed—now that he denounces himself, and I see life before me once again, the desire to live comes so strongly to this poor weak creature that my lips seem to be unsealed, and I must—I must have your love, Claire, as of old."

"Father!" cried Claire with a horrified look, as if she doubted his reason.

"Yes, you are startled; you wonder at me, but, Claire, my child, had I gone to the gallows it would have been as a martyr, as a father dying for his son's crime. Claire, my child, I am an innocent man."

"Father!"

"Yes," he cried, "innocent. You never had cause to shrink from me; and while a thousand times you wrung my heart, I said to myself, 'You must bear it. You cannot retain her love and win your safety by accusing your son.'"

"Father, you rave," cried Claire. "This hope of escape has made you grasp at poor Fred's weak self-accusation. You would save yourself at the expense of the life of your own child."

"Did I accuse him of the murder, Claire?"

"No, not till now; and oh, father, it is monstrous."

"Did he not accuse himself, stung by conscience after seeing me here?"

"It is not true. He could not have done such a thing."

"Indeed!" said Denville bitterly; "and yet I saw him leave the bedside, and stand with the jewel-casket in his hand. I say so to you, for I cannot bear it, child. Let them kill me if they will. Let them save my son; but let me, my child, let me go to my grave with the knowledge that you believe me true and innocent, and that I bore all that my son might live."

"Then you will not denounce him?"

"I? To save myself! No, though I would live. You do not believe me innocent, my child. You think me a murderer."

"Father, I believe you were beside yourself with your troubles, and that you were going to take those jewels when you were interrupted, and, in a fit of madness, did this deed to save yourself and children from disgrace."

"Claire, Claire," groaned the old man, "if you—if you only could have believed in me, I could have borne all, but you turn from me. Will you not believe in me? Have you not realised my self-sacrifice?"

"Oh, father, what can I say—what can I do?" cried Claire. "Do you not see my position? Can I think of my poor brother now as the guilty man?"

"No," he said, taking her in his arms, and trying to soothe her in her agonised grief; "it is too much to ask you, my child. It is too much for such a one as you to be called upon to even think of. I will not press you, Claire; neither will I ask you to forgive me. I could not do that now. Only try to think of me as innocent. I ask you once more, my darling; I ask you once more."

Claire threw her arms round his neck and drew his head down to her bosom.

"I am your child," she whispered softly. "Father dear, good-bye—good-bye."

"So soon?" muttered Denville. "Yes; good-bye—good-bye."

He held her hand till she was half through the door; and then, as it was closed, he tottered back to his seat, and once more sank down to bury his face within his hands.

# Chapter Twenty One
# From Prison to Prison

"Morton," said Claire hoarsely, as she returned to where her brother was waiting, "are you still strong at heart?"

"Strong? Yes," he cried. "What do you want me to do?"

"Take me to Fred."

The young officer started, but he drew a long breath and rose erect.

"Come along," he said. "Colonel Lascelles will give me an order to see him. But, Claire darling, can you bear to meet him now?"

"My own brother? Morton, could I stay away from you if sickness or a wound had laid you low?"

"Come," he said abruptly; and, taking her arm, he led her along the parade on their way towards the barracks.

Before they had gone far Morton's cheeks flushed, for he saw Lord Carboro' approaching, and he felt ready to turn out of the way.

"He will cut us dead," thought Morton. "We are disgraced for ever."

To his surprise, as they drew near, Lord Carboro' took off his hat, and held it in his hand, bowing low to Claire as she passed him.

Fifty yards further they encountered Richard Linnell and Mellersh, who, without having seen Lord Carboro's act, imitated it exactly, and drew aside to let them pass.

Morton felt his heart throb with pleasure. He had expected those who knew them to treat them slightingly, and his sister was being treated with the deference due to a queen, while he was receiving respect such as had never been paid to him before.

He held his head the higher, and gaining in confidence walked boldly on, proud of the closely-veiled figure at his side, as Claire drooped over his arm; but, as he drew nearer to the barracks, he felt a curious tremor attacking him, and it needed all his strength of mind to keep up and face his brethren of the mess.

Claire shrank more and more as they entered the gates and crossed the barrack-yard, but Morton had screwed himself up to the sticking point, and he would have died sooner than have turned tail now.

Dragoon after dragoon saluted him, and he caught sight of Sir Harry Payne, but that officer had the grace to turn off, and they reached the Colonel's quarters without an unpleasant encounter.

They were shown in at once, and without taking chairs Morton stood defiant and proud awaiting the entrance of the Colonel, and supporting his sister.

They were not kept waiting long before the Colonel entered, Morton meeting his eyes with a fiercely independent look.

He was armed against an unarmed man, for the old Colonel's first act was to place a chair for Claire, bowing to her with chivalrous deference, while directly after, in place of treating his subaltern with freezing distance, he held out his hand and shook Morton's warmly.

The young officer had truly said that he was only a boy, for this kindly act and the old Colonel's sympathetic look threw him off his balance, and his lip began to quiver and his face to change.

"You've come to ask for a pass to see your brother, Denville," said Colonel Lascelles. "Yes, of course, of course. Very sad—very painful business, my dear lad. No fault of yours, of course. Don't scruple to ask me for any assistance I can give you, my dear boy. As far as my duty will allow me, you can count upon me. There: that's it," he said, blotting a sheet of paper, and handing it promptly to the young officer, while he chivalrously refrained from even glancing at the sorrow-burdened figure at his side.

"By-the-way, Denville," he whispered, calling the young fellow aside, "you can take what leave you like now."

The flush came back to Morton's face, and he was drawing himself up, but the Colonel took one hand, while he laid his left upon the lad's shoulder.

"No, no, no: I don't mean that, my dear boy. You have behaved uncommonly well, and I never respected you half so much as I do now. No gentleman in the regiment, I am sure, will think otherwise than I do. Yours is a very painful position, Denville, and, believe me, you have my sympathy from my heart."

Morton grasped his hand firmly, and then hurried away, for he could not trust himself to speak.

Another encounter had to be gone through, though, and that was with a tall, dark officer who came upon them suddenly.

Morton flushed up again as he felt Claire start, and saw Rockley stop suddenly, as if about to speak eagerly to the shrinking girl; but he found Morton's eyes fixed upon him, and returning the look with an angry scowl he passed on.

A minute later and they were in the infirmary, where, looking white and pinched of aspect, Fred Denville lay, with a regimental nurse at his side.

The man rose, and left the side of the bed, for Claire to take his seat.

"He is to be kept very quiet, ma'am. Doctor's orders," said the man respectfully. "I shall be just outside if you want anything."

Fred was lying with his eyes half closed, but he heard the voice and opened them, recognised his visitors, and tried to raise his hand, but it fell back upon the coverlid.

"Claire?" he said in a voice little above a whisper. "An officer?"

He smiled sadly, and then seemed half choked by a sob, as Claire threw herself on her knees by him and Morton went to the other side, bent over, and laid his hand upon that lying helpless upon the coverlid.

"Fred, old fellow," said Morton in a husky voice.

He could say no more, but stood looking down upon the prostrate figure, awe-stricken at the ravages caused by the wound.

"Fred—dearest Fred," whispered Claire, kissing the hand she held.

The wounded man groaned.

"No, no," he said faintly. "You should not be here; I am no fit company for you now."

"Oh, Fred, dear Fred," cried Claire passionately, "how could you charge yourself with that dreadful crime?"

"How?" he said faintly. "Because it must have been true. The poor old man saw me there, and found my knife upon the carpet."

"It is impossible," sobbed Claire.

"I thought so once," replied the wounded man, "but I suppose it's true. I often used to think of the old woman's jewels, and how useful they'd be. It seemed so easy, too, the way up there—eh, Morton?"

"Yes, yes; but don't talk like that. Some scoundrel must have seen me climb up, and have gone there that night."

"Yes," said Fred feebly, "some scoundrel who knew the way, but who, in his drunkenness, did not know what he did, and that scoundrel was I."

"No, no, Fred!" cried Claire.

"If you did it," said Morton quickly, "what became of the diamonds?"

"The diamonds, lad?"

"Yes. Did you have the jewels and sell them?"

"Never a stone," said Fred slowly. "No, it's all like a cloud. It always is like a cloud over my mind when I've been having the cursed drink. It sends me mad."

Claire gazed at him wildly.

"You ought not to be here, Clairy. Take her away, lad. I'm no fit company for her. But tell me—the old man? They have set him free?"

"No, not yet," said Morton sadly.

"But he must be set free at once. Poor, weak old fellow! He has suffered enough. Morton, lad, go to him and try to get him out. Him kill the old woman? He hadn't it in him."

Fred Denville turned so faint that he seemed to be losing his senses, but Claire bathed his face, and he recovered and smiled up at her.

"It's hard work to tell you to go, Clairy dear, but you mustn't stay here. Say one kind word to me, though, my dear; I haven't had much to do with kindness since I left home. I'm sorry I disgraced you all so. Ask the old man to forgive me, and tell him I should like to shake hands with him once, just once, before it's all over."

"Fred, my dear brother," whispered Claire, pressing his hand to her breast, while Morton held the other.

"Ah!" sighed the wounded man, "that's better. Morton, lad, it will soon be over, and people forget these things in a few days. I'm only in the way. I always have been. You'll get on better when I'm gone."

"Hush, Fred!"

He turned his head to Claire, who was gazing at him with burning eyes that seemed drained of the last tears.

"You always were a good, true girl to me, Clairy," he whispered faintly, "and I want you to think well of me when I'm gone. I did this horrid thing, but I swear I have no recollection of it, and I never reaped a shilling advantage from the theft."

The same feeling animated father and son in this time of peril—the desire to stand well in the eyes of Claire, who seemed to them as the whole world.

"Think the best you can of me, my little girl," he whispered. "It will soon be over, and—there's one comfort—I shall die as a soldier should—do you hear, Morton? No hangman's rope to disgrace us more. I fell under fire, my lad, and I shall laugh at the judges, and prison, and scaffold and all."

"Hush! for heaven's sake, Fred!" cried Morton.

"Yes, I will. It's too much—to talk. I was in a rage with them for shooting me. It was that bully—Bray; but I forgive him, for it saves us all from trouble and disgrace. Morton, lad, don't stop in the regiment. Exchange—do you hear? Exchange, and get them away—Claire and May and the old man—to somewhere else when I'm dead."

"Fred! Brother!" wailed Claire.

He smiled at her, and tried to raise her hand to his cheek.

"Yes, little girl!" he said tenderly. "It's quite right. Cuts the knot—the hangman's knot."

There was a bitter, decisive tone in these last words, but he changed his manner again directly, and spoke gently and tenderly.

"It is no use to hide it, dear sis," he said. "I can't live above a day or two. I know I shall not, and you see it is for the best. It saves the old man, and much of the disgrace to you two. Poor old fellow! I never understood him, Clairy, as I should. Under all that sham and fashionable show he tried hard for us. God bless him! he's a hero."

"Fred, Fred, you are breaking my heart," wailed Claire.

"No, no, little one," said Fred, a nervous accession of strength enabling him to speak out clearly and firmly now. "You must be strong and brave. You will see afterwards that it was all for the best, and that I am of some good to you all at last. Try and be strong and look at it all as a blessing. Can you bring the old man here? Morton, lad, with my last breath I'll pray that you may grow up as true and brave a fellow. Just think of it, you two— that night. He saw me in the room and escape, and he held his tongue to save me! Do you remember that day, Clairy, when he found me with you and attacked me as he did? I couldn't understand it, then. Ah! it's all plain enough, now. No wonder he hated me."

"Fred, you must not talk," said Morton.

"Not talk, lad?" said Fred with a sad smile. "I've not much more chance. Let me say a few words now."

He lay silent though for a few moments, and his eyes closed as if glad of the rest; but at the end of a short space he began again in a half-wandering manner.

"Brave old fellow! Not a word. Even when they took him. Wouldn't betray me because I was his own son. Tell Claire to tell him—some one tell him—I know why. It was because I was poor mother's favourite—poor mother! How fond she was of me! The scapegrace. They always love the black sheep. Claire—fetch Claire."

He uttered this wildly, and she bent over him, trembling.

"I am here, dear Fred."

He stared at her without recognition for a few minutes, and then smiled at her lovingly.

"Only a bad headache, mother," he said. "Better soon. Don't look at me like that. I didn't mean to kill the old woman. I can't remember doing it. What a time it is since I've seen you. But look here, mother. Mind Claire. That scoundrel Rockley! I know him. Stand at nothing. Mind poor Claire, and—"

A spasm seemed to shoot through him, and he uttered a faint cry of agony as he knit his brow.

"Did you speak, dear?" he said huskily. "Have I been asleep?"

"I—I think so," faltered Claire.

"Yes, I fell asleep. I was dreaming of the poor mother. Claire dear, it would have killed her to see me here like this. There, there, it's all for the best. I want to sleep. Tell the old man he must come and forgive me before I go. Bring him, Morton, lad. No: you bring him, Claire. It will be pain to you, my child, but it is to help me. He will forgive me—brave, noble old fellow that he is—if you are standing by."

The door opened, and the military nurse appeared.

"The doctor says that you must not stay longer now, ma'am," he whispered.

"Quite right," said Fred softly, and with the manner of one accustomed to yield to discipline. "Come again to-morrow—bring the old man to me—good-bye, dear, good-bye."

He hardly turned his head to Morton, but feebly pressed the hand that held his. His eyes were fixed with a wild yearning on the sweet, tender face that bent over him, and then closed as he uttered a sigh of content with the long loving embrace that ensued.

Then, utterly prostrate, Morton led his sister from the room used as an infirmary, and across the barrack-yard to the gates where a carriage was in waiting.

Morton Denville was half stunned by the scene he had just witnessed, and moved as if mechanically, for he, young as he was, had read the truth in his brother's face and felt that even if it were possible to obtain leave, he would not probably be able to get his father to the barracks in time.

It seemed quite a matter of course that a footman should be holding the door of this carriage open, and that the servant should draw back for them to enter, close it, and then mount behind, to shout over the roof, "Mr Barclay's," when the carriage was driven off. Morton Denville said little, and did not realise the chivalrous kindness of Lord Carboro', in sending his carriage to fetch Claire back after her painful visit.

Claire saw absolutely nothing, half blind with weeping, her veil down over her face, and a blacker veil of despair closing her in on every side, as she fought and struggled with the thoughts that troubled her. She was utterly incapable of grasping what went on around her.

Now her father seemed to stand before her innocent, and her erring brother, the true culprit, having, as he had told her, committed the crime in a drunken fit. Now a change came over her, and she shuddered with horror as it seemed to her that the author of her being had made his crime hideously worse in trying to escape its consequences by charging his eldest born with the dreadful sin.

Her brain was in a whirl, and she could not think, only pray for oblivion—for rest—since her mental agony was too great to bear.

One minute she had been gazing on the pallid face of the brother whom she had loved so well; the next, darkness had fallen, and she barely realised the fact that she was handed into a carriage and driven off. All she felt was that there was a place against which she could lay her throbbing head, and that Morton was trying to whisper words of comfort in her ear.

Their departure was seen, though, by several.

Rockley, with a singularly uneasy look upon his dark, handsome face—dread, rage, and despairing love, shown there by turns—watched the brother and sister leave the barracks, cross the yard, and enter Lord Carboro's carriage, and then uttered a furious oath as he saw them driven off.

Lord Carboro' himself, too, was near at hand to see that his commands were executed without a hitch, and the old man went off thoughtfully down to the pier, to sit and watch the sea, snuff-box in one hand, clouded cane in the other.

"Poor old Denville!" he muttered softly; and then, below his breath, "Poor girl!"

Lastly, Richard Linnell and Mellersh saw Claire enter the old nobleman's handsome chariot, and a curious grey look came over the younger man's countenance like a shadow, as he stood watching the departure, motionless till the carriage had disappeared, when Mellersh took him by the arm—

"Come, Dick," he whispered, "be a man."

Linnell turned upon him fiercely.

"I do try," he cried, "but at every turn there is something to tempt me with fresh doubts."

# Chapter Twenty Two
# Nature's Temptation

Claire Denville sat back in her chair utterly exhausted, and feeling as if her brain was giving way. The news from the prison was as hopeless as ever. Fred lay lingering at the barrack infirmary; and though May was better she was querulous, and in that terribly weak state when life seems to be a burden and thought a weariness and care.

She was asleep now, and Claire had just risen softly so as not to awaken her, and make her resume her complaints and questions as to how soon her father would come back and forgive her, and when her husband would return and take her home, for she was weary of lying there.

Unreasoning in her weakness, she had that afternoon been bitterly reproaching Claire for not fetching her child, that she might nurse and play with it—at a time when she could hardly hold up her arm—and when she had been firmly but kindly refused she had burst into a torrent of feeble, querulous reproaches, which had been maddening to Claire in her excited, overstrained state.

The door opened, and Mrs Barclay's beaming countenance appeared, and she stood there beckoning with her fat finger.

"Let's stand outside and talk," she whispered. "That's right: close the door. Now then, my dear, I'll go in and sit with your sister there, for you're getting overdone; and I tell you what, it's a fine soft evening, you put on your bonnet and shawl and go and have a walk. I don't like your going alone, but just take one sharp walk as far as the pier and back, two or three times. It'll do you good."

"Have you any news, Mrs Barclay?" said Claire, ignoring the wish expressed.

"Not yet, my dear, but everybody's working for you. Now, do go."

Claire hesitated, and then in obedience to the reiterated wish she mechanically did as she was bid, and went out into the cool soft night, the beating of the waves sounding loudly on the shore, while as they broke a glow as of fire ran along their crests, flashing and sparkling with soft radiance along the shore.

But Claire saw nothing, heard nothing—neither the figure that came quickly after her as she left the house, nor the sound of steps.

For all was one weary confused trouble in her brain, and everything seemed forced and unnatural, as if it were the mingling of some dream.

Mrs Barclay had bidden her walk as far as the pier, and in all obedience she had done as she was told, reaching the pier entrance; and then, attracted she knew not how or why by the darkness and silence, she turned on to the wooden edifice, and began to walk swiftly along the planked floor.

It was very dark that night, only at the end there was a single light that shone brightly, and in her confused state this seemed to be the star of hope leading her on.

She had not had the slightest intention of going there, but in a rapt dreamy way she walked on and on, the vacant place seeming strange. The last time she had stood on the pier it had been thronged with well-dressed promenaders, but that was months—it seemed years—ago, while endless horrors had taken place since then.

How calm—and still it all was where she walked, while below among the piles the sea softly ebbed and flowed and throbbed, seeming full of whisperings and voices that were hushed lest she should hear the words they said.

She walked on and still on, and it occurred to her once that it was along here that beautiful Cora Dean's ponies had dashed, taking her over the end into the sea, from which Richard Linnell, so brave and honest, had saved her. She had often heard how the crowd cheered him—Richard Linnell. Cora loved him and was jealous of her, and yet she had no cause to be, for the events of the terrible night—the night of the ghastly serenade—killed that for ever.

Why did she think of all this now? She could not tell. It came. She felt that she was not answerable for her thoughts—hardly for herself, as she turned and looked back at the faint lights twinkling upon the Parade. It seemed as if she were saying good-bye to the town, where, in spite of the early struggles with poverty, there had been so much happiness, as in her young love dream she had felt that Richard Linnell cared for her.

Yes; it was like saying good-bye to it with all its weary troubles and bitter cares.

She walked on and on, right to the end, but the light did not shed its beams upon her now. It was no longer a star of hope. It sent its light far out to sea, but she was below it in the shade, and hope was forgotten as she leaned over the rail at the end, listening to the mysterious whisperings of the water in amongst the piles, and looking down into the transparent darkness all lit up with tiny lambent points which were ever going and coming. Now and then there would be a pale bluish-golden flash of light, and then quite a ribbon of dots and flashes, as some fish sped through the sea, but it only died out, leaving the soft transparency lit up with the faint dots and specks that were ever moving.

To her right, though, there was a cable, curving down into the sea, and rising far out, after nearly touching the sands, to ascend to the deck of a large smack aground on the bank. That rope was one mass of lambent light, a huge chain of pallid gold that glowed all round; and as Claire Denville gazed there was a rift in the clouds overhead, and from far above the rays from a cluster of stars were reflected like a patch of diamonds in the sea, and she turned shudderingly away to gaze down once more at the transparent darkness, where the moving specks seemed to have a peculiar fascination.

How the softly flowing and ebbing waves whispered below there amid the piles and down under the platform where her brother used to fish! How soothing and restful it all was to her aching head! The troubles that had been maddening her seemed to float away, and everything was calm and cool. As she stood thinking there a dreamy sensation came over her, such as comes to those who have awakened after the crisis of a fever. Hers had been a fever of the brain, a mental fever; and now all seemed so calm and still that she heaved a sigh, half sob, and the troubles died away in the past.

The transparent water into which she gazed, with its flashes of luminous splendour, seemed to grow more and more mysterious and strange. It was so like oblivion that it began to tempt her to trust herself to it and rest: for she was so weary! Trouble after trouble—the long series of cares—had been so terrible a strain that she felt that she could bear no more, and that the sea offered her forgetfulness and rest.

She did not know why she came there: it was not against her will—it was not with her will. Her mind seemed to be stunned, and it was as if her wearied body had drawn her there.

She leaned over the rail, with the cool, soft, refreshing air bathing her burning forehead, and watched one brilliant point of light—soft and lambent—that was near the surface, and then moved slowly down lower and lower into the dark depths that seemed beyond fathoming; and, as she watched it, the fancy came upon her that these points of light might be lives like hers, wearied out and now resting and gliding here and there in the soft transparent darkness at her feet.

Father—brother—sister—Richard Linnell—her past cares—all appeared distant and strange, and she had no more control over herself than has one in a dream. There was that weariness of spirit—of a spirit that had been whipped and spurred until jaded beyond endurance—that weariness that asked for rest—rest at whatever cost; and whispered that rest could only come in the great sleep—the last.

It did not seem like death, to step from the end of the pier into the dark water. There was nothing horrible therein. On the contrary, it wooed and beckoned her to its breast, offering utter oblivion when, in her more lucid moments, she felt she must go mad.

As if guided by instinct more than her own will, she turned at last from the rail and took a few steps in the darkness towards the side where the damp salt-soaked flight of steps led to the platform below—the rough landing-stage beneath where she had been standing.

Here, as she stood close to the edge with the black piles looming up around, she fancied they were the whisperers as the water heaved and plashed, and rippled and fell. There was no rail here between her and the rest that seemed to ask her to sink down into its arms, now that she was so weary, and unconsciously she was standing where her brother had stood and listened many months ago at the footsteps overhead, as he enjoyed his stolen pleasure in the middle of the night.

But there was no heavy step now—no voice to break the curious spell that was upon her, drawing her away from life, and bidding her sleep.

She was not afraid; she was not excited. Everything seemed to her dull and dreamy and restful, as she stood on the very verge of the open platform, with the water now only a few inches from her feet, leaning more and more over, till the slightest further movement would have overbalanced her, and she would have fallen in, to sink without a cry.

She hardly started as a firm hand gripped her arm, and she was drawn sharply back, to be held tightly by him who had followed her below, watching her every action and standing close behind her in the darkness with outstretched hands.

"Miss Denville—Claire—for heaven's sake, what does this mean?"

She did not struggle, but turned round slowly, and looked in the dimly seen face.

"Richard Linnell!" she said, as if wondering at his presence.

"Yes, Richard Linnell," he cried, panting with emotion. "Claire, my love, has it come to this?"

She did not shrink from him as he drew her closely to his side, and his arm clasped her waist, but gazed up at him in the same half-wondering way.

"Why are you here?" he said hoarsely. "Surely you were not thinking— oh, it is impossible."

Still she did not answer, but in a slow, dull way extricated herself from his grasp, and pressed her hands over her face, covering her eyes for a few moments till she felt his touch as he laid his hand upon her arm.

"Claire," he whispered, "you do not speak to me. Why do you not say something to drive away these horrible thoughts. You here—at this hour— alone? Is it my fate to be always misunderstanding you?"

She shuddered slightly, as if his words were reviving memories of other meetings, and now she spoke.

"I don't know why I am here," she said in a dazed, helpless way. "I have had so much trouble. I was tired!"

"Trouble!" he whispered. "Claire dearest, if you only knew how I loved you. Let me share the trouble—help you through everything."

"Hush! Don't speak to me like that, Richard Linnell," she said slowly, as if she had to think deeply before she uttered a word. "I cannot talk to you now. My head!"

She paused and gazed at him helplessly, laying her hand upon her brow.

"You ought not to have been alone," he said, earnestly. "But tell me— you were not thinking of that—"

He pointed with a shudder to the sea that whispered and hissed below where they stood.

"I don't know," she sighed, still in the same dazed way. "I came, and it seemed to draw me towards it. I am so weary—so tired out."

He caught her in his arms, and held her head down upon his shoulder, as he whispered in a voice deep with emotion:

"Weary, my poor girl, weary indeed. Now rest there, and, heaven helping me, half your trouble shall pass away. For I love you, Claire, love you with all my heart, and I too have suffered more than I can tell."

She made no resistance to his embrace, but sighed deeply, as if he was giving her the support she needed in her time of weakness; but his heart sank within him as he felt how helpless and dazed she was. She yielded to him, but it was not the yielding of one who loved, neither was there a suggestion of caress in her words. He knew that she was half distraught with the suffering that had fallen to her lot; and holding her more tightly for a moment, he pressed his lips once reverently on her forehead, and then drew her arm through his.

"I will take you back," he said.

She looked up at him, and a pang shot through his breast as he realised how weak she had become.

"Yes," she said at last, "you will take me back."

"And, Claire, are the clouds between us to pass away for ever now?" he whispered, as he held her hand.

"Clouds?" she said, as she seemed to comprehend him now. "No: they can never pass away. Mr Linnell, I am ill. I hardly know what I say."

"Then trust me," he said. "I will take you back."

"Yes—if you will," she said vacantly. "I have been so ill. I hardly know—why I am here."

"But you understand me, Claire?" he said softly.

"Yes: I think I understand you."

"Then remember this," he said. "You have shrunk from me, and there has been a terrible estrangement through all your troubles; but, mark this, Claire Denville, I love you. Let me say those simple words again, and let their simplicity and truth bear them home to your heart. I love you, as I always have loved and always shall. You will turn to me, dearest, now."

"It is impossible," she said gravely, and she seemed moment by moment to be growing clearer.

"But I love you," he pleaded.

"And they ask for my love and help," she said, with a sudden flash back into the full power of her intellect. "My poor suffering father—my sister—my wounded brother. Can you not see that there is a social gulf between us too?"

"No," he said, drawing her to him, and once more kissing her brow. "I only see the sweet, true woman who has been a martyr—I only see my love."

She did not speak for a few moments: and then the vacant manner returned somewhat, as she said to him, laying her hand upon his arm:

"I seemed drawn here. I could not help it. That would be too horrible. Take me back."

He drew her arm once more through his, and led her up the steps and back to the Barclays' house, where he paused upon the steps.

"Always yours, Claire. I am going to work again in your service. I am yours, and yours alone."

She shook her head sadly as the door was opened by Mrs Barclay, who shrank back with a smile to let both enter; but Claire glided in, and Richard Linnell remained.

"I am glad," whispered Mrs Barclay. "Why don't you come in?"

"Hush!" he whispered. "Poor girl! she is half mad with her misery. Mrs Barclay, you must not let her go out of your sight. Good-night. Good-night."

He walked rapidly away, and Mrs Barclay followed Claire into the dining-room, where the poor girl was kneeling by a chair and weeping bitterly for the lost love that she felt could never be hers; but as she wept the tears seemed to give rest and lightness to her over-taxed brain, and at last she sank fast asleep like a weary child, her head upon her old friend's lap, and her breathing coming more regularly and deep than at any time since the night of the murder.

# Chapter Twenty Three
# A Revelation

"Don't, pray don't talk to me, Mrs Barclay," said Claire piteously. "Let me lie back here and think and rest for a few minutes, and then I must go up to May."

"No, no, no, my dear; you let poor May alone a bit. She's getting on right enough, and you want more attention than she does. And don't think, my dear. Have patience. Things may turn out all right."

"No," said Claire, with a sigh. "There is no hope now."

"Oh, yes, there is!" said Mrs Barclay decisively. "Jo-si-ah says a reprieve may come at any moment, for Lord Carboro is trying might and main, and Mr Richard Linnell—ah, does that touch you?"

"No, no, hush!" cried Claire, in agony. "Don't mention his name."

"I shall," cried Mrs Barclay. "I shall say what I think will do you good, my dear. Mr Richard Linnell has been working night and day, just as he did at the trial. Now he has been getting a petition signed by everyone in Saltinville, and that's going to win, I think."

Claire caught her arm and looked at her with dilating eyes.

"Yes, I think that's going to do some good, and we've got to trust in Providence, my dear, and wait."

"Yes, yes. I do pray fervently for help."

"And you've got to rouse yourself up, my dear, and do something to keep from thinking."

"I can't—I can't, dear Mrs Barclay."

"Oh, yes, you can, my dear. Not for yourself; I want you to help me."

"Help you?"

"Yes, my dear; help me."

"I'll try," said Claire sadly.

"That's my pet; I knew you would."

She embraced Claire tenderly, and then smoothed her hair, as if proud of her.

"What shall I do?" she said to herself. "Booking? No: jools always please womenfolk. I like 'em myself."

"What am I to do?" said Claire. "I will try, Mrs Barclay. I must have been a great trouble to you."

"A great fiddlestick," cried the plump dame. "What nonsense! Now I'm going to just dust over and put down all the jools we have in the iron chest. Mr Barclay's securities, and some that he has bought. He always likes me to look over them now and then, and mark off any that have been sold or let out, and so on. You'll help me, won't you?"

"Willingly," said Claire sadly.

"That's a dear. Look there on the other side of the way. It's Mr Linnell again. He's looking up. Go to the window, and return his bow, my dear."

"No, no, I could not," cried Claire excitedly.

"Well, then, my dear, I must," said Mrs Barclay, suiting the action to the word, and not only bowing, but kissing her plump hands to Linnell again and again. "There he goes," she exclaimed. "Poor young man! I don't know whose fault it is, but some one's wrong; and I don't like to see two who ought to be helpmeets keeping at a distance for nothing."

Claire's brow contracted, but she said no word, while, after diving into a pocket somewhere beneath her voluminous skirts, Mrs Barclay brought out a bunch of bright keys, with one of which she opened a great cabinet in a dark corner of the bric-à-brac filled room.

"Here's where we keep the jools, my dear," she said, as she took another key and fitted it in a large iron safe within the cabinet. "My Jo-si-ah says that no housebreakers could open that iron chest if they tried for a week. Now, you help me. Hold your apron and I'll fill it. Then we'll lay the cases on the table and look at them, and compare them with the books, and then put 'em away again."

Claire smiled sadly as the eager little woman plunged her plump arm into the safe and brought out, one after the other, the quaint, old-fashioned morocco cases of every shape and size; and these were duly laid upon the table, on whose cloth a space had been cleared.

Along with these was a canvas bag of the kind used in a bank for sovereigns, and a couple of chamois leather bags of similar size and shape.

"That's about all," said Mrs Barclay, bustling about with her eyes beaming and her cheeks showing what an artist would term high lights. "Now we'll have a good look at 'em, my dear; all grand people of title's family jewels that they've had to sell or pledge through gambling at the tables. Ah, a very nasty sort of trade, my dear, buying and lending on them; but, as Jo-si-ah says, some people will be fools, and if he didn't make money from them other folks would."

She placed a chair for Claire, and another for herself; and then, opening a drawer, she took out a ruddy piece of wash-leather, and what seemed to be an ivory tooth-brush that had grown out of knowledge, and a nail-brush in a state of consumption.

"I always give 'em a brush up, my dear, before I put 'em away. Jo-si-ah likes to see 'em kept in good order. He says they look so much more valuable when they're brought out."

She opened one faded red case by pressing on the snap, and laid bare a diamond necklet in old-fashioned silver setting, the gems sparkling in the light as they were moved; for they were evidently of considerable value.

"There," she cried; "those once belonged to a duchess, my dear, but they're ours now. Jo-si-ah said I might wear 'em if I liked; but they're too fine for me. They'd look lovely on your soft white neck. Let me try 'em."

"No, no—pray!" cried Claire in alarm, as she shrank away with such a look of wild horror in her eyes that Mrs Barclay laid the jewels down.

"Why, my pretty!" she said tenderly, "what a fuss to make about nothing."

"Yes, yes, it was, I know," said Claire, with a forced laugh. "It was very foolish of me; but—don't—do that again."

"No; if you don't wish it, my dear, of course," said Mrs Barclay; and she looked across wonderingly at her companion, for she could not comprehend how the sight of those diamonds and the attempt to place them on her neck had recalled the back drawing-room at the house on the Parade, with the hideous old woman sitting up in bed with her jewels about her on the coverlid and on her arms and neck. The sight of diamonds had become hateful to Claire, and she was ready to leave the table, but the thought of seeming strange to Mrs Barclay restrained her.

"Poor old girl! she had to wear paste, as lots of them do when they sell their jewels, my dear. Ah, they're a beggarly set; when once they take to gambling they don't seem to be fine ladies any longer. Back you go in the box."

*Snap.*

Mrs Barclay had given the diamond necklet a brush and a rub while she was speaking; and then, taking up and opening a book, she handed it to Claire, bidding her look out for the Duchess of Duligne's diamonds, and make a pencil tick against them.

This done and the morocco case replaced in the safe, another was taken up and opened, displaying a ruby and gold bracelet.

"There, I'll put that on my wrist," said Mrs Barclay, suiting the action to the word. "I won't ask you to have it on, my dear. Some girls would want to, and wouldn't like 'em taken off again. But you're different to most people. Look at that now. Jewels always seem best against skin and flesh, but there, my gracious, how fat I am getting! Why it won't snap round my wrist! Think of that."

She laughed as merrily as a girl as she held up the glittering gems, and then started, with a loud "Lor' bless me!"

For just then there was a tremendous double knock at the door; and, jumping up with wonderful activity for one of her size, she trotted across to the window.

"Why, it's Cora Dean, my dear. No, no: don't go," she continued, as Claire rose hastily.

"I do not feel as if I could meet her, Mrs Barclay," Claire pleaded.

"But she's nobody, my dear, and she'll be so hurt if you go, for I'm sure to let out that you were here just now."

"Miss Dean, ma'am," said the servant, opening the door; and Claire's indecision was cut short by Cora going straight to her, taking her hand and kissing her, before bestowing the same salute upon Mrs Barclay.

"I am glad to see you, my dear," said the latter volubly, for she was nervously afraid that Claire would go, and of the opinion that the best way to set both at their ease was to talk.

"I ought to have been here before," said Cora, "but my mother has been ill. Don't think me unkind, Claire Denville."

She bent over and took Claire's hand, and met her eyes with a curious wistful look that was full of affection; but, as in some clear gem, such as lay beside them on the table, there was a hidden fire that kept darting forth, and that fire was the vainly-smothered bitter jealousy that was the torment of her life.

"It was very kind of you to come," said Claire quietly; and there was a coldness in her manner that seemed to make Cora's jealousy glow more fiercely, for the fire flashed up, and the wistful affectionate look seemed to be burning fast away.

It was only a matter of moments, though, for a change came over Claire. It was as if something within her whispered:

"Why should I be bitter and envious, and hate her for winning a happiness that could never be mine."

With a quick movement and a low hysterical cry, she threw her arms round Cora's neck and hid her face in her bosom, sobbing bitterly at first; and then, as Cora held her tightly in her embrace, and soothed and caressed her, the sobs grew less violent, the tears fell more slowly, and at last she raised her face and gazed in her friend's eyes, offering her lips with a simple child-like motion for the kiss in which they were joined—

"Oh—oh—oh—oh! Don't you take any notice of me, my dears," burst forth Mrs Barclay. "It's only my foolishness, but I couldn't keep it back. There, there," she cried in a choking voice, "I'm better now—I'm getting better now. I couldn't help it though. There!"

She dabbed her eyes with her scented handkerchief, and beaming on both in turns, she gave first one and then the other a hug full of affection.

"It does me good, my dears, to see you both real friends at last; and now let's be sensible and chat together till I've finished these jools, and then we'll have a nice strong cup of tea."

Neither Claire nor Cora spoke, but sat with full hearts, and with a feeling of relief stealing over them as their hostess prattled on, opening case after case, and drawing the book to herself so as not to trouble Claire.

"Look at those, my dears; real choice pearls. Ain't they lovely?" she said as she took out a ring from its tiny box. "They're small, but they're as good as good. Pearls always go best on dark people. Now just you try that on, Cora Dean, my dear. No; that finger's a little too large, and that's too small. That's it to a T; just a fit."

"It is beautiful," said Cora, admiring the pearls. "Look, Claire."

"Yes," said Claire, smiling; "they are very beautiful."

"Not as you want jools on you, my dear," said Mrs Barclay, "with a face, and rich red mouth, and throat, and hair, like you have. You want no jools to make you handsome as handsome can be."

"Oh, yes, I do, Mrs Barclay; and I did not know that you had taken to flattery," cried Cora, laughing.

"'Tain't flattery, my dear, it's truth," said Mrs Barclay; "and I can't say which is the handsomer—you or Claire Denville there—for you're both right in your own ways. You neither of you want jools."

"I do, Mrs Barclay, and I mean to have this ring if it is for sale. How much is it? It's lovely."

"It is for sale, my dear," cried Mrs Barclay; "and you shall have it and pay for it."

"And the price?"

"The price is that you're to be a good true friend to Claire Denville there, as long as you live, and,"—a hearty smack on Cora's Juno-like red lips—"there's the receipt, my dear."

"But, Mrs Barclay—"

"Not another word, my dear," cried the plump lady. "There's the little case, and—there!" she continued, taking up a pen and writing, as she muttered, "Half-hoop oriental pearl ring: Countess of Dinster. S-o-l-d. There."

She looked up, smiling with satisfaction, and busily opened another case.

"But, really, Mrs Barclay," began Cora, "such an expensive ring."

"Why, bless your heart, my dear, you don't think I look upon such a thing as that as expensive. Why, I've only to say to my Jo-si-ah I want a set of diamonds, and if they were worth a couple of thousand pounds he'd give 'em to me directly. There, I won't hear no more. These are nice, ain't they, my dears? Emeralds—real."

She held up a glittering green suite.

"Look at the flaws in them. Shows how good they are. Look at these sapphires and diamonds mixed, too. They're worth a good thousand, they are."

She spread out the beautiful stones, and Cora's eyes glistened with pleasure as case after case was opened, for it was a feast for her that she thoroughly enjoyed, while Claire sat looking on listless and sad till the task was nearly done.

"I wouldn't spend so much time over them, my dears," said Mrs Barclay, "only I think you like seeing 'em. There, now, there's only these three lots to open."

She took a wash-leather bag and opened it, to pour out some rough-looking crystals into her hand, as if it had been grain at a corn-market.

"Rough diamonds, dear," she said to Cora; and, pouring them back, she retied the bag, and took the other and served it the same. "Seed pearls, those are, and worth more than you'd think."

This bag was also retied and placed in the safe, nothing being left but the canvas packet.

"Ah!" said Mrs Barclay, "I always mean to get a case made for this lot, every time I see them. They're not much good, but it would set them off."

As she spoke she untied the bag, turned it over, and, taking hold of the bottom, shook out on the table a necklet, cross, tiara, and pair of bracelets, which tinkled as they fell on the table.

"You'll spoil them," said Cora, taking up the tiara admiringly.

"Spoil them? Not I, my dear. You couldn't spoil them."

"But they are very beautiful," said Cora, taking up the cross by the little ring at the top. "Look, Claire dear. Why, I—"

Claire turned her eyes upon them slowly, and then her countenance changed, and she uttered a cry:

"Lady Teigne's diamonds!"

# Chapter Twenty Four
# The Seller of the Gems

"Lady Teigne's diamonds!" exclaimed Claire.

"Nonsense, my dear!" said Mrs Barclay. "They're not. Now don't you get letting your poor head run upon them. Whoever did that dreadful deed took them up to London, and sold 'em, or sent 'em to Amsterdam."

"But they are," cried Claire, growing more excited. "I am sure of it. I know them so well."

As she spoke she seized the jewels, and turned them over and over with feverish haste, her face convulsed with horror.

"Nonsense, nonsense, my dear child," said Mrs Barclay.

"It is very curious," said Cora, looking at the ornaments eagerly. "I seem to have seen them before."

"Some like 'em, my dear. Lots of 'em are made and sold."

"Mrs Barclay, I know those are Lady Teigne's diamonds," cried Claire again.

"And I know they are not, my dear child. I'll tell you why: they're not diamonds at all, only some fairish imitations—paste—that my Jo-si-ah bought."

"No, no," persisted Claire; "they are valuable diamonds."

"Well, my dear, I'm not a clever woman at all; but I've had so much to do with precious stones that I can't help telling 'em directly. There's nothing valu'ble about them but the silver setting, and if you melt that down there isn't ten pounds' worth in the lot."

"Mrs Barclay—"

"Ah, I'm right, my dear. Those aren't diamonds, but paste; and I remember Josiah saying when I laughed at him, and asked him if he had been taken in—I remember him saying that they were a good-looking lot, and he should keep 'em to let on hire to some lively lady who wanted a suite, and whom he didn't care to trust with diamonds. There, now, are you satisfied?"

"No," cried Claire. "I am certain that I am right. That cross! I know it so well. I've had it in my hands a hundred times. Those bracelets, too. I have often clasped them on Lady Teigne's wrists."

"And put that ornament in her hair, and the other thing round her neck?" said Mrs Barclay, smiling.

"Yes, often; so often," cried Claire. "Oh, tell me what this means. Of whom did you buy them?"

"Well, that I can't say, my dear; but I'm going to show you that you are wrong," said Mrs Barclay, laughing and showing her white teeth. "Now look here," she continued, as she took up the necklet, and then, crossing to the safe, she picked out an old morocco case, which she laid upon the table. "Open that, my dear," she continued, turning to Cora. "There's a necklet in there very much like this."

Cora pressed the snap spring, and, in obedience to a nod from Mrs Barclay, took out a brilliant necklet and laid it upon the table.

"There, my dears," cried the plump little woman; "those are diamonds! Look at them. Those are brilliants. Look at the fire in them; and now lay these beside them. Where's the fire and bright colours? They'd light up and look shiny by candle-light; but, though they'd deceive some folks, they wouldn't cheat me. My Jo-si-ah has shown me the difference too often. There, then, take my word for it, and let's put them away."

"No, no," cried Claire wildly. "I feel as if I have found out something that might clear up a mystery. I dread to inquire further, but I feel as if I must. Mrs Barclay—dear Mrs Barclay—it seems shocking to contradict you so flatly; but you are wrong—I am sure you are wrong. Those are indeed Lady Teigne's diamonds."

"Now, bless us and save us, my dear, dear child, look here," cried Mrs Barclay, taking up the two necklets, one in each hand, and breathing upon them. "I know these things by heart, my dear. My Jo-si-ah has taught me; and a fine lot of trouble he had, for I'm a stupid old woman. Now look there."

She breathed on a couple of the largest stones again, and held them out in the light.

"Now see how the breath goes off them, my dears. See the difference? Those are brilliants. These that you say are Lady Teigne's diamonds are only paste—paste or glass, as the Italians call it. They make lots of 'em very cleverly, and they're shiny and bright, but they are not precious stones. Now then, are you satisfied? Shall I put 'em all away, and ring for tea?"

"No," said Claire, trembling; "I am not satisfied; and though I feel as if I were going to find out something horrible, I must—I must go on."

"Well—well—well, then, my dear, so you shall go on. I'll do anything to humour you, and try and make you a bit happier. Now, then, what's to be done? Let me warn you, though, that I'm right, and those are not diamonds at all, only bits of glass, with some tinfoil behind to make 'em shine."

Claire eagerly examined the jewels again one by one.

"Yes—see—both of you," she cried excitedly; "there is the tiny slip of card I put under that snap, because the spring had grown so weak; and there should be a little scratch and a chip in one of the big diamonds in the tiara. No—no—I can't see it," she said hurriedly.

"A scratch and a chip on a diamond!" said Mrs Barclay, smiling. "Oh, my dear, my dear!"

"Yes. There are the marks," cried Claire excitedly. "Look, both of you, look!"

"Well, so they are, my dear," acquiesced Mrs Barclay. "Well, that is strange! But that don't make 'em diamonds, you know. It only proves what I said—that they are paste."

"They were Lady Teigne's jewels," cried Claire; "and I always believed them to be diamonds."

"Well," cried Mrs Barclay, "and some one killed that poor old creature for the sake of getting a few bits of paste. Ugh!"

She threw down the necklet she held with a look of disgust. "If I'd ha' known I wouldn't ha' touched 'em. My Jo-si-ah couldn't ha' known, or he wouldn't ha' bought 'em. This must be cleared up."

She went toward the bell, but Claire followed and caught her arm.

"What are you going to do?" she said, with an ashy face.

"Ring and ask my Jo-si-ah to come up and talk this over. We don't deal in stolen goods."

"No; don't, don't."

"But we must find out where he bought the things."

"No, no! I couldn't bear to know," faltered Claire. "No, Mrs Barclay, pray don't ask."

"Oh, my poor darling! Catch her, Cora, my dear," cried Mrs Barclay, as Claire staggered back, half fainting, and was helped to the sofa, and fanned and recovered with smelling-salts.

She was just getting rid of the deadly hue when the door opened, and Barclay came in with a bluff "How do, ladies? Why, hallo! what's the matter?"

"Hush! she's coming round," said Mrs Barclay.

"That's better. Why, what are you doing with these things?"

"I had them out, dear, to check off and brush a little. Claire was helping me."

"Mr Barclay," said Claire, rising, and taking a step or two to the table, and speaking with a forced decision that startled her hearers, "I must speak. I must know. Tell me—"

She faltered, and pressed her hands to her brow, shivering and turning ghastly pale again.

"Oh, my dear!" cried Mrs Barclay; "she's going to faint!"

"No, no," said Claire, in a weak voice. "Don't touch me. I must speak—I must know. Mr Barclay," she cried, picking up the jewels, "where did you get these diamonds?"

"These, my dear?" said the money-lender, taking them from her. "Not diamonds at all—paste."

"There!" cried Mrs Barclay triumphantly.

"But where—where did you get them? Pray, pray speak. It is agony, this suspense."

"Get them, my dear? Don't take it like that. Why, what's the matter?"

"She says—" began Mrs Barclay.

"They are Lady Teigne's jewels," cried Claire. "Tell me, how came you by them?"

"Bought 'em, my dear, of Fisherman Dick—Miggles, you know; him as your brother Morton went fishing with."

"Yes," cried Cora. "I remember now, he brought them to us. He said he dredged them up in his shrimp net off the end of the pier."

"That's what he told me too, I remember," said Barclay.

"And he thought they were mine," said Cora. "He brought them with the carriage clock and my bag, but, of course, they were not mine."

Fisherman Dick—her brother—dredged up off the end of the pier! It was no elucidation of the mystery, Claire felt, as she stood there trembling.

"Lady Teigne's jewels?" said Barclay, turning them over, and speaking in his blunt way. "Then whoever killed the poor old woman found out that these things were good for nothing, and threw them into the sea."

"Oh, my dear, my dear!" sighed Mrs Barclay. "Don't, pray don't faint."

Poor Claire did not hear her, for as she realised that here was perhaps a fresh link of evidence against her father, a link whose fitting she did not see, her brain reeled and she would have fallen had not Cora been close at hand.

"Can I do anything?" said Barclay in his abrupt way.

"Yes," cried Mrs Barclay sharply. "Go. Can't you see we must cut her laces?"

"Humph!" ejaculated Barclay thoughtfully; "Lady Teigne's jewels! I never thought of that. No wonder. It was diamonds missing—not paste thrown off the pier."

He shook his head as he reached the door, and stood with the handle in his hand.

"Fisherman Dick, eh? Well, I'll go and see what he has to say."

# Chapter Twenty Five
# The Tough Witness

"Shall I go alone?" said Josiah Barclay, as he stood upon his doorstep. "No, it's wise to keep your own counsel sometimes, but at others it's just as well to have witnesses. Who shall I take? Richard Linnell," he said, after a pause. "He's the fellow. I'm afraid, though, it looks worse for the old man than it did before. Dick Miggles is as honest as the day as long as he is not smuggling; and he would no more think of choking an old woman than flying. I shouldn't like to be the revenue officer opposite to him in a row if Master Dick had a pistol in his hand; but he would consider that to be a matter of business. Yes: it looks worse for the old man after all."

Barclay walked sharply down to the Parade, and went up to the house where Mrs Dean was seated at one of the windows, bemoaning the absence of Cora, and murmuring at her sufferings, as she leaned back flushed, and with her throbbing head in her hand.

For she was very ill, and very ill-tempered, consequent upon her complaint—a weakness and succumbing of her fort, after a long and combined attack made by veal cutlets, new bread, and port wine.

She saw Barclay come up, and declared that he should wait for his rent this time if she died for it.

To her great disappointment, as she felt just in the humour, as she termed it, "for a row," Barclay stopped below in Mellersh's room, where Richard Linnell was seated with the Colonel.

"Business with me, Mr Barclay?" said Linnell, flushing. "Yes, I'll come out with you. No, I have no secrets from Colonel Mellersh."

Barclay looked sharply at the Colonel, and the latter glanced at his nails and smiled.

"Dick," he said, leaning back in his chair, "Mr Barclay is asking himself whether Gamaliel is a scoundrel, and Paul is a young fool to trust him."

"No, I wasn't, Colonel," said Barclay warmly. "You're a little too much for me, sir, and though you shy the New Testament at me like that (and I never read it), perhaps, money-lender as I am, I'm as honest a man, and as true a friend as you."

"No doubt about it, my dear Barclay," said Mellersh with a sneer.

"I wasn't thinking about Gamaliel, or Paul either, sir; but, since you will have it I was asking myself whether you—a clever card-player—"

"Say sharper, Barclay."

"By gad, I will, sir," cried Barclay, banging his fist upon the table—"a clever sharper—were making believe to be this young gentleman's friend for your own ends."

"Mr Barclay!" cried Richard indignantly.

"Let him be, Dick; I'm not offended. Barclay's only plain-spoken. The same thing, Barclay, my dear fellow, only I put it more classically. Here, I'll leave the room, Dick."

"No; stop," said Richard quickly. "Mr Barclay, I have told you that Colonel Mellersh is my best friend. Please say what you have to say."

Barclay looked ruffled and bristly, but he mastered his anger, and said sharply:

"I want you to go down with me, Mr Linnell, as far as Fisherman Dick's."

Richard Linnell stared and looked grave, as he dreaded some fresh trouble and complication.

"What for?" he said sharply.

"Because I believe you take an interest in Miss Claire Denville," said Barclay; "and there's something fresh about that murder affair."

He went on and told what had occurred at his house.

"Plain enough," said Mellersh. "The man who did the murder found out that the jewels were false, and he took them and threw them into the sea."

"Yes," said Barclay drily, "I found all that out myself, Colonel. Hang it, gentlemen, don't let's fence and be petty," he continued. "Colonel Mellersh, I beg your pardon, sir, and I ask your help, both of you. What's to be done? I bought those sham diamonds of Fisherman Dick, who found them, I suppose, when he was shrimping, and took them to Miss Dean—brought them here, you know."

Mellersh and Richard Linnell glanced sharply at each other.

"Thought, you see, that she lost them at the time of the accident. Well, suppose I tell this, it may make the matter worse for poor old Denville. What would you do?"

"See Fisherman Dick. Perhaps your surmise about the shrimping is wrong. The smuggling rascal may know something more."

"Will you come along the cliff with me, then?"

Richard Linnell jumped up, and Mellersh remained—as he was going to dine at the mess. A quarter of an hour later they were at the fisherman's cottage, where Mrs Miggles raised her eyes sharply from the potatoes she was peeling, while Dick was engaged in teaching their little foster-child to walk between his knees.

"Morning, Dick," said Barclay, as the great fellow gave them a comprehensive nod, and looked from one to the other suspiciously, Mrs Miggles gouging out the eyes of a large potato with a vicious action, while her heart beat fast from the effect of best French brandy.

Not from potations, for the sturdy, smuggling fisherman's wife revelled in nothing stronger than tea; but there were four kegs in the great cupboard, covered with old nets, and a stranger coming to the cottage always seemed to bear a placard on his breast labelled "gaol," and made her sigh and wish that smuggling were not such a profitable occupation.

"We want a few words with you, Miggles," said Barclay sharply.

"Right, sir. Fewer the better," said the fisherman surlily, for the visit looked ominous.

"You brought some ornaments to me one day, and I bought them of you. You remember—months ago?"

"To be sure I do. You said they was pastry."

"Paste, man, paste."

Fisherman Dick had a thought flash into his head, and he gave his knee such a tremendous slap that the child began to cry.

"Here, missus, lay holt o' the little un," he cried, passing it to her, as she gave her hands a rub on her apron—almost pitching it as if it had been a little brandy keg. "Here, I know, gentlemen," he continued, "them jools has turned out to be real, and you only give ten shillings."

"All they were worth, man. No; they've turned out to be what I told you—sham."

"Oh!" said Fisherman Dick in a tone of disappointment. "Hear that, missus? Only sham."

"But we want to hear how you found them."

"How I foun' 'em? Well, you've got 'em; that's enough for you, arn't it?" he grumbled.

"No. You must speak out—to us mind—and let us know—in confidence—all about it."

"I don't know nothing about 'em at all. I forgets."

"No, you don't. You dredged them up, you said, when you were shrimping and searching for Miss Dean's bag—after the accident."

"How do you know?" growled the fisherman fiercely.

"You told Miss Dean so when you took them to her."

"And how do you know that?"

"You told her so when you took them to her, and she told me," said Barclay.

"Then she told you wrong," said Fisherman Dick sulkily. "It warn't then."

"Look here, my man," said Barclay. "You may not know it, but very likely you will find yourself in an awkward position if you do not speak out."

"Shall I?" growled the man defiantly.

"Yes; a very awkward position. You know that Mr Denville is lying under sentence of death for the murder of Lady Teigne, and stealing her jewels?"

"Oh, yes; I know all about that," growled the fisherman.

"Well, then, what will you say if I tell you that those ornaments you sold me have been identified as Lady Teigne's jewels?"

Fisherman Dick's jaw dropped, and curious patches and blotches of white appeared in his sun-browned face.

"Oh, Dick! Dick!" cried his wife, "why don't you tell the truth? No, don't: it may get you into trouble."

"I ain't going to speak," growled Dick. "'Tain't likely."

"Hush, Barclay," whispered Linnell, taking off his hat as Claire Denville came up hurriedly, leaning on her brother's arm.

She caught Barclay's hand quickly, and said in a hurried whisper:

"You are inquiring about that, Mr Barclay? Have you found out anything?"

"No; the fellow will not speak," said Barclay pettishly.

"Then stop—pray stop!" said Claire. "Don't ask—don't ask him any more."

"My dear Claire, this is madness," cried Morton excitedly. "We must know the truth."

"No, no," said Claire faintly. "It is better not."

"I say it is better out. You foolish girl, it is our last chance for him."

"Morton," whispered Claire; "suppose—"

"Better the truth than the doubt," cried Morton. "You Dick Miggles—"

"Stop!" cried Richard Linnell. "Mr Denville, your sister's wishes should be respected."

Claire darted a grateful glance at him, and then her face contracted, and she turned from him with a weary sigh.

"Mr Linnell," cried Morton, "I wish to spare my sister's feelings; but it is my duty as my father's son to prove him innocent if I can, and I'll have the truth out of this man."

"All right, Mr Mort'n," said Dick. "Don't be hard on a fellow. You and me used to be good mates over many a fishing trip, when you used to come down o' nights out o' the balc'ny."

Morton turned a horrified look upon Fisherman Dick, as the idea flashed across his brain, that the man who knew so well how he came down, must have known the way up. It was but a passing fancy, for there was that in the rough fisherman's countenance that seemed to disarm suspicion.

"Well, what's the matter now, Master Mort'n?"

"I want you to speak out, Dick."

"Morton—brother!" whispered Claire appealingly.

"Be silent, Claire," he replied angrily. "Now, Dick, speak out. You, Mrs Miggles, you are telling him to be silent. I will not have it. Now, Dick, how did you get those jewels?"

"Shrimped 'em. Off the pier."

"And how came they there?"

"Chucked in, I s'pose," growled the fisherman. "How should I know?"

"Stop!" cried Morton suddenly. "Let me think—my head is all confused, Mr Barclay—so much trouble lately, but I seem to recollect—yes. Dick Miggles, you know; some one—that night we were fishing down among the piles under the pier."

"Yes, I recklect oftens fishing along o' you there, Master Mort'n."

"Yes, but one night—when I stole down, soon after that terrible business. Why, you recollect, Mr Linnell. You caught me."

"Yes, of course. I recollect," said Linnell eagerly.

"Dick Miggles and I were fishing that night under the pier, and a man came and threw something in."

Claire turned ghastly pale, and Linnell stretched out his hand to catch her, but she waved him off and stood firm.

"You recollect, Dick?"

"No," said the fisherman sulkily. "I don't recklect."

Claire uttered a low moan. It was horrible, and she suffered a martyrdom as she stood there, helpless now to speak or resist, only able, with her hearing terribly acute, to listen to her brother dragging out from this man perhaps some fresh token of her father's guilt.

"You do recollect," cried Morton fiercely. "You got up and looked between the planks, and you said he had thrown something into the sea."

"Oh—ah—yes—I recollect now: some one come and threw a stone in."

"Some one would not come down to the end of the pier to throw in a stone," said Barclay drily.

"No," said Morton; "and Dick looked up and watched and saw who it was. He pretended he couldn't see—"

Claire's heart sank lower and lower. It was too horrible.

"But I'm sure he could."

"No, Master Mort'n, I couldn't see."

"I noticed your manner then, Dick. I'm sure you did see, and that's why you did not speak."

"What's why?" growled Dick, assuming a vacant air.

"You knew who it was, and that something was thrown in that you meant to dredge for, and you did and found those jewels."

Fisherman Dick was posed, and he rubbed his boots together; but he looked more vacant than ever.

"You don't want to be taken to prison and made to speak, Dick?"

"No!" shouted Mrs Miggles, "and he shan't go."

"Then speak out, Dick," cried Morton; but the rough fisherman only frowned and tightened his lips.

"No; I don't 'member," he said, shaking his head.

"You do; and you saw who it was. Speak."

"Morton!" gasped Claire, staggering to him, and throwing herself on his breast. "I cannot bear it. For God's sake, stop!"

"No," cried the lad; "for my father's sake I'll have the truth. You, Dick Miggles, I order you to speak."

For the first time in his life, as Morton Denville stood there erect and stern, he looked a man.

"Can't," said Dick Miggles. "Don't know."

"You do, you coward!" cried Morton. "You will not speak for fear of getting into trouble. Look at the trouble we are in, and you might clear us."

"Morton, dear Morton!" moaned Claire, with horror-stricken face.

"Silence, sister!" cried Morton, throwing her off. "He shall speak: if it was my own father who threw those things into the sea that night. But it was not. It was some man with a heavy tread; and he stopped and did what my father never did in his life. He was smoking as he stood above our heads, and he got a light and lit a fresh cigar."

"Oh!"

It was a low, piteous wail, full of relief from Claire. It could not have been her father, then, and she leaned helpless on Barclay's arm.

Morton tried to help his sister, but she smiled at him sadly as she endeavoured to rise, and he turned to Fisherman Dick.

"Come, Dick," he said, "we used to be good friends and fishermen together."

"Ay, lad, ay, so we did," said the rough fellow, with a smile.

"Then will you not help me now I am in such trouble?"

"Ay, lad, I'd like to; but I don't see how I can."

"Dick Miggles, you're a coward," cried Morton. "When I was a boy—"

"Nay, nay, Master Mort'n, take that back again. No coward."

"Yes: a coward," cried Morton angrily. "When I was a lad, how many times did I know about cargoes being run, and your house being crammed with spirits and tobacco and lace and silk?"

"How many times, my lad?"

"Yes, how many times? Wasn't I always true to you as a mate I fished with?"

"Yes; that you was, Master Mort'n: that you was."

"And now you see my poor old father condemned for a crime he did not commit, and that must have been done by the wretch who threw those jewels into the water. You know who did it. You saw him that night, and you will not speak."

"Dursn't, my lad, dursn't," growled Miggles.

"You did see him, then?"

Dick Miggles looked in all directions to avoid his questioner's eye, but in vain: Morton went up close to him, and took him by the thick blue woollen jersey he wore, and held him.

"You did see him?"

"Well, all right, then; all right, then, Master Mort'n. I did see him," growled Miggles, "but I won't say another word."

"You shall, if I tear it out of you," cried Morton. "Now then: who was it?"

"Dunno!" growled Miggles.

"You do know, sir. Speak out."

"I can't, Master Mort'n, sir. I dursn't. It would get me into no end of trouble," said Miggles desperately. "I can't tell ye. I won't, there!"

He threw Morton off and folded his arms upon his breast, looking at all defiantly.

"I suppose you know, my man," said Barclay sternly, "that you will be summoned as a witness before the judge, and forced to speak?"

"No judge won't make me speak unless I like," said Miggles defiantly. "I tell you all I won't say another word and get myself into trouble, so there!"

Just then Claire took a step or two forward, laid her hands upon Dick Miggles' broad breast, and looked up in his great bronzed, bearded face.

The fisherman winced, and his wife hugged the child to her, and uttered a low sob.

"My poor dear father is lying in prison under sentence of death—my poor grey-haired old father," she said softly. "Perhaps a word from you will save his life—will save mine, for—for my heart is breaking. I could not live if—if—I cannot say it," she sobbed in a choking voice, as she sank upon her knees and raised her clasped hands to the great fellow. "Pray, pray, speak."

Fisherman Dick's face worked; he stared round him and out to sea; and then, with a low, hoarse sob, he roared out:

"Don't, Miss Claire, don't; I can't abear it. I will speak. It was that big orficer as fought the dool with Mr Linnell here."

"Rockley!" cried Morton wildly.

"Ay! Him. Master Mort'n. I see him plain."

No one spoke, but Linnell involuntarily took off his hat, and Barclay did the same, while Morton stood for a few moments looking down at the rapt countenance of his sister, as with eyes closed and face upturned to heaven she knelt there, apparently unconscious of the presence of others, her lips moving and slowly repeating the thanksgiving flowing mutely from her heart.

No one moved as they stood there in the broad sunshine at the edge of the chalk cliff, with the clear blue sky above their heads, the green down behind, and the far-spreading glistening sea at their feet. Then Morton Denville softly bent his knee by his sister's side, and to Richard Linnell the silence seemed that of some grand cathedral where a prayer of thanksgiving was being offered up to God.

"And may I be forgiven, too," he muttered, as he looked down on that worn upturned face with the blue veins netting the temples, and the closed eyes, "forgiven all my cruel doubts—all my weak suspicions of you, my darling! for I love you with all my heart."

Claire rose slowly from her knees, taking her brother's hand, and a slight flush came into her cheeks as she saw the reverent attitude of all around.

She looked her thanks, and then turned to Miggles, catching his broad rough hand in both of hers, and kissing it again and again.

"May God bless you!" she whispered. "You have saved my father's life."

She let fall the hand, which Miggles raised and thrust in his breast, in a strange, bashful way. Then, turning quickly to Morton, she took his arm and looked at Barclay.

"Mr Barclay, will you do what is necessary at once? My brother and I are going over to the gaol."

# Chapter Twenty Six
# Brought Home

"Gentlemen," said Colonel Lascelles, "I am going to ask you to excuse me. You know my old fashion—bed betimes. Rockley will take the chair, and I hope you will enjoy yourselves. Good-night."

The grey-headed old Colonel quitted the mess-room, and the wine was left for the card-tables, after the customary badinage and light conversation that marked these meetings.

It had been a special night, and a few extra toasts had been proposed, notably the healths of Sir Matthew Bray and his lady, it having leaked out that the young baronet had at last led the fair Lady Drelincourt to the altar, with all her charms.

Sir Matthew, prompted a great deal by Sir Harry Payne—who had but lately rejoined the regiment, looking pale and ill—had made his response, and he was a good deal congratulated, the last to speak to him about his noble spouse being Sir Harry.

"Why, Matt," he exclaimed, "you look as if you were going to be hung. Aren't you happy, man?"

"Happy!" said Sir Matthew, in deep, melodramatic tones. "You speak as if you had not seen my wife."

Sir Harry stared him full in the face for a few moments, and then burst into a hearty laugh, but winced directly, and drew in his breath sharply, for the knife Louis Gravani had used struck pretty deep.

Card-playing went on for a time, the stakes being light, and then succeeded a bout of drinking, when, with a contemptuous look at Mellersh, Rockley, who had been drinking hard, and was strange and excitable, called upon the party to honour a toast he was about to propose.

"Claire Denville," he cried in a curious, reckless tone which made Sir Harry stare.

Mellersh involuntarily glanced round, as if fearing that Richard Linnell was present.

"Well, Colonel," said Rockley mockingly, "you don't drink. Surely you are not trying to steal away my mistress."

"I? No," said Mellersh. "I did not know you had one."

"Hang it, sir!" cried Rockley, "I have just given her name as a toast. Do you refuse to drink it?"

"Yes," said Mellersh coldly. "It seems to me bad taste to propose the health of a lady whose father is under sentence of death, and whose brother is dying not many yards away."

"Curse you, sir! who are you, to pretend to judge me?" cried Rockley furiously. "Gentlemen, I protest against this sort of thing. What was Lascelles thinking about to invite him, after what has taken place between us?"

"Here, Rockley, be quiet," said Sir Matthew.

"I shall not," cried Rockley. "It is an insult to me. The Colonel shall answer for it, and this Mellersh too."

"Nonsense!" cried Sir Harry. "Nonsense, man; you can't quarrel with a guest. Never mind the toast. Sit down, and let's have a rubber. Rockley's a bit excited, Mellersh. Don't take any notice of a few hot words."

"Silence!" cried Rockley, whose voice was thick with the brandy he had been imbibing day by day. "I want my toast drunk as it should be—Claire Denville."

"Sit down, man," cried several of his brother-officers. "Here, let's have a rubber. Sit down, Rockley, and cut. Come, Mellersh."

The latter shrugged his shoulders, and allowed himself to be drawn into a game, cutting, and finding himself Rockley's adversary.

He was singularly fortunate, and in addition he played with the skill of a master, the consequence being that he and Sir Harry Payne won.

Rockley rose from the table furious with suppressed anger, and, catching up a pack of cards, he would have thrown them in Mellersh's face had not Sir Harry struck at his arm, so that the cards flew all over the room.

Mellersh turned pale, but a couple of the most sober officers drew him aside, Sir Matthew joining them directly.

"Don't take any notice, Mellersh," he said. "We're all sorry. Rockley's as drunk as an owl. They're going to get him off to bed."

"It was a deliberate insult, gentlemen," said Mellersh quietly.

"Yes, but he doesn't know what he's about," said Sir Matthew. "We all apologise."

Meanwhile the rest had summoned several of the regimental servants to help in getting Rockley from the room; but he resisted till, seeing that his case was hopeless, he suddenly exclaimed:

"Well, then, I'll go, if you'll let me propose one more toast."

"No, no!" was chorused.

"Then I shan't go," cried Rockley; "I'll stop and see it out."

"Let him give a toast," said Sir Harry, "and then he'll go. On your honour, Rockley?"

"On my honour," he said: and he seemed to have grown suddenly sober. "Fill, gentlemen. The toast is a lady—not Miss Denville, since it offends Colonel Mellersh. I will give you the health of a lady who has long been one of my favourites. Her health even that arch sharper will not refuse to drink—my mistress, Cora Dean."

In rapid succession, and in the midst of a deep silence, the claret in Colonel Mellersh's glass, and the glass itself, were dashed in Major Rockley's face.

Rockley uttered a howl of rage that did not seem to be human; and he would have sprung at Mellersh's throat had he not been restrained, while the latter remained perfectly calm.

"There is no need for us to tear ourselves like brute beasts, gentlemen," he said. "Major Rockley shall have the pleasure of shooting the arch sharper—myself—where you will arrange—to-morrow morning; but before I leave I beg to say that Miss Dean is a lady whom I hold in great honour, and any insult to her is an insult to me."

"Loose me, Bray. Let me get at the cowardly trickster and cheat," yelled Rockley. "He shall not leave here without my mark upon him. Do you hear? Loose me. He shall not go."

He struggled so furiously that he freed himself and was rushing at Mellersh, when the door was thrown open and the grey-headed old Colonel of the regiment entered.

"What is this?" said the Colonel sternly. "Major Rockley, are you mad? I have business, sir, at once, with you."

Rockley stared from one to the other, and seemed to be sobered on the instant.

"Business with me?" he said quickly. "Well, what is it? Payne, I leave myself in your hands. Now, Colonel, what is it?"

The old Colonel drew aside and pointed to the door.

"Go to my quarters, sir," he said sternly. "But you should have some one with you beside me. Sir Harry Payne, you are Major Rockley's greatest intimate. Go with him."

Sir Harry was, after Mellersh, the most sober of the party, his wound having necessitated his being abstemious, and he turned to the Colonel.

"He was very drunk," he said. "We'll get him to bed. I'll talk to Mellersh when he is gone, and nothing shall come of it."

"You have misunderstood my meaning, Payne," said the Colonel sternly. "I am not interfering about a card quarrel, sir, or a contemptible brawl about some profligate woman. This is an affair dealing with the honour of our regiment, as well as Major Rockley's liberty."

A spasm seemed to have seized Rockley, but he was calm the next moment, and walked steadily to the Colonel's quarters, not a word being spoken till the old officer threw open the door of his study, and they were in the presence of Lord Carboro', Barclay, Morton Denville, and the Chief Constable.

The Colonel was the only one who took a chair, the others bowing in answer to the invitation to be seated, and remaining standing.

"Now, Mr Denville," said the Colonel, "Major Rockley is here: will you have the goodness to repeat the words that you said to me? I must warn you, though, once more, that this is a terrible charge against your brother-officer, and against our regiment. I should advise you to be careful, and unless you have undoubted proof of what you say, to hesitate before you repeat the charge."

"Sir," said Morton, standing forward, "I am fighting the battle of my poor father, who has been condemned to death for a crime of which he is innocent."

"He has been tried by the laws of his country, Mr Denville, and convicted."

"Because everything seemed so black against him, sir, through the devilish machinations of that man."

"Be careful, sir," said the Colonel sternly. "Once more, be careful."

"I must speak out, sir," cried Morton firmly. "I repeat it—the devilish machinations of this man—who has been the enemy and persecutor of my family ever since he has been here."

"To the point, sir," said the Colonel, as Rockley stood up with a contemptuous look in his dark eyes, and his tall, well-built figure drawn to his full height.

"I will to the point, sir," said Morton. "I charge this man, the insulter and defamer of my sister, with being the murderer of Lady Teigne!"

"Hah!"

It was Major Rockley who uttered that ejaculation: and, springing forward, he had in an instant seized Morton Denville by the throat and bore him against the wall.

It was a momentary burst of fierce rage that was over directly; and, dropping his hands and stepping back, the Major stood listening as Morton went on.

"Taking advantage of the similarity of figure between himself and my unfortunate brother, he took Frederick Denville's uniform one night for a disguise, and to cast the suspicion upon an innocent man, should he be seen, and then went to the house and killed that miserable old woman as she slept."

"You hear this charge, Rockley?" said the Colonel.

"Yes, I hear," was the scornful reply.

"Go on, Mr Denville: I am bound to hear you," said the Colonel. "What reason do you give for this impossible act?"

"Poverty, sir. Losses at the gaming tables. To gain possession of Lady Teigne's jewels."

"Pish!" ejaculated Rockley, with his dark eyes flashing.

"Those jewels proved to be false," continued Morton, "and at the first opportunity Major Rockley took them, in the dead of the night, and threw them from the end of the pier into the sea."

"How do you know that?" said the Colonel.

"I was on the platform beneath, fishing, sir; and the fisherman I was with dredged them up afterwards, and sold them to Mr Barclay."

"Yes," said that individual. "I have them still."

"Bah! Absurd!" cried Rockley, throwing back his head. "Colonel Lascelles, are you going to believe this folly?"

"I am powerless, Major Rockley," said the Colonel in a quick, sharp manner. "This charge is made in due form."

"And it is enough for me, sir," said the constable, stepping forward. "Major Rockley, I arrest you on the charge of murder."

Rockley made a quick movement towards the door, but stopped short.

"Pish! I was surprised," he exclaimed, as the constable sprang in his way. "What do you want to do?"

"Take you, sir."

"What? Disgraced like this?" cried Rockley furiously.

"Colonel, you will not allow the insult to the regiment. Give your word that I will appear."

"I am helpless, sir," cried the old Colonel.

"Place me under arrest then, and let me appear in due time."

"I claim Major Rockley as my prisoner, sir," cried the constable stoutly. "I have a warrant in proper form, and my men waiting. This is not an ordinary case."

"Oh, very well," cried Rockley contemptuously; "I am ready. The charge is as ridiculous as it is disgraceful. I presume that I may return to my quarters, and tell my servant to pack up a few necessaries?"

"Of course; of course, Rockley," said the Colonel. "There can be no objection to this."

He looked at the constable as he spoke, but that individual made no reply. He placed himself by Rockley's side, and Sir Harry Payne went out with them.

"I don't believe it, Rockley," cried the latter. "Here, I'll stand by you to the end."

Rockley gave him a grim nod, glanced sharply round, and then strode out to his own quarters only a few yards away.

"Well, gentlemen," said the Colonel, looking from one to the other; "this is a most painful business for me. Mr Denville, as your father's son, I cannot blame you very much, but if you had been ten years older you would have acted differently."

"Colonel Lascelles," said Lord Carboro' coldly, "I do not see how Mr Morton Denville could have acted differently."

"I will not argue the point with you, my lord," said the Colonel. "May I ask you to—My God! What's that?"

It was a dull report, followed by the hurrying of feet, and the excitement that would ensue in a barrack at the discharge of fire-arms.

Before the Colonel could reach the door, it was thrown open, and Sir Harry Payne staggered in, white as ashes, and sank into a chair.

"Water!" he exclaimed. "I'm weak yet."

"What is it? Are you hurt?" cried the Colonel.

"No. Good heavens! how horrible," faltered the young man with a sob. "Rockley!"

"Rockley?" cried Morton excitedly.

"He has blown out his brains!"

# Chapter Twenty Seven
## A Long Adieu

Major Rockley's tacit acknowledgment of the truth of the charge against him, and the piecing together of the links, showed how, on the night of Lady Teigne's death, he had been absent from the mess for two hours, during which Fred Denville lay drunk in the officers' quarters—made drunk by the Major's contrivance, so that his uniform could be used. How too, so as further to avert suspicion, the Major had the fiendish audacity to take the party to perform the serenade where the poor old votary of fashion lay dead.

The truth, so long in coming to the surface, prevailed at last, and Stuart Denville, broken and prostrated, found himself the idol of the crowd from Saltinville, who collected to see him freed from the county gaol.

"To the barracks, Claire," he whispered. "Let us get away from here."

They were at the principal hotel, and Claire was standing before him, pale and trembling with emotion.

"Your blessing and forgiveness first," she murmured. "Oh, father, that I could be so blind!"

"So blind?" he said tenderly, as he took her in his arms. "No: say so noble and so true. Did you not stand by me when you could not help believing me guilty, and I could not speak? But we are wasting time. I have sent word to poor Fred. My child, I have his forgiveness to ask for all the past."

They met the regimental surgeon as they drove up.

"You have come quickly," he said. "Did you get my message?"

"Your message?" cried Claire, turning pale. "Is—is he worse?"

The surgeon bowed his head.

"I had hopes when you were here last," he said gently; "but there has been an unfavourable turn. The poor fellow has been asking for you, Miss Denville; you had better come at once."

He led the way to the infirmary, where the finely-built, strong man lay on the simple pallet, his face telling its own tale more eloquently than words could have spoken it.

"Ah, little sister," he said feebly, as his face lit up with a happy smile. "I wanted you. You will not mind staying with me and talking. Tell me," he continued, as Claire knelt down by his bed's head, "is it all true, or have they been saying I am innocent to make it easier—now I am going away?"

"No, no, Fred," said Claire; "it is true that you are quite innocent."

"Is this the truth?" he said feebly.

"The truth," whispered Claire; "and you must live—my brother—to help and protect me."

"No," he said sadly; "it is too late. I'm glad though that I did not kill the old woman. It seemed all a muddle. I was drunk that night. Poor old dad! Can't they set him free?"

"My boy!—Fred!—can you forgive me?" cried Denville, bending over the face that gazed up vacantly in his.

"Who's that?" said the dying man sharply. "I can't see. Only you, Clairy—who's that? Father?"

"My son!—my boy! Fred, speak to me—forgive—"

There was a terrible silence in the room as the old man's piteous cry died out, and he sank upon his knees on the other side of the narrow bed, and laid his wrinkled forehead upon his son's breast.

"Forgive?—you, father?" said Fred at last, in tones that told how rapidly the little life remaining was ebbing away. "It's all right, sir—all a mistake— my life—one long blunder. Take care of Clairy here—and poor little May."

"My boy—the mistake has been mine," groaned Denville, "and I am punished for it now."

"No, no—old father—take care—Clairy here."

He seemed to doze for a few minutes, and Denville rose to go and ask the surgeon if anything could be done.

"Nothing but make his end as peaceful as you can. Ah, my lad, you here?"

"Yes," said Morton. "How is he?"

"Alive," said the surgeon bluntly; and he turned away.

Fred Denville seemed to revive as soon as he was left alone with his sister; and, looking at her fixedly, he seemed to be struggling to make out whose was the face that bent over him.

"Claire—little sister," he said at last, with a smile of rest and content. "Clairy—Richard Linnell? Tell me."

"Oh, Fred, Fred, hush!" she whispered.

"No, no! Tell me. I can see you clearly now. It would make me happier. I'm going, dear. A fine, true-hearted fellow; and he loves you. Don't let yours be a wrecked life too."

"Fred! dear Fred!"

"Let it all be cleared up now—you two. You do love him, sis?"

"Fred! dear Fred!" she sobbed; "with all my heart."

"Ah!" he said softly, with a sigh of satisfaction. "Ask him to come here. No; bring the old man back—and Morton. Don't cry, my little one; it's—it's nothing now, only the long watch ended, and the time for rest."

In another hour he had fallen asleep as calmly as a weary child—sister, father, and brother at his side; and it seemed but a few hours later to Morton Denville that he was marching behind the bearers with the funeral march ringing in his ears, and the muffled drums awaking echoes in his heart—a heart that throbbed painfully as the farewell volley was fired across the grave.

For Fred Denville's sin against his officers was forgiven, and Colonel Lascelles was one of the first to follow him to the grave.

# Chapter Twenty Eight
# The Eve of the Finish

"A letter, Claire, so painful that I shrank from reading it to you, only that I have no secrets from my promised wife."

"Does it give you pain?" said Claire, as she looked up in Richard Linnell's face, where they sat in the half-light of evening, with the sea spread before them — placid and serene as their life had been during the past few weeks.

"Bitter pain," he said sadly, as he gazed at the saddened face, set off by the simple black in which she was clothed.

"Then why not let me share it? Is pain so new a thing to me?"

"So old that I would spare you more; and yet you ought to know my family cares, as I have known yours."

"May I read?" said Claire softly, as she laid her thin white hand upon the letter.

He resigned it to her without a word; but as she opened the folds:

"Yes; read it," he said. "It concerns you as much as it does me, and you shall be the judge as to whether the secret shall be kept."

Claire looked up at him wonderingly, and then read the letter aloud.

It was a passionate appeal, and at the same time a confession and a farewell; and, as Claire read on, she grew the more confused and wondering.

For the letter was addressed to Richard Linnell, asking his forgiveness for the many ways in which the writer, in her tender love and earnest desire for his happiness, had stood between him and Claire, ready to spread reports against her fame, and contrive that Linnell should hear them, since the writer had never thoroughly known Claire Denville's heart, but had judged her from the standpoint of her sister. It had been agony to the writer to see Linnell's devotion to a woman whom she believed to be unworthy of his love; and as his father's life had been wrecked by a woman's deceit, the writer had sworn to leave no stone unturned to save the son.

At times the letter grew sadly incoherent, and the tears with which it had been blotted showed its truthfulness, as the writer prayed Richard's forgiveness for fighting against his love and giving him such cruel pain.

"Colonel Mellersh will explain all to you," the letter went on, "for he has known everything. It was he who saved me from further degradation, and found the money to buy this business, where I thought to live out my remaining span of life unknown, and only soothed by seeing you at times — you whom I loved so dearly and so well."

Claire looked up from the letter wonderingly, but Linnell bade her read on.

"Colonel Mellersh fought hard against my wishes at first, but he yielded at last out of pity. I promised him that I would never make myself known—never approach your father's home—and I have kept my word. Mellersh has absolved me now that I am leaving here for ever, and I go asking your forgiveness as your wretched mother, and begging you to ask for that of Claire Denville, the sweet, true, faithful woman whom you will soon, I hope, make your wife.

"Lastly, I pray and charge you not to break the simple, calm happiness of your father's life by letting him know that his unhappy wife has for years been living so near at hand."

"But, Richard," cried Claire, "I always thought that—that she was dead."

"He told me so," replied Linnell sadly. "She was dead to him. There, you have read all. It was right that you should know. Colonel Mellersh has told me the rest."

Linnell crumpled up the letter, and then smoothed it out, and folded and placed it in his breast.

"It is right," he said again, "that you should know the truth. Mellersh is my father's oldest friend. They were youths together. When the terrible shock came upon my father that he was alone, and that his wife had fled with a man whom he had made his companion after Mellersh had gone upon foreign service, his whole life was changed, and he became the quiet, subdued recluse you see."

Linnell paused for a few minutes, and then went on:

"Mellersh had idolised my mother when she was a bright fashion-loving girl; but he accepted his fate when she gave the preference to my father. When he came home from India and found what had happened, and that this wretch had cast her off, he shot the betrayer of my father's name, and then sought out and rescued my mother, placing her as you have read, at her desire, here."

"But, Richard dear, I am so dull and foolish—I can only think of one person that this could possibly have been; and it could not be—"

"Miss Clode? Yes, that was the name she took. My mother, Claire. What do you say to me now?"

Claire rose from her seat gently, and laid her hand upon her arm.

"We must keep her secret, Richard," she said; "but let us go to her together now."

"Then you forgive her the injury she did you?"

"It was out of love for you; and she did not know me then. Let us go."

"Impossible," he said, taking her in his arms. "She has left here for ever. Some day we may see her, but the proposal is to come from her."

They did not hear the door open as they stood clasped in each other's arms, nor hear it softly closed, nor the whispers on the landing, as one of the visitors half sobbed:

"Ain't it lovely, Jo-si-ah? Did you see 'em? If it wasn't rude and wrong, I could stand and watch 'em for hours. It do put one in mind of the days when—"

"Hold your tongue, you stupid old woman," was the gruff reply. "It's quite disgusting. A woman at your time of life wanting to watch a pair of young people there, and no candles lit."

"Hush! Don't talk so loud, or they'll hear us; and now, Jo-si-ah, as it's in my mind, I may as well say it to you at once."

"Now, look here," said Barclay in a low voice, in obedience to his wife's request, but speaking quickly, "I've been bitten pretty heavily by the fellows in the regiment that has just gone, so if it's any new plan of yours that means money, you may stop it, for not a shilling do you get from me. There!"

"And at your time of life, too! To tell such fibs, Jo-si-ah! Just as if I didn't know that you've made a profit of Sir Harry Payne alone, enough to cover all your losses. Now, look here: I don't like little Mrs Burnett, or Gravani, or whatever her name is, but seeing how she's left alone in the world, and nobody's wife after all, and poor Mr Denville is poor Mr Denville, and it's a tax upon him, and you're out so much, I've been thinking, I say—"

"Wouldn't do, old lady. She's not the woman who would make our home comfortable; and besides—"

"But she's so different, Jo-si-ah, since she has been getting nearly well."

"Glad of it, old lady. Hope she'll keep so. But you forget that Claire will soon be leaving home, and—"

"What a stupid old woman I am, Jo-si-ah! Why, of course! Her place is there along with her father; and it's wonderful how he pets that little child. There now, I'm sure they've had long enough. Let's go in and tell them the news."

This time Mrs Barclay tapped at the door softly, before opening it half an inch and saying:

"May we come in?"

Her answer was the door flung wide, and Claire's arms round her neck.

"We've come to tell you that we've just seen Lord Carboro', my dear, and he told us that he'd heard about your brother from the Colonel of his new regiment, out in Gibraltar, and that he's getting on as well as can be."

# Chapter Twenty Nine
# A Tale that is Told

It was just such a visit that Mrs Barclay paid Claire Denville about a fortnight later; and after one of her extremely warm embraces, she exclaimed: "Guess."

"Guess what, Mrs Barclay?"

"Who's married. There, you needn't blush, my dear, because yours is fixed all right at last, but you'll never guess who."

"Then tell me," said Claire, smiling. "No, guess."

"I cannot. There are so many."

"Then I will tell you. No, no: you're too late," she cried, as Richard Linnell hurriedly entered; "I've brought the news."

"You've told her then that Cora Dean is married?"

"Now what a shame, Mr Richard," cried Mrs Barclay. "I hadn't time to say it, but I was just going to tell her. But she doesn't know who to, and I will tell her that. Colonel Mellersh, my dear."

"Colonel Mellersh!" cried Claire.

"Yes," said Richard Linnell. "I have just received this from him. A message from them both."

Claire opened her lips to speak, but her eyes fell upon Richard Linnell's thoughtful face, and it was he who spoke next, and said slowly:

"No: now I come to think of it all, I am not surprised."

Of course, Saltinville talked a great deal about this match, but the worthies of the place talked more about another wedding that took place six months later—a wedding at which Lord Carboro' insisted upon being the bridegroom's best man.

It was upon that occasion, after returning from the church, that Lord Carboro' took a casket from his pocket and placed it in Claire's hands.

"The old jewels, my dear, that I have prized because you refused them once before. God bless you! and I know He will."

The old man turned quickly away with his face working, and crossed to the Master of the Ceremonies, who was looking very much his old self, in his meagrely furnished drawing-room, and tapped him half angrily upon the shoulder.

"Hang it all, Denville," he cried, "can't you see I've forgotten my snuff-box, and am dying for a pinch? The old box, sir—His Royal Highness's box. Hah! That's better," he ejaculated, after dipping his thin white finger and thumb in the chased gold box, "a friend at a pinch, eh, Denville, eh? Damme, sir, your young wits and beaux don't often beat that, eh? The old school's passing away, Denville, eh? passing away."

"With the noblemen who are your lordship's contemporaries."

"Tut-tut-tut! Denville, don't. Never mind the lordship. We must be better friends, man—better friends for our little fag ends of troubled lives. Hush! No more now. This is the bride and bridegroom's day."

There were many strangers who, visiting Saltinville, were ready to smile at the tottering white-haired beau, so elaborately dressed, and who, not from need, but from custom, clung to his old habits and received visitors as Master of the Ceremonies still. It was a quaint old fiction, and he used to glory in his fees, now they were only wanted for a purpose he had in view.

There were other laughs too ready to be bestowed upon the palsied old nobleman in the dark wig, who met the Master of the Ceremonies every morning on the Parade, and took snuff with him as they flourished their canes, and flicked away fancied spots of dust. Their high collars and pantaloons and Hessian boots, all came in for notice. So did those wonderful beaver hats, black for winter, white for summer, which were lifted with such a display of deportment, in return to the salutes of those who were taking the air. It was always the same: they met at the same hour, at the same spot, took snuff, chatted upon the same themes, and then strolled down to the end of the pier talking of how "times have changed, sir: times have changed."

"Who's him, sir—old chap in the black wig, and a face like a wooden nut-cracker? Oh, he's old Lord Carboro'."

"And the other?" said the stranger, who had been questioning Fisherman Dick, as the old men passed them by.

"T'other, sir? Ah, I could tell you a deal about him. That's the Master o' the Ceremonies, that is. I could tell you a long story about he."

And so he did.